CLAIM NO EASY VICTORIES

THE LEGACY OF AMILCAR CABRAL

EDITED BY
FIROZE MANJI & BILL FLETCHER JR

Published by
Council for the Development of Social Science Research in Africa (CODESRIA)
www.codesria.org
and
Daraja Press
www.daraja.net

Library of Congress Cataloguing-in-Publication is available from the Library of Congress

British Library Cataloguing-in-Publication Data A catalogue record of this book is available from the British Library

ISBN: 2869785550
ISBN-13: Print: 9782869785557;
e-book: 978-2-86978-556-4

CONTENTS

ACKNOWLEDGMENTS

The editors wish to thank Kenny Desain, Maggie Dessain, and the CreateSpace editor for their assistance with copyediting, Fernanda Mendy, the late Sputnik Kilamba, and Victoria Bawtree for translations, and to contributing authors for their enthusiasm and commitment to this project.

The publication of this book was made possible by a grant from the Rosa Luxemburg Foundation, Senegal.

AUTHOR BIOGRAPHIES

Senai Abraha is a PhD candidate at Kennesaw State University's International Conflict Management Program. He is currently writing his PhD thesis, entitled "Modeling Peacekeeping: the Case of Canada Examined." Senai earned his master's degree in international development management from the University of Bradford in the UK and his bachelor of arts in business management. He has conducted research on various African development and security issues and has presented this work in different arenas, including the annual China Goes Global conference at Harvard University and the Black History conference at Atlanta. Senai speaks Amharic, Tigrigna, and English fluently and has a basic grasp on French, Spanish, and German.

Makungu M. Akinyela, is an associate professor in the Department of African American Studies at Georgia State University. He is a family therapist practicing in Georgia. He has published and lectured on critical African-centred theory, critical pedagogy, and cultural democracy, particularly as these issues relate to mental health. He is the son of Mississippi civil rights activists and came of age during the Black Power movement in Los Angeles, California. He became a student activist under the mentorship of the Revolutionary Action Movements House of Umoja and the African People's Party. As a political activist, he was a founding member of the Coalition Against Police Abuse (CAPA) in Los Angeles, the New African People's Organization, and the Malcolm X Grassroots Movement.

Kali Akuno is an organiser, educator, and writer for human rights and social justice. He is an organiser for the Malcolm X Grassroots Movement (MXGM) (see www.mxgm.org) and former codirector of the US Human

Rights Network (see www.ushrnetwork.org). Kali also served as the executive director of the Peoples' Hurricane Relief Fund (PHRF) based in New Orleans, Louisiana, after Hurricane Katrina and was a cofounder of the School of Social Justice and Community Development (SSJCD), a public school serving low-income African-American and Latino communities in Oakland, California. He is the author of several critical works including, *Born of Struggle, Implemented through Struggle, Let Your Motto Be Resistance,* and *Operation Ghetto Storm*. Kali can be reached at kaliakuno@gmail.com.

Samir Amin is an Egyptian Marxist economist and director of the Third World Forum in Dakar, Senegal. He is one of the world's greatest radical thinkers—a creative Marxist who went from communist activism in Nasser's Egypt, to advising African socialist leaders such as Julius Nyerere and being a leading figure in the World Social Forum. Samir Amin's ideas were formed in the heady ferment of the 1950s and 1960s, when Pan-Africanists like Kwamah Nkrumah, Nasser, and liberation movements thrived across the continent from South Africa to Algeria. His major works include *Capitalism in the Age of Globalization* (1996), *Delinking—Toward a Polycentric World* (1990), *Eurocentrism* (1990), *Re-reading the Post-war Period* (1994), and *The People's Spring: The Future of the Arab Revolutions* (2012).

David Austin is the author of *Fear of a Black Nation: Race, Sex, and Security in Sixties Montreal.* He is also the editor of *You Don't Play with Revolution: The Montreal Lectures of C.L.R. James.* He currently teaches in the Humanities, Philosophy, and Religion Department at John Abbott College in Montreal.

Ajamu Baraka is a veteran grassroots organiser whose roots lie in the Black Liberation Movement. An activist and organiser for over forty years, Baraka has been at the forefront of efforts to develop and apply a radical people-centred human-rights framework to social justice organising and advocacy in the United States over the last two decades. Baraka has appeared on a wide range of print, broadcast, and digital media and is a contributing writer for various publications, including Black

Commentator, Commondreams, Pambazuka, Counterpunch, and Black Agenda Report. Baraka is currently an associate fellow at the Institute for Policy Studies (IPS) in Washington, DC and is editing a new book on human rights in the United States entitled, *The Struggle for People-Centred Human Rights: Voices from the Field.*

Miguel Barros is a research associate at the National Institute of Studies and Research (INEP) of Guinea-Bissau and the current executive director of Tiniguena. Miguel's own activism began within Tiniguena's youth movement, the New Generation of Tiniguena, for which he served as coordinator from 1999 to 2002. Miguel has represented Tiniguena in national and international networks focused on the struggles surrounding extractive industries and biodiversity.

Jesse Benjamin is coordinator of the African and African Diaspora Studies Program and an associate professor of interdisciplinary studies and sociology at Kennesaw State University. He is a sociologist and cultural anthropologist and is actively involved in a wide range of teaching and research endeavors surrounding identity and history in East Africa and the Middle East, as well as critical race theory in North America and around the globe. He is a member of the board of directors of the Walter Rodney Foundation.

Angela Davis is an American political activist, scholar, and author. She emerged as a nationally prominent activist and radical in the 1960s and had close relations with the Black Panther Party through her involvement in the Civil Rights Movement. Prisoner rights have been amongst her continuing interests; she is the founder of Critical Resistance, an organisation working to abolish the prison-industrial complex. Her membership in the Communist Party led to Ronald Reagan's request in 1969 to have her barred from teaching at any university in the state of California. She was tried and acquitted of suspected involvement in the Soledad brothers' August 1970 abduction and murder of Judge Harold Haley in Marin County, California.

Demba Moussa Dembélé is director of the African Forum for Alternatives in Dakar, Senegal. He is author of *Samir Amin: Organic Intellectual Dedicated to the Liberation of the South*, CODESRIA, Dakar, 2011.

Jacques Depelchin was Hugh Le May Fellow at Rhodes University from July through December, 2012, and is a visiting professor in the history department of Universidade Estadual de Feira de Santana in Bahia, Brazil.

Mustafah Dhada, FRSA, FRAS, is the author of *Warriors At Work: How Guinea Was Really Set Free* (Niwot: University of Colorado Press, 1993), now out of print. He was born in Búzi, Mozambique, attended the School of African and Asian Studies at the University of Sussex as an undergraduate, and graduated with a doctorate from Oxford. He teaches African and Middle Eastern history at California State University, Bakersfield campus, and is presently finishing a monograph on the subject provisionally entitled, *The Wiriyamu Massacre and the End of the Portuguese Empire in Mozambique* (London: Bloomsbury Academic Press, 2014). He can be reached at dhada@mindspring.com. For additional biographical details visit, http://csub.academia.edu/MustafahDhada/About.

Jean-Pierre Diouf is a librarian at the Council for the Development of Social Science Research in Africa (CODESRIA) since 1987. He holds a master degree in information science from the Cheikh Anta Diop University, Dakar (Senegal) and master degrees in marketing, communication and in project management from ISM, Dakar (Senegal). Jean-Pierre Diouf's areas of interest are research libraries, the introduction of marketing tools in libraries and the research methodology in libraries.

Aziz Salmone Fall teaches political science, anthropology, international relations, and international development at McGill University and the Université du Québec à Montréal (UQAM). Fall is a former coordinator of the Quebec anti-apartheid network and a current member of GRILA, Group for Research and Initiative for the Liberation of Africa, where he coordinates CIJS, the International Campaign Justice for Sankara, a collective that includes twenty-one lawyers. It is the first international African campaign to successfully bring a case of impunity in the murder of a head of state before the United Nations. Fall is also president of the Internationalist Centre, CIRFA. http://www.azizfall.com

Mireille Fanon-Mendes-France, daughter of Frantz Fanon, is president of the Frantz Fanon Foundation (http://frantzfanonfoundation-fondationfrantzfanon.com) and a member of the Expert Working Group on Afro-Descendents of the UN Human Rights Council. She has been a professor at the University Paris V, Descartes, in France and a visiting professor at the University of California, Berkeley in international law and conflict resolution. She has also worked for UNESCO and the French National Assembly. She is author of several articles on human rights and humanitarian law, as well as on racism and discrimination. In 2009, she received the Human Rights Award from the Council for Justice, Equality, and Peace.

Grant Farred teaches at Cornell University. His publications include *What's My Name? Black Vernacular Intellectuals* (University of Minnesota Press), *Phantom Calls: Race and the Globalization of the NBA* (Prickly Paradigm), and *Long Distance Love: A Passion for Football.* His forthcoming works include *In Motion, At Rest: The Event of the Athletic Body* (University of Minnesota Press, 2014) and *Conciliation* (Temple University Press).

Bill Fletcher, Jr. is a racial justice, labor, and international activist based in the United States. He is an editorial board member of BlackCommentator.com; senior scholar with the Institute for Policy Studies; the immediate former president of TransAfrica Forum; the coauthor (with Dr. Fernando Gapasin) of *Solidarity Divided*; and the author of *They're Bankrupting Us—And Twenty Other Myths about Unions*. He can be reached at billfletcherjr@gmail.com. His website is www.billfletcherjr.com. He is on Facebook and Twitter.

Hashim Gibrill is an associate professor and former chair of the Department of Political Science, Clark Atlanta University, and an adjunct professor at Spelman College. Previously, he taught at Bethune-Cookman College in Florida, the University of Maiduguri in Nigeria, and in England. He teaches courses in international relations, African politics, comparative politics, and political research methodology. Dr. Gibrill received his postsecondary education at the University of Reading in England, the University of Birmingham in England, and Atlanta University (now Clark Atlanta University).

Lewis R. Gordon is a professor of Philosophy and African American Studies with affiliation in Judaic Studies at the University of Connecticut at Storrs and the Nelson Mandela Distinguished Visiting Professor at Rhodes University in South Africa. His books include, *An Introduction to Africana Philosophy* (Cambridge UP, 2008). Professor Gordon's biographical information, a list and selection of his publications, his blog, and selections of his archived interviews, videotaped lectures, and audio-lectures are available on his website: http://lewisrgordon.com/

Nigel C. Gibson is the director of the honors programme at Emerson College in Boston and an honorary research fellow at the School of Development Studies at the University of Kwa-Zulu Natal in South Africa. His most recent books are *Fanonian Practices in South Africa: From Steve Biko to Abahlali base Mjondolo* and *Living Fanon: Global Perspectives*, which he edited to mark the fiftieth anniversary of Fanon's death.

Patricia Godinho Gomes is a researcher scholar in African studies at the University of Cagliari, Italy. She graduated from the University of Lisbon (ISCSP) in international relations (1995) and received her doctororate in History and Institutions of Africa (PhD, 2003) from the University of Cagliari. She is currently carrying on research in gender studies (women in liberation struggle movements, politics, and the informal economy) and in postcolonial state crisis issues. She has published the book on Guinea-Bissau liberation struggle entitled, *Os Fundamentos de Uma Nova Sociedade. O PAIGC e a Luta Armada na Guiné-Bissau*, Torino: Harmattan Italia, 2010. She is also coeditor with Christian Muleka Mwewa and

Gleiciani Fernandes of the book entitled *Sociedades Desiguais: Género, Cidadania e Identidades*, Nova Harmonia (Brasil), 2009.

Adrian Harewood is a writer and journalist with the Canadian Broadcasting Corporation (CBC). Before making the move to television in October, 2009, Adrian spent three years as the host of Ottawa's favorite afternoon radio programme, *All in a Day*. He has a keen interest in community involvement and volunteers his time in both Montreal and Toronto. He is a past board member of Central Neighbourhood House in Toronto and served on the board of Head and Hands, helping to provide youth services in Montreal. Adrian was also a youth programme worker providing counseling for at-risk students in six Toronto high schools. He lives in Ottawa, Canada.

Augusta Henriques is the cofounder and former secretary general of Tiniguena, an organisation in Guinea-Bissau dedicated to the preservation of biodiversity through citizen action and cultural emancipation. The name Tiniguena translates into "this land is ours" in the local Cassanga language. Augusta is also a founding member of COPAGEN, a West African network organised to promote ecological agriculture and family farming and resist land grabbing and the introduction of genetically engineered seeds into Africa. She has devoted her life to working for social change and peace in her own country and nurturing solidarity for justice with others around the world.

Molly Kane is former Executive Director of the international feminist social justice organization, Inter Pares, from 1996 to 2009. During the academic year 2005-06, she was a visiting adjunct assistant professor in the department of Global Development Studies, Queen's University. Since leaving Inter Pares she has worked with the ETC Group, Pambazuka News and Development and Peace. She is Researcher in Residence at CIRDIS – UQAM, (Centre International de recherche en développement international et société, Université du Québec à Montréal).

Wangui Kimari is a Pan-Africanist from Kenya who organises with Bunge La Mwananchi (People's Parliament) in Nairobi and with the Network For Pan-Afrikan Solidarity in Toronto (NPAS). She is also an anthropology student who has done solidarity work with, and research on, Afro-Brazilian organisations in Salvador, Brazil. Her present research looks at the legacy of colonial urban planning in Nairobi and the violence, surveillance, and displacement it has required, particularly in the city's poorer urban settlements. Her writings have appeared in *Pambazuka News*, *Black Agenda Report*, and Rabble.ca.

Redy Wilson Lima is a professor at the University of Santiago and associate researcher at the Instituto Superior de Ciências Jurídicas e Sociais of Cape-Verde (US/ISCJS, Cape-Verde).

Ameth Lo is a Senegalese-born Pan-Africanist militant residing in Toronto, Canada. While studying computer science at the University of Montpelier in France, graduating in 1990, he became active in student politics. He pursued advanced studies in Paris, where he helped to organise OSEA (Organisation for Unity of Students of African Ancestry), a student organisation based at Jussieu University that drew most of its members from Africa and the French-speaking Caribbean countries. OSEA's mission was to build and promote ties between Africa and the Caribbean. Moving to Montreal in 1993, Ameth joined GRILA (Group for Research and Initiatives for the Liberation of Africa) and in 1995 founded its Toronto chapter. He is a regular host on GRILA's weekly radio show *Amandla!*.

Richard A. Lobban, Jr. is a lifelong Africanist, professor emeritus of anthropology and African studies, former chair at Rhode Island College, and vice president of the Rhode Island Black Heritage Society. He began studying Africa in 1961 at Bucknell University. He received an MA focusing on the study of Nigeria from Temple University in 1968 and a PhD from Northwestern University in 1973, focusing on the study of Sudanese Nubians. In 1964 he worked in Tanzania with FRELIMO.

During the war in Guinea-Bissau he crossed that nation with the PAIGC guerilla army and reported on the last major battle at Guiledge. He also reported on the wars in southern Sudan and Eritrea. His *Historical Dictionary of Guinea-Bissau* with Peter Mendy is soon to be in its 4th edition.

Filomeno Lopes is a writer and journalist at *Radio Vaticana*. He is the author of a number of works on philosophy and African geopolitics.

Brandon D. Lundy is associate director (interim) of the PhD programme in International Conflict Management and an assistant professor of anthropology in the Department of Geography and Anthropology at Kennesaw State University, Georgia. He received a PhD from both SUNY at Buffalo, New York, and *Université des Sciences et Technologies de Lille* (USTL), France, in 2009. His current research focuses on the effects of globalisation on ground-level livelihoods in Guinea-Bissau, West Africa. Dr. Lundy is coeditor of *Teaching Africa: A Guide to the 21st-Century Classroom* (IUP, 2013). He has published articles on fishing sector reform, tourism, cashew production, and immigration and deportation, all focused on Lusophone West Africa and its diaspora.

Firoze Manji is head of CODESRIA's Documentation and Information Centre. He is the founder and former editor in chief of *Pambazuka News* (www.pambazuka.org) and Pambazuka Press/Fahamu Books (www.fahamubooks.org), and founder and former executive director of Fahamu, Networks for Social Justice (www.fahamu.org). Amongst other books, he coedited *African Awakening: The Emerging Revolutions* (Pambazuka Press, 2011) with Sokari Ekine. He is an associate fellow at the Institute for Policy Studies (IPS) in Washington, DC, visiting fellow at Kellogg College, University of Oxford, and board member of the Institute for Agriculture and Trade Policy.

Perry Mars is currently a professor in the Department of Africana Studies at Wayne State University. His particular academic specialty is Caribbean politics and culture, focusing on such themes as the Caribbean Left,

Labor-Political Relations, and Ethno-Political Conflicts and Conflict Resolution. His books include *Ideology and Change: the Transformation of the Caribbean Left*, jointly published by Wayne State University Press and The Press University of the West Indies in 1998, and an edited book (with Professor Alma Young) entitled *Caribbean Labor and Politics: Legacies of Cheddi Jagan and Michael Manley,* also published by Wayne State University Press in 2004.

William Minter is editor of the AfricaFocus Bulletin (http://www.africafocus.org). His most recent book is *No Easy Victories: African Liberation and American Activists over a Half Century, 1950-2000*, coedited with Gail Hovey and Charles Cobb, Jr.

Explo Nani-Kofi is director of Kilombo Community Education Project, London, and the Kilombo Centre for Civil Society and African Self-Determination (www.kilomboeducation.org), Peki, which jointly publishes the *Kilombo Pan-African Community Journal* as well as hosts and produces the *Another World is Possible* radio programme on GFM Radio, London (www.gfmradio.com). He also writes for www.counterfire.org.

Nyameko Barney Pityana is a human rights lawyer and theologian in South Africa. He is an exponent of Black theology. He was one of the founding members of the South African Students' Organisation of the Black Consciousness Movement with Steve Biko. He was appointed a member of the South African Human Rights Commission in 1995, and served as chairman of the commission from 1995 to 2001. Professor Pityana became vice chancellor and principal for the University of South Africa in 2001 and held the position for nine years. He is currently the rector of the College of the Transfiguration (Anglican) in Grahamstown.

Maria Poblet was raised in Buenos Aires but politicized in East Los Angeles. Maria is a nerdy Latina rooted in the San Francisco Bay Area. Building off a decade of radical community organising and movement-building work, she led the merger of the Latino organisation she built with a Black organisation, forming a single, multiracial powerhouse called Causa Justa, which translates as "Just Cause" (www.cjjc.org). She is passionate about building an internationalist social movement and works towards this goal through the Grassroots Global Justice Alliance and various independent left projects. She has a blog on www.OrganizingUpgrade.com. Before organising, she was artistic director of Poetry for the People and had the honor of being mentored by June Jordan.

Reiland Rabaka is an associate professor of African, African-American, and Caribbean studies in the Department of Ethnic Studies and the Humanities Program at the University of Colorado at Boulder, where he is also an affiliate professor in the Women and Gender Studies Program and a research fellow at the Centre for Studies of Ethnicity and Race in America (CSERA). He is the author of ten books, including *Africana Critical Theory* (2009); *Forms of Fanonism: Frantz Fanon's Critical Theory and the Dialectics of Decolonization* (2010); *Against Epistemic Apartheid: W.E.B. Du Bois and the Disciplinary Decadence of Sociology* (2010); *Hip Hop's Inheritance* (2011); *Hip Hop's Amnesia* (2012); and *The Hip Hop Movement* (2013).

Asha T. Rodney is a senior partner in the law firm of C F Brock & Associates. She holds a wide range of experience in capital defense, criminal defense, civil litigation, professional defense, appeals, contract negotiation, arbitration, probate, and real estate. She is trained in alternative dispute resolution and is a certified mediator. She is a member of the board of directors of the Walter Rodney Foundation.

Patricia Rodney is the CEO of Partners in Health, Education, and Development, a domestic and international public health consultancy organisation. She has spent the last fifteen years in academic public health at the Morehouse School of Medicine where she had held the positions of assistant dean for Public Health Education and professor. She is chair of the board of directors of the Walter Rodney Foundation.

Carlos Schwarz da Silva was born in Bissau. He conducted his primary and secondary studies both in Bissau and at the Lyceum Camões in Lisbon. During the time of his studies, his father was arrested by the Portuguese political police (PIDE), because he acted as lawyer for the nationalist militants of the liberation struggle. He studied as an agronomist and devoted himself to leading the student anticolonial and antifascist struggle. He then joined PAIGC. In 1975 he returned to Bissau and contributed to the creation of the Department of Agricultural Research, which he has run for seventeen years. He helped create the NGO Action for Development, which intervenes in the most isolated regions of the country. In 1999 he was part of the Government of National Unity as minister for infrastructure.

Helmi Sharawy was professor of Afro-Arab Political Thought at JUBA University during the1980s. He is former director of the Arab and African Research Centre, Cairo, and a member of the executive committee of CODESRIA. He was coordinator for the African Liberation Movements offices at the African Association under the auspice of the President's Office of African Affairs (1960 to 1975), and served as consultant to the ministry of Sudan, Egyptian Integration Program (1975 to 1980). He is the author of several books on African thought and culture written in both Arabic and English, including *Angola Revolution* (1978), *Arabs and Africans Face to Face* (1985), *Israel in Africa* (1986), *Culture of Liberation* (2002), *Africa in Transition for 20-21st Century* (2008), and *The Sudan: On the Cross Roads* (2011).

Olúfémi Táíwò is a professor of philosophy and global African studies and director of the Global African Studies Program at Seattle University, Washington. His research interests include the philosophy of law, social and political philosophy, Marxism, and African and Africana philosophy. Táíwò is the author of *Legal Naturalism: A Marxist Theory of Law* (Cornell University Press, 1996); *How Colonialism Preempted Modernity in Africa* (Bloomington: Indiana University Press, 2010), and *Africa Must Be Modern: A Manifesto* (Ibadan: Bookcraft, 2012).

Walter Turner is professor of social sciences and contemporary African affairs at the College of Marin in Kentfield, California, and is a leading authority on contemporary African affairs. He hosts and produces the weekly Pacifica radio programme *Africa Today*. He has worked as a journalist in South Africa, Kenya, Cuba, Nigeria, and Venezuela and led study delegations to Cuba, Jordan, Syria, Mali, Senegal, Vietnam, Kenya, Mexico, Haiti, Venezuela, South Africa, and many other parts of the world. He was media director for Nelson Mandela's visit to California in 1990. Amongst other publications, he is a contributing author in *No Easy Victories: African Liberation and American Activists over a Half Century, 1950-2000* (2007). He is the recipient of numerous awards, including the Martin Luther King Humanitarian Award and the Golden Bell Award.

Stephanie Urdang is a South African living in the United States. Since immigrating to the United States in 1967, her career has included working as an activist, journalist, consultant to the United Nations on gender and development and gender and HIV/AIDS, and cofounding an NGO that supports women living with AIDS who were raped during the Rwandan genocide in 1994. She is author of *Fighting Two Colonialisms: Women in Guinea-Bissau*, Monthly Review Press, 1979, and *And Still They Dance: Women, War, and the Struggle for Change in Mozambique*, Monthly Review/Earthscan,1989. She has also written numerous articles, both popular and academic. She is currently working on a memoir that explores the forces that contributed to the downfall of apartheid.

Chris Webb is an MA candidate in the Development Studies Graduate Program at York University in Toronto. His current research examines the restructuring of agricultural labor in the Western Cape province of South Africa and the response of trade unions. He is active in international solidarity campaigns to support South African workers and has written extensively on social movement struggles in postapartheid South Africa. He serves as contributing editor at *Canadian Dimension* magazine and on the editorial board of *Nokoko*, Carleton University's African Studies Journal.

Nigel Westmaas is a researcher and activist currently teaching in the department of Africana studies at Hamilton College, New York. His research interests include social movements in Guyana and the Caribbean and the history of the newspaper press in Guyana. He has published articles in journals and newspapers including "Resisting Orthodoxy: Notes on the Origins and Ideology of the Working People's Alliance" in *Small Axe*. He is coeditor of a booklet on *Guyanese Periodicals: 1796-1996*. His research and cowritten commentary on *Marcus Garvey in British Guiana* for the University of California UNIA Papers project was published in 2011. Westmaas is a political activist in Guyana's Working People's Alliance (WPA), the organisation in which the late Walter Rodney was a leading member.

Amrit Wilson is a writer and political activist. Her books on African politics include *The Threat of Liberation: Imperialism and Revolution in Zanzibar* (forthcoming) London: Pluto Press, *The Challenge Road: Women in the Eritrean Revolution* (1991) Trenton NJ: Africa World Press, *US Foreign Policy and Revolution: The Creation of Tanzania* (1989) London: Pluto Press. She also coedited *The Future that Works: Selected Writings of A.M. Babu*, (2002) Trenton, NJ: Africa World Press.

PREFACE

Why Shine The Light on Cabral?

Why, in 2013, shine the spotlight on personalities who, in their time, marked their own epoch? Is it the date of the anniversary of their death? One could be content with just organising a few ceremonies, but to truly commemorate men like Amílcar Cabral involves much more than carrying out the pleasant task of remembering them over cocktails or establishing them in some pantheon. These would be acts that run counter to the great contributions that they have made.

The current crises of African democracies coincide with a simultaneous crisis in representation and political leadership. But they also coincide with the crisis of the Western economic system, as well as the Western desire to recolonize all or part of the world in the name of the fight against terrorism and the financial crisis, not even sparing the South Africa of Nelson Mandela. All this justifies not only commemorating these anniversaries but also questioning the legacy of the men and women who have fought and thought about alternatives for Africa.

While today in most African countries there is a return to authoritarian regimes, the popular uprisings in Tunisia and Egypt have inaugurated a second phase of the postindependence period, that of the eruption of the population into politics and their demand not to be neglected any longer in the crisis of the neoliberal model. As for alternatives for the African continent—those of Amílcar Cabral, of Nyerere, of Thomas Sankara, and of Patrice Lumumba—in rereading the works of those who participated in the decolonisation of the continent, one cannot help but be struck by the transformations in the aspirations of people for change and for challenging the recolonization process, as is illustrated, for example, by the crises in Mali and Côte d'Ivoire.

Our revolutionary leaders died prematurely or were assassinated because they upset the reprehensible intentions of projects supported by colonialism, because they denounced the strategy of those who assumed themselves to be the victors, and finally because they promoted another social project for the people who had been newly liberated. These men tirelessly wrote and worked to ensure that the subjection of peoples to alien subjugation, domination and exploitation constitutes a denial of fundamental human rights, is contrary to the Charter of the United Nations and is an impediment to the promotion of world peace and co-operation.[1]

They held high the hope of leaving the deep night behind, to paraphrase one of Achille Mbembé's most recent works. [2] However, a little more than fifty years after Africa's decolonisation, the imperial and neocolonial order continues to maintain most of humanity in destitution and exploitation, continually subjecting them to the ugliness of the world disorder.

It is true that domination has somewhat changed its forms, but those who are experiencing the injustice, violence, alienation, and exploitation are tragically discovering that they are still considered a "Third World" for oligarchies who are all the more powerful now that they are international. The right of peoples to self-determination— a pillar of international law that formed the political and juridical basis of the decolonisation process for which people fought—has been emptied of its substance by the promotion and implementation of an unjust and illegal economic order that has involved privatization and the commodification of almost all aspects of life, as well as the militarization of international relations.

Amílcar Cabral's projects never saw the light of day; the deviations of the postcolonial states proved too powerful. Independence remained unachieved, and instead of working towards the emancipation of peoples, they have resulted in recolonization in novel forms, under which peoples

---

1 Declaration on the Granting of Independence to Colonial Countries and Peoples, adopted by General Assembly Resolution 1514 (XV) of 14 December 1960

2 Achille Mbembé, Sortir de la grande nuit: essai sur l'Afrique décolonisée, Editions La Découverte, October 2010

are subjected to a globalised neocolonial order based on the domination of plutocracies over exploited and despised populations. The decolonisation era, according to Frantz Fanon, should have changed the world order, [3] but it has not been a "programme of absolute disorder" [4] that required calling into question the entire colonial situation.[5] The last have not become the first. [6]

There are several possible explanations for this, the most important of which is that the national elites and politicians of the Global South, including in Africa, preferred to submit and force their peoples to submit to the interests of the old colonizers. Thus they have never broken with the Western power centres, either through the official structures or through informal networks. As both Fanon and Cabral have pointed out, the lack of practical links between the elite and the social movements, their laziness and their cowardice at the decisive moment of the struggle always give rise to tragic mishaps. The power systems have been shown for what they are, systems of oppression and pillage for which "the right to development stems only from an ideological commitment, which is unrealistic, if not Third World archaism, that dates from the 1970s." [7] Hence the new stage of imperialism consists—through globalisation and with the help of certain politicians—of opening up the markets of the less developed countries to the multinationals. It is the movement towards the liberal integration of the economies of the planet to establish their hegemony definitively, and it constitutes the historical stage of a global market dominated by the financial sphere.

Our politicians refuse to see the African continent as being confronted by the same enemy. On the one hand, they have acknowledged and accepted the carving up of the continent through the imposition of artificial borders representing competing colonial interests, which developed independently of the Black consciousness concept that was sustained by

3 Frantz Fanon, *The Wretched of the Earth*, Grove Press, New York, 2007

4 ibid.

5 ibid.

6 ibid.

7 Robert Charvin, L'investissement international et le droit de développement, L'Harmattan, 2002

Amílcar Cabral as well as by Steve Biko, for whom "the basic tenet of Black consciousness is that the Black man must reject all value systems that seek to make him a foreigner in the country of his birth and reduce his basic human dignity." [8]

It is not then by chance if these men who, based on their struggles for the liberation of their countries, were thinking beyond these countries and rapidly subscribed to the liberation struggle of the whole African continent. Did Amílcar Cabral not say, in his speech at Dar es Salaam, that "no one can doubt, among our people—as among all other African peoples—that this war for national liberation in which we are engaged belongs to the whole of Africa"?

While the neocolonial structures are not the only explanation for the failure of independence, this last half-century has shown the effectiveness of the time bombs bequeathed to us by the colonial powers. The topicality of Amílcar Cabral and many others who saw only the first glows of the deceptive dawn of African independence is that they always highlighted the mechanisms of domination, exploitation, and alienation. The paths that they proposed for emancipation from an absurd and criminal social, political, and economic system remain the path for the emancipation of everyone; ultimately, the liberation of man and his de-alienation remain the final objective of political struggle.

To revive their thinking involves the painful process of opening our eyes to the brutality of the world, acknowledging the most hideous aspects of this reality, and realizing that the work that they started has not been completed. Indeed it is far from being completed. New forms of colonization have appeared, as those in power always seek to accelerate their own development to the detriment of other peoples.

But Western systems are showing signs of running out of steam. They are no longer able to guarantee the requirements for human dignity and human progress (if indeed they have ever been able to).

So the resistance continues, but it now has an advantage—these men revealed the traps that are lying in wait for the movements. They also put

---

8 Speech made in 1976

forward the conditions that should favour the process of emancipation of human societies in order to free both the colonized and the colonizer from their alienation. Emancipation has yet to arrive.

Their thinking and their actions force us to open our eyes to the tragic dawn for Africa and the rest of the world and to continue the path towards liberty and de-alienation.

Rereading Amílcar Cabral today means confronting the great issues that caused him and others to stand up and to walk with their companions along the new path conducted by 'Africana' thinking. It also means understanding that the change in paradigms that they advocated are relevant both to the present fight against the old regime and for a new order that sees man no longer in the terms imposed by humanism but by those aimed at building a new humanity.

SECTION I:

INTRODUCTION

I. INTRODUCTION

AMÍLCAR CABRAL AND THE STRUGGLE OF MEMORY AGAINST FORGETTING

Firoze Manji and Bill Fletcher Jr.

On the grounds of the military headquarters of Guinea-Bissau stands the mausoleum of Amílcar Cabral. To pay your respects, you must apply for permission in writing to the military well in advance. All being well, you will receive a letter letting you know the date and time you may visit. You'll be told that you need to bring flowers that must be purchased at a shop just opposite the entrance to the base. Some sixty dollars later, you appear at the gate of the guarded camp where you still must negotiate permission to enter. Finally, the gate opens and senior military personnel and armed guards escort you to the mausoleum at the rear of the base where they will want to pose for photographs.

Beside the large glass and concrete structure bearing the remains of Cabral is a row of brass plaques marking the graves of some of his comrades, leaders of the PAIGC who also gave their lives in the struggle for liberation. If you should ask why the mausoleum is located on the military base, you'll be told it is for "security reasons." And if you ask how the ordinary citizens of Guinea-Bissau might come to pay their respects to Cabral, the military guards will tell you that everyone is free to come whenever they want.

After returning to the streets of Bissau, one must ask why Amílcar Cabral's mausoleum is so heavily guarded. What do the military fear? Has it something to do with the fact that they are themselves the descendents of those who participated in Cabral's assassination? Do they perhaps recognise that the power of memorials is more about the future than the past? "The pile of stones thus marks both an act of deliberate remembrance and an act of deliberate forgetting."[9] How ever did Amílcar Cabral end up here?

Perhaps this guarded site of remembrance is a fearful symbol of the profound importance of Cabral's work and achievements as an extraordinary leader intimately associated with the revolution that resulted in the defeat of Portuguese colonial power in Guinea-Bissau and Cape Verde and the downfall of fascism in Portugal.

January 20, 2013, marked the fortieth anniversary of the assassination of Amílcar Cabral, agronomist, militant, theoretician, poet, and revolutionary. An internationalist, Cabral was instrumental in the formation not only of the PAIGC (Partido Africano da Independência da Guiné e Cabo Verde: African Party for the Independence of Guinea and Cape Verde) but also of MPLA (Movimento Popular de Libertação de Angola – Partido do Trabalho: People's Movement for the Liberation of Angola – Workers Party) and FRELIMO (Frente de Libertação de Moçambique: Front for the Liberation of Mozambique).

Despite the vast literature available by and about Cabral, the memory of his contributions to the struggles for liberation has faded, disintegrating alongside his bodily remains.

"The first steps in liquidating a people," wrote Milan Kundera, "is to erase its memory ... the struggle against power is the struggle of memory against forgetting." The publication of this book is an attempt to contribute to the struggle of memory against forgetting. It is not merely a romantic enterprise—though there is much to be ardent and emotional about in the recollection of the ideas and achievements of Cabral. We are convinced that Cabral's writings are as relevant today as ever, perhaps even more so. The goal of independence, of achieving the means by which the dispossessed and disenfranchised are able to reclaim their destinies and determine their futures, remains as necessary today as it was in Cabral's time.

9 M. Atwood, *The Blind Assassin*, Toronto: M&S, 2000, p 12

Anyone reading Cabral's writings today will be struck by the importance he placed on understanding a people's history and, as the contemporary manifestation of that accumulated history, culture. Cabral was aware that without its history, a people had no future. Cabral once wrote,

> There is a preconception held by many people, even on the left, that imperialism made us enter history at the moment when it began its adventure in our countries.... We consider that when imperialism arrived in Guinea it made us leave history—our history.... The moment imperialism arrived and colonialism arrived, it made us leave our history and enter another history.

Of course, there have been dramatic political changes since colonial times brought about by the mass upsurges that characterized the movements for independence, although the territorial boundaries for exploitation established by the Berlin Conference have remained largely intact. However there are striking parallels between the conditions of the colonial era and those that prevail today. The colonial territories were zones of plunder, pillage, and production of primary products for imperial centres.

Today, there is a significant comprador class, nurtured over the past four decades, that has a direct material interest in the perpetuation of these social relations of production and control of the state. The scale of the extraction of wealth from Africa has grown, bringing new euphemisms; plunder and pillage go by the name of "investment" or "development of natural resources"; "civilizing the native," once the justification for the work of missionaries, is today called "development," the justification for the aid industry and its coterie of consultants and international development NGOs.

It is a sad truth that we are often quick to lay the blame for assassinations and coups d'état at the hands of imperialist agencies such as the CIA, M16, PIDE, etc. There is little doubt that such agencies have played a significant role, and it is well known that the Portuguese secret service, PIDE, was implicated in the assassination of Cabral. We are slow, however, to acknowledge the role played by those within the ranks of inspired leaders. Whether we are talking of Patrice Lumumba, Kwame Nkrumah, Thomas Sankara, Amílcar Cabral, Steven Biko, or a host of others who led movements that threatened the hold of empire, betrayal has always come from within. Cabral himself was assassinated by his own colleagues, albeit with the support of PIDE. It is said that he responded to the first shot by turning to his assassin, saying that this was no way to resolve differences.

Like many others, Cabral realized that revolutionary movements need to win over sections of the petit bourgeoisie—the so-called "middle classes"—whose skills and knowledge could serve the movement so long as they were able to commit class suicide. Torn between finding freedom from colonial oppression through association with the forces of liberation and the attraction of the privilege, wealth, accumulation, and self-aggrandizement offered in the wake of independence, this historically vacillating class has always been notoriously unreliable. And the story of postindependence Africa is replete with examples of betrayals and treachery.

Over the last thirty years, African countries, like others in the Global South, have experienced a reversal of many of the gains of independence, gains that had been won through anticolonial revolutions only after the loss of so much blood and so many lives.

Beginning in the early 1980s, the same set of social and economic policies—the so-called structural adjustment programmes—was implemented by African governments, opening avenues for capital expansion through the extreme privatization and liberalization of the national economies. The result of these neoliberal policies has been an ever-increasing gap between the haves and the have-nots. A small minority, whose interests and enterprises were closely associated with the multinational corporations and financial institutions, have become obscenely rich, while the standard of living of the majority and value of the wage for those lucky enough to find work, has declined rapidly. Unemployment, landlessness, and homelessness are the lot of the many.

Accompanying this vast accumulation by dispossession—of land, utilities, services, and natural resources—are two other forms of dispossession that deserve more attention. The first is a process of political dispossession: African governments have become more accountable to international corporations, banks, international financial institutions, and international aid agencies than to their own citizens. The right to self-determination that so inspired the movements for independence has eroded with the lack of any formality or constitutional adjustment.

Secondly, the period is characterized by a dispossession of memory effected by a ruling elite who wish to airbrush from history their own betrayals. They have been assisted in that process by corporate media and changes in curricula in primary, secondary, and tertiary education and in the day-to-day political discourse that have all but eliminated awareness of the history of anticolonial struggles and the heroism of an entire generation.

The writings of Amílcar Cabral offer a profound understanding of this almost forgotten epoch and the historical mission of anticolonial movements across the continent and indeed throughout the Global South. A people without a history is a people without a future. The converse is also true; it is only through having the courage to invent the future that it is possible to appropriate our history and place our short lives within an epochal movement for the liberation of all humankind. It was this extraordinary grasp of his historical mission that makes Cabral so relevant and so inspiring today.

Why now?

Guinea-Bissau and Cape Verde are tiny places, yet their histories resonate far beyond their borders and hold relevance to struggles for liberation across the continent as well as the Black liberation movements in the Americas. Cabral's work and life hold a special meaning, and it was this meaning that drew the two of us to contemplate this volume and to seek out a broad array of respected writers to paint the picture of Cabral and reflect on his legacy and the ongoing struggles for liberation and transformation in the African world.

Cabral emerged on the international scene in the midst of sweeping changes in the Global South. Struggles for independence and national liberation were underway. By the mid- to late 1960s, however, it was becoming clear that, as Samir Amin has pointed out, three general crises were unfolding: the crisis of the Soviet project (and more generally, the crisis of socialism); the crisis of the national populist projects in the Global South; and the crisis of Western social democracy. These crises were not always easy to identify, in part because of the dynamism that existed in the Global South and the growing stands of nations and peoples against imperialism. The crisis of socialism was not always easy to identify, because the critics of the road taken by the then Soviet Union—whether they identified that road as socialist-yet-problematic, capitalist, or deformed—could still frequently point to other experiments in social transformation that followed—or appeared to follow—a different course.

Cabral did not speak explicitly to what we may now call *the crisis of socialism*. He was also very careful regarding rendering verdicts on the work of other national populist projects.[10] That said, within Cabral's work, one sees valuable insights into both, a point that comes through to the reader in studying this volume.

With regard to socialism, although Cabral certainly used terminology associated with Marxism (e.g. "modes of production"), he grounded his revolutionary theory in the experiences of the masses fighting Portuguese colonialism. Though he occasionally applauded other revolutionary leaders, one does not find in Cabral a near religious faith in individual great thinkers but instead the use of such thinkers—and their work—as a jumping off point in creating and advocating revolutionary theory and practice for Guinea-Bissau.

To the fury of partisans on different sides, Cabral took no stand on the split between the Communist Party of China and the Communist Party of the Soviet Union. Though a close ally of the Cuban revolution, he differed from the approach favored by the Cuban party and government during much of the 1960s called the "*foco* theory," a view frequently associated with Ernesto "Che" Guevara.[11] Certainly

10 "National populist" can be considered a generic term within which one includes national liberation struggles and other forms of anti-imperialist national movements that, while generally tending to the Left, were not, themselves, anticapitalist.

11 The "foco theory" suggested that a small guerrilla band could act as the political-military hub of a revolution, effectively dispensing with a mass-based radical party or mass-based revolutionary front.

some of his silence reflected the need of the Guinean national liberation struggle to assemble a wide swath of allies, but Cabral's stance was not based solely on diplomacy but also on establishing the legitimacy of the Guinean experience as a source of not only revolutionary inspiration but theory as well.

Though identified as a party and holding to the form of a party, Cabral's PAIGC was more akin to a national liberation front. Amongst other things this meant that while the PAIGC was committed to national liberation and social transformation, there was never total agreement as to the full nature of the postcolonial society, irrespective of the anti-imperialist language of the time. This point cannot be overemphasized, because Cabral was not speaking only his own thoughts but was representing and leading a consensus within, for lack of a better term, a revolutionary movement. He was not, in other words, an individual public intellectual who said or wrote what was on his mind, but instead, and in each case, he had to think of the dynamics that were unfolding within his movement.

The nature of the dynamics within the PAIGC, which are addressed directly and indirectly within this volume, are additionally important because they shift discussions concerning Cabral's murder and the later reactionary turn of the PAIGC (and government of Guinea-Bissau). Rather than an exclusive focus on "agents" and "traitors," a more comprehensive analysis helps us better understand the question of class struggle within revolutionary movements and in postrevolutionary societies. As we noted earlier in this introduction, class forces that had interests that were not consistently revolutionary found in Cabral and his work a threat to their own class and/or individual projects.

In Cabral we see an indictment of not only those who subsequently murdered him, but also those, both in Guinea-Bissau and in other parts of Africa, who undermined national populist and socialist projects. In Cabral's works, and in the historical details of PAIGC's efforts in the anti-Portuguese struggle, one witnesses a profoundly democratic practice. The PAIGC was rooted amongst the masses, and an immense amount of time was dedicated to educational work amongst the people in advance of the armed struggle, as well as during the course of the armed struggle. Institutions were established in the liberated zones that placed power in the hands of ordinary people, in most cases, for the first time in their lives. Many traditional practices were challenged, but they refused to succumb to a love affair with everything modern.

One of the most important examples set by Cabral and the PAIGC was that of nation-building. As this volume establishes, the building of the revolutionary movement was actually the building of the Guinea-Bissau and Cape Verdean nations. It meant respecting the multiethnic nature of Guinea-Bissau and Cape Verde, as well as the need to transcend ethnic identity and match it—rather than replace it entirely—with a national identity. This task has been one of the most difficult within Africa and has been the source of much backsliding and suffering over the last forty years.

A final general point is related to the character of the PAIGC and the revolutionary movement. The death of Cabral left the movement in Guinea-Bissau and Cape Verde in much worse shape than at first appeared to be the case. The fact that subsequent to Cabral's murder the movement went forward, declared independence from Portugal, and was prepared to assume power, masked a deeper challenge. There was an insufficient leadership cadre within the movement to provide the ideological and practical guidance to the revolutionary process that unfolded after independence. As so often happens, there was an understandable overreliance on the wisdom of the leader, in this case Cabral, when that wisdom so desperately needed to be spread. This can be contrasted, for instance, with the Vietnamese revolutionary movement that was able to survive the death of Ho Chi Minh, in large part due to the actual collective nature of the leadership of the movement. This does not suggest that there is no role for exceptional leaders within such a movement. Nevertheless, as the history of the twentieth century certainly shows, the revolutionary process must involve the building of collective and capable leadership as well as serious attention towards the creation of successors.

This volume

In this volume we have sought to present to the reader a four-dimensional view of Cabral, the fourth dimension being *time*, or in this case, context. It is not just that there are differing points of view on the significance of Cabral, it is also important for the reader to appreciate the complexities and contradictions that existed within Cabral and the revolutionary movement. As such, this volume is divided into several parts.

We begin the book with discussions on the legacy of Cabral. It is, in our opinion, critical to jump to the present, as it were, and immediately engage the reader with why Cabral remains important to this day. From legacy we move to reflections on Cabral, some of which are very personal. As with legacy, the authors endeavor to focus the reader on the current applicability and relevance of Cabral.

The third section is on Cabral, women, and emancipation. We had hoped to have additional articles here, and we believe this topic to be especially important for a myriad of reasons. During much of the period of the vibrant national populist projects, there was a masculinist tendency within the progressive movements that promoted male leadership to the exclusion of women, and additionally subordinated the struggles against male supremacy to the national, popular struggle. Though frequently tolerated in the name of national liberation and independence, such masculinist tendencies served as a cancer in the revolutionary movement. The articles in this section help us to not only understand Cabral and the question of gender but to more generally understand the challenge that exists in conducting struggles that, by their very nature, are multidimensional.

Our fourth section concerns Cabral and the Pan-Africanists. This is especially timely given efforts over the past several years to renew Pan-Africanism and, in fact, generate a twenty-first century Pan-Africanism. Cabral was an important, though frequently overlooked, Pan-Africanist. His work in connection with all of the Portuguese African colonies is often either poorly understood or taken for granted, rather than grasped as a very practical and quite revolutionary Pan-Africanism. Additionally, Cabral's Pan-Africanism was controversial in that it was "nonracial" (antiracist) in the sense in which the South African movement came to define the term. Pan-Africanism for Cabral, in other words, was not about skin colour, nor was it about a romanticization of the African past. It was truly about a revolutionized African world and the creation of connections that could link popular democratic forces to combat colonialism and neocolonialism. Cabral was intolerant of those who thought that one's colour or point of origin automatically qualified them to be an African freedom fighter. The authors in this section help us to understand this matter in greater depth.

The fifth section—focusing on culture and education—will certainly attract many readers who are familiar with Cabral's quite famous article on culture and national liberation. Many of us on the political left have been exposed to cultural caricatures from within our respective movement, i.e., 'cardboard' approaches to popular culture in the name of building a revolutionary alternative. Cabral took on the question of culture by beginning with the cultures that exist and insisting that the revolutionary forces understand them and build upon them. Yet contrary, once again, to those who romanticized—if not mythologized traditional cultures—Cabral examined them dialectically, understanding the contradictions that exist within all cultures and seeking out the democratic component upon which a new framework could be built. Of particular importance in this section is the discussion of how Cabral's thinking remains alive and vibrant in the chants and songs of RAP music in Guinea-Bissau.

The sixth section concerns Cabral and the African American struggle. This topic is highlighted in this volume because of a particular role that Cabral and his work played in the transformation of a major component of the Left of the Black freedom struggle in the United States of America. Cabral's vision of Pan-Africanism and his refusal to romanticize the past challenged the Black Left in the United States to develop a more advanced and radical politics grounded in the realities of America. This did not mean that there were automatic answers to the challenges faced in the United States, nor did it mean that those who sought out Cabral came to the same conclusions. Rather it meant that Cabral posed questions through his theory and practice that, while sometimes creating ideological discomfort, forced the Black Left in the United States to rethink its conditions and role.

We end the volume with a selected bibliography as a means of encouraging the reader to go forward with the study of Cabral, using our volume as a starting line, perhaps, or rallying point, rather than as a finish line.

Our hope is that you find this book to serve as an introduction, or reintroduction, to one whom global capitalism would rather we forget. However, the legacy of Cabral does not allow the amnesia to be complete, as the essays in this volume demonstrate so eloquently. Understanding Cabral sheds light on the revolutionary process and the necessity to ground that process in the creation of radical theory based on the actual conditions within which a movement is attempting to develop. That linkage is never complete, however, until it is joined to the actual practice of revolutionary politics and the construction of organisations that can advance such politics. The inspiring signpost for such a task has two words emblazoned upon it: ***Amílcar Cabral.***

SECTION 2:

THE LEGACY OF AMÍLCAR CABRAL

2. NO EASY VICTORIES

SOME REFLECTIONS ON AMÍLCAR CABRAL'S LEGACY

Nigel C. Gibson

The problem of the nature of the state created after independence is perhaps the secret of the failure of African independence.
—Amílcar Cabral, "Connecting the Struggles"

Struggle is daily action against ourselves and against the enemy.
—Amílcar Cabral, "Our Party and the Struggle Must Be Led by the Best Sons and Daughters of our People"

A rigorous historical approach is similarly needed when examining another problem related to this—how can the underdeveloped countries evolve towards revolution, towards socialism? There is a preconception held by many people, even on the left, that imperialism made us enter history at the moment when it began its adventure in our countries. This preconception must be denounced: for somebody on the left, and for Marxists in particular, history obviously means the class struggle. Our opinion is exactly the contrary. We consider that when imperialism arrived in Guinea it made us leave history—our history. We agree that history in our country is the result of class struggle, but we have our own class struggles in our own country; the moment imperialism arrived and colonialism arrived, it made us leave our history and enter another history.
—Amílcar Cabral, "A Brief Analysis of the Social Structure"

Amílcar Cabral is a theorist on par with Frantz Fanon. But unlike Fanon, Cabral is a theorist who has not travelled well.[12] In contrast to the 1970s and 1980s, Cabral's name is rarely heard in university classrooms or NGO offices today. Perhaps as an outcome of the period of the "Washington consensus"—the collapse of statist Communism and the hegemony of neoliberal capitalism—there have been no new interpretations of Cabral in English for over twenty years.[13] Although often reduced to a footnote in the textbooks of postcolonial theory, the questions he raises about culture and social transformation are not simply echoes of Fanon. And the case he makes for the "weapon of theory," linked to his critique of Eurocentric history and the necessity for African theorists to think Africa from African realities, remains highly relevant. Theory for Cabral was intimately connected to current realities and practices. It was worked out collectively in the struggle. Thus much of his writing is educational, taken from lectures given in seminars and talks with party militants, while his longer, more polemical and theoretical pieces are presented at international venues (at the UN, in Cuba, and in the United States) and emphasize the importance of practice.

Liberation, Cabral argues, does not only mean recovering history but also making one's own history, putting an end to the idea of being at the back end of Europe's history. Today, Africa still seems to be beholden to the Global North, and even as its looks east, it does the bidding of hegemonic global capitalism. Even if models of development don't slavishly follow Europe, Africa remains dependent along capitalist lines, always subject to theories conjured up in the North, which, from pharmaceuticals to economic models, are often first tested out in the Global South.

12 In the social sciences, Fanon like Cabral was also dismissed as a bygone third world ist by the 1980s, and without the new interest in *Black Skin White Masks* in literary studies that became essential to the emergence of postcolonial studies as a field, he too would have become simply an historical footnote. Within postcolonial studies Cabral's name is often associated with Fanon's, as in Fanon and Cabral wrote on national culture, but without much specificity.

13 See Mustafah Dhada, *Warriors at Work*. Niwot, Colorado, USA: Colorado University Press, 1993 and Patrick Chabal, Patrick. *Amílcar Cabral: Revolutionary Leadership and People's War*. New York and Cambridge: Cambridge UP, 1983.

Cabral's background as an agronomist helped to form his analysis and informs his concept of theory as practical. During the struggle, armed militants were taught farming techniques that would help the local population, who in turn would help feed the militants. Barter systems were introduced in liberated areas to provide traditional staple goods, freeing local economies from colonial-mediated markets. Cabral took seriously the importance of material reality and the Marxian idea of material conditions shaping consciousness, but he was not a determinist. As he argued, "We put ourselves in the position of people who came to learn with the peasants, and in the end the peasants were discovering for themselves why things had gone badly for them" (1969d 159). He believed in Fanon's Marxian notion that people change as they make history, and on that basis considered that the "class suicide" of the petit bourgeoisie was possible. This oft-repeated phrase actually expresses part of Cabral's philosophy: As a class, the petit bourgeoisie is defined by its small-mindedness, individualism, and egotism; thus such a suicide had to be social and was possible only within the context of social change created by a revolution. At the same time, because the petit bourgeoisie was materially weak, class suicide was not possible without their will to suicide. Thus, he maintained, just as the petit bourgeoisie's struggle against colonialism could free it of its narrow class interest, political education—through literacy programmes and collective discussion—could help bring masses of pauperized rural people into the struggle as actors, uncovering the "germs of resistance" in the cultures of peasants and the urban poor.

The Question of Organisation: Returning to the Source

As an African nationalist, African Marxist, and leader of the Marxist-Leninist (democratic-centralist) party, Cabral reflects quite a different historical moment. Yet the question of organisation and its relation to the principles of "revolutionary democracy" (see Cabral 1979d) remains important today. Critical of those armchair radicals who plotted revolutions in the colonial metropoles, on one hand, and of those who thought that power came out of a barrel of a gun, on the other, Cabral was a humanist and anti-elitist. Political practice, he maintained, depended on continually "returning to the source," i.e., the grassroots popular struggle. Rather than repeating a catechism of shibboleths, such an anti-elitist principled practice must be constantly worked out.

In contrast to Guevarism (and the focoism that was fashionable at the time),[14] which reduced theory to guerilla war, Cabral insisted on the necessity of revolutionary theory: "It is true that a revolution can fail, even though it be nurtured on perfectly conceived theories, [but] nobody has yet successfully practiced revolution without a revolutionary theory" (1979e 119). However, this did not mean that theory could simply be applied to a situation; it was intimately connected with local situations and experience, and indeed, he maintained, reflecting on practice itself "gives birth to a theory."

Thus, taking part in a revolution undergirded Cabral's concept of theory. Let us not forget that he devoted his adult life to decolonising Africa, spending ten years in the armed struggle. And what had started as a poorly armed group led by Cabral won a resounding victory against Portuguese imperialism, sparking a revolution in the colonial metropole.

Cabral's wonderful phrase, "claim no easy victories," resonates critically with contemporary struggles, which, amplified in the age of Twitter and the Internet, grab the imagination and often gain rapid support, only to quickly dissipate. Rather than the end of ideology, our globally connected age requires a critique which begins from concrete and locally grounded analyses and historically informed reflections that help a movement anticipate problems and contradictions, so that it isn't merely responding in the moment. Faithfully describing a situation helps to provide solidarity in the face of setbacks and leads to a wider and at the same time more nuanced understanding of what is at stake. Cabral understood that the defeat of colonialism was only one part of the struggle. He adamantly maintained that the colonial state could not be taken over, and remained confident that a new state, synonymous with the liberated areas, was emerging through the

14 It should be noted that Cabral's paper "The Weapon of Theory" was delivered at the first Tricontinental Conference in Havana in January 1966.

struggle. Sadly, his murder foreshadowed the stillbirth of the new society that he gave his life for.

Class Struggle and History

"My own view," Cabral argued in 1967, "is that there are no real conflicts between the peoples of Africa. There are only conflicts between the elites" (Davidson xii). In the context in which he was fighting, Cabral placed tremendous importance on national culture being created through the struggle. This concept of national culture included an analysis of the material reality of the people and the ways in which they worked on the land (collectively) but were forced to trade (individually) within a colonial system. Aware of the many different local realities, the Cabralian task was to uncover these facts and *make conscious* these living realities. Using Marxian categories in an analysis of the social structure, Cabral made an important contribution to social theory, insisting on "the existence of history before class struggle" (1979e 125). He brilliantly challenged the unthinking determinism of the Left in his "Brief Analysis of the Social Structure," quoted above, and thus rejected any notion of historical stages that would necessitate capitalist phases.

Because the "land does not have [very wide] class differences…and the better-off classes who have most resources are small in number,"[15] he considered "tribal" identity a lingering issue. Arguing that the material basis for the "tribal" system no longer existed in Africa (1969c 144), Cabral asserted that the system continued to exist because its "superstructure" was supported by colonialism. But as much as he directed his argument against the colonialists, he was particularly critical of "detribalized individuals or groups within the national liberation movement" (1979c 85) who, he argued, manipulate "tribal" identities "opportunistically" for their own interests. Continuing to be concerned that ethno-politics was being reproduced inside the party (1979c 89), he changed tack, no longer sending militants as party representatives

15 He did, however, continue to argue that class contradictions remained important.

to recruit chiefs from their own tribe. In retrospect, however, such a tactical change was clearly not enough to address "the internal contradiction in the economic, social, cultural (and therefore historical) reality of each of our countries" (1969b 91-92). Nonetheless, Cabral understood that liberation could not be introduced by a party.[16] Rather, to be truly national, liberation could only emerge from mass activity. It was through the struggle itself that local cultures could be celebrated and enlivened and that a national culture could emerge; indeed, Cabral believed, it would be woven together through the national struggle. It was the unity of the struggle against militarily superior Portuguese colonialism that made it winnable, because this unity would create new solidarities. That is to say, grounded in and part of the struggle, which was, in short, a political struggle for "dignity"—the "culture of masses in revolt"—new identities emerge (1973a 69). Cabral speaks of identity as "in a state of permanent evolution" (see 1973a 64) and, as a constantly changing expression of the multicultural character of society. Thus what was alive in local culture and what could be a mobilizing element were its songs, dances, and languages. Cabral's insistence that "we defended these cultural differences with all our strength, but we also fought with all our strength all divisions on a political level" (see 1969d) indicates how he understood culture, in contrast to chauvinism, as something alive and open. And reminding us of the weapon of theory, he added, "we can only transform our reality, on the basis of detailed knowledge of it...its various internal contradictions...and our own efforts" (1979e 122). Thus, culture alone does not equal the new society, and theory, as a product of praxis, becomes the continual work of facing new contradictions.

16 Lenin (1965 135) also insisted, against leaders of his own party, that "Socialism cannot be implemented by a minority, by the Party." And believed, like Cabral that "it can be implemented only by tens of millions when they have learned to do it themselves."

Return to the Source and the Dangerous Petit Bourgeoisie

The struggle against colonialism was a struggle for liberation and dignity.[17] Cabral argued that the question of returning to the source "does not arise for the masses of these people, for it is they who are the repository of the culture and at the same time the only sector who can preserve and build it up and make history" (1973a 61). But it would be mistaken to take "the return to the source" as a return to some kind of tradition and custom. It is not a substitute for the struggle but part of a political commitment to the popular struggle, to make history.

First, the return to the source means to deny "the pretended superiority of the culture of the dominant power." Rejecting the idea that the unschooled and illiterate masses are backward and unthinking is merely a first step of "re-Africanization,"[18] which could be "completed only during the struggle, through daily contact with the mass of the people and the communion of the sacrifices which the struggle demands" (1979f 145). The identification with the people cannot be based on individual whim, otherwise it is "nothing more than an attempt at short term benefits—knowingly or unknowingly a kind of political opportunism" (1973a 63). In other words, "the return to the source" cannot be reduced to cultural identification but has to become ongoing political praxis (see also Fanon, 1968, "On National Culture"). The petit bourgeoisie's revolutionary voluntarism is down to this: only through active and absolute identification with the struggle is class suicide possible.

---

17 So Cabral argued in the speech "Identity and Dignity in the Context of the Liberation Struggle" given at Lincoln University (an historical Black university in Pennsylvania, USA that Nkrumah attended in the 1930s and where Cabral was awarded an honorary doctorate).

18 Cabral's idea of "Re-Africanization of the mind" (1969f 76) challenges the colonised elite (the petit bourgeoisie) to dissociate themselves from colonial culture and instead direct their attention to the lived experience of the people in revolt. This "return to the source" is not an individual act, but one mediated by the party/organisation. The return to the source is a manifestation of the class suicide of the bourgeoisie. And as the social individual emerges through these new relationships with the people and their land, there is also an intimation of a critique of the party/state formation.

As in other struggles against colonialism, the fragmented petit bourgeoisie, especially the small numbers of colonially educated elites, played a role completely out of proportion with its size. Indeed it was from this class faction that Cabral and many of the leaders of the movements against Portuguese colonialism emerged.[19] Others were drawn to negritude and Pan-Africanism, which Cabral dismissed as desperate expressions of bitterness and frustration arising from their isolation from the real lives of the people (see 1973a 62). Likewise, claims to tradition were equally, if not more, problematic, and cultural identification alone was not "an act of struggle." For the petit bourgeoisie, Cabralian commitment (moral and social) in its most materialist sense, had to be class suicide (1973a 69, 63). Thus rather than a united front against colonialism (or a strategy of stages of struggle), class suicide was possible because of the very marginality and powerlessness of the petit bourgeoisie. This "suicide," or perhaps better, an absolute commitment to social and national liberation, was a slow and uneven process, Cabral warned. In a schematic way, measured by attitudes to the struggle, Cabral delineated three groups: a minority reactionary procolonialist group, a majority who are hesitant and indecisive, and lastly a majority who are committed to liberation (1973a 63-4). Yet it was from within this section of the petit bourgeoisie, namely those dedicated to the liberation struggle, that the real internal contradictions emerged.

---

19 Speaking (at a conference in Dar-Es-Salaam in 1965) of his experiences as a student in Lisbon, Cabral said that "[we were] influenced by current events which were shaking the world, and began to discuss … what could today be called the re-Africanization of our mind. Yes, some of those people are here in this hall … Augustinho Neto, Mario de Andrade, Marcelino Dos Santos … Vassco Cabral and Dr. Mondlane." Clearly "Re-Africanization of our minds" was not simply a cultural revolution or a negritude (though echoing Césaire's "Return to the Native Land" he adds that "we have not invented many things … but we do have our own hearts, our own heads, our own history) but an armed struggle to "return to our history" our hearts and our heads (see Cabral 1969 76-78).

Cabralian Pitfalls

The question, "what kind of society do we want to create," is often occluded by the urgency of the immediate situation. However, the same dialectic of regression that has affected revolutions led by democratic-centralist organisations can affect highly democratic, grass-roots social movements. In other words, the form of organisation in and of itself does not determine the success of a liberation movement. It is the question of what happens after "victory" that matters, and willing away the problems and principles involved in the building of democratic institutions can be disastrous. And thus we are back to Cabral's point about theory as the weapon.

Cabral did not think that independent movements could take over the colonial state apparatus and use it for its own purposes. It wasn't the colour of the administrator that was the issue, he argued, but the fact that there *was* an administrator (1979a 60). About this, Cabral was unequivocal, and he recognised the state as "the most important problem in the liberation," arguing that "in order to make everything possible for our people" the colonial state had to be totally destroyed (1973b 83). But what about new institutions that would not simply be representative but would be controlled by the people from the bottom up?

Despite the debilitating legacies of colonialism and the neocolonial danger, Cabral maintained that the central threat to building a new society on the basis of mass participation was internal. Implicit in Cabral's thinking is the view that there is an intimate connection between the nature of the state created after independence and the disproportionate role played by the petit bourgeoisie in the liberation struggle. In other words, in contrast to Cabral's delineation, the latter could support the struggle for independence and betray the social revolution (1969 b 110). Indeed, it was from amongst some of the armed leaders of the revolution that the greatest threat would grow.

Shying away from developing blueprints for the future, Cabral considered the future in the present as a practical issue of institution building in the liberated zones. In contrast to the parasitic and authoritarian colonial state, he claimed, "we are creating the state through the struggle. We now have popular tribunals...and the peasants participating by electing the courts themselves" (1973b 84). Indeed, as early as 1965, he argued, "Our party always thinks it is the development of the struggle that determines our political comportment. And now we realize that we have in our country a state, we have all the instruments of the state in the liberated areas" (Cabral 1965). In his lecture on revolutionary democracy in 1969, he added, "Revolutionary democracy demands that...at all costs the people feel that it is they who have the power in our lands in their hands. Up until now they have not felt this very much. In the liberated areas some comrades have usurped this power of our people" (1979d 97).

Concerned with the immediate struggle against colonialism, Cabral did not theorize this further and failed to follow up on his concern that the internal threat would manifest in "opportunists" inside the party. The problem was not simply that the party took sole power with the end of colonialism, but that the revolutionary council became a power unto itself. Additionally, Cabral always insisted that the armed struggle was not militarist and that military objectives were always secondary to political objectives, but the military (an institution which was stronger, more disciplined, and better organised than any other after independence) essentially became a political body. Challenged by the desperate socio-economic crisis, and increasingly centralized and isolated from the mass of the people, the party and military became the battlefield of contending petit bourgeois interests. It was inevitable that coups would follow.

It is of course always easier to look back on these developments with a clear view and dismiss Cabral's anticolonial, nationalist, and Marxist party politics as ideas from another time. Certainly, Cabral's appreciation of the work of revolutionary theory as a weapon did not—indeed, perhaps could not—theorize what would happen after the end of Portuguese rule. This marks the difference between Cabral's moment and our postcolonial moment. But despite massive movements for change, the development of a theory which engages the internal contradictions of decolonisation conceptually continues to be a challenge. Just as a new society cannot be introduced by a party or by a revolutionary council, it is equally mistaken to believe that autonomous movements alone equal a new society. Rather it is from this contradiction that the movement towards liberation evolves. Shaping the future depends on praxis and conscious action that includes theoretical reflection grounded also in the archive of thinking Africa's liberation—of which Cabral's work is an irreducible part. What we take from Cabral forty years after his death is that the development of liberatory theory is intimately connected to movements for freedom and the contradictory processes of the creativity of cognition. In such contexts, "struggle is daily action against ourselves and against the enemy" (1979b 65). *A luta continua.*

Bibliography

Cabral, Amílcar. 1965." Liberating Portuguese Guinea from within," interview with Frene Ginwala, The New African 85 (June). Available at http://pzacad.pitzer.edu/NAM/newafrre/writers/ginwala/ginwalaQ.htm

Cabral, Amílcar. 1969a. "Brief analysis of the social structure in Guinea" (1964) in *Revolution in Guinea.* London: Stage 1 pp. 56-75.

Cabral, Amílcar. 1969b. "The weapon of theory" (1966) in *Revolution in Guinea.* London: Stage 1 pp. 90-112.

Cabral, Amílcar. 1969c. "Practical problems and tactics" (1968) in *Revolution in Guinea.* London: Stage 1. pp. 134-151.

Cabral, Amílcar. 1969d. "Towards final victory" (1969) in *Revolution in Guinea.* London: Stage 1. pp. 156-164.

Cabral, Amílcar. 1969e. "The nationalist movement of Portuguese colonies" (1965), in *Revolution in Guinea.* London: Stage 1 pp. 76-85.

Cabral, Amílcar. 1971. *Our People are Our Mountains.* London: Committee for Freedom in Mozambique, Angola & Guiné.

Cabral, Amílcar. 1973a. "Identity and Dignity in the Context of the National Liberation Struggle," in *Return to the Source*. New York: Monthly Review Press, pp. 57-74.

Cabral, Amílcar. 1973b. "Connecting the Struggles: an informal talk with Black Americans," in *Return to the Source*. New York: Monthly Review Press, pp. 75-92.

Cabral, Amílcar. 1979a. "To start out from the reality of our land—to be realists," (1969) in *Unity and Struggle: Selected Writings on Amílcar Cabral* New York: Monthly Review. pp. 44-63.

Cabral, Amílcar. 1979b. "Our Party and the struggle must be led by the best sons and daughters of our people," (1969) in *Unity and Struggle: Selected Writings on Amílcar Cabral* New York: Monthly Review. pp. 64-74.

Cabral, Amílcar. 1979c. "Not everyone is of the Party," (1969) in *Unity and Struggle: Selected Writings on Amílcar Cabral* New York: Monthly Review. pp. 83-92.

Cabral, Amílcar. 1979d. "Revolutionary Democracy," (1969) in *Unity and Struggle: Selected Writings on Amílcar Cabral* New York: Monthly Review. pp. 93-97.

Cabral, Amílcar. 1979e. "Presupposition and objectives of national liberation in relation to social structure," (1966) in *Unity and Struggle: Selected Writings on Amílcar Cabral* New York: Monthly Review. pp. 119-137.

Cabral, Amílcar. 1979f. "National liberation and culture," (1970) in *Unity and Struggle: Selected Writings on Amílcar Cabral* New York: Monthly Review. pp. 138-154.

Davidson, Basil. 1979. "Introduction" in *Unity and Struggle*: Selected Writings on Amílcar Cabral New York: Monthly Review.

Fanon, Frantz. 1968. *The Wretched of the Earth*. New York: Grove.
Lenin, V.I. 1965. *Collected Works*, Vol. 27. Moscow: Progress Publishers

Meinkel, Deirdre. 2006. "Culture and Process in the Thoughts of Amílcar Cabral," in *The Life, Thought, and Legacy of Cape Verde's Freedom Fighter Amílcar Cabral* edited by John Fobanjong and Thomas Ranuga. Lewiston: Edwin Mellen.

3. CLASS SUICIDE

THE PETIT BOURGEOISIE AND THE CHALLENGES OF DEVELOPMENT

Samir Amin

Amílcar Cabral belongs in the pantheon of African freedom fighters. Leading a liberation struggle was only one of his achievements. He also had the best ideas for the construction of a modern, democratic, peoples' state, which would deliver on real and sustainable development.

Cabral's Thesis: The Suicide of the Petit Bourgeoisie and the National Question in Cape Verde and Guinea-Bissau

When France, Britain, and Belgium accepted the principle of political decolonisation in 1960, Portugal refused to go along. National liberation movements had no other alternative than to wage an armed struggle. War always opens up real possibilities for the radicalisation of politics, but by the same token, it also lends itself to romantic illusions. A good many of the supporters of such movements in Africa and outside Africa (especially amongst Western "third-worlders") encouraged such illusions.

Although Cabral did share some of these illusions, I think his position needs to be seen in the light of the challenges faced by African peoples as they sought to shed the huge burden of colonialism. I will expand on that after first discussing Cabral's views in the context of ulterior developments in the countries concerned, Cape Verde and Guinea-Bissau, and other former Portugese colonies. The validity of some of Cabral's theories can be put into question today.

One of Cabral's theories that needs to be re-examined is that of the "suicide of the bourgeoisie as a class." Certainly, the conditions thrown up by war often facilitate the display of the finer qualities of human nature, which even the petit bourgeoisie share. Courage, solidarity, and permanent contact with the peasant masses can help erase previous prejudice and ignorance.

But I remain unconvinced that once independence has been gained, social realities would change in the direction of an end to inequality: the advantages to be procured from positions of leadership are inevitably reserved for a minority, even if this group includes cadres drawn from the grassroots. The fight for socialism, in my opinion, is a very long war; the uncontestably progressive historic role of national liberation movements notwithstanding, the signs were already there in the hierarchies created and the manoeuvring that went on at their very heart of these groups. The Soviet Communist Party model adopted by these groups also cemented these attitudes. How many militants, even the most courageous, could behave like unconditional or even fawning believers towards the national or local leadership? Some of the people I knew to be amongst the best militants, the most sincere towards the people, the most courageous on the military front, were sent to the front line—to a certain death in some cases—while the "chiefs" remained safe from risk. I saw then that "the petit bourgeoisie was not ready to commit suicide."

The other question concerns the Guinea-Bissau/Cape Verde issue. I do not think the people of these two colonies constituted one nation—they are quite distinct. Guinea-Bissau is part of West Africa—a multiethnic African country, similar to others in the region. Cape Verde is totally different. It was in the Cape Verde islands, which the Portugese inhabited from the moment they discovered them, that they later perfected the formula which was used to build America—a slavery driven plantation colony that was part of the Euro-Atlantic mercantile system. The formula was in fact defined to the last detail by the founders of the Portugese (and later Spanish, British, and French) colonisation of the Americas—slave trade, colonisation, creolisation of the colony and its administrative structures. Cape Verde is the ancestor of the Antilles and Brazil.

The electoral defeat suffered by the PAICV (Partido Africano da Independência de Cabo Verde: African Party of Independence of Cape

Verde) at the hands of the Creole petit bourgeoisie—and bourgeoisie—which had not participated in the liberation struggles—calls for a reinterpretation of what that society really is. This is certainly sad, because whatever its limits and the errors of government, it is to the PAICV that Cape Verde owes its very existence. It was the PAICV that gave its starving and barefoot people land and education. So why was it defeated? For one, it underestimated the role of the church. But there was also the arrogance in the daily behaviour of former brave fighters who had joined the administrative service. This was the explanation given to me by Pedro Pires, the PAICV general secretary. Yet the PAICV had several remarkable cadres it could count on, many more than in other African countries. I would say the same about the leftist opponents within the PAICV, who, having adopted the Maoist line, were disliked by the PAICV leadership to the point that many of them were forced to flee into exile in Portugal before returning later to the country. A page needs to be turned on these quarrels. What is important is to reconstitute a broad leftist front united around a minimal programme but retaining its diversity on the basis of mutual respect of the various groups or tendencies involved. I do not hesitate to say that this broad democratic front could include some elements who contributed to the victory of the Right, either through pique or through being constrained by the PAICV's triumphant sectarianism.

Independent Guinea-Bissau quickly became like other countries in the region, dubbed "less developed" by Western agencies—that is, extremely dependent on foreign aid for the survival of their miserable state apparatus, after having given up on the project launched by Cabral and the armed resistance.

Angola and Mozambique

Though Cabral was not chiefly responsible for what happened in Angola and Mozambique, he does share the responsibility with the first generation of leaders of liberation movements in Lusophone Africa, all of whom shared his idea of the suicide of the petit bourgeoisie.

Angola was as problematic as Guinea-Bissau, albeit in a different manner. The MPLA was well implanted in the capital and especially in the educated classes, often metisse, a fact that the antiwhite, antimetisse nationalist demagogues didn't hesitate to exploit. The MPLA was also convinced that only a socialist path would meet the demands of the people and included several militants who had been politically trained in the Portuguese Communist Party. The FLNA and UNITA were only tribal organisations, built around a demagogic chief with absolute power and with no political programme. Obviously, they were anticommunist, and they were ready to make any and every compromise with Washington. Mobutu, and even the PIDE (the Portuguese political police), in turn saw these groups as useful pawns against the MPLA. Later, when the elections pitted the MPLA against UNITA (the FLNA had disappeared in the unrest), voters said they preferred the "thieves" (MPLA) to the "assassins" (UNITA). It is true that during its fifteen years in power in Luanda, the MPLA had changed, and that corruption has become generalised. UNITA fighters continued their murderous tactics in the zones they controlled. This didn't prevent Western media from spewing their ire on MPLA leaders (who were not very democratic, it is true) while eulogising Savimbi, the leader of the assassins. (Was he then a democrat?) Nevertheless the FLNA and UNITA existed, and UNITA is still around.

A stormy meeting erupted at the OAU at the end of 1974 when it was time to recognise the national liberation movement as the representative of the Angolan government. The first thing I observed was the noisy interference from the Soviet representatives, present in great numbers in OAU corridors. They, and a few allied African states, declared that since the MPLA was the sole force on the ground, only it had the right to form the legal government of the country. In my opinion, this position created more problems than it solved. Moreover, it was wrong, and everyone knew it. The United States was more subtle and allowed this point to be made by its allies.

Then it was China's turn to meddle, not wanting to allow only the Soviets and Americans to have a say in the matter. The Chinese proposals—very unofficial and, in my opinion, initially reasonable—called for a coalition government of all three organisations in order to avoid a civil war. I myself heard the Chinese ambassador say that "if the MPLA is really that strong, it will take on board the others and lead them; if it is not, a coalition government appears even more crucial." However, soon after, China's anti-Soviet feelings began to drastically colour its own approach.

There was an MPLA government in Luanda which, even if it did not control the entire country, had reconciled itself to the perspective of war to finish off UNITA. Since it was receiving Soviet military aid (Cuba's troops came in only later), China decided to continue backing UNITA (as it had done before 1972, supposedly in order to prevent the pro-Soviet MPLA from having sole domination). It thus found itself on the same side as the United States and South Africa, which had spared neither financial nor military support to the murderer, Savimbi. Mario de Andrade told me much later that the coalition government would have been the best solution, but he wasn't sure whether it would have been possible. Washington was intent on sabotaging the idea. Nonetheless, had such a compromise been possible, it would have prevented seventeen years of useless war. At the end of this tragic period, the Soviet Union no longer existed, Cuba had pulled back (after delivering a resounding defeat of the South African invasion which was truly magnificent), the apartheid regime had disappeared, and the MPLA no longer troubled Washington (although the United States never forgave them and still harbours ill-will to all those who dared to resist it). Savimbi's heirs were also still around, so there was no other option than to accept to negotiate and create a coalition government. What a sad ending.

Things appeared much simpler in Mozambique. FRELIMO was the only national liberation movement. The problems appeared later, after liberation. I had frequent meetings in Dar es Salaam with the future vice president, Marcelino dos Santos, along with Aquino da Braganca (who died in the plane accident that killed President Samora Machel) and with the party ideologue, Sergio Vieira.

Their excesses came after liberation. Since FRELIMO was essentially a northern-based group, it was ill-prepared to control the situation in Maputo and to absorb the influx of the petit bourgeoisie who had not participated in the war but who had provided a mass of cadres. They were rapidly promoted to replace the exodus of the Portuguese. One "leftist excess" was the party's response to its authority being challenged through unpopular measures such as collectivisation. Hard on the heels of this came the new war started by the South African backed RENAMO (Resistência Nacional Moçambicana: Mozambican National Resistance). While it was evident that the "partisans"' of this party, acclaimed by Western "democrats," were nothing but vulgar assassins without any programme whatsoever, the emergence of this party was a direct result of the mistakes made by FRELIMO. The capitulation which followed the Nkomati accords (1987) with South Africa and the opening of negotiations with RENAMO, along with the adoption of multiparty politics, had a predictably catastrophic effect—collapse.

The huge damage caused by the triumphant ideology of NGOs as representatives of civil society has been forcefully denounced by the Swede, Abramson (1999). It is obvious that these NGOs were for the most part a supplementary tool in the arsenal of foreign reactionary forces (the promoters of the "new neoliberal world order"—without government!) created and manipulated by them and supported by the local corrupt bourgeoisie. They hardly represented the authentic voice of the people.

Angola and Mozambique have become "ordinary" African countries, members of the regional grouping called SADC. They are now firmly within the orbit of South Africa, which, although free of the noxious apartheid, nonetheless has an expansionist agenda in southern Africa to the benefit of Anglo-American capital, as has been well documented by Hein Marais (1996).

This analysis of the internal policies of the countries concerned—whose margin of manoeuvre was reduced to zero by their alignment with the demands of imperialist globalisation—necessarily includes a discussion of the kinds of regional groupings that were formed and which, far from supporting the elaboration of an authentic and independent development project, were in fact content to serve as transmitters of imperialist domination.

The Political Economy of Africa in the Global System

It is usually claimed that Africa is "marginalised." The phrase suggests that the continent—or at least most of it south of the Sahara, except perhaps South Africa—is "outside" of the global system, or at best integrated into it only superficially. It is suggested also that the poverty of African people is precisely the result of African economies not being sufficiently integrated into the global system. I wish to challenge these views.

Let us consider first some facts that are rarely mentioned by the incense-bearers of current globalisation. In 1990 the ratio of extra-regional trade to GDP was for Africa 45.6 percent while it was only 12.8 percent for Europe, 13.2 percent for North America, 23.7 percent for Latin America, and 15.2 percent for Asia. These ratios are not significantly different from those prevailing during the twentieth century. The average for the world was 14.9 percent in 1928 and 16.1 percent in 1990.[20]

How can we explain this curiosity that Africa is apparently even more integrated in the world economic system than any other developed or developing region? Of course the levels of development, as measured by per capita GDP, are highly unequally distributed, and, from that point of view, Africa is the poorest region in the modern world system, its GDP per capita amounting only to 21 percent of the the world average and 6 percent of that of the developed centres. The high proportion of Africa's extra-regional trade with respect to its GDP reflects the small size of the denominator of the ratio. Simultaneously the exports (as well as the imports) of Africa represent only a minute proportion of the world's trade. And this is exactly the reason that Africa is considered "marginal" in the world system, i.e. having little importance. "The world could live easily without Africa."

The concept that a country or a region qualifies as marginalised if its quantitative weight in the global economy is small, assumes implicitly that the logic of the expansion of the global capitalist economy pursues the maximisation of production (and therefore also of trade). This

20 Serge Cordelier, *La mondialisation au delà des mythes*, La Découverte, Paris 1997, p. 141. All figures from WTO 1995.

assumption is utterly wrong. In fact, it matters little that Africa's exports have represented only a minute part of world trade, yesterday and today. Capitalism is not a system which sets out to maximise production and productivity, but one which chooses the volumes and conditions of production *which maximise the profit rate of capital.* The so-called marginalised countries are, in fact, the super-exploited—in a brutal manner—and, therefore, they are impoverished countries, not just countries located at the margin of the system.

The analysis needs therefore to be completed on other grounds. The relatively modest ratio for the developed areas—North America (United States and Canada) and Western-Central Europe (the European Union, Switzerland, and Norway) is associated not only with the highest levels of development but also with a qualitative characteristic that needs to be spelled out: *All developed countries have been built historically as autocentred economies.* I introduce here that essential concept which is ignored by conventional economics. *Autocentred* is synonymous with being essentially "inward-looking," as opposed to being *autarcic* (closed). That means that the process of capitalist accumulation in those countries which have become the centres of the world system has always been—and I submit continues and will continue to be so for the foreseeable future—simultaneously inward looking and open, even in most cases aggressively open (i.e., imperialist). That means that the global system has an asymmetric structure: the centres are inward looking—autocentred—and simultaneously integrated in the global system in an active way (they shape the global structure). The peripheries are not inward looking (not autocentred) and therefore integrated in the global system in a passive way: that is, they "adjust" to the system, without playing any significant role in shaping it. That vision of the real world system is totally different from the one offered by conventional wisdom which superficially describes the world as a "pyramid," constructed of unequally wealthy countries ranking from the lowest levels of GDP per capita to the highest.

My conclusion from this conceptualisation is that all the regions of the world (including Africa) are equally integrated in the global system, but they are integrated into it in different ways. The concept of "marginalisation" is a false one, one which hides the real question. What we need to ask is not to what extent are the different regions integrated, but rather *in what ways are they integrated.*

As indicated earlier, the degree of integration in the world system has not significantly changed throughout the whole of the twentieth century, as is suggested by the dominant, fashionable discourse on globalisation. There have been ups and downs for sure, but the trend which reflects the progress of the degree of integration has been continuous and rather slow, not even accelerating over the last decades. That does not exclude the fact that globalisation—which is an old story—has developed through successive phases that should be identified as qualitatively different from each other, each focusing on the specificities of the changes commanded by the evolution of the centres of the system, i.e., by dominant global capital.

On the basis of the methodology which I have suggested, let us now look at the various phases of Africa's integration in the global system and identify the specific ways in which integration has operated during each of the successive phases.

Successive Phases of Integration

Africa was integrated into the global system from the very start of the emergence of that system in the mercantilist period of early capitalism (the sixteenth, seventeenth, and eighteenth centuries). The major periphery of that time was colonial Americas, where an outward looking export economy was established, dominated by European Atlantic merchant capitalist interests. In its turn that export economy, focused on sugar and cotton, was based on slave labor. It was through the slave trade that large parts of Africa south of the Sahara were integrated into the global system in a most destructive way. The subsequent "backwardness" of the continent is in good part due to that form of "integration" which led to a decimation of population to such an extent that it is only recently that Africa has begun to recover the proportion of the global population of the world it probably had in the 1500s. The Atlantic slave trade resulted in the dismantling of earlier larger state formations that were replaced by smaller brutal military systems that were permanently at war with each other in the supply of slaves for the slave trade.

In America itself, the mercantilist form of integration in the world system destroyed the potential for further development in many regions. During that phase of early capitalism, the highest rates of growth were achieved in areas such as the Caribean, Northeast Brazil, and the southern flank of the North American British colonies. No doubt if experts of the World Bank had visited these places at the time, they would have written about the "miracle": the value of Saint-Domingue's exports of sugar was, at the time, larger than the total exports of England. The experts would no doubt have concluded that New England, which was building an autocentred economy, was on the "wrong track." Today, Saint-Domingue has become Haïti, and New England has become the Unites States of America!

The second wave of integration of Africa into the global system was that of the colonial period, roughly from 1880 to 1960. Once conquered, it was necessary to "develop" Africa. At this juncture comes in both the reasoning of world capitalism—what natural resources do the various regions of the continent possess—and the conditions prevailing amongst existing African societies. We need to take into account here the three models of colonisation that operated in Africa. First, the trading economy that incorporated the small peasantry into the world tropical products market by subjecting it to the authority of a market controlled by oligopolies, making it possible to reduce the rewards for peasant labor to a minimum and to waste the land. Second is the example of the exploitation of the economy of southern Africa's reserves organised around mining and supplied with cheap labor provided by forced migration coming precisely from those inadequate "reserves" which served the purpose of enhancing the perpetuation of traditional rural subsistence. And third, the establishment of the economy of pillage which the concessionary companies embarked upon by taxing without the return of a farthing and reaping products picked from afar, in a context in which local social conditions neither permitted the establishment of "trading posts," nor were there mineral resources sufficiently and economically abundant enough to justify the establishment of reserves that could furnish them with abundant manpower. The pillage of the Congo basin belongs to this third category.

The results of this mode of insertion into world capitalism were to prove catastrophic for Africans. First, it delayed—by a century—any commencement of an agricultural revolution. It enabled surplus to be extracted from the labour of the peasants and from the wealth offered by nature without making any investments in terms of modernisation (no machines or fertilizer), without genuinely paying for the labour (with the social cost of reproduction of labour being borne by the noncapitalist agricultural social formation), without even guaranteeing the maintenance of the natural conditions of reproduction of wealth (pillage of the agrarian soils and the forest). Simultaneously, this mode of development of natural resources tapped into the framework of the unequal international division of labour that excluded the formation of any local middle class. On the contrary, each time that the latter started the process of formation, the colonial authorities hastened to suppress it.

As a result most so-called "least developed countries" today are, as is well known, located in Africa. The countries which make up this "fourth world" are, for the large part, countries destroyed by the intensity of their integration in an earlier phase of the global expansion of capitalism.

Bangladesh, for example, the successor state of Bengal, was once the jewel of British colonisation in India. Others have been—or still are—peripheries of peripheries. Burkina Faso, for example, has supplied most of its active labor force to Côte d'Ivoire. If one takes into account that the two countries constituted at the time a single region of the capitalist system, the achievements of the Ivory Coast "miracle" would have had to be divided by two. Emigration impoverishes those regions from which labour flows and thus reduces the social cost of reproduction of labor in the receiving country. The young are lost to the supplying country at the moment when they become potentially economically active. And the social cost of supporting the old is pushed back on to their country of origin when they return home. Such costs, much greater than the "money orders" or "remittances" sent home to their families by emigrants, are almost always forgotten in the calculations of our economists.

There are in fact very few countries which are "poor" and nonintegrated or little-integrated into the global system. Perhaps, until recently, one might have included the north of Yemen or Afghanistan as examples of places that were little-integrated. The integration of these regions that is happening currently is similar to what happened elsewhere at an earlier period, producing nothing more than a "modernisation of poverty"—the shantytowns taking on the landless peasants.

The weaknesses of the national liberation movement and of the inheritors of the colonial states date back to this period of imperial fashioning. They are, therefore, not the products of the pristine precolonial Africa,as the ideologies of global capitalism seek to portray them and from which they derive legitimacy through their usual racist discourse. Indeed the precolonial formations had long ago disappeared in the storm of integration. The "criticisms" of independent Africa, of its corrupt political middle classes, its lack of economic direction, the continuation of its rural community structures, etc., all ignore the fact that these features of contemporary Africa were in fact forged in the period between 1880 and 1960.

No wonder, then, that neocolonialism has perpetuated these same features. The form that this failure took is well illustrated by the limitations of the Lome Agreements that have linked sub-Saharan Africa to the European Union. These agreements have perpetuated the old division of labor, relegating independent Africa to the production of raw materials at the very time when—during the Bandung period (from 1955 to 1975)—the Third World was embarking elsewhere on an industrial revolution. They cost Africa close to thirty years at a decisive moment of historic change.

Undoubtedly, African ruling classes were partly responsible for what was going to begin the involution of the continent, especially when they joined the neocolonial camp against the aspirations of their own people, whose weaknesses they exploited. The collusion between African ruling classes and the global strategies of imperialism is, however, certainly the ultimate cause of the failure.

Political Independence

Having attained political independence, from around 1960, the peoples of Africa embarked on development programmes, the main objectives of which were more or less identical to those pursued in Asia and Latin America, notwithstanding the differences in ideological discourses that accompanied them. This commonality can be readily understood if we recall that in 1945, practically all countries in Asia (excluding Japan), Africa (including South Africa), and Latin America (although with a few nuances) were still bereft of any industry worth this name—except in mining here and there. The populations were largely rural and governed by archaic regimes dominated by land-owning oligarchies or colonial regimes (Africa, India, Southeast Asia). Beyond their great diversity, all the national liberation movements had the same objectives of political independence, modernisation of the state, and industrialisation of the economy.

There is today a great temptation to read this history as if it were a stage in the expansion of world capitalism, which was said to have performed more or less certain functions related to primitive national accumulation, thereby creating the conditions for the next stage, which we are now supposed to be entering into, marked by the opening out to the world market and competition in this field. We should not yield to this temptation.

The dominant forces in world capitalism have not "spontaneously" created the model(s) of development. "Development" was imposed on them. The vision of "development" was a product of the national liberation movements of the contemporary third world. I want to stress here the contradiction between the spontaneous and immediate trends of the capitalist system, which are always guided only by the short-term financial gain that characterises this mode of social management, and the longer-term visions that have guided the rising political forces, which are fundamentally in conflict with the former. This conflict is certainly not always radical, and capitalism certainly seeks to adjust itself to it, even profitably. But it only adjusts to it; it does not generate the movement.

All liberation movements in Africa shared this modernist vision which I qualify as *capitalist*. It is capitalist by the nature of its concept of modernisation. It is expected to produce the relationships of production and the social relationships that are basic and peculiar to capitalism: the wage relationship, business management, urbanisation, patterns of education, and the concept of national citizenship. No doubt other values characteristic of advanced capitalism, like those of political democracy, are woefully lacking. All countries of the region—radicals and moderates—chose the same formula of the single party, the holding of farcical elections, and the naming of a "founding father" of the nation, etc. In the absence of a middle class of businessmen, the state—through its technocrats—was expected to be a substitute for that class. But sometimes, where it existed, the middle class would be held in suspicion on account of the priority that it would give to its immediate interests over the longer-term ones. Suspicion became, in the radical wing of the national liberation movement, synonymous with exclusion. This radical wing then believed, naturally, that its project was that of "building socialism," and it consequently took up Soviet ideology.

If we consider the criterion of national liberation movements, that is "nation building," the results are on the whole questionable. The reason is that, whereas the development of capitalism in an earlier period supported national integration, globalisation operating in the peripheries of the system today works, on the contrary, in the opposite direction—towards breaking up societies. However, the ideology of national movements ignored this contradiction, having been immersed in the bourgeois concept of "catching-up" or "making up for a historic backwardness." It conceived this "catching-up" as being possible through a passive participation in the international division of labour, without trying to modify it by delinking.

There is little doubt that, depending on the specific characters of precapitalist, precolonial societies, the tendency towards disintegrating had a more or less dramatic impact. In Africa, whose artificial colonial borders did not respect the previous history of its peoples, the disintegration wrought by the development of capitalist peripheries made it possible for ethnicism to survive and proliferate, despite the efforts of the ruling class to get rid of its manifestations in the immediate postindependence period. When the crises came, destroying suddenly the increase in the surplus which had enhanced the financing of transethnic policies of the new state, the ruling class itself broke up into fragments which, having lost every legitimacy based on the achievements of "development," then sought to create for themselves new political bases associated with ethnic retreat.

While a small number of countries in Asia and Latin America embarked during those "decades of development" in the second half of the twentieth century in a process of industrialisation (which turned out, in some cases, to be competitive in global markets), in Africa "successful development" (in fact growth without development) remained within the old division of labour, i.e., largely producing only raw materials. Oil-producing countries are typical examples (other major mineral resources, such as copper, suffered a long structural demand crisis), but so also are some of the "tropical agriculture" producers, such as Côte d'Ivoire, Kenya, and Malawi. These are often presented as "brilliant successes." In reality, they have no future; they belonged to the past from the very start of their prosperity. Most of these experiences turned out to have unsuccessful growth, even within the limits of the old division of labour. This is the case for most of sub-Saharan Africa. These difficulties were not the product of "bad policies," but rather of the prevailing objective conditions of the period. In fact, this type of development had already existed during the colonial times and reached its ceiling by 1960. This is the case of Ghana. And the Ivory Coast "miracle" was just a matter of "catching up" with colonial West African coast achievements!

Reversals in the Balance of Forces

What followed the erosion of the national development projects of the 1960s and 1970s is well documented.

The starting point was the brutal reversal in the balances of social forces, to the benefit of capital, which occurred in the 1980s. Dominant capital, as represented by the transnational corporations, moved into the offensive, operating in Africa through the so-called "structural adjustment programmes" enforced throughout the continent since the mid-1980s. I say "so-called" because in fact those programmes are more conjunctural than structural, their real and exclusive target being the subordination of the economies of Africa to the constraint of servicing the high external debt, which in its turn, is to a large extent the very product of the stagnation which started appearing in the least-developed countries along with the deepening crisis of the global capitalist system.

During the two last decades of the twentieth century, average rates of growth of GDP have fallen to roughly half of what they had been in the previous two decades. This was the case for all regions of the world, Africa included, with the exception of East Asia. It was during that period of structural crisis that the external debt of third world countries (and Eastern Europe) started growing dangerously. The global crisis was, as usual, characterised by growing inequality in the distribution of income, high rates of profits, and therefore a growing surplus of capital which cannot find an outlet in the expansion of the productive systems.

As a result, financial alternative outlets had to be created in order to avoid a brutal devalorisation of capital. The United States deficit and the external debt of third world countries were responses to the financialisation of the system. The burden had reached unsustainable levels. How could a poor African country earmark half or more of its exports simply to pay the interests of such debts, and simultaneously be pressured to be "more efficient" and to "adjust"?

Let us remember that, after World War I, the payment of Germany's reparations represented *only 7 percent* of the exports of that industrialised powerful country. Most economists at that time considered the level too high: they considered that the "adjustment" of Germany's economy to it to be impossible. Germany could not adjust to a loss of a mere 7 percent of its export potential, but Tanzania is supposed to be able to adjust to a loss of 60 percent.

The devastating results of these policies are well known today: economic regression, social disaster, growing instability, and even sometimes total disruption of whole societies (as in Rwanda, Somalia, Liberia, and Sierra Leone). During the whole of the 1990s, Africa's rate of growth in GDP per capita has been negative (-0.2 percent). Africa is alone in having such a negative growth rate. As a result, Africa's share of global trade decreased. That fact is precisely what is being qualified as being a reflection of its "marginalisation." Instead, one should speak here of the dramatic malintegration of Africa into the global system. Conventional neoliberal economists pretend that this is only a "hard transition" towards a better future. But how could it be? The destruction of the social tissues of a country, the growing poverty, and the regressions in education and health, all of these situations cannot prepare a better future; they cannot help African producers to become "more competitive" as is demanded of them. Quite the opposite!

This neocolonial plan for Africa is indeed the worst pattern of integration in the global system. It cannot produce anything but further decline in the capacity of African societies to meet the challenges of modern times. For sure, these challenges are to some extent new, relating to the long-run possible effects of the ongoing technological revolution (informatics), and through them, the effects on the organisation of labour, its productivity, and new patterns of the international division of labor. However, all these challenges are manifested in the real world in the conflicting strategies. For the time being, the dominant segment of global capital—the transnational corporations—appears to dictate what is favourable for the progress of its particular strategies. African peoples and governments have not yet developed counterstrategies of their own, similar, perhaps, to what East Asian countries have been trying to push ahead with. Globalisation does not offer to Africa any solutions to its own problems. Foreign direct private investments in Africa are, as everybody knows, negligible and exclusively concentrated in mineral and other natural resource sectors. In other words, the strategies of transnational corporations do not help Africa move beyond the pattern of international division of labour belonging to the remote past. From an African perspective, the alternative has to be built in a way that combines the building of autocentred economies and societies with participation in the global system.

This general law is valid for Africa today as it has been throughout modern history for all the regions of the world.

It is still too early to know whether African peoples are moving towards that goal. There are talks today of an "African Renaissance." No doubt that the victory of the African people in South Africa, i.e., the breakdown of the apartheid system, has created positive hopes not only for that country but also throughout large parts of the continent. But there are not yet visible signals of these hopes crystalizing into alternative strategies. That would require dramatic changes at national levels, going far beyond what is generally suggested under the headings of "good governance" and "multiparty democracy," as well as at regional and global levels. Another pattern of globalisation would therefore gradually emerge from those changes, making possible the correction of Africa's malintegration into the global system.

Africa in the International Context

From 1960 to 1964, independent Africa was divided into two camps. One was the Casablanca camp (Egypt, Morocco, Guinea, Ghana, and Mali) that considered that the independence "granted" had not resolved the question of national liberation. They thought that the Monrovia camp (all the other countries satisfied with the situation) were neocolonial states. But they all came together within the OAU, which was set up in 1963. All of independent Africa also belonged to the Movement of Nonaligned States, created in Bandung in 1955 and whose spirit found strong echoes, not only amongst the people, but also within ruling classes and governments.

Severely weakened by the legacy of colonialism, the new Africa was fragile, and African societies faced a serious threat of disintegration. The dominant discourse blamed this on the "lack of maturity" of these countries, with the implicit assumption that independence had been given prematurely. The real reason for the crisis was glossed over, namely, the market. On its own, the market functions like a centrifugal force, one that disintegrates. It only ceases to do so when it is controlled by the state. In economies such as those in Africa, fragile both because of colonialism and before that the slave trade, this disintegrating effect was even more devastating than elsewhere. There was no system of production worth the name, and the market doesn't create it. It is incumbent on the state (an instrument of society and the result of social compromises that determine its character at any given time of its evolution, even if it was capitalist in nature) to create a system of production in line with its ideology. If this is not present, market forces simply exploit the disparate segments of a system, which, because it doesn't really exist, cannot put up any resistance. "Compradorisation" is the social, political, and ideological form that takes shape when there is no state to play that role. Africa doesn't suffer from too much government; it has only had bad "comprador" rule.

Neocolonialism can only operate where there is permanent crisis. This is why it met with successive waves of nationalist and populist revolts. The first, represented by Nkrumah's Ghana, Modibo's Mali, Guinea, and Congo, had barely died down when it was the turn of uprisings in West Africa, in Benin, then in Burkina Faso, and then once again in Ghana and Mali, as well as in Tanzania and Ethiopia in East Africa, in Madagascar, and then in southern Africa.

This is not Africa's failure; it is capitalism that has failed to offer anything remotely acceptable to Africa. Today, the Bandung page has definitively been turned, and the impasse has never been as dramatic. The frontal assault on the peasantry, the cornerstone of the World Trade Organization's liberalisation policies, has accelerated the transformation of the continent into desolate countryside and urban slums. The migratory pressure that has ensued (the new boat people) is an inevitable consequence. But the European refrain remains stubborn—the only way African states can cooperate is to police their own frontiers.

The Imperialist Management of Postcolonial Africa

Regionalisation in Africa is mere window dressing

The principal aim of the Organisation of African Unity (OAU) (which later became the African Union) was political, created to support on the one hand the liberation struggles in Lusophone Africa, Zimbabwe, Namibia, and South Africa, and on the other hand to contain and resolve intergovernment conflicts. In this respect, the OAU was a weak substitute for Pan-Africanism.

During the "development decades" (the 1960s and 1970s), the OAU's duties were relatively easy, because at the time, most governments had some popular legitimacy. The fruits of development strengthened the legitimacy of the former national and transethnic liberation movements, which had now become ruling parties. The development of political parties was also in tandem with the emergence of a nascent middle class (a product of the progress of education) who soon developed a vast clientele in the lower classes.

The political situation today is tragically different. The erosion of people-centred development models and the diktat of liberal globalisation have brutally delegitimized the majority of African states—even the so-called democracies or facades of democracy which have followed in the wake of autocratic nationalist and populist rulers. They have been unable to restore the legitimacy of governments, as they are simply incapable of providing their people with any kind of social progress. Africa has entered a phase of involution characterised by what is wrongly called "internal tribal wars." These are not conflicts whose real origins lie in ethnic hostility, but rather conflicts fabricated by warlords who want to get their hands on the country's resources (petrol, diamonds, etc.) and, therefore, deliberately stoke ethnic tensions. Called to the rescue, the OAU, or even the UN, have proved themselves to be totally impotent in such situations—witness the disastrous results of the intervention of ECOMOG (Economic Community of West African States Monitoring Group) in Liberia and Sierra Leone. Under such conditions, the very idea of regionalisation is nonsense.

There are several organisations of subregional cooperation, of which the leading ones are ECOWAS (Economic Community Of West African States) in West Africa, SADC (Southern African Development Community, which replaced SADCC, the Southern African Development Coordination Conference) and COMESA (Common Market for Eastern and Southern Africa, which followed the PTA, Preferential Trade Area) in southern and east Africa, CEAO-UMOA (Communauté Economique de l'Afrique de l'Ouest-Union Monétaire Ouest Africaine) and UDEAC (Union Douanière et Économique de l'Afrique Centrale) in the francophone countries, and SACU (Southern African Customs Union) and CMA (Common Monetary Area) in the Rand zone. There were also the branches of the big global institutions (such as the African Development Bank, a quasi branch of the World Bank) and other more minor institutions (the Mano River Union, the Community of the Great Lakes, the Inter-government Committee for Sahel, etc.). It is worth noting that the seemingly strongest regional institutions are those that are linked to either France or South Africa (before and after apartheid).

Immediately after the independence of its African colonies, France made sure that they remained within the francophone structure, whose rigid rules excluded any autonomy in the area of financial management. This is a colonial vestige doomed to extinction under the triple onslaught of the replacement of the franc by the Euro, liberal globalisation, and African involutions. But if the system were to collapse, there is nothing that could replace it effectively, either at the level of the countries concerned or of the regions they are part of.

In southern Africa, the conventions that govern customs and monetary union between South Africa on the one hand, and Lesotho and Swaziland on the other, cannot be classified as regional cooperation, because the imbalance between the dominant partner and the other countries is so flagrant. SADCC (Southern African Development Coordination Conference), which had been set up in the apartheid era to enable southern African countries to free themselves of their dependence on Pretoria, was itself transformed after the fall of apartheid into a new organisation (SADC), which now incorporates South Africa. But this new South Africa intends to pursue the same policies towards its neighbours, over whom it has a huge industrial advantage. The question is: Will they accept this unequal partnership indefinitely?

The results achieved by these African subregional organisations of cooperation/integration are meagre, to say the least. Trade has remained negligible and the intraregional movement of capital, nonexistent. The adhesion of African countries to the principles of free trade espoused by the new World Trade Organisation can only aggravate the deceptive spin-offs of "opening up trade." The OAU's economic role was diluted by virtue of Africa's active participation in the Non Aligned Movement and the Group of 77 at the UN and the establishment of a "common front," representing the demands of the South as opposed to those of the North in the global economic order. Nonetheless, the OAU tried to convince member states to adopt development plans that would favour regional integration and industrialisation.

These dangers were quickly recognised by the World Bank. The famous Berg report (1981) was an immediate response to the Lagos Plan and has since become the bible of the World Bank, international cooperation institutions, and governments. The only alternative offered by the Berg report was to continue the kind of "specialised development" based on Africa's "natural" advantages, in other words, to remain within the old formula of agro-mining. The weakness of the OAU's proposal was their ignorance that its implementation required an active role on the part of the state. However, the rent-owners who became the ruling classes in the African states have neither the means nor the will to go down any other path other than the agro-mining sector from which they draw their wealth. "Regionalisation" in this condition is not at the centre of their concerns, nor is it at that of the dominant forces in the global system. It is mere window dressing.

The European Union-ACP: Africa, the Caribbean, and the Pacific

The EU-ACP grouping may occupy a minor positon on a global scale, but it has real importance when it comes to the analysis of the place of Africa in the world system.

From the outset, the aim of the Lome accords was not to use external relations to effect an economic, political, and cultural transformation to the benefit of the African people, but only to reinforce Europe's position in the world order, on the economic as well as geopolitical stage. In other words, the "development" aspect was only secondary, and considered less important than the political aspect. The goal above all was to support "moderate" governments and to encourage such tendencies elsewhere. This in effect meant to subvert nationalist aspirations, which might have been tempted to use Cold War rivalry to their advantage.

In the neoliberal era, the reorganisation of Euro-African relations has taken place within the framework of the WTO, thus consolidating the monopolies exercised by the power centres in crucial areas, including the access to natural resources and the creation of new technologies, as well as control of the monetary and financial system. From this perspective, the only use of regional associations is their capacity to provide the most profitable returns for multinational oligopolies.

Resistance to this kind of thinking could develop in Africa for the following reasons:

i) The regions and those countries unlikely to provide dividends are automatically excluded from the potential benefits of regionalisation;
ii) The growing polarisation and exclusion will generate further migrations, which will be even more difficult to manage because neoliberalism bans the free circulation of workers;
iii) This plan implicitly integrates military alliances, which makes recalcitrant countries from the South vulnerable.

The way it has been conceived, the regionalisation of Euro-African relations is perfectly compatible with the management of internal conflicts that erupt in an Africa that has been marginalised by social disintegration.

It was clear that during the 1960s and 1970s, the underlying thread beneath the various cooperation conventions between the EU and African nations was the European concern to maintain its supply of tropical agricultural produce, as well as of mining and petroleum resources. In tune with the WTO rhetoric, Europe threw its weight behind the structural adjustment panacea that was being proclaimed as the universal economic cure. Local authorities sometimes tried to resist, because these policies were alienating much of their base, thereby undermining their legitimacy. However, the external debt burden and government corruption further reduced their capacity to fight back and to implement any corrective measures, thus forcing them to submit to the daily orders from international institutions tasked with dealing with the crisis. The so-called "initiative for severely indebted poor nations" formulated by the World Bank and enforced by the European Union, is part of the plan to recolonise the continent.

The fruits of this association are not sweet. The gap between per capita GDP in sub-Saharan Africa and that in other developing countries has been steadily increasing. Add to this the flight of capital from Africa abroad (to the North, especially Europe) which overtook the amount of capital coming in, both public and private. Moreover, instead of the much-vaunted redistribution of income, i.e., the trickle-down effect, there was only more inequality, which in turn resulted in a huge wastage of investments (because priority was given to expensive investments destined for the privileged classes).

The marginalisation of Africa in international investments is the final nail in the coffin. Even though the European Union provides half the external financial needs of ACP countries, the proportion of aid could only be maintained by increasing the amount of public aid, while at the same time the opening up of African economies resulted in the disinvestment of private capital.

Finally, the European Union doesn't seem to have an environmental policy which takes into account dealing with the destruction of the environment in Africa. In the current negotiations between the European Union and ACP (African, Caribbean and Pacific Group of States) countries under the aegis of the Cotonou convention, ACP formulated the *directives,* but the *mandate* was set down by the European Commission. According to a study commissioned by the Cotonou Monitoring Group, conducted by the European Research Office, there are quite a few differences between the two sides but not on substantial issues. The negotiations focus on the modalities of the implementation of free-trade zones with Europe from 2008, which presupposes an accelerated rate of intra-African economic integration. There is growing resistance to these projects (called APER, Annual Performance Evaluation Report), which are very reminiscent of the colonial equation between Europe and Africa. Voices are being raised with authority and resonance at African social forums and at the assemblies of peoples' movements. This resistance has also echoed with some governments, especially Nigeria.

A defining characteristic of our times is the way agriculture is being transferred by the mounting penetration of international and local capitalism. In Africa, this pressure translates into dispossessing the majority of the continent's farmers who still benefit, albeit under dramatically changed conditions, from access to land. The agrarian question (in the sense of access to land by all farmers) is at the heart of the challenge to marry democratisation and social progress. Imperialist capitalism is incapable of providing a solution to this crucial problem for societies in Africa, Asia, and Latin America. The aim of the "land privatisation" model proposed—or rather imposed—is to maximise profits for transnational agro-businesses such as Monsanto, as well as for more recently arrived local capitalist farmers. International "cooperation" encourages all initiatives that are geared towards this objective and discourages any attempts to express the resistance of the farming majority.

This offensive to globalise agriculture marched in tandem with that of the WTO, with fake promises that the markets of both the North and South would be opened up for trade of food and agricultural products. At the centre of the dispute between Northern countries (the United States and Europe are in total agreement over this, despite some minor disputes) and the Global South is the issue of agricultural subsidies. Small wonder the WTO was at a total impasse in Doha. The sharp rise in prices of food products highlights the gravity of the underlying institutional drama.

The aim of major capitalist countries has always been to gain exclusive control of the globe's principal resources, including petrol and uranium, and to prevent their competitors (China in particular today) from getting the same. This concern is at the heart of the "cooperation" accords between Europe and Africa. Niger for example has been flooded with "aid" aimed primarily at corrupting the government—not to address the fact that it is one of the poorest countries on the continent—and to prevent a nationalist party from taking over the country and its uranium mines (now controlled by the French Commission on Atomic Energy) located in a region situated between Algeria, Libya, and Nigeria.

The Rhetorical Packaging of the Discourse on Euro-African Cooperation

On the one hand, there is the usual mantra of democracy, good governance, poverty reduction, and humanitarian aid, and on the other hand, there is the reality, which makes for double standards. This has to do with finding ways to manage conflicts (and not codevelopment) which are a result of the deliberate exclusion of Africa from the concert of nations. NEPAD (New Partnership for Africa's Development) did not produce any results either; it was just another kind of rhetoric.

The Alternative: South-South Cooperation in the Perspective of Delinking

If the Global South wants to go on the offensive, it has to destroy the monopolies that are the means by which imperialism perpetuates itself.

For the oligopolists of the new financial plutocracy to remain in power, they have to maintain control of the financial weapons through which they exercise their monopoly, both internally (which allows them to rake in substantial profits) and internationally (in order to keep the periphery submissive). The compulsive need for capitalist centres to retain exclusive control of the planet's natural resources is simply not viable. It is put into question by the development of the South. The WTO's attempts to monopolise technologies and information by reinforcing industrial and intellectual property rights will certainly end in failure, if only because many Southern countries have mastered these new technologies.

The South is not the same place as it was during the Bandung era, when it was totally devoid of any means of autonomous development. Today, it can easily outstrip the North and develop new kinds of cooperation, including in trade and technology. "Bandung-II," whatever the form it might take, is already in the works.

Defeating imperialism with its new "advantages" means choosing an autocentred development delinked from the global system. Once again, I do not mean this in the sense of an absurd and completely closed economy, but in the way I have defined it as the rejection of submission to the pressures of external relations, thus prioritizing internal development and social progress. This is a non-negotiable precondition.

Delinking can only be possible when the party in power (as opposed to comprador governments) benefits from the support of a genuine social base. This is as true today as it was in the past. Certainly, delinking has evolved over the years. In the Bandung period, it was synonymous with industrialisation within a strictly national framework, even in modest-sized countries. While it can remain national for continent-sized countries, it requires now other forms of intense regional cooperation between partners based on the complementarity of smaller nations. This is not a "common market" model, but rather one of associative partnerships with an economic dimension (planned, in the sense that peoples' demands are incorporated into government policies). ALBA (Alianza Bolivariana para los Pueblos de Nuestra América, or the Bolivarian Alliance for the Peoples of Our America) is perhaps the first example of this kind of association.

What Conclusions Should One Draw from this Discussion?

A close look at the developments discussed suggests that the achievements appear meagre and that the expectations of the glorious struggles waged by their people were not met. The petit bourgeoisie in none of these countries has committed suicide, but has instead become the backbone of a pathetic comprador government, devoid of a political programme and functioning under imperialist—especially European—domination.

Cabral tried mightily to avoid such an outcome and for this he amply deserves to be called one of the most audacious leaders of the first generation of African freedom fighters.

Cabral didn't just put forward a facile theory on the "suicide of the petit bourgeoisie"—he spelled out the conditions. For Cabral, the decisive role played by the peasantry in the anticolonial war would lead to a massive social bloc, bringing together peasant leaders and intellectuals, and thereby neutralising, as it were, the passive segments of the petit bourgeoisie. Cabral didn't just theorise, he actually implemented it in the liberated regions of Guinea-Bissau.

Similarly, I perfectly understand the impulse behind Cabral's espousal of the Guinea-Bissau/Cape Verde one nation idea. Colonisation has always divided peoples, pitting one ethnic group against the other. All liberation movements took the opposite position, rightly affirming the unity of the people. In this sense, the peoples of Guinea and Cape Verde were related peoples, united against a common enemy— "one people," almost. However, the quasi-negation of the diversity inherent in the African peoples inevitably had negative consequences, because once the euphoria of independence had subsided, the politicians who emerged from the petit bourgeoisie, which did not commit suicide, proceeded to restore their image and substituted the development process, which had lost credibility, with a new legitimacy based on diversity—ethnic and other kinds.

The history of contemporary Africa is that of the battle between progressive forces, which from 1960 to 1980 (the Bandung era) wanted to rebuild their countries and for this reason chose an independent, potentially socialist path (Mali, Ghana, Tanzania, Ethiopia, Madagascar, Benin, Congo Brazza, Burkina Faso, etc.) and those forces on the side of neocolonialism, backed by foreign powers. The liberation movements in the Portuguese colonies and Cabral's philosophy and actions were at the forefront of progressive forces during that period. I have written about this battle in *L'Eveil du Sud* and at this juncture would like to recall the reasons why those movements ran out of steam, creating in the process the conditions for the recolonisation that is still prevalent. Imperialism today needs Africa for its natural resources, and the peoples of Africa are impediments to the exploitation of that wealth.

Africa has to begin the second wave of liberation, which can only advance if it is a two-pronged approach:

a) Embark on the audacious campaign of industrialisation, which barely took root during the Bandung era and,
b) Insure that this industrialisation goes in tandem with the reconstruction of a peasant economy based on the access of all to land.

On these two points, Cabral's thought has never been as relevant.

Bibliography

Abramson, D.M. 1999. "A Critical Look at NGOs and Civil Society as Means to an End in Uzbekistan,"in Human Organization. 58(3), 240-50.

Amin, Samir (2008). *L'Eveil du Sud*, chap 2 ; Le Temps des Cerises, Paris.

Amin, Samir et al. (2005) *Afrique: Renaissance ou exclusion programmée;* Maisonneuve et Larose, Paris..

Amin, Samir (2012). "Contemporary Imperialism and the Agrarian Issue"; *Agrarian South*; Sage, Inaugural issue.

Tandon Yash, *Enfinir avec la dépendance à l'aide*; Cetim, Genève 2009 (English: Pambazuka 2008)

Marais, Hein (1996). *South Africa, Limits to Change*, Zed, London.

4. AMILCAR CABRAL AND THE PAN-AFRICAN REVOLUTION

Ameth Lo

This past October marked the twenty-fifth year since our brother and comrade, Thomas Sankara, died in the most unfortunate and tragic circumstances. African peoples are still traumatised by the experience of losing someone like Sankara, who was brutally assassinated on October 15, 1987, as he was heading for a meeting of the governing council. Since then, Blaise Compaore's comprador regime has reintroduced neocolonial-type development policies that make Burkina Faso completely subordinate to the interests of Western imperialist powers. Having been one of the first to attempt a real "delinking" from the global capitalist system in the postindependence era, Sankara incarnates continuity with the thought, as applied to the specific conditions of Burkina Faso, of one of the most eminent revolutionaries of the twentieth century: Amílcar Cabral.

Like Sankara, Cabral was taken from us on January 13, 1973, in similar conditions. This year's fortieth anniversary of his assassination will be commemorated across the world by Pan-Africanist and progressive people. For sixteen years (from 1957 to 1973) Cabral devoted his life to the liberation of the peoples of Guinea-Bissau and the Cape Verde islands. Sixteen long years during which he led the PAIGC (African Party for the Independence of Guinea-Bissau and the Cape Verde Islands), which successfully liberated two thirds of the national territory under colonial rule. Despite the presence of 30,000 Portuguese troops, the colonial power was unable to prevent the inexorable march to independence, and Cabral's political project was able to gain ascendance over the repression. At a time when the world capitalist system is entering a new phase of global redeployment, when the wretched of the earth reformulate their aspirations and strategies in a situation marked by the vacuum left by the collapse of the so-called Socialist Bloc, a reappraisal of the thought of Amílcar Cabral is indispensable. That at least is the attempt of this contribution dedicated to the cause of the Pan-African Revolution. To best understand Cabral's thought and praxis, it is necessary to see them in their historical context—social, economic, and political—of which he was a product.

Historical Context

Guinea-Bissau is a country with a total area of 40,000 square kilometres and a population estimated at 500,000 people in 1960. Situated off the western coast of the continent with Senegal to the north, Guinea to the south, and the Atlantic Ocean to the west, Guinea-Bissau faces Brazil, to which much of the population must have been deported during the period of slavery. The impact of this transatlantic trade (also known as triangular trade: Africa, Europe, Americas) can still be seen in the low population density in the subregion. Goree Island, which lies off Dakar (the capital of Senegal), was the point of departure for the forced transportation of millions of Africans (men, women, and children) on a journey without return.

This first painful and tragic experience of contact between the African populations and Portugal triggered a long process of resistance, which culminated four hundred years later in the first national uprising against the stranglehold of Western imperialism (mainly Euro-American) on the country's natural and human resources. In the meantime, in 1885 the Berlin Conference had officialised the division of the continent into different zones of influence carved out by European colonial powers, namely France, England, Portugal, etc. In 1703, England, desperate to stem France's expansion in the region, signed the Metwen accord, which meant supporting the colonial ambitions of Portugal (itself a kind of British semicolony) in Guinea-Bissau and the Cape Verde islands. The triangular trade mentioned earlier was replaced by colonialism, which was to last until the declaration of independence of Guinea-Bissau and the Cape Verde islands on September 24, 1973. Portugal, a country backward in economic and cultural terms (more than 50 percent of the population was illiterate in 1965), which also ruled Mozambique, Angola, and the islands of Sao Tome and Principe, had committed one of the worst crimes against humanity since the Second World War. At the start of the fifties, a catastrophic situation prevailed in Guinea-Bissau and the islands. With an economy solely based on the cultivation of groundnuts, a massive famine aggravated by recurring droughts decimated the Cape Verde islands (10,000 dead between 1948 and 1959).

Desperate people began fleeing to neighbouring countries. Thousands of people were recruited by the colonial administration and sent to work in the plantations of Angola as migrant workers in conditions akin to slavery. The country, devoid of even the most basic public infrastructure, was on the verge of explosion. The forced cultivation of groundnut as a monocrop exacerbated the chronic lack of basic foodstuffs, with all the attendant consequences: malnutrition, vitamin deficiencies, etc. Life expectancy at the time was thirty years. The conditions were ripe for mass mobilisation, which began well before the actual start of hostilities between nationalist forces and Portuguese colonialists. The Portuguese administration, despite its control over a few chiefdoms and some segments of the petit bourgeoisie, was finding it increasingly difficult to maintain its previous style of exploitation, based mainly on taxing the peasants and overexploiting the tiny working class in urban centres. The resistance of the African peoples has been an uninterrupted phenomenon throughout their interaction with imperialism—the uprisings of different ethnic groups (balantes, mandjaks, pepels, etc.) are evidence of this. This resistance will only end with the physical extermination of the oppressed group in question.

It became a life and death struggle between two antagonistic forces in permanent conflict—the oppressor and the oppressed. It was total war, which took different forms—refusing to pay taxes, passive resistance, and armed struggle—depending on the set of contradictions in play, and which continued until the defeat of one side. The nature of this struggle was entirely determined by the historical conditions of the conflict. The so-called "pacification" period only ended at the beginning of the nineteenth century, when Portugal finally exercised more or less full control over the national territory. But this was short lived. In 1957 a strike organised by the workers of Port Pidjiguitty ended in a bloodbath at the hands of the Portuguese military—fifty dead and over three hundred people wounded. The intensification of the repression resulted in the first armed attacks by the national liberation movement led by Cabral and the PAIGC on January 23, 1963. Nationalist forces felt that, at this stage of popular resistance, only an armed struggle would bring down Portuguese colonialism. Amílcar Cabral's emergence on the scene as the incarnation of the aspirations of the people of Guinea-Bissau and the Cape Verde islands has to be seen within this historical context, the dialectic of oppression and resistance. Throughout his short life, Cabral was able to articulate better than anyone else his people's thirst for the recovery of their fundamental rights—the right to live in respect, dignity, and peace, without any form of exploitation and oppression.

Amílcar Cabral: A Pan-African Revolutionary

Amílcar Cabral was born on September 12, 1924. His father, a teacher by profession, was from the Cape Verde islands, while his mother (like millions of African women then and now) worked several jobs in order to make ends meet and belonged to what one could call the middle class in a colonial context. Cabral had access to a Western-style education at the missionary-run school in Bissau. After completing his secondary studies, he embarked for Lisbon to study agronomy and met students from the Portuguese colonies of Angola and Mozambique. This period also saw the consolidation of the power of the fascist Salazar regime in Portugal. Huge swathes of Portuguese society, reeling under poverty and military repression, emigrated to France, Spain, and Italy. In the absence of any room for political expression, universities became the hotbed of the antifascist resistance.

His involvement in the antifascist struggle as part of the student movement gave Cabral an understanding of some of the revolutionary theories that had emerged at the turn of the century. World War II, which resulted from the contradictions inherent in the development of world capitalism, had a profound impact on the minds of colonised peoples across the globe. In Europe, the FEANF (Federation of Black African Francophone Students) and the publishing company Presence Africaine, along with the IASB (International African Service Bureau, based in England) led by George Padmore in collaboration with Kwame Nkrumah and C.L.R James, became increasingly vocal about the question of decolonising Africa. Padmore had just broken off with the Third Socialist International, which wanted to focus on the struggle against "fascist imperialist powers" (Italy, Germany, and Japan) and not against the "democratic" imperialist powers, such as France and England.

The holding of the Pan-African congress in Manchester in 1945 marked a qualitatively new phase in the struggle for self-determination. In Lisbon, meanwhile, Cabral and his friends, such as Agosthino Neto and Mario De Andrade, felt that it was time to set up an independent organisation bringing together the citizens of "Portuguese speaking" colonies, away from the control of the euro-centric Left. It is against this backdrop that Cabral and his friends began their political education, with the aim of national liberation. Influenced by the emergence of "negro-African" literature, they were convinced that only a "return to the roots" would enable the movement to be in total symbiosis with the deepest aspirations of the peoples of Africa. In Cabral's words,

> Our work consists of researching our African roots again. And this has been so fantastic, so useful and heavy with consequences that even today the founders of this group are all leaders of liberation movements in the Portuguese colonies.

This quote shows how highly developed Cabral's political understanding was and also reveals clearly what he intended to do.

They felt that the "return to roots" was one of the preconditions for an effective alliance between the petit bourgeois intellectual class and the African masses. After university (around 1949 or 50), Cabral decided to return to Guinea-Bissau with a clear idea in his head to contribute to the liberation of his people.

However, it is one thing to identify a political project, it is another to clearly understand the social terrain in which the struggle is to take place and, therefore, to identify the means, tactics, and strategies to be adopted. The success of a national liberation struggle depends not only on a deep understanding of the mechanisms of enslavement used against the exploited masses but also on devising a strategy that will overturn the power relations between the oppressor and the oppressed, the adoption of the right strategy at the right moment, in a specific social context. These strategies have to be based on the concrete realities of the dominated people. This is what Cabral devoted the rest of his life to. The depth of his political thought in conjunction with what he achieved in the objective conditions prevailing in Guinea-Bissau and the Cape Verde islands make him one of the greatest theoreticians of the anti-imperialist struggle in Africa and the world in general.

Cabral and the Class Struggle in Africa

According to Cabral, the "class" socio-economic phenomenon in a given society is a fundamental consequence not just of the progressive development of productive forces but also of the distribution of wealth. He suggests a reformulation of the idea that "class struggle is the driving force of history," because such a conception of history implies that the history of peoples only begins with the emergence of the class phenomenon and consequently class struggle. This hypothesis would exclude the entire history of humanity from the discovery of hunting, the invention of agricultural techniques, to the appropriation of land for private use. It would also deny the peoples of Africa (but also the first nations in the Americas and other places) the fact that they had a history before their first contact with Western imperialism.

There is growing scientific evidence that the appearance of class was a gradual phenomenon, marked by slow fluctuations, and that only when a certain degree of accumulation had been reached was there an emergence of class and class conflict. This was Cabral's point of departure for his analysis of the class phenomenon in the context of African history, and specifically that of Guinea-Bissau and the Cape Verde islands. But he insisted that such an analysis only made sense if it served the goals of national liberation; otherwise, it would be mere rhetoric and intellectualisation. Because of its socio-economic structure, Guinea-Bissau is representative of many African countries today—a multiethnic and multireligious mosaic of people who are mostly rural and illiterate, with urban centres surrounded by poverty stricken areas inhabited mainly by people who fled the precarious conditions of life in their villages and found themselves in the trap of a colonial (or neocolonial) economy without any opportunities for employment. The African petit bourgeoisies played a key role in the organisation of the liberation struggle. Created out of thin air by colonialism, this social category was the only one with the political understanding to comprehend the nature of imperialist domination. However, the very nature of the petit bourgeoisie explains its limitations in the challenge of national reconstruction.

As Frantz Fanon noted in the *Wretched of the Earth*, "the national bourgeoisie which comes to power, uses its class position aggressively to confiscate all the positions left vacant by the departure of the colonialists." Cabral comes to more or less the same conclusion when he says that in order not to betray the goals of the national liberation struggle, the petit bourgeoisie has only one option—to reinforce their revolutionary consciousness, reject demands and attempts at "bourgeoisification" from fellow class members, and identify themselves with the working class and not impede the revolutionary process. Speaking at the conference of solidarity with the peoples of Africa, Asia, and Latin America held in Cuba in January 1966, he said, "To play its role in the struggle, the revolutionary petit bourgeoisie has to be capable of 'class suicide' and be reborn as part of the revolutionary working class, identifying entirely with the aspirations of the people to whom they belong." While the colonial and neocolonial situations are similar in their foundations (complete dependence on the former colonial power), Cabral outlines two phases in the national liberation struggle. According to him, the struggle consists of a national phase, and, more important, a social phase. Each phase is distinct because of its specific historic task, as well as the class alliances and organisational structure required to carry out the project successfully. The national phase implies the recovery of national sovereignty or independence, whereas the social phase in fact determines the real nature of liberation. Is the newly created nation really in a position to determine its own destiny?

The PAIGC, under the leadership of Cabral, proved that the only way to answer this question was not only to combat the enemy on all fronts but to also create a new mode of living in the liberated areas through radical transformation of the economic, social, and cultural structures inherited from colonialism. This meant the construction of new schools and hospitals, the integration of women in all spheres of community management, combating systematically those Africans who chose to ally themselves with colonialism, and finally to channel the emergence of a national culture cleansed of stultifying pressures from within or without. A thorough analysis of the relations between the various social categories at play at the national and international levels will ensure the recovery of the wealth of the nation and its just and equitable redistribution.

Despite numerous successes, Cabral and the PAIGC had to face major challenges that threatened to derail the revolution and that were internal, such as economic underdevelopment and the ensuing social deficit, the scars of tribalism that had been created or exacerbated by Portuguese colonialism, and a host of external factors linked to international power relations. On the tribal question, Cabral always said,

> The existence of tribes appears to be a major contradiction only for opportunists, generally detribalised individuals or groups. Class contradictions, even at an embryonic level, are more important than contradictions between tribes.

The Role of Culture in the National Liberation Movement

As mentioned earlier, the petit bourgeoisie was the only social category capable of taking over the colonial state apparatus in the postindependence period. Sometimes allied with the masses and at others with imperialism, its hesitations are directly linked to the fundamental contradiction it faces permanently—satisfy its class ambitions and simultaneously deal with the most urgent demands of the rural and urban masses who had not fought merely for a flag and a national anthem but for a concrete improvement in their living conditions. Far from being homogenous, the petit bourgeoisie can be divided into three sub-groups.

The revolutionary petit bourgeoisie:

> This consists of a minority (often intellectuals, civil servants, teachers, etc.) who, after the huge sacrifice of the "return to roots," were successful in identifying with the masses and their culture, history, and aspirations. It was also the most dynamic element within the national liberation movement. Cabral and the most important leaders of the PAIGC belonged to this class.

The alienated petit bourgeoisies:

> This is another minority group (Black skin, white mask). It categorically rejects the idea of independence and believes that the future of their people depends on their association with the colonial powers. This is a desperate group, and there is no way of convincing them of their peoples' capacity to take their destiny into their own hands. If they had the means, they wouldn't hesitate to leave the country after independence like some Algerian intellectuals did after the victory of the FNL (National Liberation Front).

The silent majority:

> This last group (the majority) constantly fluctuates between the first two. Most opposition leaders in the continent today come from this category. Sometimes they are in open rebellion against the government and sometimes allied with it for a slice of the

> "national cake," but they do not have any deep vision for the transformation of African societies. Their opportunistic attitudes have a negative effect on the masses, who in the absence of alternatives keep their distance from all political parties.

To understand the role of culture as a fundamental part of the resistance of the oppressed, it is important to analyse it in relation to the different social categories present at any given time in the society concerned—culture, not as an abstract receptacle, but as a dynamic synthesis of the historical reality (material and spiritual) of a human group at any given time. In Cabral's words,

> Culture, whatever its ideological or idealistic characteristics may be, is an essential part of the historical process. It has the capacity (or responsibility) to develop and nourish those elements that will ensure the continuity of history and at the same time determine how society will progress or regress.

To see culture as a reflection of historical reality, which is determined by the development of productive forces, is to distinguish the culture of the masses from that of the African petit bourgeoisie. Indeed, it is evident that the Rasta culture is not that of the Jamaican elite. Five hundred years of European domination have not significantly changed the culture of the African masses.

Nevertheless, the African petit bourgeoisie, constantly humiliated by the West, is always on the edge in the context of the national liberation struggle. It has no other alternative other than to identify with one side of the conflict. The psychological trauma that results explains the desire to reconnect with the people. Thus emerges a discourse based on the concept of culture and the need to return to one's roots. A need not shared by the majority of people, because they are the carriers of that culture and hence the generators of history.

It is in this sense that the development of the Afro-centrist movement in the African diaspora needs to be understood. To be viable for current generations, it has no other choice than to situate the struggle for a cultural renaissance within the larger national liberation movement. As Cabral said,

> The return to the roots is not and cannot by itself signify an act of struggle against foreign domination (colonialist/racist) but neither does it mean a return to tradition. It is a practical response to a concrete and historical need that results from the implacable contradiction between a colonized or (neocolonial) society and the colonial power, between the exploited masses and the foreign classes.

For him the "return to the roots" phenomenon can only be realized if the African petit bourgeoisie get directly involved in the daily struggle of the popular masses. As he said, "the masses reject both the domination of foreign culture and foreign exploitation."

The cultural struggle, therefore, also has to be political, with the aim of creating an environment conducive to the free cultural expression of the oppressed. This can only be possible if the people retake control of their own development. Though the bulk of Africans have not been significantly affected by the culture of the dominating power, it has to be noted that there is no single culture in society. This explains the difference in attitudes towards the national liberation struggle between individuals belonging to the same social class. African societies can be broadly divided into two categories:

Societies with horizontal social structures (without government):

> These societies are based on the collective ownership of the factors of production and have a matrilineal social structure. Social stratification is often based on age. They were the ones who put up the most armed resistance to colonisation. Armed resistance ended with what the colonialists called the 'period of pacification.' From the outset, such societies were key players in the national liberation struggle.

Societies with vertical social structures:

> These societies are highly hierarchical, with women at the base of the social ladder. They are ruled by a chief with real power. Some of these chiefs were co-opted by the colonial administration to pre-empt any form of interethnic alliances. This was the case with some of the Fula chiefs in Guinea-Bissau. The breakdown of some societies from the first category through the imposition by colonial authorities of customary chiefs (who belonged to different ethnic groups) led to tensions between some ethnic groups. In some cases, this led to cracks within the nationalist ranks. However, it is important to underline that at first contact with the Europeans, the "phenomenon of tribalism" as some have called it, was already on the way out. The movement was towards large, multiethnic nation-states—the Ghanaian empire and the Mandingo Empire on the west coast of the continent are examples. It was the "divide and rule" policy of the colonialists coupled with the opportunistic manipulations of the African ruling classes that led to the resurgence of so-called ethnic conflicts during the colonial and neocolonial periods. But this cannot and should not mask the fact that, objectively speaking, the contradiction between ethnic groups is minor compared to that between the African masses and imperialist powers and the ruling elites they are in tandem with.

Cabral and Today's Challenges

Cabral's works are experiencing a resurgence in popularity amongst youth across the spectrum. That's probably happening because, at the moment, everything in Africa and the world feels as if it's up for grabs. Across West Africa, there is a cleverly orchestrated redeployment of imperialist forces, abetted by national office-holding elites, aggressively appropriating farmland for multinational corporations. In the long run, their success risks turning back the clock on one of the key objectives of liberation struggles—the right of populations to reclaim their means of production as a precondition to making their freedom a fact.

The subregion in general, and in particular Guinea-Bissau, is at the centre of significant turmoil, which threatens the stability of the whole region. Symptoms of these conflicts, such as a growing drug trade, with routes running from Latin America to Europe, are now beginning to surface. Nor can we afford to ignore the particular brand of strife evolving before our eyes in northern Mali, threatening to put the whole subregion at risk. Some of the conflicts we are seeing involve multiple players (such as the United States, France, amorphous Jihadists, drug traffickers, etc.). These groups sometimes work with each other, when their interests coincide, but at other times they compete for control of the area's vast, superabundant reserves of natural resources (gold, oil, and uranium) or for a strategic base from where to operate. Amongst the other cards on the table is a global capitalist system built upon a nonsustainable consumerist model of ever-increasing greed, which is presently undergoing a crisis because it lacks the reserves of energy and minerals with which Africa is so richly endowed.

Today, after fifty plus years of nominal independence, one cannot deny that the persistence of these pitfalls reflects the reality that the national liberation movements, led by nationalists like Cabral, failed to meet all their projected objectives, although they were able to realize certain significant achievements. In fact, the risks to stability persist. Imbalances between urban and rural sectors are intensifying, creating a situation of flux with two parallel streams. One current is expressed as a huge exodus of peasants from the country to the city in search of better living conditions. The other is experienced as a wave of African youth with blurry vision, lured by mirages from the West that often come framed within patterns of suicidal emigration (across the burning desert or high seas) towards countries in the North.

Just how did we get to this situation, in spite of the enormous sacrifices embraced by leaders like Cabral so they could free their people from all forms of domination and exploitation? What constraints inhibited the national liberation movements and made them turn away from the social transformation that would lead to genuine revolution? What internal contradictions favored the liquidation of leaders like Cabral when they headed those movements?

These are questions that demand an answer if we are to benefit from the lessons of the past and be in a position to sharpen our clarity and consciousness for the battles to come.

"The Cancer of Betrayal"

In Guinea-Bissau's case, the process of weaving deep and radical transformation into the social, political, economic, and cultural fabric was stopped dead in its tracks at the dawning of independence with the assassination of Cabral. When, in November 1980, Nino Vieira engineered the first coup, he ushered in an era of serial coups that plunged the country into chronic instability. Strangely, Cabral had been prescient in that regard and had warned as much in his famous speech ("Cancer of Betrayal") in Conakry at Kwame Nkrumah's funeral. I'll let him speak for himself: "…how far and to what extent is the treason in Ghana linked to class struggle, the very structure of his society and its institutions, including armed forces within the context of a newly-independent state?"

Reading Cabral's words, it's evident that he had a good grasp of the significance of those internal fissures in African society that could be manipulated to derail the transformation process in which nationalists were embedded as liberation wars evolved. In one sense, neocolonial armies can provide a template for what occurred, since they play a pivotal role in undermining several progressive experiments on the continent, such as Mobutu's assassination of Lumumba in the DRC, the assassination of Sankara in Burkina Faso, Eyadema's overthrow of the government in Togo, and the ousting of Nkrumah in Ghana. The examples are endless.

Accompanied by his wife, Anna Maria, Amílcar Cabral returns from a reception at the Roumanian Embassy in Conakry during the hours of darkness between the nineteenth and twentieth of January, 1973. There's a man named Inocencio Kany lying in wait, together with another male named Mamadou Touré, a bodyguard in charge of Cabral's security, and they try to kidnap him. When Cabral fights them off, Kany shoots him down in cold blood. The attacker is subsequently arrested and summarily executed before those who gave him his marching orders can be revealed. Cabral's assassination only serves to indicate the tip of the iceberg lying beneath a much more complex state of affairs.

The PIDE's secret services, some possible connexions within the PAIGC political apparatus, and elements within the Sekou Toure's regime are suspected.

Feeling caught in a vise, Conakry, host to hundreds of PAIGC officers and members, hunts down suspected party members. Sékou Touré has Aristides Pereira, José Araujo, and Vasco Cabral, who were escaping by boat to Bissau, arrested and appoints a commission of enquiry.

An impressive list of suspects surfaces in the course of an extended and painful period of spying and settling of accounts within the entrails of the PAIGC, without getting us any closer to the truth. Forty or so individuals are held responsible for a vast conspiracy hatched by the PIDE—the International Police for the Defence of the State. Dozens of individuals will pay with their lives, demonstrating the extent to which treason wormed its way into the ranks of both Cabral and his allies. Regarding the circulation of damaging rumours, as well as attempted plots against his person, Cabral had already, during the preceding months, put a residential surveillance system in place against certain conspirators, fearing the development and proliferation of ethnic disputes between Cape Verdeans and the inhabitants of Guinea-Bissau.

Disdainful of violence, devoted to antiracism and revolutionary democratic ideals, Cabral willingly exposed his soft underbelly to his murderers, who were still unable to prevent the crumbling of the Portuguese colonial army, the revolution from below, or the advent of sovereignty for Africa's Portuguese colonies.

Arguably, the contradictions inherent in building any society create conditions which imperialism can use to advance its own agenda. It has usually done so in collusion with reactionary local elements located at the very heart of the movement itself, engineering assassinations like the one that cost Cabral, Lumumba, Sankara, and many other patriots their lives. Cabral always warned against a central role being played by the military in carving out the political vision of the movement and instead insisted that once independence was won, most of the freedom fighters should return to the land and become involved in the production sector. Sadly that never happened in Guinea-Bissau, where Nino Vieira's coup put the military in power to head of government and brought the nation to its knees.

On the other hand, on Cape Verde Island, where those who led the country to independence were from the same original PAIGC party led by Cabral, the transition to independence was more stable. The presence of the military outside the daily run of the state apparatus spared the country some of the unproductive traumas just described in the case of Guinea-Bissau. To some extent, another contributing factor to this relative stability is an incoming flow of money sent from abroad by its dynamic diaspora, mainly based in Europe and the United States, or revenues generated by a vital tourism sector. Both elements helped Cape Verde maintain a relative stability compared to its neighbours.

To contribute to the stability of the newly independent African country, the neocolonial army needs to be radically transformed and its mission focused around peoples' collective security at the regional level. In times of peace, such a reformed army should be involved in social transformation projects, alongside the civilian population, in building bridges, schools, roads, reforestation, etc. In fact, the "military" should be subordinated to the "political," as previously envisioned by Cabral, to prevent it from being the factor that will trigger or spread the "cancer of betrayal."

On a fundamental level, therefore, it is imperative that progressive forces across the continent reconnect with the militant tradition, providing political and ideological training of their members. Doing so can be a way of helping growing numbers of our youth to learn how to identify the challenges we face as peoples, as well as to be conscious of the presence amongst us of various internal and external forces whose interests run counter to an ongoing evolution of our struggle towards a future that will bring progress, social justice, and freedom, Cabral's overriding preoccupations during his leadership of the PAIGC.

Conclusion

What we have learned suggests, therefore, that there is no way around the need of a rigorous analysis of the configuration of the different social classes within our social formations. Cabral initiated this pioneering work in the course of his endeavours across the country as an agronomist and agricultural engineer. Those experiences no doubt grounded him and gave rise to the accuracy of his political vision, while informing the practical steps he took in service to the struggle of the PAIGC.

Cabral, who led the national liberation struggle in Guinea-Bissau and the Cape Verde islands so brilliantly for more than a decade, has left a glorious legacy, and I would like to zero in on three important aspects.

Firstly, that no matter how revolutionary the leadership of the movement may be, the success of the struggle hinges on an effective symbiosis with the masses—peasants, workers, and youth. This fusion can only take place if the intelligentsia identifies itself with popular culture. A thorough knowledge of African languages is another must as a communication tool if there is to be true political mobilisation. Far from being static, popular culture is in perpetual evolution and conditioned by the mode of production prevalent in any given society. Cabral understood the dialectics of expanding capitalism at the centre and increasing impoverishment of the periphery. He revolutionised the theory of class struggle and the battle against imperialism in general. Cabral's "Unity and Struggle" is akin to "Pitfalls of National Consciousness" in Fanon's *The Wretched of the Earth*.

A second fundamental aspect of his work is his contribution to Pan-Africanism as a political ideology for the liberation of oppressed Black people. He proved through his own experience that, however revolutionary a theory may be, it is doomed to failure if it is not based on a profound understanding of the mechanics of transformation. While it is true that a revolutionary theory is indispensable for the revolution to take place, it is not sufficient for the uprising to be successful. The dialectic between theory and practice was always a constant element in Cabral's thought and actions. Its international dimension notwithstanding, in practice this theory is always specific to the local conditions where the struggle is taking place and cannot be simply exported. "National Liberation and Culture" and "Identity and Dignity in the Context of National Liberation" represent the culmination of Amílcar Cabral's intellectual legacy. These two texts highlight the dynamic character of the culture of the African peoples' struggle and offer an exceptional analysis, not seen since Fanon, on the role of the intelligentsia in the process of struggle and the psychological progression that underlies the decision by a section of the intellectual elite to commit to the struggle and break decisively with the dominant discourse.

Today in 2013, Africa is once again in the throws of recolonisation, more subtle than before, which has drawn the continent into the global capitalist system as a subjugated entity. The euphoria which preceded the dismantling of the former Eastern Bloc has begun to show its limits. Beyond the ideological propaganda spread by the new means of communication, which have a global reach, the peoples of Africa know now more than ever that there can be no solution to the crisis without a process of revolutionary transformation with a clear Pan-Africanist orientation.

A luta Continua!

References

Cabral, Amílcar: *Le pouvoir des armes.* Francois Maspero, Paris 1970

Cabral, Amílcar: *Return to the Source.* African Information Service New York 1973

Cabral, Amílcar: *Combattant pour la cause du peuple.* Agence de presse Novosti Moscow 1973

Cabral, Amílcar: *Unité et Lutte Volume II : La pratique Révolutionnaire.* Francois Maspero Paris 1975

Cabral, Amílcar: *Unité et Lutte Volume I : L'Arme de la Théorie.* Edition Francois Maspero Paris 1980

5. AMILCAR CABRAL

AN AGRONOMIST BEFORE HIS TIME[21]

Carlos Schwarz

At twenty-eight years of age in September 1952, a few months after completing his studies, Amílcar Cabral, the agronomist, returned to the land that had witnessed his birth.

In his mind he certainly carried the words that his father, Juvenal Cabral, wrote in the book *Memórias e Reflexões* (Memories and Reflections), when he settled in Bissau in 1911:

> [after] having left the naked rocks of *Paria Negra,* of *Achada Grande,* of *Lazareto,* and whose severe and sad aspect, seems to symbolize the suffering and pain, my eyes, amazed, had contemplated without ceasing the paradisiacal majesty of the flora that, in a mysterious way seems to emerge from the sea! Leafy trees all over, pretty and strange shrub that, verdant, spread in the ground like carpets on the floor. All this is opulence and vigor, it is wonder that enchants, it is wealth that seduces and predisposes a youngster to face life with optimism in this country.

21 To the memory of my father Arthur, who, since my childhood stimulated me (without me understanding) to follow the ways of agronomy. To my mother, Clara, who was always solidly behind my options, and at whose hands I saw, for the first time, and still during the times of the dictatorship, as the symbols of the PAIGC. To Isabel, my forever strong and engaged companion in this difficult but extraordinary walk. To my children, Cristina, Ivan, and Catarina, who courageously and without hesitation shared the political upheavals of the life their parents chose. To my granddaughters, Sara and Clara, with the hope that one day they will be able to live in tranquility in the adjourned land, as Cabral dreamt.

This vision of his father must have influenced Amílcar Cabral to opt to exercise his profession in Guinea. There was also the fact that, at the time, agriculture in Cape Verde was proscribed to abandonment, as most of the men emigrated northward (the United States, Portugal, and Holland) for survival and livelihood, while others, since the end of the nineteenth century, sought Guinea especially for the cultivation of sugar cane, almost always associated with the production of *aguardente* (overproof rum). An agronomist who in fact wanted to exercise his profession would have to opt for Guinea, where everything could be made—everything had to be made—and where almost all of the inhabitants were small "native" farmers.

His first wife, Maria Helena Rodrigues, a sylviculturist who joined him three months later, would for the first time come to know the city of Bissau, then a small urban centre with very few inhabitants. It was spread into two distinct zones. On one side was the so-called "civilized" colonial city that included the *Amura* fortress, the area now known as *Bissau Velho* (Old Bissau), the port of *Pindjiguiti*, and the Avenue of the Republic—today Amílcar Cabral Avenue. This avenue extended to the monument *Esforço da Raça* (Effort of the Race) and the Governor's Palace, then under construction. The other part, surrounding the centre, was the so-called "native" part, preponderantly inhabited by the *pepel* ethnic group.

It was in the colonial part that the few intellectuals present in the country lived, and where the large foreign firms such as NOSOCO and SCOA, to which were added Portuguese trading houses (A.C. Gouveia, Alvaro Camacho, and *Sociedade Comercial Ultramarina*, amongst others), as well as an enormous pleiade of Lebanese small traders like Mamud ElAwar, Aly Souleiman, Michel Ajouz, etc.

In the rest of the country, the trade of products and basic goods were primarily secured by *djilas*, itinerant traders who traveled all over the country by bicycle and canoe.

So-called "native" agriculture, practiced for about 3,000 years, centred around the cultivation of rice, for consumption within the rural communities, and production of the export crop, *mancarra* (peanuts/groundnuts), stimulated by the foreign companies who export it to

Europe (raw or as oil). The *mancarra* cycle started in the zone of Buba, stimulated by Germans and leaving an easy trail to identify—through the erosion and degradation of the soil that it provoked—and passed on to Bolama, northern Oio, Bafatá, and Gabú.

Official services of support to the farmers were practically nonexistent or inoperative, confined within the administrative and technical infrastructures already in place. No centre of experimentation, staff training, or marketing existed.

This is the global context that Cabral encountered upon his arrival in Bissau; he arrived, as he said, "to live his time," to initiate the political challenges of the struggle for independence, to defend a development centred in agriculture, and to promote the dignity of the Guinean people.

He and Maria Helena settled themselves in the house assigned to the director of the Experimental Farm of Pessubé (then situated very far from the centre of Bissau) in a poor neighborhood at the periphery, an isolated zone and of difficult access. The farm comprised four hundred hectares of land, where a large number of essential forests existed and a small number of fruit species like the cocoa palm.

At this time, when he starts to exercise his profession, Amílcar is convinced that the independence process will unfold peacefully, in the form it will proceed in other African countries, and he decides to start the construction of the new *conceptual agricultural building* to gradually substitute for the existing colonial model.

The Pessubé Farm will be his point of departure, to start putting in practice a strategy in three principal stages that he considers important for the development of Guinean agriculture. The first one is to transform the Farm from a mere unit of vegetable production, destined for the colonial political and administrative authorities of the praça (city) and a place for picnics and recreation walks, into a centre of agricultural research—a tool to improve and modernize the production of the farmers.

Cabral conceives and applies a programme of experimentation based on the identification of cultivation techniques for different types of farming (compass, land demarcation, fertilization, and sowing period), of tests for various adaptations (rice, sugar-cane, mancarra, banana, cotton, and horticultures), of plagues and illnesses, valorization of local varieties of certain species like "jute," and the introduction of new species such as sesame, soy, and sunflower.

Work to take advantage of the farmlands of the *Granja* starts, using innovative criteria that conforms with the nature of the soil and its capability, betting on its organic fertilization based on the dung of the animals of the cattle farm, in the consociation of cultivations (cassava-banana trees), identification of plagues and illnesses, and the characterization of the different varieties of each species.

He initiates, for the first time, publication of the results of experiments and reflections on Guinean agriculture, creating for this purpose the quarterly *Boletim Informativo* (Information Bulletin) of the Experimental Farm of Pessubé, in which, besides the description of activities, he proposed reflection on important themes, such as "mechanized farming," the "groundnut rosette virus," and the "farming of jute."

With notable regularity, five *Boletins Informativos* were published beginning in November 1952.

The second was to tear down internal walls within which the agricultural services were confined, to approximate them to the farmers, who should be the main beneficiaries.

More than the saying of the time that "agriculture is the base of the economy," Cabral clearly defended the notion that "agriculture is the real economy of Guinea," for which it was important for the services to get close to the small farmers. It was in this way that the *Granja de Pessubé* started to carry out tests and gain agricultural experience in the stations of Bula, Safim, Bigene, Nhacra, and Prábis, making what nowadays is called "trials in peasant setting" as a form of testing its adaptability to different ecological conditions and farming systems of the agriculturalists.

The FAO agricultural census project, approved by the Portuguese government in 1947 and soon put in the drawer where it slept for more than four years, was quickly retaken by Cabral a few months after his arrival at Pessubé, which he studies, plans, and executes. The census was, for him, not only a set of tables and numbers but also the possibility to read, comprehend, and act on the prevailing agricultural dynamic.

This work allowed him to define in precise form the contribution of different Guinean ethnic groups to agricultural production, serving to this day—after sixty years—as a basis for understanding the production systems and farming practiced by them.

In other words, the census made the agricultural services leave their ivory tower and land in the fields of the farmers, confronting them with the reality that they had to serve and make possible the search for solutions to their fundamental problems and the modernization of agriculture.

The third was that of the interaction of Guinean farmers with those in the neighboring countries of the sub-region. Conscious that the reduced number of technical personnel and the constant lack of resources would hinder the realization of agricultural research that could bring useful and practical results to farmers, Cabral encouraged the coming to Pessubé of various technical entities, such as the French pedological mission of Dakar, sugar-cane specialists, entomologists, etc.

The participation of Amílcar Cabral in the International Conference Groundnut-Millet, realized in Bambey, Senegal, in 1954, where he presents a paper on "*Queimadas e Pousios no Ciclo Cultural Mancarra-Milheto*" (Forest Fires and Fallow Land in the Farming Cycle of Groundnut-Millet), is eloquent proof of his strategy of researching the results of the experiments of older foreign stations, with greater numbers of technicians, and marking the presence and capacity of Guinean technicians in the scientific circuits of the subregion, aspects that he considered determinant for the postindependence period.

Internally, he started creating a nucleus of technical personnel who could guarantee the continuity and strengthening of these programmes. Amongst them, two stand out. Bacar Cassamá, agricultural monitor of the farm, is the first person he got close to and with whom he would create a friendship and confidence until the end of his life. Cassamá was tall, strong, serious, slow to smile, and with whom Cabral would repeatedly have quarrels, quarrels that they always overcame, because for Cabral the best form of being honest was to clearly tell the "engineer" his position and what he thought. Cassamá never bent over backward and continued to be Cabral's friend and faithful to the PAIGC, even after the *coup d'état* of Nino Vieira, when there was an attempt to erase Cabral from the history of Guinea-Bissau. Cassamá ended up dying in 2012, forgotten and abandoned by his friends; but Cassamá had remained loyal to Cabral more than anyone else.

Júlio Antão de Oliveira Almeida, a practicing farmer in the Granja, ended up being present at the founding of the PAIGC in Bissau, in September of 1956, and in the subsequent activities. He died in Portugal after independence in 1982.

For two and a half years, Cabral traveled all over Guinea, observing, studying, and writing on facets of Guinean agriculture. One can cite the study of forest fires and fallow lands in Fulacunda. Determinant was the realization of the agricultural census, when, as head of a technical team, he contacted farmers, community leaders, young people, and women. He understood the different logic of thought and action of each ethnic group, its potentialities and weaknesses, and, above all, its most pressing priorities in the promotion of its way of life.

In March of 1955, Cabral left Bissau in an Air France plane by order of the colonial political government authorities that accused him of exercising conspiratorial activities for the independence of Guinea. He was authorized to visit Bissau annually, which he took advantage of in 1956 in order to collaborate with other nationalists in the founding of the PAIGC on a day in September that later ended up being arbitrarily fixed as the nineteenth. Also in 1959, at thirty-five years of age, he came to Bissau in the year of the massacre at the port of Pindjiguiti, a determining moment for Cabral in his understanding that the conquest of independence would have to be obtained by armed struggle and not by the peaceful resistance for which he always strived.

After he was expelled from Guinea, Cabral continued to develop his agronomical activity in Portugal and Angola, always dedicating himself to reflection on Guinean agriculture, published in the journal AGROS of the *Associação de Estudantes de Agronomia* (Association of Students of Agronomy) he wrote, *A agricultura na Guiné, algumas notas sobre as suas características e problemas fundamentais* (Agriculture in Guinea: Some Notes about its Characteristics and Fundamental Problems).

In 1960, stimulated by the independence of Guinea-Conakry, and for the "no" vote delivered to France in 1958, he decided to establish himself in Conakry, sure that it was the ideal place, especially because Senegal had decided to accede to independence. The vicissitudes that the guerrillas underwent in this country during the eleven years of struggle showed that his vision was correct.

A few years before his assassination in 1972, conscious that the military victory was a given fact and would appear in the short run, he started to dedicate more of his time to the conception of the future state of Guinea-Bissau, maintaining agricultural reform as a key element. The stay in Conakry allowed him to identify the real dangers which the new country would confront in the postindependence period. The dangers included the "attractions" that the city of Bissau would have for many in the leadership of the guerrillas and the tendency for leaders to engage in intrigues and political plots. The other danger was the inevitable forgetfulness and gradual distancing of the leaders from the populations that had participated in the armed struggle. One of the ideas that Cabral was developing when he was assassinated was the creation of different governmental ministries, one in each of the regional capitals of the country. It would keep the leaders close to the citizens, forcing them to resolve the concrete problems of the people and diminish the risk of *diz que diz* (he said, she said), sterile conflictuality, and political intrigue. It was a return to the agronomist thesis that the technicians and decision-makers should not lock themselves behind doors but should be close to the beneficiaries of their work.

The Agronomist Thought of Cabral

Cabral's first great and decisive rupture with established concepts was made in the beginning, when he was still formulating his thesis in the Alentejo (in southern Portugal). At the time, he invigorated the principle that the advance of agriculture would be made exclusively through the introduction of new agricultural techniques. Later, they would come to designate this option as the "technological package." Cabral, while recognizing the necessity to make use of alternative techniques, centres in man the challenge of the agricultural evolution. Colonial agriculture was based exclusively on the work of specialists in illnesses of the coffee tree, of the soil, etc., without agriculture being seen as a set of components in which the principal actor is the farmer, an active subject interested in his own evolution. Cabral breaks with the colonial model and integrates the human element, the farmer, as the determining element in the modernization of agriculture; the introduction of new agricultural techniques would be the answer to the problems experienced by the farmers. During these times, as a consequence of the dominant vision, farmers were easily blamed for the poor utilization of specialists' techniques, without understanding that the crux of the problem resided in the technicians not comprehending the real priorities of the farmers. It is curious to note that nowadays, technicians appear in Guinea-Bissau with a (ridiculously) opposite perspective, stating that technical innovations are not necessary, that the farmers need to be left to themselves, asserting that they have practiced farming for millenia and, therefore, already know everything they need to know.

For Cabral, the modernization of agriculture was believed to start with knowledge of the agrarian systems and not from the compartmentalization of the disciplines of agriculture, where one runs the permanent risk of having a limited vision and ignorance of local challenges. Cabral espoused the thesis that one should simultaneously have a global concept of the challenges of agriculture and a realistic sense of responding with practical answers to the necessities of the farmers. In other words, it was these concepts that should determine the agricultural agenda, and not the strategies of the colonial metropolis, to determine *mancarra/peanut,* cotton, coffee, cacao, etc., as the species to develop in the different colonies.

Cabral was the first to question the system of agriculture based on monoculture, at that time it was *mancarra*, which represented a danger to the economy as the annual crop price fluctuations in the external markets put the farmer in a situation of dependence, risk, and uncertainty. Monoculture also subjects farmers to the possibility of not having a financial alternative to meet their food needs in a bad agricultural year. Furthermore, in the case of *mancarra*, monoculture provoked an irreversible degradation of the soil, especially through erosion. This consequence was not only true at that time, but it was also apparent in the postindependence period, where today Guinea-Bissau is condemned to monoculture that oppresses the cashew farmer. For Cabral, it was necessary "to diversify production, to not depend only on one product."

The importance of implanting a "system of research-popularization" was assumed from the beginning of Cabral's activities as an agronomist. The transformation of the status of the *Granja de Pessubé* into a centre of agricultural experimentation, as well as the creation of a network of dispersed posts in the country for the realization of trials of varietal adaptation, proves the importance of the dynamic "experimentation-dissemination" in the modernization of Guinean agriculture. It was in this form that the first results of the realized trials soon became shared and used.

The dangers and limits of agricultural mechanization (Cabral refers only to motorization, not animal traction) were exhaustingly addressed in a 1953 text, since he was confronted immediately upon his arrival in Bissau with a thesis very much in vogue that attributed the backwardness of Guinean agriculture to the non-use of farm tractors.

He called attention to various aspects of technical and socio-economic order, including that of the majority of agricultural soils (slopes and upland) being of shallow useful depth and with a tendency for erosion, so that the use of the soil for tractors could prove to be prejudicial. There existed the wrong idea that, with mechanization, the incomes of the farmers would increase, whereas the most that would happen was merely an increase in production. Thus mechanisation starts by being a cultural question that demands from the farmer a relationship with the tractor and its engine, the need for maintenance, proper functioning, planning, programming, purchasing of spare parts, tractor drivers, and mechanics, all of which takes time and consolidates itself gradually. Finally, the financial sustainability of the tractor is tied to its use in commercial farming, which could devastate the security of family farming production and consequently of the country.

The indiscriminate "recovery of *bolanhas* (paddy fields)" to increase the cultivated land and gain political dividends was challenged by Cabral, who held that the great issue facing Guinean agriculture was finding a way to increase the income of farmers, in order to have more production and not to risk only increasing the cultivated areas. In the recovery of the *bolanhas*, the case is even more pertinent, since they require soils with specific characteristics, in particular acidity and salinity levels that render farm land unviable or low-yielding, not justifying the investment. He argued that it was pointless to try to recover paddy fields when the only result is the reduction of rice production. Curiously, to this day, this issue is still on the agenda, with decision makers and financial sponsors showing up to invest in the recultivation of *bolanhas* of doubtful value.

The fight against the degradation of soils caused by cultivation practices that increased erosion, the choosing of crops that reduced the land's fertility, an increase in forest fires, and the reduction of the recovery time allowed for the fallow fields to regenerate the most fragile soils, was another struggle undertaken by Cabral. He conducted various local studies and wrote on the studies undertaken in Fulacunda (in the Quinara region of southern Guinea-Bissau), insisting on the need for modifying farming techniques to contribute to the reduction of the risks of erosion and reinforce the land's fertility.

It is interesting to note the environmental preoccupations of Cabral at a time when such concerns had not caught the world's eye, and his defense of a more advanced and holistic view of agriculture is still neither understood nor accepted by some fundamentalist ecologists. For Cabral, "*man is also nature,*" and as such is perceived as something that contributes to the denegration of environmental resources. Ironically, humans were also seen as indispensible to nature's preservation, according to the different systems of production and use that humans made of ecosystems. "Environmentalist" Cabral was noted especially for his reservations about mechanization and concern over soil erosion, uncontrolled forest fires, fallow lands, lack of collective cultivation, and a reduced practice of naturally fertilizing of the soils. He did not consider the farmer an anti-environmentalist that needed to be "educated"—a concept still defended today by developmentalists—but as the deciding factor in the productivity and health of agriculture.

This set of theories, that Amílcar Cabral defended in a pragmatic way, shows to what extent he was an agronomist before his time; with him still around, the post-independence era would have been very different.

The Struggle for Independence as an Integrated Development Programme

The way in which Cabral addressed the implementation of the agricultural census shares the guiding principles that drove him to the struggle for independence. In the census he was confronted with scanty human resources, a lack of logistical means, and sparse finances, but this did not impede him from moving forward with enormous success. In fact, he was so successful that even today, sixty years later, he remains the source for any serious information needed on the subject. Furthermore, the struggle initiated with scarce resources was equally a success, because it rested on the will, determination, conviction, and competency of those involved. Cabral conceived a strategy of valorization of the few resources that existed, conditioning the rhythm of advance and progress towards obtaining the largest increase that could be made. During the whole period of the armed struggle, this was a sacred principle for Cabral, consubstantiated in the watch words, "Do not make a step bigger than the leg."

Cabral opted for the gradual involvement, through phases, of the peasants in the evolvement of actions to the extent that the protagonists would acquire competencies and knowledge without ever being in a hurry to accelerate the rhythm of implementation and end up "detaching" themselves from the rural militants. He never pressed for a dynamic that burned bridges or that demanded of the peasants, the largest source of combatants, activities for which they were not yet prepared, staking everything on their organisation and capabilities. As happened in agriculture, the armed struggle started with simple actions, providing immediate results that excited and mobilized the participants, who would then go on to understand and assume the mechanisms of conception and decision-making, gaining organisational maturity that allowed them to assume new responsibilities.

As happens in agricultural associations, it is important to have small, dynamic, and consequential leadership groups and not have plethoric militant directorates as a means of making everyone participate. When the group is large, the delegation of responsibilities starts pushing responsibilities to others, often resulting in the leadership becoming unbelievers and inconsequent leaders. Privileging the decentralized creation of various groups, according to their activities, in which the leaders will be involved by their engagement, stimulates capacity for team work, mobilization of human resources and pragmatic creativity in the conduction of actions, making territorial occupation more tenable.

At the beginning, a process of innovative development is always small, so that Cabral was obliged to start small and to evolve gradually to end up with a large number of simultaneous, coordinated, and reciprocally-potential initiatives. It would have served nothing to start at full speed, managing many initiatives at the same time, in a short time and without experienced local cadres, only to lose direction and fall into discredit. The decentralization of the action groups insured that the best militants were quickly recognized and that they acquired greater power of initiative without being tied to a centralized and weighty structure.

For a process of development to be independent, it should involve the most diversified foreign partners possible, for which he was never limited to the East (China, USSR, and others of the Warsaw Pact), sensitizing Western countries like Sweden and militant organisations in the United States, Germany, France, etc. Cabral, just as he was opposed to monoculture, relied heavily on a diversification that allowed him to guarantee *the independence of thought and action of the PAIGC*, and to bypass the Sino-Soviet conflict, which occasionally avoided many serious problems.

Although Amílcar Cabral had given, for obvious reasons, particular attention to the armed front, he conceived the struggle for independence as a process where all the components of human life—health, education, justice, trade, culture, local knowledge, international sensitization, infrastructures, and agriculture—assumed equal importance. His training and practice as an agronomist certainly contributed to this perception that he did not desire militarists but "armed militants"; that is, reminding all that the weapons were only one circumstantial and that most important was the integral development of the country. The future came to show dramatically that Cabral lost his bet. If during the struggle he was the political commissioner who directed the military commander, a few years after independence, the soldier considered himself to be the only one responsible for the success of the armed struggle.

So dramatic are the consequences, when Cabral always saw himself as a profoundly antimilitarist person. From the outset he tried to persuade the movement for independence to unfold in a peaceful way, without resorting to war; it was a position not accepted by Salazar, leader of one of the most retrograde dictatorships of Europe. Throughout the eleven years of war, he always reaffirmed his readiness to negotiate, since, as he always said, "both sides speak Portuguese and could understand each other quickly". During the struggle, he reached the point of giving a rigorous order that the *Ponte de Saltinho* (Saltinho Bridge), over the *Corubal* river, should not be destroyed, in spite of the military benefits that could be gained by the guerrillas in impeding a north-south linkage for the colonial troops. He justified this decision by asking: "And after independence, where are we going to find funds for its reconstruction?"

Other Agronomic Works

Besides the work realized in Guinea-Bissau, Amílcar Cabral undertook agronomical activities in Portugal, Angola, and Germany, from March, 1955, when he and Maria Helena were "expelled" from the country after two and a half years of intense work.

There are numerous technical documents produced by Amílcar Cabral at the time, relative to those countries, having as objectives: to gain financial resources that allowed him to live with dignity; to practice his profession, earning new knowledge and experience; to await the moment to "leap" to the interior of Guinea-Bissau to pursue the struggle for independence, which he started to organise as soon as, finishing the course, he left for Bissau.

Final Note

After the liberation of Guinea-Bissau in 1974, I saw only one person, Luis Cabral, Amílcar's brother and the first president of the republic, who understood Cabral's agronomist thought. He invested seriously in agriculture, launching numerous projects and constantly following up enthusiastically, as well as encouraging the technical actors. Examples include frequent visits to the *Contuboel* rice-growing centre, where, besides the research introduced for the first time in Guinea-Bissau, there was rice cultivation during the dry season, as well as the public production company of hens and eggs.

After him, no other president was interested or dedicated to the promotion and modernization of Guinean agriculture.

Bibliography

Estudos Agrários de Amílcar Cabral, INEP, (1988)

Juvenal Cabral, *Memórias e Reflexões*, Instituto da Biblioteca Nacional, Cabo Verde (2002)

Luís Cabral, *Crónica da Libertação*, O Jornal, 1984

Acknowledgments

For the elaboration of these brief notes, I sought the information and opinions of people who helped us and to whom we are very much indebted and grateful.

I'd like to thank the numerous veterans of the struggle for the independence of the Matas de Cantanhez (Forests of *Cantanhez*), the first liberated zone, who have shared the stories of their lives, their villages, and the leaders who established guerrilla camps.

Also to Bacar Cassamá, monitor of the *Granja de Pessubé* and veteran of the first hour, with whom I regrettably have not talked for a while.

To José Araújo, the PAIGC leader who told us when we were in the leadership of JAAC (Youth of the Party) about many of Amílcar Cabral's thoughts, especially what he was planning for the post-independence period.

To Flora Gomes, filmmaker and former student of the Escola Piloto (Pilot School) in Conakry, who lived closely with Cabral and who much supported and contributed to the elaboration of these notes, giving us the hope that they can be useful in creating the "film of his life," entitled, *Amílcar Cabral.*

To Clara Schwarz Da Silva, early friend of Amílcar and Maria Helena, who undertook the translation of the texts "Feux de Brousse et Jachères dans le Cycle Culturel Arachid-Mils" and "À Propôs du Cycle Cultural Arachide-Mils en Guinée Portuguaise," both presented by Cabral in the Arachide-Mils Conference in Bambey, Senegal, in 1954, and who kindly provided unpublished photographs in which Amílcar Cabral is present and which form part of her personal collection.

6. THE CABRAL ERA

STRATEGIC AND FOREIGN POLICY OBJECTIVES

Richard A. Lobban, Jr.

Introduction

The period of the 1950s and 1960s in the world was characterized by intense Cold War rivalries, polarization, tensions, and a fearsome arms race for atomic weapons on the land, air, and seas. In Africa, this strategic battle was played out with proxy partners and strange alliances. Formally, the sides were drawn sharply between NATO (the North Atlantic Treaty Organization, founded on March 18, 1949) and the Warsaw Pact (the Soviet Union and Eastern European allies). Portugal, a colonial power and fascist dictatorship at the time, as well as a state formerly sympathetic to Nazism, was determined to join NATO. Officially, NATO equipment and training should have been relegated to European defense, but clearly, American funds, equipment, and training (seen with my own eyes) got into Africa, as that continent was perceived as a battle ground for the proxy forces in the Cold War.

This was the era of coup d'etats, assassinations, armed insurgents in a variety of battles for decolonisation, national self-determination, and anti-apartheid struggles, a time when logic, history, and ideology would suggest that the United States be on the side of liberation; viewed in a Cold War lens, however, African anticolonial movements (PAIGC, FRELIMO, MPLA, SWAPO, ZANU, ZAPU) and antiracist (ANC, PAC)[22]

22 PAIGC: Partido Africano da Independência da Guiné e Cabo Verde; FRELIMO: Frente de Libertação de Moçambique; MPLA: Movimento Popular de Liberta-

insurgents were seen as alarming "terrorist" threats. Anticolonial wars in Southeast Asia were other major pivot-points in world history at the time. History will judge these events.

I first went to Africa in 1964 to work on a project building a school and teaching biology in Tanzania for refugees from South Africa, Mozambique, and Namibia. One of our neighbors was Dr. Eduardo Mondlane (PhD Northwestern University, Professor at Syracuse University), who was a founder and first president of FRELIMO. Needless to say, he was an impressive man driven by the noble mission to decolonise Mozambique ("Portuguese East Africa"). I continued with my formal education in African studies (MA from Temple in 1968 on Yoruba in Nigeria; PhD from Northwestern in 1973 on Nubians in Sudan). Inspired to carry on with liberation support work, I joined the Southern Africa Committee in New York as a staff writer. Each of us had a specific African nation as our assignment for monthly reporting on political and military affairs. It happened, partly because of the large Portuguese community in New England, that our contingent focused on Angola, Mozambique, Guinea, Cape Verde, and Portugal. Other staff writers wrote on Zimbabwe (Southern Rhodesia), Namibia (South West Africa), and South Africa.

So it happened that I was assigned to cover the national liberation war in Guinea-Bissau. In the fall of 1972, I worked with the New England PAIGC Support Committee. I spoke publically on the anticolonial struggles and met with Gil Fernandes who had graduated from the University of New Hampshire and become an activist for the PAIGC. I arranged with him to go to Guinea-Bissau as a journalist in 1973 to cover the war. He indicated that I could meet Amílcar Cabral, PAIGC secretary general, on that occasion. Actually Cabral came to the United States in the fall of 1972 to speak at various forums, including Lincoln University, but since I knew I would meet him in person next year, I skipped that opportunity...to my lasting regret. Cabral was murdered on January 20, 1973, in Conakry.

ção de Angola – Partido do Trabalho; SWAPO: South West Africa People's Organization; ZANU: Zimbabwe African National Union; ZAPU: Zimbabwe African People's Union; ANC: African National Congress; PAC: Pan Africanist Congress

PAIGC Foreign Policy

The African Party for the Independence of Guinea-Bissau and Cape Verde (PAIGC) was formed in 1956 at the height of Cold War polarization. The PAIGC was strongly opposed to apartheid and white settlers in southern Africa. Although Portugal was under the fascist rule of the Estado Novo governments of Salazar and Caetano and was sympathetic to the Nazis, it remained neutral in World War II, and later joined the North Atlantic Treaty Organization (NATO). These postwar years also saw widespread decolonisation by England and France.

In Guinea-Bissau the struggles were not simple, as there were political proxy rivalries and a lack of regional support. Guinea-Bissau's neighbors were unwilling to provide supplies and training for the PAIGC guerrillas; Senegal's leadership was cautious, given ongoing associations with France; radical anticolonial Guinea-Conakry was suffering from virtual paranoia because of coup attempts, repression, and invasions. Consequently, much of the early military training for the PAIGC was in the Maghreb. I understand that some initial military training for the PAIGC soldiers took place in Morocco and Algeria. Once the war was underway, training for FARP (Regular Armed Forces) and FAL (militias) took place in the liberated zones. Advanced training for selected officers was in the Soviet Union, Cuba, and the People's Republic of China.

PAIGC hoped that peaceful protest could lead towards decolonisation, as it had elsewhere in Africa in the 1950s and 1960s. But this was not to be. The turning point was at the Pijiguiti strike and massacre of August 3, 1959. After the deaths of an estimated fifty workers, the PAIGC determined that the path to freedom would be forged by protracted, armed struggle; they were joined also by the MPLA (Angola), FRELIMO (Mozambique), and the MLSTP (Movement for the Liberation São Tomé and Príncipe) under the overall umbrella of the CONCP (Conference of Nationalist Organizations in the Portuguese Colonies).

Gradually, small guerilla units were turned into FAL (local militia forces) and FARP (regular army forces). The few initial weapons were replaced and expanded by 1966, with more small arms, light weapons, mortars, bazookas, small portable canons, and 75mm recoilless rifles. This military technology came from the African Liberation Support Committee, the Soviet Union (and Warsaw Pact allies), China, and the Arab world. The Portuguese weapons came from the NATO allies.

Tactics and Strategies in the War of National Liberation

Despite a very long tradition of Guinean resistance to the Portuguese, with the last battle of colonial "pacification" as recent as 1936, there was no direct hope of defeating heavily armed Portuguese colonial forces. Consequently, a strategy of protracted insurgency was determined to be the only way forward. The colonial enemy would be worn down and vanquished by a thousand stings of guerrilla insurgency, as inspired by Soviet, Chinese, Cuban, Vietnamese models.

The military strategy of the Portuguese was essentially to secure the capital and the major towns and establish forward operating bases (FOB) to secure the borders and send out counterinsurgency patrols. This strategy might avoid the overextension of military resources and personnel, but over the long term it was a defensive strategy that had difficulty in taking the war to the insurgents. Politically, colonialism had lost legitimacy through the United Nations declarations on the Rights of National Self-Determination. On the side of the PAIGC insurgency, the strategy was to create liberated zones in the rural areas that the Portuguese could not easily attack and be able to hold. The more these zones could be secured, the more local economy, and health and educational services could be created to rival the skimpy provisions in these areas by the colonial administration.

Certainly, in the historical rearview mirror, these two different strategies, played out over many years, almost guaranteed the final outcome. The tactics employed, however, would shape the winners and losers. Needless to say, the events that unfolded in the postcolonial period were a separate matter.

The 1973-1974 Turning Points: The Battle of Guiledge

By 1973, some 81,000 refugees fled to Senegal from the northern areas of Guinea-Bissau, and thousands had also fled from the south to Guinea-Conakry. The assassination of Secretary General Amílcar Cabral on January 20, 1973, in neighboring Conakry, was a body blow against the organisation he had founded. It is a tribute to his organisational skills and the structure of the PAIGC that the political and military battles could advance so significantly in the next few months and that the war of national liberation against colonialism went on to achieve its primary objective. Gains on the battlefield had already created tremendous pressures in the colonial capitol of Lisbon itself. MFA (*Movimento Forças Armadas*) officers sprang into action on April 25, 1974, and brought the five centuries of the Portuguese empire tumbling down.

One of the first major post-Cabral events was termed "Operation Amílcar Cabral." This was designed to show the occupying forces that the insurgency was not going to be set back by the loss of their top leader. Luís Cabral (Amílcar's half-brother) and Aristides Pereira, the new secretary general, had to do something, and they took immediate action.

After meeting with Luís Cabral in Dakar and riding down south with him to the Casamance, we met the PAIGC officials at Ziguinchor to prepare for a tour in the liberated areas of the Northern Front with two other journalists. We left Ziguinchor by truck and took the main road east towards Kolda. Getting off the truck, we walked into the heavy forest on the south side of the road. Thus, in June of 1973, I began a month-long walk across Guinea-Bissau, from north to south, on foot and by canoe.

The issues, events, and context were defined, first of all, by the murder of PAIGC Secretary General Cabral and the subsequent judgments and executions of his murderers. This is entirely another subject for analysis and consideration. Only eleven days after Cabral was killed, Ernestina ("Titina") Silla was killed in combat in the Northern Front, on January 31, 1973. She was a leading member of the CSL (Superior Council of the Struggle).

These grave blows against the PAIGC demanded a severe military response, so as not to lose the rapidly building political momentum on the battlefield. So it came to be that the FARP (Peoples' Revolutionary Armed Forces) unit launched multiple attacks in February at Portuguese fortifications at Farim in the north front and at Catio, Cadique, and Guidage in the south. In March, 1973, the Soviet Union introduced to the FARP units SAM-7s (Surface to Air Missiles) that could be handheld and had heat-seeking offensive capacity to be used against jet aircraft and helicopters.

In that month the Portuguese lost some twenty aircraft; their air supremacy was, astonishingly, curbed in a short while. Amongst the losses was the celebrated Portuguese Air Force Lieutenant Colonel Almeida Brito, whose Fiat G-91 was shot down at Medina Boé. In April, FARP units re-engaged with a renewed heavy attack at Guidage, and in May FARP soldiers struck again at Bula in the north front, and Catio and Guidage in the south. On the twenty-fifth of the same month, FARP launched Operation Amílcar Cabral against the frontier fort at Guiledge. With blow after blow, and using SAM-7s against Portuguese air power, this base was finally captured, with major Portuguese losses in life and war material.

The Fort of Guiledge

Guiledge was five hundred meters (close to a quarter of a mile) on each side. It was densely encircled by rows of barbed wire. Generators electrified flood lights and motion detectors in the nighttime; the barbed-wire fences were augmented by antipersonnel mine fields. At each corner of the base there were heavy mortar emplacements. Dug-in subterranean bunkers provided protection for the soldiers and officers assigned to this forward-operating base. At times there were also tanks, armored personnel carriers (APC's), and open military transport trucks for troops and crews to move from Guiledge to the fort at Gadamael. Ammunition dumps were also dug in to store sufficient rounds and shells to the defending soldiers. Just outside of the barbed wire there was even a small airfield, and when I visited there was the wreckage of a military spotter plane. To top this off, there were field howitzers that could lob artillery shells towards areas where FARP units were believed to be massing or firing.

This was not all. The Portuguese also employed many punitive measures, including "counter-terror" espionage, torture, collective punishment, terror and threats (I saw people with ears cut off), a pass system, parallel to apartheid, and *aldeamentos* (concentration camps for rural relocation). While not on the same scale as the Italian repression in Libya, it was torn from the same pages of brutal European colonial fascism in Africa.

This stout defense was a challenge to FARP units, but multiple regional attacks were demoralizing to the beleaguered Portuguese, who felt more and more isolated. The next step was to cut off the Portuguese air support and supply with the use of the Soviet "Estrella" (SAM7's). Supplies, air spotting and intelligence, and firing on FARP ambush-and-attack positions became more and more difficult for the Portuguese defenders. Then FARP brought their 60mm mortars, 80mm canons, and small arms fire in a final blow against Guiledge.

The commanding Portuguese Major at Guiledge finally called for a full-scale retreat and attempted to flee to Gadamael on May 25, 1973. However, FARP engineers had anticipated this decision and the route they would have to take, so some eighteen antitank mines placed along the escape road destroyed the exiting trucks and killed twenty-six Portuguese soldiers.

From there I took a ride on one of the captured vehicles and then on to the border with Guinea-Conakry. After a long ride to the capital, I met Aristides Pereira in Conakry. He was still nursing his wounded wrists, injuries inflicted during his capture by the same assassins of Cabral. He indicated the spot surrounded by white stones where Cabral had fallen and Pereira had been kidnapped and taken by ship back towards Bissau, until he was rescued by a joint Guinean-Soviet rescue force.

In June there were more attacks at Gadamael, followed by the Second National Congress (held in liberated areas) from July 18-22 of 1973 at Medina Boé. The decisions taken then and there led to the September 24, 1973, Declaration of Independence; the Portuguese governor,

Antonio de Spinola, was relieved of his post. The ground was shaking, and on November 2, the United Nations called on Portugal to cease its military actions in Guinea-Bissau. The Portuguese were virtually in a state of shock and intransigence, so the FARP units of the PAIGC attacked Bula in the north and Bafátá in the east on November 6, just to push their point that colonialism was over. Fellow Africans had no trouble in rising to this request and on November 19, Guinea-Bissau was admitted as the forty-second member of the Organisation of African Unity. The pressures for change mounted.

At last, younger officers, though very tired from the endless colonial wars, seized power in Lisbon on April 25, 1974, in the name of the MFA (Armed Forces Movement) and not only toppled Portuguese colonialism in Africa and Asia, but brought about the fall of the fascist state of Portugal. After further negotiations in Angola, Cape Verde, São Tomé, and Príncipe and Mozambique, Portuguese colonialism in Africa was done, and on September 14, 1974, Portugal's new MFA leaders recognized the new Republic of Guinea-Bissau. On October 15, 1974, the last Portuguese soldiers left Guinea-Bissau. The colonial era was terminated. In retrospect, this was the last major and decisive battle of eleven years (frim 1963 to 1973) of war. On September 24, 1974, the PAIGC celebrated it first full year of national independence.

Here are some notes from my diary entry.

June 30, 1973, Saturday:

At 1930h we found a couple of people who said that a 30-minutes-walk would bring us to Guiledge—the recently fallen Portuguese post- (visit by only 2 foreign journalists). We pushed on in the dark and reached this destination at 2000h—making 11 hours of march today and with 7 ½ hours of yesterday we marched 18 ½ hrs within 2 days-I won't say that it was exactly a pleasure trip.

Thus tonight I am sitting at a Portuguese officer's table writing my notes. Although it is dark it is very clear that this base (now defended by a PAIGC "Bigroup") is very extensive-with a great number of military structures and houses for civilians. It is pointless to write more now when tomorrow's light will permit much closer examination and photography. However, I just comment that this is a dramatic end to 3 ½ weeks of travel in liberated Guinea. Tomorrow night a PAIGC truck will come and take us to Canjambari, from there to Boke and Conakry for some cold drinks and hearty meals which I have savored in my mind these past weeks. We ate our a supper of meat and rice which I devoured in quantities as great as the water I required. Then straight to bed.

July 1, 1973, Sunday:

I didn't sleep because of noise and mosquitoes but it didn't matter anyway since the captured Berliet (French) truck arrived at 0200. After some discussion it was decided that I could not remain (for security reasons) but might be able to return. The heavy military truck was loaded with Portuguese artillery shells and ammunition boxes to be taken to Canjambari. At 0330h we left and very shortly came to the place where a series of 18 anti-tank mines had killed 26 Portuguese soldiers and which led to the demoralization immediately before the evacuation.

We arrived at Canjambari at 0530h. It is a major and extensive PAIGC base area defended by DCA (which has been shooting short bursts from time to time). There are Russian trucks and jeeps as well as the material captured at Guiledge.

This was to be a major turning point. Tragic, destabilizing events that unfolded in the coming decades were most disquieting after such a long struggle; but at least, now, Guineans could make their own mistakes and not have to deal with colonial rule ever again.

Captured armored vehicle, Guildege

Captured armored vehicle, Guildege

Captured artillery, Guildege

Captured Mercedes truck, Guildege

Portuguese Pirates of Guildege

Raising the PAIGC flag, Guildege

Richard Lobban with PAIGC guerrillas, Guildege

Wreckage at Guiledge, 1973, Guildege

7. THE WEAPON OF THEORY

AMÍLCAR CABRAL AND AFRICANA CRITICAL THEORY

Reiland Rabaka

> *Always bear in mind that the people are not fighting for ideas, for things in anyone's head. They are fighting to win material benefits, to live better and in peace, to see their lives go forward, to guarantee the future of their children ... We do not fall back on clichés or merely harp on the struggle against imperialism and colonialism in theoretical terms, but rather we point out concrete things... Hide nothing from the masses of our people. Tell no lies. Expose lies whenever they are told. Mask no difficulties, mistakes, or failures. Claim no easy victories...*
>
> —**Amílcar Cabral**, ***Revolution in Guinea***

Introduction: Cabral, Critical Biography, and Critical Theory

The Cape Verdean and Guinea-Bissaun revolutionary, Amílcar Lopes Cabral, connects with and contributes to the discourse of Africana critical theory in several poignant, provocative, and extremely profound ways. First, it should be mentioned that "although he did not start out or train as a philosopher," Cabral, according to the Nigerian philosopher, Olúfémi Táíwò (1999), "bequeathed to us a body of writings containing his reflections on such issues as the nature and course of social transformation, human nature, history, violence, oppression and liberation". Second, and as eloquently argued by the Eritrean philosopher, Tsenay Serequeberhan (1991), Cabral's ideas led to action (i.e., actual cultural, historical, social, and political transformation, and ultimately revolutionary decolonisation and liberation) and, therefore, "represents the zenith" of twentieth century Africana revolutionary theory and praxis (p. 20).[23] Third, and finally, his writings and reflections provide us with a series of unique contributions to critical theory, which—in the fashion of W.E.B. Du Bois, C.L.R. James, Claudia Jones, George Padmore, Aimé Cesaire, Léopold Senghor, Louise Thompson Patterson, Frantz Fanon, Malcolm X, Stokely Carmichael, Amiri Baraka, Angela Davis, and Walter Rodney, amongst others— seeks to simultaneously critique racist capitalist and racial colonialist societies.

Cabral's biography has been documented by Mario de Andrade (1980), Patrick Chabal (2003), Ronald Chilcote (1991), Mustafah Dhada (1993), Oleg Ignatiev (1975, 1990), and Jock McCulloch (1983b) and, consequently, need not be rehearsed in its entirety here. That said, at this juncture what I am specifically interested in are those aspects of his life and legacy that impacted and influenced his contributions to Africana critical theory. As Chabal (2003) observed in his pioneering work, *Amílcar Cabral: Revolutionary Leadership and People's War*, Cabral's revolutionary theory and praxis are virtually incomprehensible without critically engaging his gradual and often extremely interesting growth from nonviolent student militant to internationally acclaimed revolutionary leader.[24]

23 Serequeberhan extends and explicates the thesis that Cabral "represents the zenith" of twentieth century continental African anticolonial political philosophy in *The Hermeneutics of African Philosophy* (1994), and specifically chapter 4, "The Liberation Struggle: Existence and Historicity," (pp. 87-116). Cabral is also a major presence in his volume entitled, *Our Heritage* (2000), and specifically chapter 6, "The Heritage of the Idea: Violence, Counterviolence, and the Negated," (pp. 59-72).

24 As I am here only concerned with Cabral insofar as his intellectual life and political legacy are understood to connect and contribute to the development an Africana theory critical of contemporary culture and society, I shall forego a detailed discussion of his biography. Readers seeking further biographical treatments of Cabral, besides the main sources listed in the text, are also admonished to consult: Chabal (1980, 1983), Comitini (1980), Dadoo (1973), Davidson (1969, 1981, 1984), Fobanjong and Ranuga (2006), Goldfield (1973), Lopes (1987, 2006, 2010), McCulloch (1983), Nikanorov (1973), Rahmato (1982), Sigrist (2010), and Táíwò (1999).

Born of Cape Verdean parents in Bafata, Guinea-Bissau, on September 12, 1924, Cabral's parents exerted an enormous influence on him. His father, Juvenal Antonio da Costa Cabral, was born on São Tiago Island, Cape Verde. The senior Cabral's family were landowners and, therefore, considered "well-to-do" by local standards. As a result, he was afforded a "proper education," as with the other members of his family (Chabal, 2003, p.29). Juvenal Cabral had early ambitions to become a priest and was summarily sent to seminary in Portugal following a glowing stint in secondary school. It is not clear whether Juvenal's studies in Portugal awakened his sense of anticolonialism and Africanity or whether it was the racial climate and rigid religious curriculum of seminary, but what is certain is that he became a "politically conscious man who did not hesitate to speak his mind" (p. 30). For instance, on one occasion he sent a letter to the minister of colonies deploring what he understood to be the complete absence of government assistance in alleviating the catastrophic effects of drought, going so far as to suggest several remedies. On another occasion he wrote an article expressing his disdain for the colonial government after a house collapsed in an overcrowded part of Praia, the capital of Cape Verde. He went further to criticize the inhuman conditions in which Cape Verdeans had to live because they were forced to flee the countryside and come to the already overcrowded city to find food and work.

Chabal persuasively argues that it was Cabral's father who gave him his first lessons in political education, a point further corroborated by Dhada (1993, pp. 139-140). Juvenal Cabral also instilled in Amílcar a profound sense of the shared heritage and struggle of Guinea-Bissau and Cape Verde. He wrote poetry, polemics, and expressed an uncommon and long-lasting interest in the agricultural problems of Guinea-Bissau and Cape Verde. Juvenal, a renowned and well-respected school teacher, possessed a deep "sense of intellectual curiosity and rigour, a respect for academic pursuits and for the written word," which he consistently stressed to Amílcar, amongst his other children (Chabal, 2003, p. 30). While it cannot be said that Juvenal Cabral was a revolutionary nationalist by any standard, it does seem clear that he may have planted, however nascent, the seeds of nationalism in the fertile soil of his young son's heart and mind.

As it was with his father, Cabral's mother, Iva Pinhal Evora, was born on São Tiago Island, Cape Verde. However, unlike his father, she was born into a poor family which stressed hard work and piety. If Cabral's father bequeathed to him political education, a love of poetry, and an interest in agriculture, then it can be argued that his mother provided him with a very special sense of self-determination, discipline, purpose, personal ethics, and an unshakeable iron will. For a time, Mrs. Cabral made good and was an entrepreneur, the proprietor of a shop and a small *pensão* (hotel). When she and Juvenal Cabral separated in 1929, things took a turn for the worse financially. She lost her business and worked as a seamstress and laborer in a fish-canning factory to support her family. Even still, her earnings were "barely sufficient to feed the family and there were days when they went without food." Chabal (2003) poignantly observes that though "Amílcar's family did not starve like so many Cape Verdeans, they were very poor" (p. 31). He went on to emphasize, "Cabral never forgot the difficulties of his early years and later spoke of poverty as one of the reasons which had led him to revolt against Portuguese colonialism" (p. 31). The hardships he witnessed his mother endure and overcome, caring for him and his siblings, undoubtedly influenced his views on gender justice and, most especially, women as cultural workers and revolutionary comrades in the national liberation struggle (Cabral, 1979, pp. 70-71, 86, 104; see also Chabal, 2003, p. 107, 118; Campbell, 2006; Gomes, 2006; Urdang, 1979).

Cabral and Cabo Verdianidade: From Innocuous Anti-colonial Student-Activism to Revolutionary Democratic Socialist African Nationalism

In discussing Cabral's early life, and especially the influence of his parents on him, it is also important to point out that he was home-schooled until the age of twelve. Though he did not enter primary school until he was twelve, Cabral is reported to have "thrived on education, and from the very beginning he was clearly an excellent student." One of his former primary school classmates, Manuel Lehman d'Almeida, recalled that Cabral was "by far the best student and that he passed his secondary school entrance exam with distinction" (Chabal, 2003, p. 31). His school records support d'Almeida's claims and lucidly illustrate that Cabral completed his studies at the *liceu* by the age of twenty, which would mean that he finished four years of primary school and seven years of secondary school in an astonishing eight years! During the last couple of years of his studies at the *liceu* Cabral became aware of the Cape Verdean literary renaissance and cultural movement commonly known as Cabo Verdianidade (essentially Cape Verdeanness), which was primarily an outgrowth of the journal, *Claridade*. In many senses Cabo Verdianidade was the Cape Verdean version of the Harlem Renaissance and Negritude Movement, both of which strongly influenced its writers.[25]

Cabo Verdianidade was unique in that its writers for the most part broke with Eurocentric models and themes and, in a move that must be understood to be extremely bold for the time, turned their attention to Cape Verdean subjects, particularly ordinary people's life-worlds and lived-experiences: from drought to hunger, from migration to mild critiques of colonial miseducation, and from starvation to other forms of deprivation. Even so, more similar to the Negritude Movement than the Harlem Renaissance, Cabo Verdianidade was limited by its intentional aim at readers well-versed in colonial history and culture. To make matters worse, it was essentially escapist, expressing an intense cultural alienation that did not in any way promote anticolonial consciousness or decolonisation, nonviolent or otherwise. Much like the early issues of Negritude's *Présence Africaine*, then, Cabo Verdianidade's *Claridade* explored ethnic, racial, and cultural politics in a vacuum, as opposed to connecting the intersections and political economy of ethnicity, race, racism, and colonialism, with the machinations of modern white supremacist capitalism.

---

25 For further discussion of *Claridade* and the Cape Verdean literary renaissance and cultural movement, and for the works that influenced my interpretation here, see Alfama and Laban (2006), Bettencourt and Silva (2010), Brennand (1996), Ferreira (1986), Hamilton (1975), Moser (1992), and Rector and Vernon (2012).

The first generation of Cabo Verdianidade writers established their journal, *Claridade*, in the 1930s, but by the 1940s a new cohort of Cape Verdean writers founded the journal *Certeza*. The *Certeza* writers introduced two elements into Cape Verdean consciousness that foreshadowed the future emphasis on national liberation and national culture. The first element involved their critical calling into question of Portuguese colonialism in Cape Verde and an unswerving emphasis on the necessity for political action, though not necessarily decolonisation, as later conceived by Cabral and his revolutionary nationalist comrades. For these writers, Marxism rather than neorealism provided their theoretical framework and political orientation. The second element, connected in several ways to the first, revolved around this group's stress on *returning* Cape Verdeans *to the source* of their history, culture, and struggle: Africa.[26]

As we have witnessed with the writers of the Cabo Verdianidade Movement, at this time most Cape Verdeans understood themselves to be Europeans, and the Cape Verdean archipelago to be Portugal's most prized overseas islands. The *Certeza* writers went beyond the *Claridade* collective by unequivocally emphasizing their African ancestry and longstanding connections with continental African history, culture, and struggle. Ironically, Cabral had completed his studies and had left Cape Verde by the time this new movement was underway. However, he did keep track of it from abroad, and noted that it had the potential to lead to anticolonial consciousness and an openness to nationalist ideas.

In the autumn of 1945, at the age of twenty-one, Cabral trekked to Portugal to pursue a five-year course of study at the Agronomy Institute at the Technical University of Lisbon. He attended university on a scholarship provided by the Cape Verdean branch of Casa dos Estudiantes do Império (CEI), the House of Students from the Empire, a colonial government financed social development centre for students from Portugal's

26 For further discussion of the *Certeza* writers and the Cape Verdean literary renaissance and cultural movement, and for the works that influenced my interpretation here, see Afolabi (2001), Afolabi and Burness (2003), Araujo (1966), Arenas (2011), Batalha (2004), Burness (1981), Chabal (2002), Peres (1997), and Vambe and Zegeye (2006).

colonies. His scholarship remitted his tuition and supplied him with a very modest stipend of 500 escudos, which was later increased to 750 escudos. His meager stipend was, of course, not enough to live on, so Cabral tutored and took various odd jobs to supplement his income, all the while consistently maintaining the highest marks of his class. Even in light of all of this, Cabral found the time to participate in university affairs, metropolitan politics, and sundry extracurricular activities, most notably: the Radio Clube de Cabo Verde, the Radio Club of Cape Verde; Comissão Nacional para Defensa do Paz (CNDP), the National Commission for the Defense of Peace; Lisbon's Maritime Centre and Africa House; the Centre for African Studies (CAS); Movimento Anti-Colonialista (MAC), the Anti-Colonial Movement; and Comité de Liberação dos Territórios Africanos Sob o Domíno Português (CLTASDP), the Committee for the Liberation of Territories Under Portuguese Domination.

Indeed, Cabral was a multidimensional student-activist, although an extremely cautious one. Dhada (1993) contends that Cabral may have "stayed clear of subversive politics, largely for cautionary reasons—perhaps for fear of losing his scholarship or being hounded by the Portuguese secret police, Policía Interncional para a Defensa do Estudo (PIDE)," the International Police for the Defense of the State; the very same secret police who would, two decades after he earned his degree in agricultural engineering, mercilessly assassinate him (p. 141). Perhaps Cabral sensed his imminent future fate, but even still, harassed and hounded by the Portuguese secret police, he managed to graduate at the top of his class on March 25, 1952. This was a real feat, especially considering the fact that he was the only student of African origin in his cohort. Out of the 220 students who began the rigorous five-year course of study with Cabral, only 22 were awarded degrees as agronomists or, rather, agricultural engineers.

One of the students with which Cabral developed a lasting rapport was Maria Helena Rodrigues, a silviculturist who was born in Chaves, northern Portugal. One of only 20 women admitted in Cabral's initial cohort of 220 students, Rodrigues and Cabral became study partners and, after earning their degrees, husband and wife. With his studies completed and a new wife by his side, Cabral applied for a position in the

Portuguese civil service and was "ranked as the best candidate, but was denied the post because he was Black" (Chabal, 2003, p. 39). This insult served as a yet another reminder that Portuguese colonialism was inextricable from Portuguese racism. He then did what so many colonial subjects are forced to do when their dreams of escaping the hardships of their colonized homelands have been dashed: he returned to his native land convinced that he could make a special contribution to its development. In a word, he was doggedly determined to decolonise Cape Verde and Guinea-Bissau.

Cabral gained employment as a "grade two agronomist" with the Provincial Department of Agricultural and Forestry Services of Guinea at the Estação experimental de Pessubé, a research complex not far from Bissau. He was second in command and, from all the reports, seems to have thrown himself into an agricultural census of Guinea-Bissau commissioned by the Lisbon-based Ministry for Overseas Territories. It was through this massive undertaking that Cabral become intimately familiar with the people and land in whose interest he would soon wage a protracted people's war for national liberation. He began the study in late 1953, traveling more than 60,000 kilometers, and collecting data from approximately 2,248 peasants. By December, 1954, he presented his and his team's findings to the colonial authorities. The report was subsequently published in 1956 as a 200-page document. It featured statistics and analysis pertaining to Guinea-Bissau's agricultural demography, which the colonial government promised the United Nation's Food and Agricultural Organization it would use to better grapple with droughts and famine—amongst other issues—besetting Guinea-Bissau.

Cabral was afforded considerable expertise carrying out the agricultural census. In fact, Chabal went so far to contend that, "few twentieth-century revolutionary and guerrilla leaders were in the enviable position of having such a specialized and detailed knowledge of the country in which they proposed to launch a people's war" (p. 53; Forrest, 1992; Mendy, 2006). Along with his work for the colonial government, Cabral made many political contacts with both Cape Verdeans and Guinea-Bissauns. Many initially outright rejected his ideas on decolonisation, but after he discursively provided examples, often with empirical and irrefutable evidence (e.g., disenfranchisement, deprivation, starvation, lack of education, and violent government repression), usually over a prolonged period of time (i.e., usually several weeks or months), they were persuaded to seriously contemplate radical political alternatives as solutions to the problem(s) of Portuguese colonialism. It is here that Cabral excelled, clandestinely making contacts with civil servants and entrepreneurs, as well as urban workers, peasants, and villagers.

Initially Cabral was open to using every available legal means of bringing about an end to Portuguese colonialism. To this end, in 1954 he formed a sports, recreational, and cultural club for local youngsters, with the ultimate aim of using it as a front to promote nationalism, political education, and anticolonial consciousness-raising, as had been successfully done in "British" and "French" Africa (Alegi and Bolsmann, 2010; Black and Nauright, 1998; Darby, 2002; Koonyaditse, 2010). For instance, after a game of football, Cabral and his colleagues would retire to a more private place supposedly to discuss how each player could improve their skills; what really took place were intense and eye-opening discussions about African history, culture, and struggle, and the nefarious nature of Portuguese colonialism and racism. The club and its secret meetings gained considerable notoriety in and around Bissau and, as a result, were insidiously infiltrated by the Portuguese secret police's informers and swiftly terminated on government orders. Consequently, Cabral was forced to leave Guinea-Bissau and permanently banned from residing there again. He petitioned for, and was granted, annual visits to briefly see his mother and other family members.

At this point the dye was cast, and Cabral let go of any lingering hope that Cape Verde and Guinea-Bissau could be liberated using the constitutional or legal decolonisation path. It was, therefore, on one of his colonial government-sanctioned visits to Guinea-Bissau, on September 19, 1956, that Cabral, Luiz Cabral (his brother), Aristides Pereira, Fernando Fortes, Julio de Almeida, and Eliseu Turpin founded the Partido Africano da Independência e União dos Povos da Guiné e Cabo Verde (PAIUPGC), the African Party for the Independence and Unity of Guinea-Bissau and Cape Verde. Later the name was slightly altered to Partido Africano da Independência da Guiné e Cabo Verde (PAIGC), the African Party for the Independence of Guinea-Bissau and Cape Verde. Over the next seventeen years of his turbulent life, Amílcar Cabral would not only bring Portuguese colonialism to its knees and lead the people of Guinea-Bissau and Cape Verde to national liberation, but he would also reconstruct and redefine what it means to be a revolutionary nationalist *and* revolutionary humanist. Though there are many who argue that Cabral was not necessarily a theorist, and more a guerilla leader and military strategist whose work is confined to the national liberation struggle of Cape Verde and Guinea-Bissau, my work—especially in *Africana Critical Theory* (2009) and *Forms of Fanonism* (2010b)—challenges these assertions and illustrates several of the ways in which Cabral's "organic intellectual" life and political legacy continues to contribute to radical politics, critical social theory, and revolutionary movements, Africana or otherwise.[27]

In *Social Movements, 1768-2004* (2004), noted political sociologist Charles Tilly essentially argued that social movements are most often made up of ordinary people, rather than members of the politically powerful and intellectually elite, and it is these "ordinary people," these "organic intellectuals"—à la Antonio Gramsci's provocative work in his *Prison Notebooks*—who collectively think, act, and speak in the best interest of, and in concert with everyday average people—the so-called "masses." Gramsci (1971) famously contended that "all men are intellectuals," but "not all men have in society the function of intellectuals" (p.9). It is extremely important to emphasize this point, because neither the African masses nor the squalid shacks and shantytowns they have been callously

27 For further discussion of Cabral's social and political thought, as well as his conceptions of revolutionary nationalism and revolutionary decolonisation, and for the works which influenced my interpretation here, see Abdullah (2006), Bienen (1977), Chilcote (1991), Fobanjong (2006), Lopes (1987, 2006, 2010), McCollester (1973), McCulloch (1983), Mendy (2006), Nzongola-Ntalaja (2006), Rahmato (1982), Rudebeck (2006), Vambe and Zegeye (2008), and Wick (2006).

quarantined to have been recognized for their intellectual activities and positive cultural contributions.

Although "one can speak of intellectuals," Gramsci declared, "one cannot speak of nonintellectuals, because nonintellectuals do not exist." In point of fact, "there is no human activity from which every form of intellectual participation can be excluded: *homo faber* cannot be separated from *homo sapiens*," which is to say, the "primitive man" (*homo faber*) cannot be completely divorced from the evolution of the much-vaunted "wise man" (*homo sapiens*). Intellectuals do not simply inhabit college campuses and highbrow cafés, then; they can also be found in each and every country in Africa, including the villages, slums, ghettoes, and shantytowns. Right along with "men of taste," Gramsci included "philosophers" in his conception of "organic intellectuals," contending:

> Each man, finally, outside his professional activity, carries on some form of intellectual activity, that is, he is a 'philosopher,' an artist, a man of taste, he participates in a particular conception of the world, has a conscious line of moral conduct, and therefore contributes to sustain a conception of the world or to modify it, that is, to bring into being new modes of thought (9; see also 3-43).[28]

Africana critical theorists, and Cabral in particular, may not be understood to be "philosophers" in the Western sense of the term, but no mistake should be made about it: *the Africana tradition of critical theory, a tradition predicated on the pronouncements and practices of continental and diasporan African organic intellectuals, is undeniably philosophical in that it articulates and actively helps to bring into being a new "conception of the world" and "new modes of thought" free from Eurocentrism, racism, sexism,*

28 For further discussion of Antonio Gramsci's life and legacy, especially his conception of the "organic intellectual," and for the works which influenced my interpretation here, see Adamson (1980), Boggs (1976), Fiori (1990), Francese (2009), Germino (1990), Gramsci (1977, 1978, 1985, 1995, 2000), Holub (1992), and S.J. Jones (2006).

heterosexism, colonialism, and capitalism, as well as other forms of modern and postmodern fascism and imperialism.

Not Knowledge for Knowledge's Sake, but Knowledge for Life and Liberation's Sake: Cabral, Africana Philosophy, and Africana Critical Theory

Cabral presents Africana critical theory with several significant challenges. Particularly, his lifework necessitates a fundamental rethinking of critical theory in general and, more specifically, the discourse and development of Africana critical theory. Cabral's thought serves as a cue and calls for a more "concrete"—as opposed to "abstract"—philosophy, an *Africana philosophy of praxis*: a historically-nuanced, culturally-grounded, and politically-charged form of critical social theory that speaks to the special needs of continental and diasporan Africans. Eschewing the scholasticism and abstract system-building of the bulk of European and European American-trained philosophers of African descent, Cabral constantly developed accessible critical theories of: the changing conditions of contemporary society; the prospects of Pan-African democratic socialist revolution; revolutionary decolonisation; revolutionary re-Africanization; revolutionary nationalism; and revolutionary humanism. He was ever concerned to utilize theory (i.e., philosophy) as a weapon against imperialism, and to unite it with the emancipatory aspirations and efforts of his specific struggling people and racially colonized humanity as a whole. Cabral always admonished intellectual-activists to be critically cognizant of our particular circumstances and situations, but, as revolutionary humanists, to remain open to learning what we can from the lived-experiences and experiments (e.g., social, political, and cultural experiments) of others. In his own weighted words:

> The experience of others is highly significant for someone undergoing any experience. The reality of others is highly significant for one's reality. Many folk do not understand this, and grasp their reality with the passion that they are going to

> invent everything: "I do not want to do the same as others have done, nothing that others have done." This is a sign of ignorance. If we want to do something in reality, we must see who has already done the same, who has done something similar, and who has done something opposite, so that we can learn something from their experience. It is not to copy completely, because every reality has its own questions and its own answers for these questions....there are many things which belong to many realities jointly. It is essential that the experience of others benefit us. We must be able to derive from everyone's experience what we can adapt to our conditions, to avoid unnecessary efforts and sacrifices. This is very important. (Cabral, 1979, pp. 49-50)

In good dialectical fashion Cabral suggested that we start with our own circumstances and situations, but maintain an *epistemic* and *experiential openness*, and be willing and able to appropriate and adapt the advances or breakthroughs of others as they pertain to our circumstances and situations, as these advances and breakthroughs could in many instances aid us in avoiding "unnecessary efforts and sacrifices." He firmly warned us "not to copy completely," because our lived-reality, that is our concrete conditions and unique historical happenings, are distinct from those of any people in any other age. We are to always remember that "every reality has its own questions and its own answers for these questions." Here, this caveat should also be connected to Cabral's (1971, 1972, 1973, 1974, 1975, 1979) discussion of the plurality of African histories, cultures, and struggles. Indeed, Cabral and his comrades provided solutions to many problems, crucial answers to several critical questions, but contemporary critical theorists must be cognizant of the fact that Cabral and his comrades provided solutions to the particular problems they were faced with in their specific historical moment, as they were confronting the conundrums of an extremely particular, if not peculiar, form of racial colonialism: Portuguese colonialism. Cabral (1972) critically contended:

> We, peoples of Africa, who are fighting against Portuguese colonialism, have suffered under very special conditions, because for the past forty years we have been under the domination of a fascist regime…Portugal is an economically backward country, in which about 50 percent of the population is illiterate, a country which you will find at the bottom of all the statistical tables of Europe….Portugal is a country in no position at all to dominate any other country (p. 78; see also da Ponte, 1974; Ferreira, 1974; Meintel, 1984; Morier-Genoud and Cahen, 2012).

This means, then, that it is equally important for contemporary critical theorists, Africana or otherwise, to critically bear in mind that, however attractive Cabral's thought, no matter how fervently we believe it to speak to the special issues we are confronted with in the twenty-first century, his contributions to critical theory cannot provide us with the concrete and nuanced historical understandings necessary to develop revolutionary movements, that is, national and international liberation struggles aimed at altering the new and novel social and political problems of the present.

There simply is no substitute for contemporary critical theorists practicing conceptual generation; no problem-solving proxy for our solemn development of new theory geared towards, not only gauging but changing contemporary societies, bringing into being a new humanity, new societies and, perhaps even, a new world culture and civilization grounded in and growing out of various trans-ethnic traditions of revolutionary decolonization, revolutionary humanism, revolutionary democratic socialism, critical multiculturalism, racial justice, gender justice, women's liberation, freedom of sexual preference, and religious tolerance, among others.

However, even in light of all the critical observations above, I continue to believe that Cabral's theoretic-strategic framework is extremely useful for those critical theorists concerned with, not merely colonialism, neocolonialism, and postcolonialism, but also racism, critical race theory, revolutionary nationalism, revolutionary humanism, re-Africanization, and the critique of capitalism and class struggles in contemporary society. His theoretic-strategic framework, indeed, does offer critical concepts and innovative analytical categories; it does, in fact, provide a wide-range of principles and prospects that make intelligible the constantly changing character of contemporary colonialism, capitalism, and racism. Further, it seems to prophetically prefigure and point to new, untapped types of revolutionary social and cultural movements, and even goes so far to suggest several distinct directions for future radical political struggle.

Cabral's theoretic-strategic framework is distinctive in that it audaciously challenges contemporary theorists to actually, ontologically speaking, *be* simultaneously "critical" *and* "theorists," "intellectuals" *and* "activists." It explicitly asks that "critical theorists" embrace the dialectical task of transforming themselves and their societies, which, once again, are situated in specific historical moments, with concrete conditions, and particular social and political problems. Corroborating Cabral and, in a sense, updating his thesis that "every reality has its own questions and its own answers for these questions," the Ghanaian philosopher, Kwame Gyekye (1995), has stated: "Philosophers belonging to a given culture or era or tradition select those concepts or clusters of concepts that, for one reason or another, matter most and that therefore are brought to the fore in their analysis" (p. 7). These "concepts and clusters of concepts" are employed, insofar as specific philosophers understand them, to offer the most compelling and comprehensive means to alter contemporary societies and, even more, contemporary "souls," following the fundamental thrust of Du Bois's contributions to critical theory (see Rabaka, 2007, 2008, 2010a). Gyekye (1997) commented further:

> If one were to examine the cultural and historical setting of the intellectual focus, concerns, and direction of the individual thinker, one would be convinced, beyond doubt, that philosophy is a conceptual response to the basic human problems that arise in any given society in a given epoch. Such an examination would reveal that philosophers grapple at the conceptual level with problems and issues of their times, even though this does not mean that the

> relevance of their ideas, insights, arguments, and conclusions is to be tethered to those times; for, more often than not, the relevance of their insights and arguments—or at least some of them—transcends the confines of their own times and cultures and, thus, can be embraced by other cultures or societies or different generational epochs. In others words, a philosophical doctrine may be historical, that is, generated originally in response to some historical events or circumstances, without our having to look on it as historicistic, without our having to confine its significance simply to those times of history when it was actually produced....the fact that the philosophers who produced the ideas and arguments were giving conceptual response and attention to the experiences of their times needs to be stressed and constantly borne in mind: it was the problems of the time that constituted the points of departure for their reflective analyses....(p. 19)

Cabral impels Africana critical theory to consider the concrete conditions of philosophical settings, reminding us that it may be extremely useful to acknowledge and engage the fact that, and the manner in which, philosophy is inextricable from notions of, most especially, "tradition," but also "history" and "heritage" as well. Another Ghanaian philosopher, Kwasi Wiredu (1991), has asserted that "the philosophy of a people is always a tradition," and that a tradition "presupposes a certain minimum of organic relationships among (at least some of) its elements" (p. 92). He went on to observe: "If a tradition of modern philosophy is to develop and flourish in Africa, there will have to be philosophical interaction and cross-fertilization among contemporary African workers in philosophy" (p. 92; see also Wiredu 1980, 1995, 2004).

In as much as it is reputedly a "return" to the history and culture of African peoples, Cabral's critical return to the source(s) suggests in no uncertain terms that Africana critical theory of contemporary society concern itself with the deconstruction of European-derived continental and diasporan African philosophical discourse, and the reconstruction of a decolonised and re-Africanized critical theory and praxis tradition.

The deconstruction of European-based continental and diasporan African philosophy presupposes that modern workers in Africana philosophy, and Africana Studies in general, have the conceptual and analytical skills and tools to undertake such an endeavor. Further, this endeavor, being nothing less than what has been aforementioned and outlined in the preceding paragraphs as "Africana critical theory," must always and at its core—as a critical self-conscious and critical self-reflective effort—be willing and able to critique and correct its own subjective settings, concrete conditions, and insidiously inherited Eurocentric philosophical influences, as well as other imperialist intellectual influences, which in many, if not in *most* instances keeps it from *doing* what Gyekye (1997), amongst others, understands the fundamental tasks of philosophy to be: (1) provide people with "a fundamental system of beliefs to live by"; (2) determine "the nature of human values and how these values can be realized concretely in human societies"; (3) speculate about "the whole range of human experience" by providing "conceptual interpretations and analysis of that experience, necessarily doing so not only by responding to the basic issues and problems generated by that experience but also by suggesting new or alternative ways of thought and action"; and, (4) offer "conceptual responses to the problems posed in any given epoch for a given society or culture" (pp. 15, 23, 24, 27).

To speak of an Africana critical theory in the contemporary moment means nothing less than speaking of, and actively engaging in, the critique, appreciation, appropriation, and disruption— if need be—of hitherto "traditional" or, even more, abstract academic and Eurocentric, European-influenced forms of continental and diasporan African philosophy and conceptual generation. As Cabral's critical theory suggests, the engagement of any form or field of knowledge should always and ever be, not for scholasticism, abstract system-building, or simply nostalgia's sake, but in the interest of real, live, suffering and struggling women, men, and children; in a word, *not knowledge for knowledge's sake, but knowledge for life and liberation's sake*. Again, Gyekye offered Africana philosophers advice: "philosophical knowledge and insight should benefit the society as a whole, not [merely] the philosophers personally" (p. 18). As philosophers of African origin and descent continue to rescue and rediscover, as well as critically engage and (re)interpret various philosophical systems and traditions, we must be vigilant, remaining consistently conscious of the fact that no matter which form or field of philosophy we feel compelled to engage, it is our solemn duty, as "philosophers," even more, as organic intellectuals and critical theorists of contemporary society, to do so in the revolutionary spirit of Amílcar Cabral—as well as W.E.B. Du Bois, C.L.R. James, Claudia Jones, George Padmore, Aimé Cesaire, Léopold Senghor, Louise Thompson Patterson, Frantz Fanon, Malcolm X, Stokely Carmichael, Angela Davis, and Walter Rodney, amongst others—seeking solutions to the enigmatic issues of our epoch; always and ever, willing and able to criticize and offer alternatives and correctives to contemporary crises and conundrums.

**Bibliographic references can be found in the Select Bibliography in Section 8.*

8. "WEAPONS OF THEORY"

EMPLOYING AMÍLCAR CABRAL IN THE PRESENT

Nigel Westmaas

So say the elders: "The deeds of a man are greater than the details of his birth"

—Maasai Proverb

The year 2013 marks the fortieth anniversary of the assassination of the Guinea-Bissau revolutionary and intellectual Amílcar Cabral. Like murdered leaders and activists everywhere, he left an influential ideological and political legacy in revolutionary struggle and organisation. Cabral was a "poet, agronomist, fighter and theorist," one who approached life "dialectically—on the one hand he was an intellectual and theorist, on the other, he was an organiser and unifier."[29] He was also a significant and brilliant military strategist who fought a successful war of liberation from the Portuguese.

In spite of his relatively short lifetime, Cabral's many speeches, books, and key defining themes testify to the significant body of political wisdom his legacy provides. While the main foundation and detail of the content is relatively unknown, his work, while mainly situated on the struggle in Guinea-Bissau and African liberation, left us powerful lessons on revisiting our ideas on organisation and theory.

In the significant body of revolutionary theory and practice, Cabral embraced certain memorable phrases that address larger and deeper issues.

---

29 Ronald Chilcote, "The theory and practice of Amílcar Cabral: Revolutionary implications for the third world" (1984) *Latin American Perspectives* Vol II No 2.

These titles, found in his important published work, include "return to the source" and "weapons of theory" and proffer much for progressives today. In many respects, Cabral was in advance of his time in political culture, addressing strengths and weaknesses of the personal and political, pursuit of collective leadership, and in demonstrating magnanimity in releasing prisoners of war of the Portuguese state. Cabral wrote in the context of 1960s and 1970s, but his wisdom remains pertinent—even as the era of the mass political and social movements of all shades and types, either in the form of Lula's Brazilian trade union movement or guerrilla warfare participants such as Cabral's own PAIGC, have either dimmed or retreated from the prevailing shock of globalisation and the predominant position of international capital. Meanwhile, the "shining cities," the favelas, dungles, and the old hamlets of indignity and poverty, are as present as ever. Few now address global poverty as a phenomenon originating in the ideological and structure of world capitalism. Poverty is relegated to the problem of the individual. Strident anticolonialism and anti-imperialism have receded, been sidelined or disappeared completely from the public narrative as active challenges to global capitalist supremacy. New forms of global psychological warfare and hegemony are being waged against the undeveloped world and leftist organisations, or against isolated labor and political struggles. Now the era of celebrity humanism, the "lone redeemers," and the important but insufficient charitable war on poverty—no substitute for social justice—is upon us.

I contend that you can find the broad span of Cabral's ideas in several constructive themes. One is Cabral's practical application of context for any struggle. Many progressives have been prone to the unchanged catch phrases and jargon of the formal Left. World reality is more multifaceted and requires, as Cabral once stated, strong doses of "reservations about the systematization of phenomena." [30]

"In reality,"he argues, "the phenomena don't always develop in practice according to the established schemes."[31] This advice is very, very crucial in the present. It is almost tautology to affirm that the world has

30 Richard Handyside, Ed. *Revolution in Guinea (1969)* p.141

31 Ibid, p. 141

changed since the Cabral era. Socialism and national liberation struggles have failed to come to terms with the new "present."

The truth, as Cabral would concur, is complex. It is likely that the present world conjuncture has more to do with the combination of global capitalist hegemony, the import of novel social and political context, and the accretion of errors made by the global Left in countering the rise of capitalism. One of the most important points Cabral consistently made is the need for vigorous and bold reappraisal and assessment of the strengths of both the philosophy and political praxis of modern social movements:

> We base our struggle on the concrete realities of our country. We appreciate the experiences and achievements of other peoples and we study them. But revolution or national liberation is like a dress which must fit to each individual's body. Naturally, there are certain general or universal laws, even scientific laws, for any condition, but the liberation struggle has to be developed according to the specific conditions of each country.[32]

Noted author and activist Arundhati Roy writes of the new philosophy of capitalism and ways in which social and political movements of justice and equality have been sidelined, incorporated, disbanded, or misrepresented with the power of global capital:

> Corporate-endowed foundations administer, trade and channelise their power and place their chessmen on the chessboard, through a system of elite clubs and think tanks, whose members overlap and move in and out through the revolving doors. Contrary to the various conspiracy theories in circulation, particularly among left-wing groups, there is nothing secret, satanic, or freemason-like about this arrangement. It is not very different from the way corporations use shell companies and offshore

32 Cabral, (1973) *Return to the Source: Selected Speeches of Amílcar Cabral.* pp. 86-87

> accounts to transfer and administer their money—except that the currency is power, not money. [33]

Newer assessments of the strengths and weaknesses of the liberation struggles of the past and present have never been more critical. Another page from Cabral's philosophy is crucial here. In one of his many memorable insights, Cabral argues that "the leadership of the (liberation) movement must have a clear notion of the value of the culture in the framework of struggle and a profound knowledge of the culture of their people, whatever the level of economic development"[34]

This reappraisal also extends to the enemy. For too long the organised Left has examined the imperial world as static formation. Using what I would describe as Cabral's flexible weapons of theory—the focus of modern day progressives and leftists should bear in mind some requirements (not necessarily on order of priority) of the present time. First is to build links and allies across the previously dogmatic division and ideological lines in the sand and update their responses to local and global forces of conservatism. Second is to be aware and open to the new social media and its potential in attracting modern youth.

Third is the necessity for conscious appreciation of the intersections of race, class, and gender and the need to proceed with the active, acknowledged parity of these areas in the assessment of social and political life in any part of the globe. In his own fight against Portuguese racism, Cabral afforded his own take on the struggle against race: "in combating racism we don't make progress if we combat the people themselves. We have to combat the causes of racism. If a bandit comes to my house and I have a gun, I cannot shoot the shadow of the bandit; I have to shoot the bandit. Many people lose energy and effort, and make sacrifices combating shadows. We have to combat the material reality that produces the shadow."[35]

---

33 Arundhati Roy, (2012) "Capitalism: A Ghost Story" *Outlook India*, March 26

34 *Amílcar Cabral: Unity and Struggle – Speeches and Writing*. New York: Monthly Review Press, 1979. p.143

35 *Return to the Source- Selected Speeches*. New York: Monthly Review Press, 1973. p. 77

Fourth is the obligation to unearth new and creative ways of highlighting poverty and other social ills that progressives and revolutionaries have always challenged. In like vein, we require uncommon ways of restoring and raising public consciousness about social exclusion and local and global poverty. Recall the lessons of history. Progressives must apply pressure, no matter how seemingly innocuous. In the nineteenth century, Victorian reformer Charles Booth's creative demographic of London poverty provided the antipoverty forces with a boost at a time when mass immiseration was largely ignored.[36] Today the technology of social media at the disposal of the progressive movement is far more favorable than in the Victorian era.

In the age of a dominant Western political and cultural narrative, it is likewise crucial to draw on contradictions in the system rather than attempting to transmit pure ideological messages and universalized responses to everything. In other words, avoid the pitfalls of what is described as the "incoherent Left."[37] Here even the use, by example of method, of comparative humor is instructive. The Daily Show's Jon Stewart's intelligent technique of the use of the "enemy's" voices (especially Fox News) or statements to highlight their own contradictions, could well be studied by the Left. One critic offered the notion that "alternative journalism, one that uses satire to interrogate power, parody to deconstruct contemporary news, and dialogue to enact a model of deliberative democracy…"[38] would be a powerful tool in the hands of progressive forces.

Finally, there is need for caution against the dangerous assumption that the global imperial and neoliberal rule is implacable, unyielding and immune to defeat. There are many cracks in the empire, and more will

---

36 **Charles Booth** (1840–1916) was an "English social investigator" who pioneered, or helped pioneer, the social survey method. His extensive statistical study of poverty in London, showing "its extent, causes, and location" was published as *Life and Labour of the People in London*

37 See Todd Gitlin, "The Incoherent Left" (2011) *Chronicle Review*

38 Geoffrey Baym, "The Daily Show and the Reinvention of Political Journalism" Paper presented at the 3rd annual Pre APSA conference on Political Communication, Chicago, 2004

appear. Sometimes history unfolds in a "Black Swan" moment.[39] New forces are emerging in different forms and places. They are not viewed as a universalistic solidified whole. As witnessed in Latin America, the African continent and Asia, new social and political movements have emerged to challenge neoliberal capitalism and imperialism. On the fortieth anniversary, let the last words go to Cabral.

> You see therefore the importance of knowing our reality and of knowing also all the realities. It is for us to know where ours is among the others, for us to know our total strength and our total weakness… Only in this way we can see the actual situation.[40]

References

Chabal, Patrick, (1983) Amílcar Cabral: Revolutionary Leadership and Peoples War. Cambridge: Cambridge University Press

Return to the Source- Selected Speeches by Amílcar Cabral. (1973) New York: Monthly Review Press

Amílcar Cabral: Unity and Struggle – Speeches and Writing. (1979)New York: Monthly Review Press

Chilcote, Ronald (1984) "The Theory and practice of Amílcar Cabral-Revolutionary Implications for the third world." Latin American Perspectives, Issue 41, Vol 11 No 2

Revolution in Guinea. Selected Texts by Amílcar Cabral (1969).New York: Monthly Review Press,

39 According to a Penguin review (2007) of Nassim Nicholas Taleb's book the *Black Swan*: a "Black Swan is a highly improbable event with three principle characteristics: it is unpredictable; it carries a massive impact; and, after the fact, we concoct an explanation that makes it appear less random and more predictable than it was."

40

Arundhati Roy, (2012) "Capitalism: A Ghost Story" Outlook India, March 26,

Geoffrey Baym, "The Daily Show and the Reinvention of Political Journalism" Paper presented at the 3rd annual Pre APSA conference on Political Communication, Chicago, 2004

Gitlin, Todd "The Incoherent Left" (2011) Chronicle Review

9. SONS OF THE SOIL: CABRAL AND SARAMAGO

Sons of The Soil

At first glance, the revolutionary from Guinea-Bissau and Cape Verde, Amílcar Cabral, and the Portuguese Nobel Laureate and novelist, José Saramago, have at least one thing in common. The obvious thing that they share, of course, is their politics. They are both, in their own way, radical leftists. Saramago was an avowed communist—some critics deem his communism to have been "libertarian," others dubbed him an "unflinching communist," still others considered him an anarcho-communist. Saramago joined the Communist Party of Portugal in 1969 and remained a member until his death in 2010. Cabral, of course, was the founder and leader of the Partido Africano da Independência de Guiné e Cabo Verde (PAIGC); in his colleague Mário de Andrade's terms, "For Guineans and Cape Verdeans, he is the founder of the nation and the guide."[41] Cabral was a radical socialist, a socialist deeply rooted in the struggles of his people, in Africa, and, as his two addresses to the United Nations (1962 and 1972) make clear, an African socialist with a global sensibility.

Cabral's is an internationalism that begins, saliently, in no less a place than the imperial centre, Portugal. "I wish to reaffirm my people's solidarity," he says in his "Second Address before the United Nations," "not only with the fraternal African peoples of Angola and Mozambique but also with the people of Portugal, whom my people have never equated with Portuguese colonialism."[42] No surprise, of course, that Cabral would declare his solidarity with those in Angola and Mozambique, not

41 Mário de Andrade, "Biographical Notes," *Unity and Struggle: Speeches and Writings*, Amílcar Cabral, translated by Michael Wolfers, (Pretoria: Unisa Press, second edition, 2007) 23.

42 Amílcar Cabral, "Second Address Before the United Nations," *Return to the Source: Selected Speeches of Amílcar Cabral*, Edited by Africa Information Service, (New York and London: Monthly Review Press, 1973) 28.

only because they too were struggling against Portuguese imperialism but because he knew from his days as an activist agronomy student in Lisbon the likes of Agostinho Neto (the first president of a sovereign Angola, who became MPLA president in 1962; Cabral also worked in Angola as an agronomist) and Eduardo Mondlane (Mozambiqu—FRELIMO president from 1962 until his assassination in 1969). Salient, however, is Cabral's (in the name of the PAIGC's) insistence that the dictator António de Oliveira Salazar's Portugal must not be mistaken for the "Portuguese people;" the Portuguese people must be distinguished from the pluri-continental Portugal of Salazar's imperial imagining, the Lusitanismo—lusotropicalism—that Salazar intended to recapture the glorious, ghostly imperial past, a past Saramago so pithily mocks in *Raised from the Ground* (RG): "weep, O souls of da Gama, Albuquerque, Almeida and Noronha" (all Portuguese viceroys in India in the fifteenth and sixteenth centuries) (Saramago, 319).

However, the real bond—which will also be revealed to be a real difference—between Cabral and Saramago (at least, the Saramago of RG) is a fundamental one. As this essay will show, Cabral and Saramago, who traces his lineage to landless Azinhaga (Ribatejo Province) peasants, are men of the soil, thinkers produced out of an autochthony that is intensely rooted in the land of their various countries. This essay uses Saramago's RG to show Cabral's close bond with the soil in the moment of Guinea-Bissau and Cape Verde struggle against Portuguese imperialism, because although the novel covers a longer historical span, roughly the period of Salazar's dictatorship (1932-74), it coincides with some of the key moments in the PAIGC's campaign for sovereignty. Also, RG evokes those moments through a telling, but not complete, alienation. RG's is a Portuguese hinterland, but not one entirely removed from revolutionary developments in Africa. The PAIGC's campaign, as we will see, is unobtrusively present in Saramago's latifundio, those large, baronial estates owned by an exploitative and repressive landed gentry. The struggle in West Africa haunts, in paradoxical ways, the Portuguese political imagination. On the one hand it is used to threaten the local populace. During one small act of resistance by the latifundio's peasants, church (represented by the craven

Father Agamedes—the Roman Catholic church numbers amongst Saramago's chief political targets) and state joins forces. "Tell him your story," Agamedes urges João Mau-Tempo (the central figure in RG's main peasant family), "if you don't, the inspector will pack you off to Tarrafal" (Saramago, 240). Tarrafal was a place of terror for both PAIGC partisans and latifundio peasants, because it was a prison facility in Cape Verde, known as the Camp of Slow Death, where Salazar sent opponents of his regime. The invocation of "Tarrafal" was intended to instill fear in Mau-Tempo, no matter that he had no political "story" to tell the inspector.

On the other hand, the spectre of the PAIGC induces a political anxiety in the landowners, so much so that latifundio peasant resistance can only be understood in terms of the revolution taking place in Africa: "news comes that there has been an attack on the barracks of the third infantry regiment in Beja, now Beja is not in India or Angola or Guinea-Bissau, it's right next door, it's on the latifundio" (Saramago, 320). The MPLA or PAIGC attacks on Portuguese forces in Africa have transmuted the latifundio's peasants into a kind of "internal front"—the attack on the Portuguese state from within by those who, although they have their own historic axe to grind, acquire a revolutionary patina, appropriate or not, from without.

The effect of revolutionary Africa's "intrusion" into the latifundio casts, as this essay argues, the Portuguese peasants into the shadow of their PAIGC counterparts. And, in the period that the novel covers, there is a certain truth to the identified in that characterization. (RG was first published in 1980 and translated into English in 2012.) But in our moment a very different situation obtains, beginning with the fact that since the country became independent in 1974 no elected leader, beginning with the ouster of Luis Cabral in November 1980 in a coup by João Bernado Vieira (Bernado Vieira returned to power in 2005 after having been driven into exile, to Portugal, by the military 1999), has served out his term. After the coup of 1980, Cape Verde broke with Guinea Bissua and became independent.

In some ways, Guinea-Bissau, much more so than Cape Verde (which has a relatively stable system of government with a good economy), is an old and familiar postcolonial tale: massive failure of the state, corruption, graft, intense internecine battles arising from the mobilization of ethnic identities; in just the past four years, there has been military unrest (2010), a failed military coup (2011), a military coup (April 2012), preceded and followed by highly partisan external intervention. Currently, the principal actors in this ongoing conflict been are Guinea's regional neighbors, on one hand – Senegal, Nigeria, Ivory Coast, sometimes in the guise of ECOWAS—and the country's longtime Lusophone associate, Angola.. In other ways, Guinea's failures are signal. It has become one of the prime redoubts for drug cartels from Latin America and the cartels own a significant amount of property in the capital. Here the Angolans, who have historic links to the PAIGC, are massively culpable. The long standing relationship between Bissau and Luanda has seen Angolan elites profit immensely from their various investments in Guinea – profits from dubious sources that the PAIGC has, to say the least, done nothing to discourage. In a dozen or so years, under the leadership of the PAIGC, Guinea-Bissau and Cape Verde drove out the Portuguese and founded a sovereign state. Today, sometimes under the leadership of the PAIGC and sometimes under the auspices of the opposition, Guinea-Bissau is considered synonymous with narco-trafficking, obliterating its revolutionary past. Not entirely unusual in postcolonial Africa, but still noteworthy.

Only one thing has remained constant, or remains from the revolutionary past. As the country has lurched from crisis to crisis, one name, and one name only, is deemed worthy of invocation: *Amílcar Cabral.* Never more so than in the crisis that began in 2012 and shows little sign of abating. In a strange and uncanny way, Cabral and Saramago find themselves bonded by events in 2012, years after their deaths—deaths separated by almost four decades (Cabral, 1973; Saramago, 2010). In 2012, just months after the military coup in Guinea, Saramago's RG was translated into English, so that the magnificence of Cabral and the PAIGC's struggle is animated anew—heard, we might say, as if for the first time, so that Cabral's name is addressed to us once again, with echoes that have deadly reverberations. In the crisis that follows the coup, Cabral's name returns, yet again, to haunt, and maybe even (one can only hope) inspire the people of Guinea-Bissau and Cape Verde again. To struggle, again; to struggle as they have never struggled before. "A luta continua, continua." Is that what this uncanny coincidence of revolutionaries is urging? To turn their native land into something might be worthy of an earlier, still resilient imagining?

Names that Survive, Names that Require Fiction

Comparing the latifundio with the sea is as useful as it is useless...if we disturb the water here, the water all around will move, sometimes too far away to be seen.

—José Saramago, Raised from the Ground

...these Africans were seen by their own efforts to have wrecked the forty-year-old dictatorship of fascist Portugal and destroyed the Portuguese empire.

—Basil Davidson, Introduction, Unity and Struggle: Speeches and Writing (Amílcar Cabral)

Cabral "turns," if such a phrase might be permitted, to the land because the Marxist mode of struggle—building an organisation based on the urban proletariat—proves itself inefficacious for the PAIGC's campaign against Salazar's forces. The "massacre at Pidgiguiti" in which some 50 dock workers from Bissau were killed and more than 100 wounded, not only showed Cabral that "there was no question of choosing between a peaceful struggle and armed combat" but that "for the armed struggle...it was necessary to have a solid political base in the countryside" (Cabral, "Second Address," 16). In its own way, this is classic Marxism of "The Eighteenth Brumaire" variety—men do not make history under conditions of their own choosing. Cabral converted necessity, and the lessons of the bloody Pidgiguiti encounter, into a theoretical principle: "To start out from the reality of our land—to be realists" (Cabral, *Unity and Struggle*, 83).

Cabral's both is and is not an exercise in realpolitik. The PAIGC struggle must start from the land "because the great economic strength in our land lies basically in the countryside" (ibid). Organising the rural populace, however, presents a serious political challenge, if one that is ripe for Marxist pedagogy: "It had not been easy to convince the peasantry that they had an objective interest in joining the national liberation struggle, when their outlook was limited to a simple understanding of the difference between the price and the value of their produce" (Andrade, 33). The PAIGC proved equal to this task, because by 1972, a decade after beginning their revolutionary campaign ("ten years is…a short interval in the history of a people"), Cabral could declare to the UN that it controlled more than two thirds of their national territory, in no small measure due to the Party's ability to not only draw the peasantry into its ranks but also build the PAIGC around it (Cabral, 16).

What Cabral comes to understand is that the "reality" of the situation is a simple, yet easily overlooked, one. The land must not only be inhabited (farmed, lived on) by Guineans and Cape Verdeans, it must be acquired; the land must be brought, struggled, into sovereignty. By itself, the land is; through struggle, the land is made sovereign (Cabral is at his intellectual best when theorising the notion of struggle in its relation to unity: "Unity is a means towards struggle…It is not necessary to unite all the population to struggle in a country…a certain degree of unity is enough. Once we have reached it then we can struggle") (Cabral, "Party Principles and Political Practice," 69). Only through struggle for the land can Guinea and Cape Verde become sovereign, Cabral explains dialectically: "Unity for us to struggle against the colonialists and struggle for us to achieve our unity, for us to construct our land as it should be" (Ibid. 70). To "construct our land as it should be" is a politically-freighted phrase: it expresses the desire for sovereignty, the construction of the land of Guinea and Cape Verde as it "should be" to make of this land an independent state. It is also, of course, a declaration of independence—this land will be made as it should be—and in this way it is a final—rather than a warning—shot across the bow of Portuguese colonialism:

> The Africans of the Portuguese colonies will destroy Portuguese colonialism. It may be the last colonial regime to go, just as it is the last in terms of technical and economic development, and the last to respect the Rights of Man. But its days are surely numbered. (Cabral, "Portuguese Colonial Domination," 65).

And numbered they were, those days. As Davidson recounts it, the dictatorship's end could be traced directly the success of the PAIGC revolutionaries:

> In April, 1974, the Portuguese officers of the Movimento sas Forcas Armadas (MFA) overthrew the dictatorship on the dual slogan of 'Decolonisation and Democratisation'. Some of the most active of these officers, as they bore witness then or later, had learned their politics of liberation from the example of the PAIGC. 'The colonised peoples and the people of Portugal are allies,' declared the assembly of the MFA officers of Guinea-Bissau in a unanimous statement of June 1974: 'The struggle for national liberation has contributed powerfully to the overthrow of fascism and, in a large degree, has lain at the base of the MFA whose officers learned in Africa the horrors of a fruitless war, and so have understood the roots of the evils which afflict the society of Portugal (Davidson, 19).

Through its struggle the PAIGC made the Rights of Man philosophically available to the Portuguese people. The effect of the revolution in Africa was to enshrine democratic rights in Portugal. It does not matter where the revolution starts, its benefits are like the waters of the latifundio– sometimes felt in places too far away to be seen.

For RG's peasants, however, the MFA's slogans have a hollow ring. To begin with, they are suspicious of how the Carnation Revolution—so-called because the Portuguese people threw red carnations at the soldiers to show their support for the overthrow of the dictatorship—has conceived itself: "what kind of name is junta for a government, there must be some mistake" (Saramago, 349). More importantly, there are no material effects that improve the lives of the latifundio's peasants: "There is no work, what kind of liberation is this, people are saying that the war in Africa is nearly over, and yet the war on the latifundio rages on" (Saramago, 354). RG writes a radical role reversal: despite Cabral's assassination by PIDE agents, liberation has come to Africa. The war on Alentejo peasants, however, continues unabated, Salazar or no, Carnation Revolution or no. When Saramago writes, "they preach democracy and equality, and yet when I want work, there is none, tell me what kind of revolution is this?" he is not posing a question. He is issuing an indictment, one that is audible in Lisbon and Bissau, Porto and Praia, familiar to both the postcolonial and those on the latifundio come late to post-imperialism (Saramago, 354).

This indictment, however, applies more to Portugal than to Guinea or Cape Verde. That is because while Cabral and the PAIGC was radicalising its peasantry into a liberating force, Alentejo peasants appear to be locked into a timeless, unending servitude. There is for them, especially the Mau-Tempo ("Bad Weather") clan at the centre of RG, their radical proclivities (restrained in João's case, more explicit in his son António's) notwithstanding, a sense of perpetual burden. The Alentejo peasants stand outside history, particularly the history of their own county. The way things were before and during Salazar's republican dictatorship is almost indistinguishable from their revolutionary present. In this way, Saramago captures their survivalist tendencies best through the Mau-Tempos' autochthony: "the land shared out between the largest and the large, or, more likely, joining large with large…It took centuries to get this far, who can doubt it will always be the same?" (Saramago, 4). "This far," as the Carnation Revolution proves, isn't very far at all. The latifundio is home to generations who have barely survived: "Here they all are, the living and the dead" (Saramago, 363).

It becomes possible, because of how Saramago is aware of the world outside the latifundio in ways that the Alentejo peasants are not, to detect uncanny echoes that bring Cabral to mind, in this moment 50 years after his death, because of the revolutionary's afterlife, because of how he continues to haunt us, continues to live as a figure for political thought amongst us: "some lives are erased more completely than others" (Saramago, 340). In this regard—the resilience of the life—Cabral's accomplishment is that his life—his name—has not been "erased." It has survived him. It survives him, ever more audibly, perhaps with an unspeakable nostalgia, every time a political crisis takes place in his native land. Some names cannot be erased, no matter how many crises afflicts Guinea and Cape Verde, no matter how many times the PAIGC and its Cape Verdean successor (PAICV) fails its founder(s).

For those such as the Mau-Tempos, based on Saramago's own family's experiences, a very different case obtains. It requires Saramago's fiction to restore life to those who endured, just barely, on the latifundio, through the monarchy, Salazar's brutal republic, and the false promise of the "junta." It is fiction, more than history or the revolution, that can honour both the "living and the dead," because the life of the latifundio, as RG shows, has no end. Saramago's work is to raise the "living and the dead" from the historical dust into which they have been ground, to ensure that the lives of these people, "small and disparate, who came with the land," is not completely erased (Saramago, 4). The work of fiction is, as RG's narrator says, to find "another way to speak of all this," to restore the lives of the Alentejo peasants to the history of their own country in the ways that the peasants of Guinea and Cape Verde claimed their history from Portuguese colonialism (ibid).

Theory of Concentric Circles

If history might be understood as a theory of concentric circles, the world changes, always outward, leading from, say, one small event to a larger to a still larger one, then this is a theory that Saramago inverts in RG. In reading Saramago and Cabral together, it becomes clear that for those on the latifundio change occurs only sporadically, and then at a glacial pace. Substantive change takes place or begins far away from the latifundio, its ripples felt amongst the peasants of Alentejo as the pernicious mark of their exclusion from the events that affect their own country. The war on the latifundio rages on, and on. The world, Africa in particular, that is supposedly far away, is changing more quickly than the latifundio. At least more visibly than the Portuguese hinterland that is Alentejo. In Guinea and Cape Verde, Angola and Mozambique, the old imperial order has been toppled, the world has been stood on its head.

In Alentejo the "same people continue to dictate the laws of the latifundio so that the same people obey them" (Saramago, 354). What does it matter then that João is an incipient Marxist, that his son António and his son-in-law Manuel Espada are more forthright in their opposition to the land barons, and that his granddaughter Maria Adelaide promises even more? These people, with whom Cabral has no quarrel, are struggling to eke out a living from the land they have worked for generations. They have only a rudimentary sense of how to make their mark upon their own land. How critical then Cabral's and the PAIGC's decision to turn to the land, to raise their country from the ground the peasants work. How noteworthy the PAIGC's ability to "convince the peasantry" that the only way in which they could truly attend to their land was to make it sovereign, to make it truly theirs. Because of the deliberate ways in which Saramago sketches peasant life on the latifundio, he brings into stark relief the significance of the PAIGC's success in explicating to their peasantry the importance of thinking beyond the "difference between the price and value of their produce." The Mau-Tempos possess elements of Cabral's radicalism, but their ground has not yet been raised to his—and the PAIGC's—level. No wonder then that RG is saturated with such a wistful sense of historical incompleteness. The revolution will only come when the Portuguese peasantry rises above the ideological ground in which it was raised. In truth, the latifundio wonders: will the revolution ever come?

10. CABRAL

HIS THOUGHTS AND ACTIONS IN THE CONTEXT OF OUR TIME

Mustafah Dhada

Cabral Under Gaze

Several works[43] to date assess Amílcar Lopes Cabral, Luso-Africa's pre-eminent nationalist and thinker who spearheaded the fight to oust Portugal from Guinea-Bissau and the adjacent islands of Cape Verde. Some embed him in the context of this fight.[44] A handful focus

43 Basil Davidson, *The Liberation of Guiné: Aspects of An African Revolution.* Harmondsworth: Penguin, 1968; Gérard Challiand, *Armed Struggle in Africa: With the Guerrillas in "Portuguese" Guinea.* New York: Monthly Review Press, 1969; Lars Rudebeck, *Guinea-Bissau, A Study in Political Mobilization.* Uppsala: The Scandinavian Institute of African Studies, 1974; Oleg Ignatiev, *Amílcar Cabral, Filho de Africa: Narração Biográfica.* Lisbon: Prelo, 1975; Oleg Ignatiev, *Três Tiros da PIDE: Quem, Proquê e Como Mataram Amílcar Cabral?* Lisbon: Prelo, 1975; Stephanie Urdang, *Fighting Two Colonialisms: Women in Guinea-Bissau.* New York: Mothly Review Press, 1979; Patrick Chabal, *Amílcar Cabral, Revolutionary Leadership and People's War.* Cambridge: Cambridge University Press, 1983; J. McCulloch, *In the Twilight of Revolution: The Political Theory of Amílcar Cabral.* London: Routledge & Kegan Paul, 1983; R.E. Gallli and and J. Jones, *Guinea-Bissau: Politics, Economics and Society.* London: Francis Pinter, 1987; Ronald H. Chilcote, *Amílcar Cabral's Revolutionary Theory and Practice: A Critical Guide.* Boulder: Lynne Rienner Publishers, 1991; Joshua Forrest, *Guinea-Bissau, Power, Conflict, and Renewal in a West African Nation.* Boulder: Westview Press, 1992; and Mustafah Dhada, *Warriors At Work, How Guinea Was Really Set Free.* Niwot: University Press of Colorado, 1993.

44 B. Davidson, G. Challiand, and L. Rudebeck.

on him almost exclusively;[45] and a few discuss his political ideas.[46] The perspectives they offer vary. One set sees him as a Marxist-Leninist,"[47] a hyphenated Gramcian-Marxist, Africa's answer to Lenin,[48] a "revolutionary par excellence",[49] or as good as Karl Marx, Lenin, Trotsky and others who "left us a legacy of revolutionary experience."[50] Others, persuaded by a lack of references to doctrinal tracts in his texts, seem less convinced of his portrayal as a hard-core ideologue and find him to be a Marxist in method but not ideology; a socialist; a revolutionary democrat perhaps.[51]

The resultant portrait, however, leaves Cabral fundamentally a Marxist, but with perspectives exogenous to him unchallenged. Today, Cabral emerges a composite of twenty or more characteristics, each competing with the other for attributive supremacy in the Marxist cannon. There is evidence to suggest that Marx and Mao may well have influenced him.

But Cabral was far more complex than that. Almost all the scholars in the field acknowledge this to a degree. One or two scholars even go so far as to construct him as "Africa's philosopher King,"[52] and "the supreme educator in the wisest sense, or an empiricist devoid of ideological dogmatism and rigidity,[53] making this type of assessment in the context of revolutionary thought. One author elects to project him as a humanist, a pragmatist, an undaunted optimist at the end, a dominant, friendly,

45 Chabal and McCulloch

46 ibid.

47 J. McCulloch, p. 57.

48 ibid.

49 Gérard Challiand, "Amílcar Cabral," *International Journal of Politics*, 7, Winter 1977-1978:3.

50 Ronald H. Chilcote, *Amílcar Cabral's Revolutionary Theory*, p. 13.

51 P. Chabal, pp. 31, 37, 67, 144, 158, 167, 168, and 169.

52 C. Chapman, "Africa's Philosopher King" *The London Times Higher Education Supplement*, 19 August 1983:12

53 P. Chabal, pp. 31, 37, 67, 144, 158, 167, 168, and 169.

tolerant, charismatic leader- a teacher,[54] while another claims him to be a unifier of people.[55]

Those that see Cabral as a complex personality, above or outside doctrinal Marxism, do so as part of a discourse on the armed struggle and the diplomacy for liberation that accompanied it. These scholars focus on a specific area of his life pertinent to a given discourse.[56] Such works attempt to encapsulate Cabral in a broader context, but are seen by critics as only partially successful in capturing Cabral's essential core.[57] These works are subsequently determined as having failed to see him outside hagiography.

Cabral himself saw his leadership to fight for liberty as part of a larger whole. "Nobody is indispensable," said Cabral. "…An achievement is worthwhile to the extent that it is an achievement of many…even if one pair of hands is taken away."[58]

Placing aside Marxist influence on him, it could be argued that Cabral was Cabral, a complex meta-racial African.[59] As such, a closer look at his life and works suggests a triad governed him: external inputs, internal reflection and reflexive action. Viewed this way, he emerges deservedly complex, intact, and with a core of his own rather than that of a Marxist derivative.

No one has yet produced a full-scale, stand-alone and up-to-date biography on him, much to everyone's regret—Chabal's 1980 monograph on Cabral and Chilcote's latest[60] *Opus Bibliograficae* notwithstanding. Paulo Freire perhaps comes nearest to the jugular as does Mário de Andrade, describing Cabral holistically,[61] from inside out as it were, as a dialectically unified personality—a public figure internally balanced between words and actions.[62]

---

54 P. Chabal, pp. 31, 37, 67, 144, 158, 167, 168, and 169.

55 T. Kofi, "Prospects and Problems of the Transition form Agrarianism to Socialism: The Case of Angola, Guinea-Bissau, and Mozambique," *World Development* 9,9-10:856

56 Dhada, *WOW*.

57 Dhada, *WOW*, 139-148.

58 Amílcar Cabral, *Unity and Struggle*. London: Heinneman, 1980, 96.

59 Amílcar Cabral, *Unity and Struggle*, p. xii.

60 Ronald H. Chilcote, *Amílcar Cabral's Revolutionary Theory*.

61 Paulo Fereire, *Cartas à Guiné-Bissau de uma Expiriência em Processo*. Lisbon: Morais, 1978,18

62 ibid

Indeed, Cabral saw himself this way—as an ordinary man who lived life intensely and drew from it experiences that gave him direction.[63] His reflections informed his actions, springing forth in the end as analytical responses calibrated for praxis. Cabral was immensely creative in this way, and the balance between words and actions informed his strategies throughout his professional and political career.

To understand the context of his experience, Cabral reflected over empirical evidence, explored viewpoints in normative discourses and engaged in vigorous discussions and discords with friends living a colonial reality similar to his; all of which cumulatively neutralized the toxicity of the colonial experience mining him within.

The colonial experiences—structural, environmental, racial and creative in nature—had brought Cabral to witness poverty, drought (catalyzed by asymmetric colonial agricultural policies), economic marginality, racial profiling and preference in the Bissau civil service, abuse of the rule of law in the colonies and in the metropolis and restrictions on creative liberties in the media and the performing arts.

Furthermore, travels on professional assignments to Angola had brought him face to face with the inner workings of plantation economy, as did his travels and discussions with political activists, party officials, and networking contacts in Egypt, Guinée-Conakry, Morocco, Czechoslovakia, the Soviet Union, Yugoslavia, Senegal, Tunisia, China, and the United Kingdom and a host of other countries in Africa and Europe.[64] In Guinea itself, he and his team traveled over 60,000 kilometers, visiting 2248 hamlets[65] to produce a 200 page commissioned report evaluating the colony's agricultural demography.

These experiences and encounters, reflections and normative inputs shaped him and his thinking, which subsequently informed his strategy for national liberation from Portuguese colonialism. Cabral thus rose above his condition to serve as a normative future, a call befitting the greater good above the need of the personal and the present.

---

63 Amílcar Cabral, *Unity and Struggle*, p. xii.

64 Mustafah Dhada, "Guinea-Bissau's Diplomacy and Liberation Struggle" *Portuguese Studies Review*, IV, 1, 1995: 20-40.

65 Dhada, *WAW,* 146.

His Writings and Thoughts

One of Cabral's first most significant nontechnical texts analyzed the social structures under colonialism. It was published as a seminal paper in August 1964.[66] Cabral drew inspiration for this narrative from two sources: archival research of Portuguese colonial documents in Lisbon during his student days in the late 1940s and 1950s and studies in demographic agronomy undertaken during his stay in Bissau prior to the formation of his bi-nationalist movement. *Warriors At Work*, a monograph on the liberation struggle in Guinea-Bissau and Cape Verde, gives a detailed breakdown of Cabral's thinking here.[67] This structural analysis highlighted Guinea-Bissau as a tapestry of eighteen social segments of fragmented dependencies, serving sectors of the colonial demography in a complex structural web. Each segment was assessed according to its position and privilege under colonialism, the degree of depletion of its sovereign identity or a mixture of both. At one extreme, a segment was seen as having been denuded of a will to create transformational change, while another segment was identified as nihilistic, unable to entertain change for a future without colonialism. This sector, according to Cabral, was unwilling to engage in revolutionary actions driven by a goal for self-determination, or what he called "an individual's mastery over nature"[68] (nature here signifying the status quo).

Two years later this analysis became a blueprint for action to oust Portugal from Guinea-Bissau and Cape Verde, during the mobilization drive, which also drew on his critical readings of literary works, poetry and drama and his experience as a former radio talk show host. Again, a detailed narrative of how this campaign was executed and how it entailed performance-based canvassing are to be found documented in broad strokes in Patrick Chabal's seminal work[69] and in *Warriors At Work*,

---

66 Amílcar Cabral, "The Struggle in Guinea" *International Socialist Journal*, 1, 4, August 1964: 428-446.

67 Dhada, *WAW*, 224-226.

68 Ibid.

69 P. Chabal, *Amílcar Cabral, Revolutionary Leadership and People's War.*

though the latter engages in a more Cartesian perspective, sticking very close to the evidence while eschewing generalities lacking documentable specificity.[70]

In 1966, Cabral finally completed constructing a theoretical template for liberation, which distilled what he saw, what he learned in the field, as it were, and what he could draw from it. He revealed this template in early summer of that year during his visit to Cuba at the formation of *Tricontinental*, a Third World solidarity organisation.[71] The meeting proved critical for him and his organisation to solicit material support, much needed for the armed struggle. Cabral sought to attract donors in two ways: by demonstrating the strength behind his movement and by conveying the visionary caliber of his leadership. To this end, he delivered a tightly woven presentation suggesting his movement to be solidly grounded in sound theory. This presentation, namely, "The Weapon of Theory"[72] proved to be the first of several public texts outlining his thinking on the social construction of identity, culture, and liberty.

Three years later Cabral deployed the Weapon of Theory framework to analyze the crises that his bi-nationalist movement faced. The analysis engendered a seldom-examined five-part study on political to economic, armed and cultural types of resistance.[73] It was this analysis that helped him and his movement tackle internal dissent and external challenges related to the armed struggle against Portugal. Discourses in

70 Dhada, *WAW*, 6-7, 9-12, 214-15, 222-24,

71 Dhada, *WAW*, 177.

72 Amílcar Cabral, "The Weapon of Theory," Address delivered to the first Tricontinental Conference of the Peoples of Asia, Africa and Latin America held in Havana in January, 1996. http://www.marxists.org/subject/africa/cabral/1966/weapon-theory.htm, accessed 22 January 2013.

73 Amílcar Cabral, "Análise de Alguns Tipos de Resistência." Lisbon: CIDAC Repository, 1969; Amílcar Cabral, "Análise de Alguns Tipos de Resistência: 1. Resistência Política." Lisbon: CIDAC Repository, 1969; Amílcar Cabral, "Análise de Alguns Tipos de Resistência: 2. Resistência Económica." Lisbon: CIDAC Repository, 1969; Amílcar Cabral, "Análise de Alguns Tipos de Resistência: 3. Resistência Cultural." Lisbon: CIDAC Repository, 1969; and, Amílcar Cabral, "Análise de Alguns Tipos de Resistência: 4. Resistência Armada." Lisbon: CIDAC Repository, 1969.

this five-part study ultimately went on to inform two of his subsequent and what later proved to be final texts on identity, culture and national liberation.

One text "national liberation and culture" was delivered on 20 February 1970 at Syracuse University, a year after Eduardo Mondlane's assassination. [74] That same very text appeared in Wolfer's critical 1980 edition *Unity and Struggle*.[75] The last text "The Role of Culture in the Liberation Struggle"[76] was crafted during the summer of 1972, six months before his own assassination, at ten-thirty at night on 20 January 1973.[77]

The Syracuse text proved challenging to deliver. Up to this point, Cabral, like other Luso-African nationalist leaders, was unwelcome in the US. Cabral had visited the United States once before, in New York in 1962, to convince the UN's Fourth committee to recognise the bi-nationalist movement he was leading.[78] During the succeeding eight years, Cabral failed to gain entry into the United States; largely because the latter's NATO-based alliance with Lisbon helped the United States with its Vietnam-focused logistic needs for military facilities and bases in the Azores.

In 1970, however, things changed. A few months before the event at Syracuse, the Vatican, which was in the throes of Vatican II and which was headed by Pope John the XXIII, recognised Cabral's movement

---

74 Eduardo Mondlane was assassinated near Dar-e-Salam on 3 February 1969 at the age of 41. Mondlane was American educated with an undergraduate degree from Oberlin and a doctorate from Northeastern. He was then heading the fight to free Mozambique had been assassinated near Dar-e-Salam. See, Anon, "In Memory of Eduardo Chivambo Mondlane '53," Oberlin: Oberlin College, at http://www.oberlin.edu/alummag/oampast/oam_spring98/Alum_n_n/eduardo.html, accessed 05 November 2012. Se also, William Minter, "An Unfinished Journey," *No Easy Victories: African Liberation and American Activists over a Half-Century, 1950-2000*. Washington, DC: Africa World Press, 2007. Also obtainable at http://www.no-easyvictories.org/select/nev-front.pdf, accessed on 05 November 2012.

75 Amílcar Cabral, Maurice Taonezvi Vambe, Abebe Zegeye and Michael Wolfers, *Unity and Struggle: Selected Speeches and Writings*. Pretoria, South Africa: Unisa Press, 2008.

76 Amílcar Cabral, *Unity and Struggle*.

77 Dhada, *WAW*, 46-48.

78 Dhada, *WAW*, 179.

and those led by fellow Luso-Africans fighting for self-determination in Angola and Mozambique. Thereafter, the American position on Luso-African nationalism softened. Cabral was not only granted entry to deliver the memorial lecture, but was subsequently invited to speak to the Senate hearings on the Portuguese colonies. Put differently, both Cabral and the text were received well, given the circumstantial trajectory of his entry into the United States.

How He Viewed Culture, Identity, and Self-Determination

Cabral saw culture as a process of individual and social consciousness, resulting in a dynamic synthesis. This synthesis engaged "the material and spiritual historical reality of a society or human group" as a discourse "between man and nature as well as among men and among social classes or sectors."[79] Identity on the other hand, according to Cabral, was the affirmation or negation of characteristics by an individual along a "bio-social and historical" continuum.[80]

For Cabral, then, identity was an informed choice with which to affirm or negate a given culture. That choice was arrived at or catalyzed through a creative force. Education in its broadest sense was one such creative force, as were the fine arts and performance and radio theater. As such, this creative force played a clear multidimensional role as a rectifier of deficiencies, as a builder of capacity for choosing identity and as a tool for empirical, existential and iterative self-realignment. Whether catalyzed by forces outside one or from within, public-fora education was a trans-disciplinary key to progress. His own early multidisciplinary forays into poetry, dramaturgy, mass media arts and communication, the natural sciences and agronomy were a testament to this perspective, as was his inclination to use his colonized life as a

79 Anon, *Guinea-Bissau: Towards Final Victory! Selected Speeches and Documents From PAIGC.* Richmond, Canada: Liberation Support Movement: 1974, 46.
80 ibid.

learning process. Life-long learning therefore transcended disciplinary bounds for creative self-growth.

When fed by external reflexive forces and processed internally through iterative analysis, a white could thus claim to be an African by choice, as could a Black elect to be a European in theory. In theory only; in practice, colonialism complicated the prospect of Blacks as Europeans.

Cabral saw colonialism as a complex shape-shifter, not a zero-sum entity dominantly developing Europe, as Rodney's text would suggest. In its totality, colonialism was a force of cultural occupation in Africa. In contact with the local population colonialism pushed, tugged and pulled the social fabric of the subjugated, shaking it loose, while driving the most susceptible to socio-economic extremities and the least vulnerable—and fewer in number—towards cultural and socio-economic collusive supremacy, in cahoots with the empire.

Assimilation policies proved singularly effective in furthering imperial interests here. They formalized entries for the assimilated into the upper margins of society, Cabral suggests. By using literacy prequalifiers, colonialism targeted such individuals for colonial agency, thereby inducing "desenraizamento"—alienation through upheaval. Ultimately, with this process in place, the assimilated assumed a colonialized identity, servicing Portugal as cultural occupationists. Such individuals lived, by their very definition, on both margins of society, estranged from their own culture and on the fringe of the dominant colonial culture. Their impact on the majority was pernicious, divisive, and variegated.

It is here that a return to the source must play a role in self-determination, a first step in the struggle to decolonise. To find themselves from within and in the context of their own culture, such individuals, according to Cabral, must return to the source. They must "re-Africanize,"build a series of biosocial and historical matrices on which to begin a process of self-validation and, by linear extension, wean themselves off colonialism.

Of course there is nothing to prevent such individuals from staying put. But to do so is to continue the validation of a culturally occupying force, which in turn was antiliberation, a choice outside self-determining history. Were such individuals to commit as it were cultural "suicide,"however, they were not bound to construct a matrix from whence they originally sprang. They could turn to alternative sources of nonimperial culture, or graft a composite. In his own case he elected to re-Africanize, reclaiming his African roots while dermally retaining his Cape-Verdean socio-biological nativity. In short, he became a bi-nationalist.

It is not surprising that Cabral came to these sets of heuristic conclusions for his own process of self-determination. In retrospect, it is clear that this process was largely dictated by two sets of experiences mentioned earlier in this text. The first set sprang largely from his colonial encounters, before, during and immediately after his university days in Lisbon, before his arrival in Guinea-Bissau; and the second set emerged from the lived-in experience as a fighter leading the struggle against Portuguese colonialism.

Further, it is important to point out that Cabral here is not advocating a process of individuation, as the term is used in Jungian psychology.[81] No. He is asking that the rediscovery of the new self be part of a larger social and cultural collective. He saw individualism as a scab, residually stripping native culture of its dignity. In a sense, Cabral is therefore at odds with Senghor's idea of validation of a dominant European colonial culture, particularly one that encourages subsumption of African social-cultural realities.

Once reconstructed, Cabral envisioned such de-assimilated elites catapulting ahead to lead the party. Even here, Cabral notes with caution, this sudden rise to power was fraught with peril for the party and ultimately the nation. One such peril was nepotism. Basil Davidson chose to call it mountain-topism, a term used by the Chinese under Mao's leadership to denote corruption and graft. Cabral was astute to recognise this as a possibility within his party—and for good reason. After all, these assimilated leaders had in the past abused power as enablers of cultural occupation under Portuguese colonialism.

He was therefore right to suspect that this trend would infect his own party, which it did in early seventies as it battled the efficacy of Spinola's

81 Jolande Jacobi and R Manheim, *Complex, Archetype, Symbol In The Psychology of C. G. Jung*. London: Routledge, 1999, 113-114.

military campaign to undercut the Cabral-led gains in liberating Guinea-Bissau. Again, he used a combination of measures to combat nepotism, after having failed to eliminate it with draconian purges after public trials. The newly minted measures ranged from public fora education to workshops and problem-resolution based conferences involving party cadres as solution providers. Such tendencies, he firmly believed, could be obviated or dealt with through discipline, vigilance and public education, designed to defeat sectarianism with service for the benefit of the greater and larger whole. In effect, Cabral here was using his own version of "mini-Conference Nationale," a Magna Vox Populi, if you like—a formalized institutionally sacred space in which "the people-as-no-one" negotiated conflicts and settled pressing issues of nationalist concerns as a lived-in experience under an ideological banner.[82]

The Conclusive Context

Can Cabral's thoughts and actions address the challenges we face in contemporary nationalist politics in Africa and beyond? As stated above, for Cabral culture was a relational matrix, governing humans in their natural context, a matrix openly adaptive towards an objective. Identity was an act of volition, docking one's consciousness to a culture of choice, driven towards a purpose. Taken together, culture and identity, when operationalized this way, drove the dynamics of self-determination forward. Of course, where such dynamics derailed from its purpose, public fora or "self-determination conferences" ensured that both culture and identity were re-oriented towards the struggle for liberty under self-determination. This task of reorientation was achieved by negotiating conflicts collectively, in the Claude Lefortian sense of the world.

Put differently, the ailments festering in contemporary nationalism in Africa and globally could benefit a great deal from Cabral's ideas as praxis. His concept of culture as a malleable force for national consciousness and nation building could prove immensely useful—in resolving

82 See, Bernard Flynn, *The Political Philosophy of Claude Lefort: Interpreting the Political.* Evanston, Illinois: Northwestern University Press, 2005.

crises in ideology, in addressing atomized partisanship and in tackling conflicts festered by identity politics, race, and warring cultures. His advocacy to dock identity to culture as a Cartesian choice could facilitate greater consciousness for an all-inclusive social pluralism, a pluralism that celebrates diversity and acceptance. Such a stance would therefore render identity an act of choice and not an inheritance dictated by accidents of birth and reinforced by divisive social conditioning. His framework of a national conference could well help address broader national crises threatening the very fabric of constitutional politics, national integrity and sovereignty. This concept has recently been proposed as an idea in praxis and is to be found in a published text penned by this author on the national crises that America faces.[83]

In a few words then, Cabral is indeed relevant in the world in which we presently live.

83 For an example of how Cabral's Magna Vox Populi could be used for resolving a potential national crisis see, Mustafah Dhada, "America: Have We Crossed The Rubicon?" *Empirical*, November 2012, 39-48.

II. IN THE SPACE OF AMÍLCAR CABRAL

Helmi Sharawy

I had the opportunity, in mid-December 2012, to visit Praia, the capital of Cape Verde, where the late leader Amílcar Cabral lived for some years before moving to his mother's home on the mainland.

I remembered with some emotion the few days I had spent in the company of Cabral, only a few weeks before his tragic assassination at the frontier of his country. It was near the end of 1972, when I was a member of the Egyptian Delegation to the meeting of the Coordination Committee of the liberation of African colonies at the OAU, attended by many African foreign ministers. Cabral was furious at the meager assistance for these liberation movements, that forced many of their leaders to solicit the help of their friends in the socialist countries. Indeed, such help was forthcoming; Cabral even pledged to supply anti-air missiles if those weapons could be necessary to armed struggle. I have no idea if such promises were ever realized. What I know is that the "message" arrived and "African Party for the independence of Guinea Bissau and Cap Verde "(PAIGC) announced the unilateral independence in 1973! And in 1975 the new regime in Portugal, that succeeded Salazar, acknowledged this independence. But the high price paid for this independence was the assassination of Cabral, in Jan. 1973.

On my recent visit to Madam Anna Maria Cabral in Praia, she reminded me of her last visit to Cairo, with her late husband, only a few weeks before his fatal visit to Accra. We used to greet Cabral and other African Leaders at the African Association in Zamalek, where it was my duty as Coordinator with African Liberation Movements to arrange meetings with Egyptian intellectuals and other liberation movements. His views were rich in the fields of class analysis, national culture and the class and ethnic struggles to be expected after liberation in the continent.

This shows Cabral's important role as a man of great continental vision and not merely a leader of a small country.

During my recent visit to Praia, I found a stable liberal regime, in the sense of stability prevalent in the present global atmosphere. In Cabral's own party, only the older members and the partisans of radical change remembered his rich ideas. The national airport is named after Mandela; the university does not bear his name, and his old home in Assomada looks on a wilderness of oblivion! All this did not diminish my appreciation for the fundamental correctness of Cabral's analyses.

Strong pressures are deployed to keep the islands within the sphere of global interests, since they were employed to obstruct the movement of African boycott of the apartheid regime in South Africa. Even after independence in 1975, such pressures were sufficiently effective to keep Cape Verde from taking part in the African boycott. On the other hand, Guinea-Bissau, on the continent, languishes in its double backwardness as a Portuguese colony in Africa.

As I see it, the traditional comprador elite that Cabral warned against in Guinea-Bissau is in full power there, while the petit bourgeoisie that he hoped could play a nationalist role in both regions was simply contained by globalisation.

The realities I met there did not disprove my regrettable expectations. Emigration of thousands of Cape Verde youth to Europe, the United States, and Brazil is very active, while thousands from inside the continent take their place all the time. I asked Madam Anna Maria Cabral about the whereabouts of his daughter and his grandchildren and got the immediate answer that they were in Bissau, while she remained steadfast in Praia, to take care of, in collaboration with the activist Pedro Pires, the late president of the islands, a Cabral Memorial Foundation. She had previously spent some years as an ambassador of her country in several foreign capitals. I was happy to hear that the Cabral family was not touched by the scourge of emigration, and that they take an active part in keeping the Cabral tradition, and upholding his vision of Pan-African ideology during this second phase of African liberation movements, where Africa faces a new wave of neo-imperialism under the guise of world globalisation, as a variation of the old colonial occupation.

Such conditions give actuality to Cabral's analyses, and his concepts of national culture that are being reformulated by the colonial and traditional powers as new forms of alienation from history, under conditions of globalisation.

I review here some of Cabral's ideas, while witnessing the struggles in North Africa between the Salafist (fundamental) traditional forces and the revolutionary forces they are trying to block.

Cabral's Stance on Culture And Identity

One cannot help but share Mario de Andrade's astonishment at the importance of culture in Cabral's intellectual life and in the various steps he took in founding the African Party for the independence of Guinea and Cape Verde (PAIGC). For Cabral, the party was nothing more than one part of a cultural and political totality for the peoples of Guinea and the islands of Cape Verde. Cabral compared the process of enculturation and the role of culture in national liberation as politico-cultural osmosis. National culture is that which creates a dialectic relationship between society and history. Cabral, an agricultural engineer, compared this to a flower produced by a long process of cultivation—the passage of history itself. For Cabral, the national liberation movement was nothing more than the organised political expression of a people's culture during its struggle against the culture of the oppressors.

National identity, therefore, is the product of cultural interaction between society and history through the process of national liberation. As well as synthesizing social history, culture and dialectics, Cabral linked history with the culture of resistance. Colonialist thinking and its anthropological methodologies denied African societies their place in human history by any means other than through the colonialist process, regarded by imperialists as modernization, and by some Marxists as igniting class struggle. Cabral opposed both these explanations, as he associated colonialism and imperialism with our negation out of history, not our entry into it. For this reason national identity can only be realized through the struggle against colonialism and through the liberation movement concentrating on cultural heritage and articulating the particular characteristics of its dialectic.

The excellent text on "National Liberation and Culture" that Cabral delivered to the Tricontinental conference in Havana in 1966, and then again at the UNESCO conference of 1970, speaks for itself.

Cabral linked the analysis of society's social construct with its cultural component, and spoke of the need to give more importance to cultural diversity in political activity. In his social analysis he contributed to the evaluation of the status and roles played by the various African social classes and categories. There is no space here to discuss at length his bold rereading of Marxism, but it is worth mentioning his refusal to sanctify popular culture as it stood, pointing out that it included both positive and negative elements to be identified and filtered by the national liberation movement during the process of popular struggle.

Dealing with Cabral's treatment of the petit bourgeoisie and their status in the national liberation movement is vital when discussing his bold approach to Marxist thinking. It exposed him to attacks from both traditional Marxists—especially Leninists—and some leaders of the national liberation movement in the other Portuguese colonies.

Cabral saw the role of the petit bourgeoisie as a modern and modernizing social force that could either be exploited by colonialists to run the country or could be won over to the national liberation movement, both on the strength of their private aspirations, which could be helpful for liberation process, and also on the basis of their postindependence role as one of the forces for motivating progressive development. This is with the proviso that the national liberation movement could succeed in making this class betray their traditional role as described by certain Marxists. However, Cabral specifically meant a new culture of national liberation and the importance of the liberation movement formulating a new, wide-ranging political culture, as he was aware that cultures, in their new incarnations, would impose their own new, nontraditional classifications.

In the age of globalisation we are witnessing the marginalisation of the middle class and the end of the petit bourgeoisie, a development in the interests of the business sector that had marginalised the working class itself and then extended the scope of this marginalisation. Because of this, the elements of the informal economy have become the most wide-ranging sectors in society, confronting contemporary dialectic thought with new and complex challenges.

At the same time, and in his discourse on Eduardo Mondlane in particular, he did not reject the class nature of culture either locally or worldwide, nor the importance of modernization through which development would take place from the village through to the level of global culture.

This political Cabral is not the ideologue who adopted only the concept of the the nation and excluded social analysis, yet Cabral's conception of the unity of the nation, with all its diversity and internal conflicts, rested on a cultural and analytical approach to society and its various social formations, ie tribal and ethnic ones. I believe that analysing Cabral on the basis of his distinctive approach to the societies of Guinea-Bissau and the islands of Cape Verde is of great help when revisiting his work, and that the failure of certain national liberation leaders to follow his ideas has led African societies into a swamp of tribal and ethnic ideologies, the effects of which we still suffer from today. The attention given by intellectuals such as Edward Said to Cabral's work on national cultural resistance has made his contributions to issues of identity and national culture a rich source for prominent cultural analyses of the representation of the colonizer and colonized.

The Challenges of Globalisation: The Peoples of Second-Wave National Liberation

As Cabral himself did, I shall preface my discussion with a summary of the challenges of globalisation. Having analysed the role of capitalism in promoting strong production forces and relations in its own countries, and having described imperialism as the highest stage of capitalism, Cabral admitted that imperialism was a historical necessity, just as national liberation in its turn was a historical necessity that would destroy capitalism and bring about socialism. He then related how imperial capital never contributed to the development of production forces capable of realizing progress in colonized countries, as well as describing capitalist methods of exploitation, etc.

But what does this have to with our discussion of identities and national cultures? On this point, Cabral's thinking was more or less based on the idea of the colonial capitalist centre and the peripheries or colonized limbs; the prevalent school of thought at that time. This thinking was given credence by the relationships between the various colonialist states and their colonies. Pragmatic economics adopted a similar analysis that was validated by the presence of a number of different axes of economic power on the world level, including, of course, the socialist axis. For the international capitalist system, the actual or potential marginalisation of Africa was determined by the lack of potential for capitalist exploitation of its resources and by the fragmentation of its social classes.

Yet the political economy of capitalism has moved beyond traditional imperialism (neoliberalism) to reach new heights, and we find ourselves in a world united by brutal capitalism, a world in which Africa is no longer marginalised, but rather integrated into the world labor market. This has taken place within the framework of a neoliberal ideology that—day in, day out—churns out ideas justifying integration under the umbrella of the capitalist centre—or rather, the new empire—as it militarizes the world, unifies apparatus of control, and legalizes it all within this same ideological framework. This demands the use of intellectual weapons that deal with those national cultures and identities defended by Cabral. African thought.

Samir Amin says imperial capitalism, founded on rationalism and its sciences, offers the Third World nothing but irrationalism. We meet the old colonial rationalizations in new guises. Just as Cabral talked about expulsion from history as being a product of colonial social sciences and a colonialist tool used against our peoples, so neo-imperialism is achieving the same result deploying post-modern schools of thought to reject the very concept of historicity. And just as Edward Said has indicated that every people has its own narration, when discussing imperialism's rejection of our people's narration, so neo-imperialism denies the validity of self-sufficient narrations, or rather, only recognises one narration—its narration about itself, its culture and its identity, whilst denying the narrations of the other (i.e. our identity and culture).

In dealing with these narrations, neoimperialism is wary of the contributions of thinkers such as Cabral on issues of national identity and national cultures. This is because it fully understands the direct relationship between these identities, national liberation and the second wave of independence. It is in the interests of imperialism to disseminate more specific identities and their associated ideologies, from identities of gender, minorities and nationalities, to tribal and ethnic identities.

We are confronted by a fragmentation that can only be unified by means of a single, global centre, in which the social citizenship of a new democratic totality or pan-movement identities have no place. Cabral had assigned the national liberation movement and the liberation culture the role of gathering together social diversity within the totality of a new society. Ideologically speaking, neo-imperialism is obliged to somehow avoid discussing social and class conflict on a local or global level. Therefore it redirects its treatment into a discussion about the major civilizational types, failing to mention the great global blocs in the conflict between imperial capitalism and socialism as formulated by Cabral and others.

From here spring other ideas about the clash of civilizations, in which Africa lags far behind, and which say that we will be trapped in a never-ending cycle of conflict unless we cede victory to Western modernism. Our societies are nothing more than outdated or fragile entities that, to use Cabral's formulation—have been once more selected to make their exit from history.

Despite the fact that national identities and cultures are necessarily part of the logic of the clash of civilizations (giving this logic a chance for the moment), the main civilizational identities assigned in the context of this clash do not give us the opportunity, as Cabral would put it, to claim historical presence, but only to lose our place in history once again.

In essence, the portrayal of the world in terms of civilizations and their conflicts only leaves room for the Western "we." Following September 11, there was only room for the American identity. As the current American administration puts it, it's either us or the others, and even this is a best-case scenario, as the rest of their ideological apparatus only recognises the formulation we—the West—and the other is the rest, as the African thinker Mahmoud Mamdani put it. In my estimation, opposing this new line of thought is a natural progression from the ideas of Fanon, Cabral and Rodney.

Some African and Arab Issues

Throughout the sixties Cabral was well known in Arab-African society, making constant visits to Cairo, either to attend African or Afro-Asian conferences or to meet Gamal Abd Al-Nasser. Some of the seminal works of Cabral and his party were translated into Arabic, and he was discussed in Arabic writings on Guinea-Bissau and Cape Verde.

Intellectuals in Egypt and Lebanon were chiefly interested in his texts on national liberation and culture, *The Weapon of Theory and The Social Formation of the Society of Guinea and Cape Verde*. These texts were translated into a number of sources (see sources).

The dominance of colonial anthropology had a negative impact on the direction taken by academia in Arab universities. For example, Cabral or Mondlani were not accepted into university curricula, although political culture, through political activism, became acquainted with them both through the aforementioned texts. Arab academic culture had previously excluded the revolutionary thinker Fanon, due to the dominance of traditional Marxist thinking. Indeed, for a while Samir Amin himself was suppressed in his own country for the very same reason. However, the translation of some of Edward Said's works in the 1990s gave these texts a new lease of life, associated as they were with the slogans of national culture and resistance through culture. These slogans were adopted by national groups that were influential in opposing both treaties between

Arab governments and Israel, and the growing American influence over cultural mechanisms and the loyalties of certain intellectuals.

So here we are, appealing to Cabral's ideas at a time of rampant globalisation! His conception of culture as a dialectic bond between culture and history is well worth invoking, particularly in North Africa and the arab world where history has a particularly strong impact. At times this impact conceals the process of interaction, and at others exposes it to stagnation, known as fundamentalism (salafism) in the arab region. The Umma (nation) transcends history, society and culture to take salafism as its identity. Cultural explication is its sole methodology, whilst society, with its diversity, its historical cultures and its social classes recedes into the background. It is as if society is banishing itself from history, with history grinding to a halt at some point in time, with its religious and civilizational peculiarities described in purely cultural terms. This is the stance of Jihadist movements throughout the Islamic world, be they Wahabbi, Mahdi, Sanoosi or Fodi, all of which use the concept of ijtihad (i.e. renewal and Islamic awakening). The well-known intellectual Fawzy Mansour has described this condition as a kind of Arab departure from history, because Arab or Islamic commercial capitalism has not wanted or has not been permitted to enter the age of modern industrial capitalism. A form of self-expulsion or negation from history has taken place, pre-empting European colonial capitalism's efforts to exclude the region from the arena of dynamic progress.

Cabral's analysis of the force of national culture, which limits the extent of the defeat at the hands of the aggressor culture, may be correct here, as this is more or less what has happened. Cabral talked of the national liberation movement using culture as a tool for struggle and resistance, but was assassinated before he saw the extent of that interaction. We, on the other hand, have lived to see the reversals suffered by national culture: stagnation in the Arab world, and in Africa a programme of globalisation that has destroyed the role of the nation state and paralyzed cultural politics ever since the United States imposed sanctions against Unesco in the 1980s. Some leaders of these international organisations have tried to uphold national cultural policies that protect societies and nations from disintegrating in the face of a global culture and media.

We must not forget here that Cabral talked about the duality of the cultural and the political, and tried to conceptualize some form of positive interaction between the two. This led him to discuss the positive and negative aspects of national cultural heritage, so that it could continue to play a role in modernism and internationalism with a political, liberationist, activist awareness. Compare that to the current trend amongst the intellectuals of globalisation to reject the political on the grounds that it is comprised of defunct ideologies that fell with the Berlin wall!

Setting up barriers between culture and national politics, and the failure to analyze social and cultural diversity in the framework of the cultural totality discussed by Cabral, had two results, both of which were obvious to the national liberation movement. The first was the disappearance of a national identity in a network of specific international identities (i.e. the woman, the environment, tribal, ethnic etc.), and the second was the collapse of national identity (once again!) into a salafist past—sometimes of a religious nature, and at other times resembling a utopian golden age. All this has distanced society somewhat from the true movement for its reform, or rather, for its liberation from the new hegemony. The leading elements in society no longer strive towards a new totality, submitting instead to the following painful processes: firstly, inclusion into the world community, and secondly, violent confrontations, either from terrorism or by imposing reform by force, away from the sensitivities of rational modernism. This can be seen directly in the Greater Middle East initiatives and in imposed, formal political reform.

The Arab region, and within it, North Africa, is exposed to internal and external operations to destroy its inherited collective identity. The reason for this is the absence of a role for national political culture in activating the relationship between the Umma and society. Just as the unity of the Umma is held sacred, so—within its political structure—are the figures of the Imam, the Caliph and the just tyrant. Because of neoliberal policies, however, they have become no more than dictators, without the democratic justice and development necessary for the region's various social classes and areas.

The approach of sanctifying society's cultural component did not concern itself with a new social analysis. This analysis demanded the activation of roles for social movements and groups that expressed political, tribal or ethnic differences, allowing them to become forces for civil society, which took citizenship as a yardstick for democratic political activity, and which gathered everyone together into a renewed, modern socio-cultural totality.

In the light of static social concepts, there is no chance of entering into history with formal definitions of society, culture and democracy. For this reason, Islamists participate in the neoliberal capitalist project using the old logic of commercial capitalism, and some leftists join in the process of modernization with the logic of liberal democracy, which they played no part in renewing, and which is impossible to realize in the current social climate.

Identity and national culture have suffered savage attacks, presenting neo-imperialism with a land enfeebled and ripe for assault. For many, the settlers' colonialism in Palestine is no longer comparable to the apartheid that the African peoples resisted for so long, since the Arab liberation movement has failed to stand up for itself and the Palestinian movement itself suffers from the same corruption that afflicts neighboring Arab regimes. Similarly, many no longer consider the American occupation of Iraq as an illegal assault and occupation, but instead as part of a necessary process of sweeping away the home-grown tyranny that afflicts the region as a whole. Indeed, it is associated with the logic of modernization that, according to some, could help remove the tyranny of salafism.

Taking Africa as a whole, the concept of a pan-African movement has disappeared from political culture, just as pan-Arabism has disappeared in the north of the continent. This is because both have submitted to the absence of a duality between the cultural and the political. The words unity and union -and other expressions of cooperative Arab activity in Arab North Africa-are no longer associated with the idea of a pan-Arabic movement. This has allowed the concept of Arab-African conflict to creep into certain regions, alongside the arrival of Islamic terrorism. Yet those who concern themselves with tribal, civil and sometimes religious conflict have never thought to deal with these conflicts by raising the idea of an effective cultural and social totality.

The Arab and African mind has to understand nationalism, national culture, and national identity by understanding the objectives of globalisation, which comes armed with weapons, propaganda, and local agents.

Semi-Conclusion

To conclude my reexamination of Cabral's ideas in an age of globalisation permit me to join Mario de Andrade in offering some quotes from Cabral's works that I believe to be a valuable instrument for analysing and confronting our current circumstances, about which no more need be said!

When discussing the confrontation of colonial culture, Cabral envisioned greater objectives for cultural resistance built on the development of popular culture and authentic, positive, cultural values; a national culture, built on history and the gains of the struggle itself; a scientific, technical culture compatible with the demands of progress. Development will come about, he said, through a critical understanding of human knowledge—the arts, sciences and literature etc., and a world culture, from the perspective of a healthy integration with the world around us and a forward-looking vision for its development. The life of the African peoples confronts the challenge of imperialism. The challenge here is to fertilize history with an expression of our culture and African-ness, then to convert that into a leap forward, expressive of the culture of a liberated people

Bibliography

Andrade, Mario de: *Amílcar Cabral, Essai De Biographie Politique.* Maspero- Paris 1980.

Amin, Samir: *Toward A Theory For Culture. A Critic For Euro-Centrism* (in Arabic), Institute of Arab development- Beirut 1989.

Cabral, Amílcar: *Revolution in Guinea, An African people`s struggle*. Stage I , London 1969-71.

Cabral, Amílcar: *Unity And Struggle*. Heinemann, London.

Mamdani, Mahmood: *Good Muslim Bad Muslim, America, The Cold War, And The Roots Of Terror*. Pantheon Books, New York 2004.

Mousa, Ayda El Azab: *Guinea and Cape Verde* (in Arabic), African society, Cairo, 1978.

Sharawy, Helmi: *Culture of National Liberation* (in Arabic) Madbouli, Cairo, 2001.

12. 'THE CANCER OF BETRAYAL, WHICH WE MUST UPROOT FROM AFRIKA ...'

Aziz Salmone Fall

Treachery is a cancer we must excise by combatting impunity. On May 13, 1972, while making a speech praising Kwame Nkrumah whom he lauded as the Kilimanjaro of Afrikan revolutionary consciousness, Amílcar Cabral declared:

> President Nkrumah is the consummate strategist, inventor of Afrikan positivism, positive action and an implacable foe of neocolonialism .... All coins have two faces and all reality has a positive and negative side ... How far and to what extent was treachery able to succeed in Ghana because of class contradictions, the role of the party and other institutions including the army? We absolutely despise those who could stoop to betray Nkrumah to please imperialism.[84]

In his speech, Amílcar Cabral wondered aloud about what could be behind so many betrayals of so many of the martyrs who gave their lives in the struggle for Afrikan liberation. This was not a question that occurred to Cabral just because of Nkrumah's death. In fact the question had haunted him for quite a while and it really began to hit home as he was delivering his eulogy. Over the preceding months he had already become conscious of the foul breath of treachery all around him. Although the colonial era was over, a culture of impunity had descended across the continent, creating a climate where traitors thrived. How do we root them out, Cabral wondered?

84 Cabral's Obituary to Nkrumah, http://www.youtube.com/watch?v=rLo3Y2IG-iY and Transcription at http://mairenasolidaria.webcindario.com/escrituramecanica/Amílcarcabral.html

Does treachery flourish because of how we define who **the people** are? Or is there a link to a bigger problem stemming from how we select revolutionary leadership?

When we take into account his birth in *Bafata,* named after an illustrious Carthaginian and his childhood and youth under noxious colonialist influences that generated feelings of alienation as well as the constant temptation for the colonized to betray each other, this is someone who knows of what he speaks. To those in the underground struggle, he was *Abel Djasi*, a name meant to protect him against traitors but one that soon achieved a kind of symbolic status within the ranks of his comrades. Even so, drawing from a bottomless well of human deception, some of the very men who reverently referred to him as *O Homem Grande*—the Great One—were amongst those who would eventually betray him. Cabral knew the risk he ran, just from being aware of the long line of dead martyrs that he respected stretching backward along the road to Afrikan decolonisation…Ben Barka, Mondlane, Moumié, Um Nyobé, Rwagasoré, Lumumba, Olympio…The list was long and only grew longer after the assassination of Cabral with the addition of Ngouabi, Sankara, Machel , Dulcie September, and Chris Hani.

In the case of all of those martyrs, it was only the people in their inner circle, their intimates, who knew their secrets and could get prior knowledge of the day they would die. As the saying goes, "too much trust breeds treason." Despite it all, Cabral never gave in to paranoia and potential crime. On the contrary, he followed his natural tendency towards tolerance and unity rather than divisiveness[85], and, in the end, that was what did him in. He brought his capacity for unity to an international solidarity conference of peoples in struggle that took place in Havana in 1966. This conference was seen as a "tricontinental" resistance front. The tough stands taken at the conference faced a stiff fight or became progressively weaker, despite the fact that they were right on target. One by one, its executive secretaries, *Mehdi Ben Barka, Ernesto Che Guevara and Amílcar Cabral* were all assassinated. Hardly a coincidence!

85 Cabral on the liberation struggle, the making of the State and PAIGC' s policy, http://www.ina.fr/video/I00017312

In a stadium traumatized by Nkrumah's death, Cabral declared:

> As Afrikans we firmly believe that the dead continue to walk beside us. We are a society of both the living and the dead. At dawn every day Nkrumah will rise again in the hearts of freedom fighters and show up in their determination. Neither our liberation movements, the people of Ghana, Afrika or the progressive world will forgive those who betrayed Nkrumah. Never! [86]

The coup that toppled Nkrumah is a tortuous conspiracy with deep roots. In 1969, the Portuguese freed Aristides Barbosa and Momo Touré, two former PAIGC fighters and smuggled them out to Conakry. They became part of a grab-bag of fake deserters from the colonial army as well as various other corrupt individuals who would go into liberated zones pretending to repent, to have become reconverted nationalists or to be new recruits. Their task was to sow dissension within the ranks of their former comrades while collaborating with a branch of the PIDE-DGS, International State Defense Police controlled by the Portuguese Security Services, quite likely operating in conjunction with Germans, Italians and the French. These agent provocateurs spread discord, vilifying Cape Verdian officers who were disproportionately represented in the upper echelons of the PAIGC, exacerbating differences and exploiting the superiority and inferiority complexes that pitted the so-called "Mulattoes" and "Assimilados" from "Ethnic" Afrikans such as (Balantes, Foulas, Mandinkas, Mandjacques, etc.). Despite the popularity of the PAIGC, which reached right down to the tiny *Tabancas*—those small grassroots cells in the liberated zones, the virus of treachery continued on its insidious journey. Perfidy works by design, functioning as a series of pernicious steps.

The Portuguese had already attacked Guinea Conakry on November 22nd 1970. Operation *Mar Verde,* Green Sea, was launched on Spinola's orders. Around 400 assailants, one-third Portuguese and the rest a gang of European mercenaries with their Afrikan counterparts, including Guineans

86 Obituary, http://www.youtube.com/watch?v=rLo3Y2IG-iY

opposed to Sekou Touré, attacked Conakry. They quickly took up positions around strategic targets so they could free pro-Portuguese prisoners and take down the PAIGC. They also tried to kill Cabral as well as Sekou Touré and to free conspirators against the regime who by that time had already spent more than a year behind bars. Some Guineans were set free, the presidential palace came under attack and Sekou Touré was reported missing. Although the Guineans mounted a spirited defense, the PAIGC camp was destroyed. Cabral, who was visiting Roumania at the time, was unperturbed. Indeed, many of the Portuguese men involved boarded their boats home convinced that the operation had been successful and their Afrikan partners had seized the capital. Touré's people rescued him after answering Touré's call to arms, which he issued from a secret hideout.

In March 1972, Cabral denounced the PIDE (Polícia Internacional e de Defesa do Estado) and DGS (Direcção-Geral de Segurança) for making new attempts to assassinate him. He said, "If I am ever murdered it will be from within our own ranks. No one from outside can destroy the PAIGC, it will take one of our own to do it."

In November 1972, another attack aimed at several high-ranking PAIGC officers also failed. Cabral suffered no casualties.

On January 8, 1973, after elections in all the liberated zones, Amílcar issued a call to convene a national people's assembly. He saw it as the institution that would preside over independence. However, to the Portuguese, that became the signal to get rid of him, since his stated intention to declare independence terrified Lisbon. They were already backed into a corner since their troops were becoming increasingly disgusted with conducting its dirty war. Once again, General Spinola and Marcelo Caetano targeted Cabral for elimination. A certain Néné, in charge of PDG communications, conveyed the message to the killer commando, while Amílcar was meeting with members of FRELIMO on a visit to Conakry. Amílcar continued on to a reception at the Polish embassy in Conakry and later on that fateful night, January 20, 1973, he returned home with his wife, Maria Helena Rodriguez. With access to Cabral's personal schedule, given to them by Nabonia, someone close to him, some individuals were able to set up a roadblock on the route he was travelling on his way home. He got out of his car and appeared to recognise the individuals at the roadblock. However, the attackers seemed determined to kidnap him. He reasoned with them for a moment until the blast of machine-gun sounded in the night and tore a hole in his gut. He had had just enough time to start arguing with those who finished him off. At long last treason had met reason face to face.

The most commonly held theory was that Bissau Guineans had made a deal with the Portuguese that left the Cape Verdeans out. There was also a persistent rumour that said the plotters must also have had local co-conspirators, including the complicity of their leader, Sekou Touré. The latter mounted a spirited defense, pointing his finger instead at imperialism and the Portuguese who had corrupted the members of the party implicated in the plot. Touré's secret service rounded up the conspirators Innocent Camil (Inociencio Cani), Momo Mamadou Touré, Coda Nabonia, Carlos Pereira, (Valentino Mangana, Aristides Barboza, Jaoa Tomaz, Soares de Gama and Momo who had been expelled from the party a few months earlier for anti revolutionary activities), Lasana Bangura, Ansoumane Camara, Aleino Egora, Raphael Barbosa—ex-president of the party had become a spy for the PIDE. In his confession Valentino Mangana gave a detailed account of the plot: eliminate the PAIGC and its leader, heir to the party and independence; preserve Cape Verde as a strategic outpost for Portugal and rid Guinea-Bissau of its influential Metis leadership. Another of the plotters, Isidor Lima, who was later absolved and then banned following investigation by a different dispensation, returned home from exile in Sierra Leone years later. A huge witch-hunt tore the party apart even as Camil confessed his sins to Guinean authorities. Otelo Saraiva, a PIDE operative, later admitted, at the end of his overseas posting, that the operation had been a total failure since the objective had been to bring back Cabral alive and the PIDE men had overplayed their hand. [87]

During that period there was constant discontent in Sekou Touré's PDG camp with fratricidal conflicts breaking out between Guineans from Bissau and Cape-Verdeans who refused to take responsibility for

87 Many versions exist on this plot, among them see Lewin Andre, Ahmed Sekou Touré, 1982, Paris, l"Harmattan 2009;Chabal Patrick, Amical Cabral, revolutionary Leadership and People's war, African Studies Series, No37; Castanheira Jose Pedro, Qui a fait tuer Amílcar Cabral, Paris, Paris, l'Harmattan, 2003

the treachery. Their inter-communal turmoil remained unresolved and, directly or indirectly, continued to poison the atmosphere at the highest levels of the state in Guinea-Bissau. The presence of "Metis" Cape Verdeans who were disproportionately represented within the higher echelons of Guinea-Bissau aroused resentment within the ranks of "Aboriginal" Afrikans. Very quickly everything fell into place for the state to become the prey of a criminal cabal and a comprador mentality. This was what probably provoked the backlash which eventually culminated in Nino Vieira's coup d'Etat against Luis Cabral, Amílcar's half-brother, and down the line resulted in Nino's own assassination.[88]

But let's get back to the business at hand. A Revolutionary Investigative Commission swung into action, composed of Cuban and Algerian diplomats and Guinean Democratic Party leaders. Later on, it was augmented by delegates from Senegal, FREMILO, Egypt, Sierra Leone, Zambia, Tanzania and Nigeria.

Had Sekou Touré taken umbrage with his host and Cabral's "revolutionary aura" which eclipsed his own? Was there some link with initiatives around staking maritime claims that were open to potential competition by Portugal as early as 1962? What of the areas where Guinea Conakry was already carrying out joint deep-seas explorations with multinational corporations, even to the extent of carrying out seismic experiments the year Cabral died? What of the rumours of dreams of a Greater Guinea to which Conakry's leader clung? And yet, on the other hand, a magnanimous Sékou had also been open to joint Pan-Afrikan exploitation of the disputed oil zone in the early eighties.

As Cabral said in relation to identifying real revolutionaries at Nkrumah's funeral:

> My views on this question will help us better understand Nkrumah's outstanding achievement as well as the complexity of the

88 Conchiglia, Augusta, Guinée Bissau, Questions sir l'assassinat d'un Président, Monde Diplomatique, 12 mars, 2009 and also Tobias Engel, Au Cap-vert , la seconde mort d'Amílcar Cabral, Monde Diplomatique, Novembre 2003 ; Lourenco Da Silva, Les héros de la Guinée Bissao, la fin d'une légende, Paris, L'Harmattan, 2012.

> challenges he faced, quite often all alone. Those challenges tell us that as long as imperialism exists, any independent Afrikan state must exist as a movement for taking power or it will cease to exist. Please don't bother to tell me that Nkrumah died of throat cancer or some other illness. No, Nkrumah died from the cancer of betrayal, which we must uproot from Afrika if we are serious about eliminating imperialist domination.

Inspired by Cabral's achievements, Sankara did not fall prey to misjudging the scope of the task before him or of the fact that the people's enemies, the retrograde bourgeois cliques—would never stop trying to sabotage what had been accomplished:

> Parasitic classes that always benefited from colonial and neocolonial Upper Volta are and will forever remain hostile to the revolutionary process which we began on August 4, 1983. That is so because they remain and will forever remain attached to international imperialism by an umbilical cord. They are and will remain passionate defenders of the privileges they acquired by selling out to imperialism. Whatever we might do or say they will remain just as they are, and will never stop plotting and hatching conspiracies for reconquering their "lost kingdom." Don't expect these nostalgic folks to change their mentality or attitude. They are insensitive and only understand the language of struggle, the struggle of revolutionary classes against the exploiters and oppressors of the masses. They will no doubt find our revolution absolutely authoritarian in every way; it will in fact be an act through which the people impose their will including a call to arms.

Sankara was the last Afrikan head of state in the twentieth century who successfully tried, without going through a stage of war for national liberation, to follow in Cabral's footsteps. However, that stopped abruptly when he was betrayed by his brother Blaise Compaoré in collusion with *Françafrique*. Compaoré, the sophisticated face of treachery and willing steward of French machinations and sinister designs against the whole region, today reigns, in total impunity, as master of all he surveys. While he was the Minister of Justice, he brazenly and outrageously claimed that Sankara died of natural causes at the exact same time as eleven of his colleagues. To this very day he refuses to allow the truth about his treasonous actions to come out. While there is impunity and imperialist protection for it, treason will never end.

Impunity, either in life or in the law, is defined by what is missing. That can mean the absence of prosecutorial provisions against violators of human rights or those who neglect their civil, administrative or disciplinary responsibilities. It may also mean the absence of a properly constituted investigatory system that might lead to charges, arrest, trial, and, if parties are found guilty, conviction and appropriate punishment, up to and including compensation for the victims for having suffered prejudicial acts.

The fight against impunity means taking a holistic approach. Today impunity is enthroned in every facet of Afrikan life. That includes civil rights and political rights, as well as human rights, economic, social, cultural, gender or ecological rights. As human beings we also need to understand that we should respect the rights of all other living beings on this earth, including those who have not been given rights. This is a question of critical importance. For example, let's look at what's happening in the Congo. As the world averts its eyes with studied indifference, six million Congolese have lost their lives, sacrificed on the altar of globalisation and consumerism, largely because impunity is embedded in the system that governs their lives, and networks of transnational corporations always operate beyond the reach of any law. The laws themselves permit our resources to be pillaged and our sovereignty to be whittled away. For example, in the Maghreb, in spite of an uprising for democracy, the prevalence of impunity prevents accountability and, in the final analysis, facilitates counter-revolution. Obscurantist religious forces that fit right into the globalised security and neoliberal order gut progressive gains and betray whatever hope they bring.

My brother Demba Dembelé, who owes a debt to Cabral, as I do, has said:

> Forty years after his assassination Cabral's ideas remain more relevant than ever. His premature demise robbed Afrika's revolutionary season of one of its most prominent and original theoreticians. Cabral was a leader intimately involved in the life of the masses and imbued with the fundamental values of his people. He was both a visionary and a passionate panAfrikanist, a living symbol of the kind of leadership of which Afrika has been cruelly deprived at this time, where there are growing threats of recolonization. In fact the events unfolding in Mali as well as Libya and the Ivory Coast in 2011 revealed the impotence of Afrikan officialdom in in all its nakedness and exposing the lack of vision of the continent's leadership class, some of whom are no more than vulgar puppets of imperialist forces.[89]

I wrote these lines on the very same day we were commemorating the loss of Chris Hani, on the day when he was murdered, twenty years ago. Like all the other charismatic leaders he also understood that there was a price on his head and so took nothing at face value—and rightly so. We've all turned ourselves into targets by struggling against impunity. On the other hand, far too many of our intellectuals are willing to cut demeaning deals for a few filthy perks. How did our elites sink to such depths of consumerist greed that our people have become numbed and can no longer defend those gains carved out of the struggles that our martyrs led? We badly need to repoliticize our youth based on Pan-Afrikan ethical rules and fundamental human values. But that would demand an extensive mobilization campaign with the objective of erasing the culture of impunity, which both covers up and funds treachery.

Amílcar's assassination opened up a pernicious Pandora's box of impunity. Fratricide, pogroms, civil war and evening old scores stalk the corridors of power, while corruption, narco trafficking have also disfigured the country historically liberated by Cabral. And yet Cabral continues to

89 Demba Dembelé. http://www.frantzfanoninternational.org/spip.php?auteur90

rise above it all and his spirit transcends our struggles like a beacon on the Pan-Afrikan horizon. His anthem is and will always remain an undying flame:

Sol, suor e o verde e mar,
Séculos de dor e esperança:
Esta é a terra dos nossos avós

[Sun sweat grass and sea
Centuries of suffering and hope
These lands passed down by our Ancestors hands]

SECTION 3:

REFLECTIONS ON CABRAL

13. TO WANT AND TO LIVE

THOUGHTS FOR TODAY, INSPIRED BY AMÍLCAR CABRAL

Lewis R. Gordon

There's a Charles Mingus song, "Cumbia & Jazz Fusion" (1977), that always makes me think of Amílcar Cabral. "Mamma's little baby don't want Uncle Ben's, Aunt Jemima, and Shortbread," Mingus objected.

> Mamma's little baby wants truffles
> Mamma's little baby wants diamonds
> Mamma's little baby wants good schools so he won't act like no damn fool! ...
> Mamma's little baby wants all the fine things in life....[90]

Colonialism, Cabral and Frantz Fanon once reminded us, splits the world into two kinds of beings: Those for whom supposedly the bell of history tolls and those who are expected to manufacture the bell without glory and, at the end of the age, memory.[91]

Misguided memory leads, as well, to a story of erasure in which past aspirations are also lost. Thus, as we lament the abuses of imposed

---

90 See Charles Mingus's album, *Cumbia & Jazz Fusion* (Atlantic Records, 1977).

91 See, e.g., Amílcar Cabral, *Revolution in Guinea: Selected Texts*, trans. and ed. by Richard Handyside (New York: Monthly Review Press, 1970), *Return to the Source: Selected Speeches* (New York: Monthly Review Press, 1979), and *Unity and Struggle: Speeches and Writings*, with an introduction by Basil Risbridger Davidson (New York: Monthly Review Press, 1979), and Frantz Fanon, *The Wretched of the Earth*, trans. Constance Farrington (New York: Grove Press, 1963).

directions on our ancestors' path, we often fail to ask whether such aims were not also independently theirs.

Inspired by Cabral, Olúfẹ́mi Táíwò recently explored some of these considerations in his meditation on modernity, aptly entitled, *How Colonialism Preempted Modernity in Africa*.[92] The empirical verdict on contemporary Africa, it seems, is a conclusive judgment of failure. This failure is not, however, accidental, but an additional violation is to offer a misdiagnosis of its causes and bases of its continuation. There is, after all, so much to learn from Africa's presumed failures, especially as Jean Comaroff and John Comaroff have been arguing, much of late modernity is becoming the laboratory experiment its progenitors thought contained to latitudinal points by and below the equator and longitudinal ones confined by Atlantic and East Indian Ocean shores. What ultimately is Africa but the current state of humanity globally understood?[93] Here is the proper diagnosis, at least as articulated by Táíwò in his homage to Cabral.

First, a major mistake in understanding the contemporary situation of much of Africa is the conflation of colonialism with modernity. This leads to the response amongst many African leaders and intellectuals (some of whom are both) to the rejection of *modernity* and colonialism. Táíwò, again echoing Cabral, contends, however, that the problem isn't a consequence of colonisation and the advancement of modernization. It is one of colonisation and a deliberate aborting of the project of modernization. The abortion of modernisation served the purpose of radicalising exploitation. Cabral, we should remember, was an agronomist. He took seriously the efficacy of modern techniques in the production of a likewise organisation of life. As rural communities face the encroachment of modern political and

92 Olúfẹ́mi Táíwò, *How Colonialism Preempted Modernity in Africa* (Bloomington, IN: Indiana University Press, 2010).

93 See Jean and John Comaroff, "Law and Disorder in the Postcolony: An Introduction," in Comaroff and Comaroff (eds.), *Law and Disorder in the Postcolony* (Chicago, IL: University of Chicago Press, 2006), pp. 1–56 and the provocative, *Theory from the South: Or, How Euro-America Is Evolving Toward Africa* (Boulder, CO: Paradigm Publishers, 2011).

economic conditions, the proper response was not to hide themselves in sand but to look directly in the eyes of the modern situation.

To unpack this modern situation it is necessary to distinguish colonisation from modernization. The former was more the province of colonial administrators. The latter, historically in Africa, was more the path of Christian missionaries and Islamists. Taíwò adds to this, drawing upon recent historical studies such as the Comaroffs' *Of Revelation and Revolution*, that colonisation should be studied through further distinctions, such as settlement colonisation, political exploitation, and settlement exploitation.[94] Each has its tale, but the dynamics of political power shift according to the goals to which settlers aspire. Some, after all, were missionaries who actually believed their faith. As proselytizers, they sought converts who subsequently spread the Word. Whether they were Europeans or Africans didn't matter to many, and we often forget that the spread of Christianity in non-Christian areas was done by indigenous peoples and their hybrid, Europeanized offspring.

There were, however, settlers who didn't come to save souls, but sought instead to dominate them. Political exploitation was their proverbial cup of tea, and as that grew, the beverage turned to the intoxicating one of power. Such interests could very well have been conducted from metropolitan centres, however, but for the need for local administration, which meant the addition of settler administrators. So, while, for good or ill, one group sought to create Christians, similarly to those who sought (and continue) to create Muslims before them; another group, inspired by Lord Lugard's lessons from Britain's "mistakes" in India, emerged who did not seek the production of localized power in native hands. Cultivated dependency was the aim of this group, which meant the retardation of human relations, as

94 See Jean and John Comaroff, *Of Revelation and Revolution,* vol. 1, *Christianity, Colonialism, and Consciousness in South Africa* (Chicago, IL: University of Chicago, 1991) and *Of Revelation and Revolution*, Volume 2: *The Dialectics of Modernity on a South African Frontier*. Chicago: University of Chicago Press, 1997).

guardianship structures were put into place and asymmetric conditions of wealth followed.[95]

Cabral saw this process not only in terms of the word and the sword but also in terms of the systems through which both were to be replaced. For as proselytizing presented settler culture as divine and colonial administration as omnipotent, there was also the danger and paradox of secularized divination—as science, too, offered its colonial potential in terms of an omniscient force. To argue against science promised little more than technological peril. So, Cabral understood, as did Fanon, that demystifying science was an important task of decolonisation and liberation. But such a task needed to be done without collapsing into a normative colonial practice of guardianship. Epistemic decolonisation required, in other words, active participants, active minds, people who took responsibility for what they ought to know. So the revolutionary significance of transforming practice into praxis was posed, and how more material could such an effort be without the demonstration, from arms to cultivation of land, offered by the military forces under his leadership?

Nothing promises a future better than that which encourages participation in its making. The meditation on modernity, then, cannot be a passive or nostalgic one on uncompleted Christianity or Islam. For they, too, we should remember, were themselves products of prior conflicts on modernization. As a product of Roman conquest of Judah, the fusion that led to Christianity and Rabbinic Judaism required the price of forging the future on different terms than the normative worlds that preceded it. Many ancient peoples, crushed under the heels of Roman conquest, only saw one future: Rome's. Rome, however, didn't understand that one cannot dominate so many

95 See F.D. Lugard, *The Dual Mandate in British Tropical Africa* (Edinburgh: W. Blackwood and Sons, 1922). Lugard's counsel is well known among Africanist scholars of colonialism such as the Comaroffs and Taíwò, but see also for the context of Portuguese colonization see, in addition to Cabral's writings, Boaventura de Sousa Santos (ed.), *Democratizing Democracy: Beyond the Liberal Democratic Canon* (London: Verso, 2007).

and remain the same, and as Judah offered a different conception of the future than Rome—a linear future with an end instead of a cyclical order of constant returns—a new reflection of urgency demanded a different consideration for many under Roman rule, who now thought about nothing less than the end of the world.[96]

Islam, as we know, rejected the regulations of order afforded by Christianity and Judaism and asserted a different future without realizing that any model of perfecting the earth leads, inevitably, to questioning the practice of perfecting.[97] The future, in other words, is a question that enabled subsequent generations to question the validity of the present. And if the present can legitimately be questioned, the onus emerged from that discomfiting query rolling down the inclines of history: What is to be done?[98]

Cabral understood that whatever was to be done required addressing the many dimensions through which and in which human beings live in the world. The revolutionary task was not simply one of eliminating domination but also cultivating and building a livable world. He, an agronomist, understood that food and shelter were necessary but only partial conditions of a human world, but the future also required thought and the production of symbols that make human beings at home in their

---

96 For this pluralistic conception of modernity, see, e.g., Hans Blumenberg, *The Legitimacy of the Modern Age*, trans. Robert M. Wallace (Cambridge, MA: MIT Press, 1985); Enrique Dussel, *The Underside of Modernity: Apel, Ricoeur, Rorty, Taylor, and the Philosophy of Liberation*, trans. and ed. by Eduardo Mendieta (Atlantic Highlands, NJ: Humanities Press, 1996); Lewis R. Gordon, *An Introduction to Africana Philosophy* (Cambridge, UK: Cambridge University Press, 2008) and "Justice Otherwise," in Leonhard Praeg (ed.), *Ubuntu: Curating the Archive* (Scottsville, SA: University of KwaZulu Natal Press, 2013); and Walter Mignolo, *The Darker Side of Western Modernity: Global Futures, Decolonial Options* (Durham, NC: Duke University Press, 2012).

97 Cf., e.g., Ali Shariati, *Man and Islam*, trans. Fatolla Marjani (North Haledon, NJ: Islamic Publications International, 1981).

98 I am speaking, of course, of Vladimir Lenin's pamphlet, *What Is to Be Done?: Burning Questions of Our Movement*, trans. Joel Fineberg (New York: Penguin Classics, 1990 [original 1902]).

time. The modernization question for him, then, was not one simply of development, since even that concept, as Sylvia Wynter has shown, requires interrogating on whose terms, on whose standards, it could be made manifest.[99] The task of such inquiry is to transform the meaning of the future, with an acute understanding that every future depends on what precedes it. There is, in other words, no such thing as emerging, outside of its relations with anything else.

So, as Africa today and the Global South in general reflect on what is to be done in these early years of the new millennium, in which the acceleration of time already demands taking seriously the need to prepare for the twenty-second century, we could also reflect on what could be learned from this brilliant revolutionary cut down in 1973 at the age of forty nine.

Cabral's life and thought teach us that humanity must take seriously its responsibility for its future. To forget that this struggle involves negotiating and transforming a human world is to forestall our agency at our peril, since, as we already know from climate change and economic disaster, most, if not all of it, is in human hands. This does not mean that we have the capacity to live forever, like gods, but it does mean that we should recognize the very human limitations and struggles we face as we take on a challenging future.

99 Sylvia Wynter, "Is 'Development' a Purely Empirical Concept or also Teleological?: A Perspective from 'We the Underdeveloped' in *Prospects for Recovery and Sustainable Development in Africa*, ed. by Aguibou Y. Yansané (Westport, CT: Greenwood Press, 1996), pp. 299–316.

14. CABRAL AND THE DISPOSSESSION (DEHUMANIZATION) OF HUMANITY

Jacques Depelchin[100]

It has been pointed out that the assassination of Amílcar Cabral marked the end of a sequence of history (Michael Neocosmos), namely the end of politics through armed struggles.[101] In the process of thinking and rethinking the legacy of Amílcar Cabral, is it possible to say anything that has not been already said, either by himself, or by those who have written about him? Is it possible to go beyond just citing words and/or phrases that reconnect to his vision of an emancipated Africa? Is it possible to accept that, from the end of World War II, if not before, history has unfolded as imposed by the most powerful economic and political forces?

Discussing Amílcar Cabral, in a way, is no different from discussing other iconic and revolutionary figures whose lives were cut short precisely because of how they were perceived by their enemy. The long history of freeing Africa and Africans from the legacies of enslavement, colonisation, apartheid and globalisation seems like a never-ending task. The task

---

100 Hugh Le May Fellow at Rhodes University, July-December 2012—Visiting professor history department, Universidade Estadual de Feira de Santana, Bahia Brazil

101 For a detailed analysis of this see Michael Neocosmos's essay "Civil Society, Citizenship and the Politics of the (im)possible: Re-thinking Militancy in Africa." Today" which was first produced as a report for CODESRIA, and then appeared in *Interface: a journal for and about social movements*, vol 1(2): 263-334 (November 2009). : http://interfacejournal.nuim.ie/wordpress/wp-content/uploads/2010/11/Interface-1-2-pp263-334-Neocosmos.pdf Accessed on November 27, 2012.

could be made easier if one's understanding of the above legacies were not too intimately tied to the Enlightenment.[102]

In this essay, I would like to argue that one of the reasons Africa and Africans, and especially the poorest, are not better than they were in 1973 (and possibly worse off) has to do, in part, with an inadequate understanding of how capitalism rooted itself in Africa, while uprooting its people, its culture, its history, and, at the same time pushing the splitting of humanity to levels that will make the task of coming back together appear impossible.

While most theorizers of capitalism and the processes linked to its expansion do mention violence, to my knowledge, none has really focused on the impact of cumulative violence on both sides. In addition, most theorizers, even if they may deny this, focus on the economic and financial impact of capital. The political and ideological impact resulting from the violence has not received the same kind of attention that the equation labor-capital has received. If capital, for the sake of its survival, shall feed on states—any of them—it will do so.

The financialization of capital and the kind of impunity it rests on must be analyzed through a theorization of how violence has been exercised, while, at the same time, not being presented as violence. The towering dominance of finance capital is deeply connected with the violence present, represented, and accumulated over the years in military organisations like NATO and the nuclear arsenals of countries with nuclear capability. In turn, that latent violence, which hangs over humanity like a Damocles sword, has historical roots in processes that tend to be seen as separate. Ideologically speaking, capital and capitalism must be presented in the same light as, say, the history of the United States: the best and the greatest are considered incapable of committing crimes against humanity. The ruthlessness of capital, under any of its historical sequences, has been sanitized to the point of turning it into the "only acceptable alternative."

102 From the perspective of Africa and its history from the time of the encounter with Europe, the Enlightenment might be better described as something akin to Obscurantism. Louis Sala-Molins in *Le code noir* does not call it that, but points out how none of the philosophers associated with the Enlightenment denounced Atlantic slavery.

The political and ideological power that has resulted from the violence inflicted during slavery and colonisation deserves greater attention if the economic, political, and cultural transitions are going to be understood, whether from slavery, colonial-apartheid, or postslavery, postcolonial, postapartheid times. In a nutshell, the argument can be summarized as follows: from slavery through the current era of "globalisation," a type of power has emerged on a global scale that has not been given a name, as of yet. In addition, the cumulative effect of violence—physical and psychic—has led to the emergence of a world in which violence will often take forms that have nothing or little to do with violence as it is understood. To this kind of overwhelming power, that is almost impossible to assess, one should add the power of technology. The creative side of technology is overemphasized while its destructive capacity has been growing beyond the imaginable.[103]

For example, through advertizing (supposedly focused on creativity), consumers are led to believe that a given product (while in reality lethal for one's health) is not only desirable but also will enhance one's health and how one will feel, look, etc. Thus, while living under a socio-economic system that could be described as the most predatory in the history of humanity, humans seem to be unaware and/or unconcerned that, in the words of Aimé Césaire, "We have entered a tower of silence where we have become prey and vulture."[104] Indeed, one could convey

---

103 Interestingly, one of the persons who seemed to have seen through this confusion is Robert Oppenheimer, the lead scientist of the Manhattan Project and who, upon testing the atomic bomb at the trinity site in New Mexico, could only think of the words from the *Bagavad Gita*: "I am become death, the destroyer of the Worlds."The significance here, it seems to me, is that Oppenheimer could not find the right words from within the culture he had been born in. It could be argued that those words were thought not as an American citizen, but as a member of humanity.

104 Aimé Césaire, from "Batouque," a poem in *Les armes miraculeuses*, Éditions Gallimard, 1970, p.64.

the same idea by wondering whether capitalism has become the nicotine of humanity.[105]

If it were to be analyzed in detail, this kind of power, rooted in how capitalism has imposed itself, could lead one to conclude it has achieved the kind of dominance that Nazi leaders could not have dreamed of. Yet it would be wrong to look at the end of World War II (i.e. how it came about, as a singular turning point). What is needed is a history of transitions (from slavery to colonisation to apartheid to globalisation) of capitalism, focused on where and how the concentration of economic, political, and financial power was built.

One of the starting points has to be how the post-WWII era has been presented—by the powers that have been in control of that process—as a period that has brought greater progress, peace, and security to everyone, under the twin aegis of capitalism and the United States. This narrative must be questioned in view of the crossroads in which humanity finds itself today. Asking for the narrative to be questioned does not mean that one has reached a conclusion with regard to how one should call the times under which we are living, but questioning at all times while maintaining fidelity to humanity can be the only way of maintaining fidelity to emancipatory politics.

Cabral's famous warning about not claiming easy victory comes to mind. Yet, it could be argued that, in fact, systematically, at every transition, there has been something akin to "claiming an easy victory," or thinking that because some victories had been achieved, the rest, as Nkrumah so famously put it, will follow. In Frelimo's publication during the

105 This phrase was inspired by reading Robert N. Proctor's book, *Golden Holocaust: Origins of the Cigarette Catastrophe and the Case for Abolition*. University of California Press: Berkeley, Los Angeles, London. 2011. The violence unleashed by the cigarette companies, and the relative impunity it has encountered can only be explained by examining its rise under the protection of an economic system that, almost by definition, is considered above the laws that govern justice.

struggle, an editorial was written, very critical of Nkrumah.[106] Was Cabral thinking of Nkrumah when he issued his warning about not claiming easy victories?

As in any scientific endeavor, emancipatory processes, if they are going to be successful, can never end, if only because the temptations of one group seeking to take advantage of the rest is always going to be present. One of the difficulties, if not the principal one, is that the nature, form, and appearance of the challenges will never be the same. Thus, Samora's probing question "Who is the Enemy?" cannot ever have a prefabricated or ready-made answer. It requires a constant battle, whose shape, form, and organisation will never be the same. Sounds obvious—but is it? One of the reasons why there has been a tendency to claim easy victories (whether over slavery, colonisation, Nazism, or apartheid) comes from the imposition of historical narratives that see no connections (or very few) between these various phases, when, in reality, the connections are structural and should lead to constant re-examination.

For example, is it farfetched for an author like Claude Ribbe to look at Napoléon Bonaparte as a precursor of Hitler?[107] Ribbe's book focuses on how Napoleon ordered the restoration of slavery when he came to power. How that process was carried out may lead historians to other conclusions, but there is no doubt about how horrific it was (instructions coming from the highest levels were to make no prisoners—to asphyxiate them in massive numbers in the ships' holds before throwing the dead bodies in the ocean). Moreover, Napoleon's intentions were made clear: make the punishment as severe as possible so that the enslaved would think twice before engaging in overthrowing slavery. There are parts of the history of capitalism and/or nations that became powerful through expansion that are considered sacred and untouchable. If impunity is go-

106 See the critical editorial (on Nkrumah) that appeared in FRELIMO'S *The Mozambican Revolution* # 24. Also in the same critical vein,see Robert Fitch and Mary Oppenheimer, *Ghana: End of an Illusion.* Monthly Review Press. 1966. In fiction, see Ayi Kwei Armah's *The Beautyful Ones Are Not Yet Born* (1968). Per Ankh Publishers 2008.

107 Claude Ribbe, *Napoleon's Crimes: A Blueprint for Hitler.* 2007, ISBN 1-85168-533-2.

ing to be addressed seriously, then let it be done in a manner that does not flinch at investigating some of the most deeply embedded causes.[108]

The enemy that allowed slavery to be abolished was actually working at modernizing slavery, i.e. getting rid of those shackles that were considered as obstacles to the growth of capital. The enemy that was later defeated in Indochina, Kenya and Algeria was in the process of modernizing its arsenal. This process has nothing to do with conspiracy theory; rather it has to do with the transition from colonisation by European countries to United States capital overtaking the latter. It has to do with the obvious: reconnecting histories that have continued to be treated as separate and unrelated to each other.

The history of the politics of emancipation as it has unfolded in Africa is one that should generate a process of rethinking, à la Cabral. This would mean that emancipatory politics must understand the trajectories of colonisation, apartheid, and globalisation better than those who think that given that they always have won, there is no other lesson to learn from anyone, let alone from those who have been systematically slaughtered because their resistance was described as backward, barbarian, etc.[109]

---

108 One of the other problems in changing narratives was partly illustrated in France when, under President Chirac, a law was passed calling slavery a crime against humanity. Pierre Nora, a historian, complained that history should not be legislated. Christiane Taubira responded. Their interventions were published in the opinion pages of *Le Monde*. See: http://old.christiane-taubira.net/cms/index.php?mact=News,cntnt01,print,0&cntnt01articleid=119&cntnt01showtemplate=false&cntnt01returnid=62. Accessed on November 24, 2012. And: http://www.lph-asso.fr/index.php?option=com_content&view=article&id=4%3Apierre-nora-l-liberte-pour-lhistoire-r&catid=4%3Atribunes&Itemid=4&lang=fr Accessed on November 24, 2012.

109 This can be seen through any of the narratives, speeches, histories issued by the conquerors, affiliates and descendants, in the distant past or closer to the present as exemplified, say, by Alexis de Tocqueville's comment about abolition of slavery, Charles de Gaulle's comment on Guinée's opting out of the Franco-African community, Sarkozy's speech at the Cheikh Anta Diop Univeristy in July 2007.

1. Power, violence and impunity[110]

At the root of the long process of conquering Africa one finds violence exercised with impunity. The end result, as can be seen today, is a practice of power that, implicitly and/or explicitly, states that "power is only power if it is exercised with impunity." In order to understand this, one has to look at the cumulative violence that has been unleashed for centuries, most of which went unrecorded in the annals or archives of the conquering forces.

It is not enough to note, as most observers do today, that there are two international justice systems, one at the service of the most powerful nations, corporations and one at the service of the weakest. For the latter, an arsenal of humanitarian, charitable organisations has been put in place since the days of the abolitionist movement in England.

Humanitarianism has a history longer than the birth of the United Nations and most charitable organisations. Humanitarianism can be looked at the manner in which the most powerful show their power to the weakest. Justice that is practiced out of charity is not justice. When adjectives begin to be added to justice, such as "social justice," then one should be alerted to the fact that justice means different things to different groups of people.

For power to be exercised with impunity, the violence behind it must not be interpreted as questionable or unjust. The most powerful nations and corporations are not interested in examining the reverberations/repercussions of how they exercise their power. It has reached levels of unaccountability that are usually associated with dictatorial rule; for example, when it is decided in a given place that a group of people must be liquidated because one person has been identified as a threat to the well being of those controlling economic, political, and financial power. Such a process makes a mockery of justice and reframes the parameters

---

110 Again for the sake of avoiding claiming easy victories, and better knowing what we are up against, I strongly recommend Jaron Lanier's well-informed critique of Silicon Valley and related industries. *You are Not a Gadget: A Manifesto* (Vintage Books, Random House, 2010) seeks to draw attention to the fact that very little remains sacred. In his words: "the internet has come to be saturated with an ideology of violation… The ideology of violation does not radiate from the lowest depths of trolldom, but from the highest heights of academia." (p.65)

of international relations in a way that becomes impossible to challenge because impunity has become part and parcel of the definition of power as exercised by the most powerful.

2. Education, history

If one looks at the interest in history during the liberation struggles and the immediate aftermath, it is not difficult to notice that history was an important topic. Education was equally important. The reasons were obvious: if people were going to be mobilized to fight colonial rule, then it was necessary for them to understand its roots and how it worked, both physically and mentally.

If one takes the example of Frelimo and the teaching of who the enemy is during the armed struggle, it is not difficult to see how crucial education and history were as mobilizing weapons. When the colonised (or the enslaved) stand up and affirm themselves as not colonised, as free, they state that they count in a way that goes counter to how they had been treated by the enslavers and/or colonisers. However, that affirmation does require constant updating if the pitfall of National consciousness[111] (or claiming easy victories) is going to be avoided.

Is it not interesting that preoccupation with history and/or education tends to occur at moments of crisis or in times when there is a sense that things cannot go on as they are? Although still in power, Frelimo has adopted the dominant manners and practices of its former enemy, by relegating history, education and health to the bottom of priorities. The presupposition (from the United States to Mozambique, to DRC, to Brazil) is that disciplines (like history and education) are sought by the less intellectually gifted. According to those in power (corporations and/or state) this is as it should be, because the best brains are headed for science, Business and Law Schools.

Post-apartheid South Africa devotes 20 percent of its budget to education, and yet education continues to suffer from the apparent determination that it is not crucial for a society driven by a bottom line that has

111 As Fanon wrote about in *The Wretched of the Earth*.

stated, for centuries now, that Africa and Africans should not get the best education possible for every single person. The bottom line continues to be dictated by the notion that those who have risen to the top have done so thanks to their own merit. The idea that maintaining fidelity to humanity is crucial not just for the tiny few at the top, but for every single one, is simply anathema to those who have most benefitted from the process of dispossession and dehumanization that has taken place under capitalism.

3. Capitalism: Towards Eradicating Humanity and its History?

Over and above the typical features of capital related to the relationship between labor and capital, what takes place at the same time is a lethal process of dispossession that goes far beyond what has been understood. How lethal capitalism has been in its process of destroying humanity has not been fully understood. The discussions about whether primitive accumulation or dispossession best capture how capitalism as an economic system operates can only lead to claiming easy victories, because capitalism has impacted humans in ways that go far beyond the realm of economics.

It is not sufficient to provide a critique of capitalism by just focusing on its economic features. Sometimes it may take the voice of poets to see better through capitalism. I will refer here to just two of them: Aimé Césaire and Ayi Kwei Armah. The first, in his *Discourse on Colonialism*, articulates the interconnections between capitalism, Nazism and colonialism in a way that does not follow the usual script. He points out how the reconstruction of Europe went hand in hand with a continuation of Nazism (in the colonies). After all, it is not Hitler who proclaimed the following: "We do not aspire to equality, but to domination. The foreign-race country must become again a land of serfs, daily farm or industrial workers. The issue is not to do away with inequalities amongst people, but to amplify them and turn it into a law."[112] Ernest Renan, the Western humanist and idealist philosopher, is the author of this quote, written immediately following the end of WWII.

In a few more paragraphs, Césaire illustrates, with quotes, the ideological kinship between French thinkers and Hitler and his acolytes; between the barbarism that colonisation leads to and where Nazism led. For Césaire, both colonialism and Nazism are the by-products of a sick civilization that, in his words, "irresistibly, from consequence to consequence, from renunciation to renunciation, calls for its Hitler, I mean its punishment."[113]

From the perspective of Africa and its enslavement, Ayi Kwei Armah has written about the reality brought about by the white destroyers and the way to heal from the carnage. He has done it not only in his writing, but also in his practice as a writer, a thinker, as a sharer of his vision and understanding of the way away from the destroyers' way. In chapter 7 of *Two Thousand Seasons*, readers will find reflections that are pertinent to not claiming easy victories, as in the following lines, where he describes what a liberator is: "For he is no liberator whose skill lies in calling loudly to the bound, the trapped, the impotent enslaved, to rise upon their destroyers. The liberator is he who from a necessary silence, from a necessary secrecy strikes the destroyer. That, not loudness, is the necessary beginning." (p. 314). Farther down, he warns of more difficulties: "Dangers will be in the newness of this discovery, dangers like the headiness of too quick, abundant faith from those too long sold to despair; the pull of old habits from destruction's empire; the sour possibility of people helping each other turning in times of difficulty into people using each other to create a selfish ease… (p.315)

4. Cabral and Guiné-Bissau

As observers and scholars look today at the African continent, the general impression that emerges is certainly not the one that prevailed around 1973, just before the assassination of Cabral. Even the assassination of

112 Aimé Césaire, *Le discours sur le colonialisme.* Paris: Présence Africaine, 1955, 2004, p. 15.
113 Ibid. p. 18.

Cabral could not dampen the feeling that victory against Portuguese colonial rule was within reach. By April 1974, thanks to the pressure brought by the armed struggles in the colonies, the Portuguese army seized power and put an end to the dictatorship. With the independence of Mozambique the (September 1975) the focus shifted from ending Portuguese colonial rule to facing and defeating Ian Smith and his allies in South Africa. With the defeat of the Americans in Vietnam in 1975 it appeared as if anything was possible, including the end of the apartheid regime. There came Soweto, 1976, but soon after that (September 1977) came the assassination of Steve Bantu Biko. And it was around this time (April 1976) that the United States (under Henry Kissinger) decided that the timing of the end of apartheid had to take place according to what would be decided in Washington and London, and not by Africans.

For the purposes of this essay and the current times, there is one question that is impossible to avoid: from the days of Nkrumah's rise to power and the process of decolonisation, what is it that, systematically, has not been dealt with as it should have been? Despite the volumes written on African unity, how come everything but unity prevails? What is it that prevented thinkers like Cheikh Anta Diop, Nkrumah, Cabral, Fanon, Nyerere, Mondlane and Ruben Um Nyobe from joining their efforts? What is it that has led African political leaders to treat Cheikh Anta Diop's individual work with the same disdain that, collectively speaking, Haiti's overthrow of slavery has been treated? These questions will have to be answered sooner or later.

I mentioned earlier the fact that in the process of enslaving and colonising the continent destroyed much more than what has been acknowledged, even by leaders like Cabral. It is one thing to call for African unity, it is another to articulate it in a way that any one on the continent would immediately understand the historical, cultural, linguistic and philosophical roots of that unity; provided such articulations were rooted in an understanding and conviction that, in fact, that unity that politicians talk about has in fact been in existence through the culture, the languages, the values that can be traced back to Egyptian civilization. Although Cabral himself pointed out that the history of Africa has deeper roots than alleged by the theoretical approach framed by the history of class struggle, there is no evidence that he or his close collaborators, like Mario de Andrade, for example, took the work of Cheikh Anta Diop seriously.[114]

Today, what is the state of liberation (emancipatory politics) in countries that fought armed struggles? More broadly speaking, what is the state of the continent compared to what it looked like it might become in 1973? Can one say that the leadership in charge today has carried on, with fidelity to humanity (as envisioned by Fanon in his conclusion to *The Wretched of the Earth*) from where Amílcar Cabral and others left off?

Land grabbing in various countries is taking place as if cued by some sort of virtual replay of the Berlin Conference (more than a century later) aimed at dividing up the Continent according to the new configuration imposed by capitalism. If it is not land grabbing, laundering of the money made through drug trafficking is ensuring that capitalism takes root by any means necessary. The dispossessing or dehumanization of humanity has received a new lease of life on the continent, thanks to a renewed process of aggression against the most precious treasure held by all human beings: conscience.

5. Conclusion

For emphasis, let it be said that the focus on African history and not on history has led to a failure to understand humanity and its history as a whole. By creating area studies for the sake of producing expert knowledge on areas like Africa, the United States, and its allies (mostly former colonising countries), we created a way of looking at African history that prepared the ground for the repeated stumbling that prevented a complete and total

114 It should be noted that resistance to Cheikh Anta Diop's work significantly changed with the Cairo meeting of Egyptologists organised by UNESCO in 1974. At this meeting, Cheikh Anta Diop (and Théophile Obenga) responded to their critics. For those who are interested, see the full report of that meeting : http://unesdoc.unesco.org/images/0003/000328/032875eo.pdf Accessed on November 29, 2012.

eradication of the consequences of enslavement and colonisation.[115] When looking at the history of Africa and Africans by only concentrating on the continent, one ends up distorting that history. In turn that distortion leads to a distortion of the history of humanity, especially if, in the process, the humanity of Africans is systematically denied.

From within the emancipatory tradition there are more voices of conscience than the ones referred to in this text. At the same time, what is not sufficiently appreciated is the degree to which capitalism has come to dominate humanity's conception of itself, and its reliance on its conscience to keep coming back to its senses. Whether it was from Fanon, Ruben Um Nyobe, Biko, Sankara, Lumumba, Nehanda, or Kimpa Vita, these voices expressed what humanity has in common: conscience. While it may have been eroded to the point of giving the impression that it has disappeared, I would suspect that it never will, but if it is going to succeed in reversing the current process then there has to be a conviction that conscience is humanity's most powerful weapon in resisting its ongoing liquidation.

If Césaire's questioning of whether Nazism had ended (*Discourse on Colonialism*) had been pursued systematically, one of the possible results could have led to an understanding of capitalism as a system that modernized Nazism so that it would automatically generate mechanisms (ways of thinking) aimed at getting rid of those members of humanity that are considered worthless: the poor, the Africans, the old people, the indigenous people, street children, the handicapped, the terminally ill, etc. In other words, what can be seen today (not only through so-called globalisation) is a modernized form of Nazism in which there is no Hitler to point at as a scapegoat; capitalism seeks the same *lebensraum* that Hitler was aiming at. The difference is that capitalism has been slowly transforming humanity into its opposite by occupying all of the spaces that were once considered sacred if fidelity to humanity was going to be maintained.

115 Now, the same thinking that led to the creation of area studies has led to the creation of poverty studies (see the courses being offered, for example, at Stanford and UC Berkeley). For UC Berkeley, see the following entry: http://www.berkeley.edu/news/media/releases/2009/03/10_poverty.shtml Accessed on November 30, 2012.

15. THINKING WITH OUR OWN HEADS AND WALKING WITH OUR OWN FEET

Augusta Henriques and Miguel Barros of *Tiniguena*, Guinea-Bissau in conversation with Molly Kane [116]

Augusta Henriques: When I first learned about Amílcar Cabral, I was an adolescent studying in Portugal. I heard about the nationalist movements in my country, Guinea-Bissau, and I heard about Amílcar Cabral. I was still in Portugal studying when we learned of his death. I was not yet a very politicized person at that time, and it was still the colonial regime in Portugal. I remember that the assassination of Amílcar Cabral was the first item on the news that morning. During the revolution of 1974, I was involved as a student, and at that time our big question was how to gain the independence of the Portuguese colonies, amongst them Guinea-Bissau.

Our movement, the PAIGC (African Party for the independence of Guinea and Cap Verde), had already declared the independence of Guinea-Bissau. Independence had been planned during the lifetime of Amílcar Cabral, and the leaders had even declared liberated zones in Guinea-Bissau. So this gave us something—it set us apart from all the others. We thought it was just a question of recognizing the fact of our independence, which had been already declared and that many countries had already recognized. It seemed that all that remained was for Portugal to accept what other countries and even parts of the military within Portugal had accepted too.

I remember that at that time, we had a pride in ourselves and in Guinea-Bissau—and Guinea-Bissau and Amílcar Cabral were almost

116 Augusta and Miguel talked with Molly Kane on the living legacy of Amílcar Cabral in Guinea Bissau in interviews conducted during January and February 2013.

the same thing. All the students in our country and other Portuguese colonies, even from Portugal and many other Europeans countries, wanted to study his work. When people realized that my sisters and I came from Guinea-Bissau, we were treated with respect. So, from my point of view, the great difference between my generation and that of Miguel and my children is that at that time, being from Guinea-Bissau was a great source of pride—and that pride was thanks to the action and work of of Amílcar Cabral. For me there was never any question that I would stay in Europe. While for my children there is the question, should I stay or not? For me, no! I studied in Portugal to be educated to return and work at home.

My father and I had generational differences as well. My father was a "*metis*," and it was seen, in some way, as part of the colonial system. He was the son of a Portuguese farmer who come to Guinea-Bissau looking for a better life; born in Guinea-Bissau from an African woman, educated in Portugal, and settled back to Guinea-Bissau, my father became later a successful entrepreneur, thanks to his hard work as a self-made man. Nevertheless, most of the people thought that his enterprise benefited from the colonial system that protected those who didn't question the colonial power in Africa, while it persecuted and threatened those that struggle for liberation of their country. Due to historical reasons, my father was a Guinean connected to the Portuguese. But even though, like him, I studied in Portugal, I was more politicized when I come back to Bissau. I was related to the new social project of independence which the majority of African students embraced. So, I studied the work of Amílcar Cabral with passion. I can say that I am part of the generation of Amílcar Cabral. Everything in my life, the opportunities I had were shaped by Amílcar Cabral. The great tide that influenced my generation was a simple man who wanted to respond to his times and to his place in history. So that's how it was—each of us wanting to find our role and our place in history. We who were the youth of the generation of Amílcar Cabral embraced Guinea-Bissau with all the love that we shared with him. We made of Guinea-Bissau our home, our land, our dream, and our dream for our children.

Some of the greatest pain that we have known in our lives has been the continuing and ongoing assassinations of Amílcar Cabral. How many times has he been assassinated since his death? Who killed him? We know who killed him physically. They were arrested, judged, and executed. But who ordered it? Who from the outside? Who from the inside? It's always easier to focus on the "other," and to not look inside ourselves. But we continue to assassinate him even today, because we don't look inside. Amílcar Cabral today—where is he? His tomb is not in a civic space. He is in a military space. He is in a fortress, surrounded by the military. And the conditions imposed on visitors means that ordinary citizens never have the right to visit his tomb without the authorization of the commander-in-chief. The memory of Cabral, and that of his people, has been taken hostage by the military that he trained. But because his life was cut off before his time, his legacy continues to be killed. We have known the dream of Amílcar Cabral, we have known the death of Amílcar Cabral, and yes, we also know that Cabral still lives.

Amílcar Cabral lives in the everyday—in the responses that continue to inspire the new generation to construct our future with all the small pieces of our history broken into a thousand pieces. Amílcar Cabral inspires us. One thing he said that really had an impact on my life is that the struggle for liberation is a cultural act. I worked with Paolo Freire, who was a great admirer of the work of Amílcar Cabral. His theory of liberation was very inspired by the thinking of Amílcar Cabral. And Freire viewed adult education—my work in the early years of my adult life in Guinea-Bissau—as a cultural act as well.

Amílcar Cabral dreamed of a society in Guinea-Bissau that would be created from the best things that existed within the cultural mosaic of Guinea-Bissau. Amílcar Cabral dreamed of a country in which culture inspires what distinguishes us in relation with others. And even today where we find the strength to go forward in Guinea-Bissau, it is first amongst the people, especially amongst the rural people who produce, who feed all of us. It is the knowledge that they have developed from their work in the fields and their activity in the sea, their activity in the forests and the savannah, the knowledge that they have developed and above all the simplicity of the people of Guinea-Bissau that inspires us even today, at the individual level and in collective action. We try to bring synergy to our action to make this brilliance shine. For this we have a kind of debt to Amílcar Cabral.

I was visiting a close friend in Mali a few years ago when I was going through a difficult time in my life; I had recently lost my father, political tensions were increasing in my country, and I was feeling very sad and discouraged. My friend said to me, "Augusta, you don't have the right to let go of Guinea-Bissau; you don't have the right to be discouraged." She said, "Amílcar Cabral so inspired our generation in Mali; we studied his works in our university, we listened to the radio of PAIGC, the radio of the liberation of Guinea-Bissau. He inspired us as youth in the university. We were so proud of such a struggle in which a small and determined people, with a visionary and strong leadership, defeated a big empire with all is sophisticated armaments and generals. That was Cabral's achievement and his legacy. He made us dream! He was one of the African leaders who inspired us the most. So, no matter what country of Africa you go to, you will find a street, a square, a statue that is consecrated to Amílcar Cabral. The Guinean people do not have the right to let down these countries, for what Cabral struggled so much for and to which he committed his entire life. You must be accountable to him, to the history of your people, to Africa. And I feel you have been accountable, but much more must be done to make peace and security in our country. And I feel also you need much more solidarity from us, all African people."

Sometimes when I speak with my children I understand that they feel that my generation is responsible in some ways for letting this beautiful dream fall apart. I ask myself the question, "How could this have happened? How did we get here?" When I came back to Guinea-Bissau in 1977, at the age of twenty three, my heart so full of pride, I had so many dreams. I had the right to dream anything, to choose anything for my life. I felt there was work to do and we held our heads high when we said we were from Guinea-Bissau. We were so proud! When my daughter finished her studies in Portugal and she came home she didn't have anything like the hope that I had. What happened?

When Amílcar Cabral died he left a huge gap—like the space left in a forest when you cut down a big tree. There are no other big trees growing in that space. He was really an extraordinary person, and great visionary. He had a coherent vision, strong energy and the capacity to rally others, to make them move in the good direction. He was the first to rise and last to sleep and very demanding of himself. It was difficult to replace his leadership. After his assassination, there was such a climate of fear and disorientation in PAIGC, even amongst its most distinguished leaders, that it was almost fatalistic to take on the leadership after Amílcar Cabral.

Without his leadership, the unity of Cap Verde and Guinea-Bissau broke down. The Portuguese colonialist (and others too) took advantage of the contradictions and divided and manipulated the differences. We were not immune from human pettiness and we lost momentum. Perhaps we needed more time to achieve real independence. There were major problems and errors increasingly in the direction of the national party and we hadn't had enough quality education for running a modern state, our base was still insufficient. What was known was the colonial model of governing "la chose publique" so the old settlers ("les colons") were replaced by the new ones. And these new *colons* had some kind of complex in which they had neither the required capacities and tools to run the new state, nor the coherence of the vision of Cabral, nor the knowledge of how to run the old style colonial state.

This complex was expressed at different levels, mostly on the leading of cultural and educational policies. We have been incapable of having a coherent language policy that affirms our different languages as an important part of our identity, not only for traditional issues and oral communication. We have never been able to use our many languages to communicate information on science and education. The few attempts to introduce our mother-tongues in literacy and formal education have been criticized and marginalised by the ruling elite who are unable to understand the real meaning of cultural emancipation, who consider it is sufficient for people to write and to read in a foreign language.

So, we have never replaced Portuguese as the language of instruction even at the very basic level. This is one of the biggest reasons of the failure of our education system after independence, because we tried to extend primary education to everybody using Portuguese as the only instruction language. Worse still, this was done on the under conditions where most teachers that don't even speak Portuguese particularly well. Since neither pupils nor teachers are able to communicate well in Portuguese, everybody ends up trying to teach or to learn by memorizing words, sentences and ideas. We simply don't stimulate people's capacity for understanding or being creative, but just in memorizing.... As a result, we are trained to adopt and copy foreign ideas and solutions, most of which are not suitable to our society. Education has become a caricature that produces leaders who are unable to find solutions for our problems, unable to generate new ideas or new strategies to lead our country, and unable to present such ideas with dignity at the international level.

As we were not able to develop a culturally specific model for Guinea-Bissau; the state we have created is a caricature that has become even worse after structural adjustment. The more the leaders exploited the people the more "legitimate" they became in their own eyes.

We in Guinea-Bissau have not made peace with our history. We need put history in its place and take part in our own history. Hopefully the new generations are less affected by their relationship with the *colons* than were my generation. Young people such as Miguel and similarly for my children have their eyes on the future. Cabral gives us cause for pride and confidence to look to our future with roots deeply in our own culture but open to the good things of modernity.

Culture must not be understood merely as tradition or as something from the past. We need an open culture for an open world. We need to be strong because of who we are in ways that open us to the future. We in Tiniguena are trying now to build ownership of our land and our cultural heritage at grassroots and national levels, leading experiences that are rooted in the people, in the past, but open to the future. We are building responsible citizenship so that we are not disinherited.

But, what happened to Guinea-Bissau did not happen to Guinea-Bissau alone. What happened to countries where we had great African leaders—Kwame Nkrumah, Nelson Mandela, Julius Nyerere—great dreamers for Africa, the founders of our nations? Who are the great leaders of Africa today? Who are great leaders in the world? What are their interests? What moves the leaders of the planet today? Guinea-Bissau reproduces at a small scale, with a small population, in a small concentration everything that has happened in the world in the past forty years.

What inspired us forty years ago? What were our struggles? And now? What are the things that nourish our children? We cannot understand the history of Guinea-Bissau outside the history of Africa, outside the history of the world. We are really the reflection of how a small people, a small country, rich in biodiversity and with great cultural diversity, that has a great history that has inspired people all over the planet has been able to fall so low. That story is not ours alone. It is our common history.

Miguel Barros: My father was one of fourteen Guineans who had a postsecondary education at the time of independence. At the age of sixteen he was already organising against the education system and spent time in prison. At the time, Cabral had already conceived of a new society, a new model to put in place in society; and my father was responsible for the "people's stores" in the liberated zones. My father explained that the model of the "people's stores" was to be the new model for trade and exchange amongst the people. The people's stores provided supplies for the soldiers in the zones of combat, supplies for the people who had been victims of the violence of the armed struggle, and support to the education of cadres in the liberated zones.

I did not know Amílcar Cabral as I was born after he died. But I grew up with people who had spent a lot of time with him. My father's family participated in the resistance, even before the PAIGC. When Cabral took the leadership of the PAIGC and the PAIGC took the lead in the liberation struggle my family was close to him. I had an uncle who was a great leader in the clandestine liberation movement.

Augusta Henriques: Much of the education and organising at that time amongst the young people in Portugal took place at dances. People like Miguel's uncle came to the dances to talk with us. We had a good excuse to be together—under the colonial regime under Salazar, we did not have the right of assembly but we could go to dances. And sometimes I would ask myself why are the boys off in a corner always talking while we wanted to dance? Miguel's uncle was one of those who introduced us to the movement for liberation and to the work of Amílcar Cabral.

Miguel Barros: One of the things that I learned from my family was that Cabral said that the soldiers were the armed militants and those in the underground were the political militants. So the struggle was the inheritance of all Guineans—not just those who carried out the armed struggle, but also those who struggled in the clandestine movements outside the liberated zones, who suffered a great deal; many were even tortured and imprisoned. It was very hard at that time. Anyone who knows about the time of Salazar can speak about this. And so the struggle was the inheritance of all Guineans.

For me this is one of the great lessons in terms of how Cabral speaks to us today. He calls us to civic and citizen action. I always wear a bracelet with a saying from Cabral: *We need to walk with our own feet and think with our own heads*. But this commitment to our country Guinea-Bissau has to be long term. It is also the commitment of the African. This is why I think the slogan, "Cabral is not dead," is still powerful even if the mausoleum of Cabral is now under the control of the military. As a sociologist I carried out a study of how the youth of Guinea-Bissau have incorporated Amílcar Cabral into their lives today.[117] There has been an appropriation of the story of Cabral by the old combatants to justify a different kind of leadership around the military.

The liberalization of the political system that came with the liberalization of the economic system under structural adjustment was an important moment in the consolidation of this appropriation. Whether in Guinea-Bissau or Cap Verde, we witnessed the same phenomenon. Our

117 See Migueal de Barros & Redy Wilson Lima: *Creole RAP: Pan-Africanism of Cabral in youth music interventions in Guinea-Bissau and Cape Verde* in this volume.

activist formation and education was replaced with civic education that had been stripped of the teachings of Amílcar Cabral.

We were not able to bring the thought of Amílcar Cabral into our civic education. The education for militants that took place in the liberated zones was about understanding the theory of liberation and the vision for the new society. It was ideological education. After independence, it was thought that we no longer needed ideological education now that we had one party. So we had "civic education" that was unable to actualize the teaching of Amílcar Cabral within citizen education, not in political way.

In both Cap Verde and Guinea-Bissau when we brought in "civic education" we lost the teachings of Amílcar Cabral. In Guinea-Bissau, especially, the state abandoned education. We experienced the privatization of education and lost the memory of the history of Guinea-Bissau in our education system. My generation learned about the history of the struggles in many African countries. But the next generation has not learned of that history. When I was studying in Portugal I saw there was a huge difference in knowledge of history between my generation and those younger. And when I compare us to Augusta's generation before us I see that they were more militant. What are our ideologies now? What are our struggles? What are our achievements? This is what the thinking of Amílcar Cabral helps us to analyze. But it is what has been taken away from the younger generation by removing it from the education system.

And this role of political education that is no longer fulfilled by school is also not fulfilled by the family. Structural adjustment also weakened the family and the family has lost its capacity to take care of the political education of youth. So the younger generation takes on the thought of Amílcar Cabral through rap music. The rap musicians are the inheritors of Amílcar Cabral. Even though they did not know Amílcar Cabral and did not share in his life, Cabral is with them as a messenger of truth. And what is interesting today is that even though Guinea-Bissau and Cap Verde are no longer united by the same political movements, we find the same words in the rap of the two countries. And it is interesting that even for the second and third generation of emigrants from Guinea-Bissau and Cap Verde that are in the diaspora in Portugal, in France and elsewhere, and who are in some ways expatriated, they find their common identity in the legacy of Amílcar Cabral. So his thought continues to be very current, and interest in recuperating the works of Amílcar Cabral is growing amongst the young. One reason is that the youth do not see commitment to the long term for the future of Guinea-Bissau amongst the leadership today. And another reason is that Amílcar Cabral inspires us—he was a poet, a politician who was close to his people and his community.

One of the greatest factors of success of the armed struggle for the liberation of Guinea-Bissau and Cap Verde was that Amílcar Cabral was a leader who was very close to his communities. He knew them like the palm of his hand. So he was able to bring forth a synthesis of aspirations, from the depths of our own communities. And that was the great secret of Amílcar Cabral. And now our struggle in Guinea-Bissau is what Cabral called the "Major Programme." The minor programme was gaining independence. And the major programme was to ensure the development of the two countries, Guinea-Bissau and Cap Verde, and to struggle against all forms of colonisation, even within ourselves. We feel that the new generation is in the process of taking on this struggle.

Many of Amílcar Cabral's speeches are now accessible through the Internet. Even only ten or fifteen years ago these films were still on reels and people had no access to them. Even the music was not available. But now that is no longer the case. The Internet has made it possible to have access to all this material from the time of the independence struggle. There is a lot of musical production by young people in which they mix their music with the voice of Amílcar Cabral from the recordings that are now widely available. Their productions are widely disseminated through Facebook and YouTube.

Augusta Henriques: The new generation—not just in Guinea-Bissau—needs a new paradigm. They need to renew and nourish themselves—and they won't find that sustenance in the ugliness of much of what we encounter today. And in all the darkness of what we are going through today—physically, psychically, psychologically, the thought of Amílcar Cabral continues to be a light. A light that attracts people. The light comes from a national identity and these young people need this light to inspire them, to find themselves in the light and not in the darkness. And the darker that things become around us the more we need this light. The new rap music is a way to spread light and to galvanize the best in them. And that is why we say that the more Cabral is killed the more important the light of his life becomes. His body can be imprisoned but his thoughts are free.

Miguel Barros: The two messages of Amílcar Cabral that are to be found in almost all the new creations of the young in which they evoke Amílcar Cabral are as these.

First, *even in the most difficult conditions, nothing is impossible*. When we have a vision of what we want, when we have the will, when we have the capacity to unite, and our cause is just, we can bring about change.

And, secondly, the condition of citizenship: *think with our own heads and walk with our own feet*. And this goes beyond partisan politics. That is the power of Amílcar Cabral.

Augusta Henriques: Each of us has to live our own times with all our integrity and sincerity. We are responsible for our own time, our own era. We are not responsible for yesterday or tomorrow. We are responsible for today. And I have learned with the legacy of Amílcar Cabral to understand my surroundings. My entourage is the family from which I came into the world and the community in which I live and with which I share life and the desire to improve life, believing that change is truly within our reach. We can compromise everything but the right to dream.

We have a base that is sufficiently strong and powerful to carry us forward. We share a country. This land is ours. How many people died so that Guinea-Bissau would be a nation? We are accountable to those people. We cannot bring them back to life. But we can stop killing them. We are responsible for building the dream for which they died. We are responsible for bringing about progress for the next generation. We are living between the old and the new generations. Guinea-Bissau is a country that inspired Amílcar Cabral. It inspired the people whom Amílcar Cabral succeeded in mobilizing for the struggle that brought about the independence of Guinea-Bissau. Amílcar Cabral engaged in the struggle at the risk of his own life—knowing he could be killed from one day to the next. One could say that he was a man ahead of his time—and perhaps that is also why his influence is in many ways timeless. His vision was so unusual in looking towards the very long term, beyond his own time. And it went so far beyond his era that it created malaise around him.

Miguel Barros: Another indication of how he was ahead of his time is how he saw the role of women in society. He created the Democratic Union of Women. During the struggle he not only carried out the political education of women but also brought women into all the political and military structures. He understood the importance of the emancipation of women. In all the liberated zones the leadership structures had to have as many women as men. And this all happened amongst people without formal education. Today with all our formal education we have not achieved this kind of equality. He really was an exceptional visionary. He was able to change the game and redefine political action as protagonism.

Augusta Henriques: He was indeed brilliant with a rare intelligence of the heart as well as of the mind. He was very human. But he was still a man of his times—he made the time to exchange ideas with the other leaders in Africa and not only in Africa. Fidel Castro sent Che Guevara to Guinea Conakry where the PAIGC had a base to meet Amílcar Cabral. Che reported back to Castro that he "had been in the presence of an exceptional man," and "the only serious movement." He played an important role in the struggle of Angola. In a way he crystallized the leaders of that time. We know that those times had amazing creative energy. We had dreams and so much latitude. This was true not only for Africa, but in Africa in particular it was amongst those who finally saw that after the long era of slavery we were there! We were taking on the destiny of our peoples. It was wonderful. Amílcar Cabral himself was in some ways the great creation of his time. By advancing the struggle of a tiny little country and taking advantage of learning from the bad experiences and pitfalls of the larger countries that had already achieved independence, and from their attempts to build new nations, he was determined to not make the same errors. But he always said that it would take great sacrifice to bring about change.

I remember when independence was granted and I returned to Guinea-Bissau, I was a young bourgeois. My father was a rich man who had sent his four children to Portugal for their education. We were privileged. But I learned that Amílcar Cabral said that the petit bourgeoisie was an important element of the struggle for national independence. The great challenge would be for this petit bourgeoisie to commit class suicide later. In my point of view he was correct but … he did not see it all. Because it is not just about the petit bourgeoisie; it is about everything that existed deep in each of us of personal ambition that undermines the collective good. And that wasn't just amongst the petit bourgeoisie. There were people who came from the liberation struggle, who had been commanders and enriched themselves, becoming a new bourgeoisie and betraying their own struggle. They justified themselves, saying, "We gave up our youth to this struggle and now it's our turn to be in charge." Very quickly they forgot the lessons of their history. One of the great sorrows of Guinea-Bissau is that some people used our history, our roots, to take power but not to inspire us, not to lead us to a better place, to protect us, but just to serve their own entourage. If we are not capable of leading a social project to which people can adhere, we fall back on ethnic and community identity to establish legitimacy.

I have studied the thought of Amílcar Cabral and have tried to live according to his teaching. I have succeeded in bringing the good things that I have from my past into a commitment to the future of Guinea-Bissau. I can say that for myself, Guinea-Bissau—the project of Guinea-Bissau as Cabral dreamed—is half of my life. When I returned to Guinea-Bissau after independence and saw the problems of my country I felt them deeply as something intimate and personal. I made getting to know my people and my country my first task and to take responsibility for my inheritance, not just as responsibility but also as a privilege. I think I am lucky. Choosing one's destiny, embracing one's destiny, choosing what one does, what one struggles for, what one gives, and what one doesn't do is a privilege. I had this privilege thanks to people like Amílcar Cabral. His example and his thinking inspired me to play my part in my time to contribute something to inspire Guineans. In some ways I think the organisation I helped to create and where I have worked, *Tiniguena*, inspires Guineans. And that is my legacy, my own way of being Cabral. I think all of us keep a bit of Cabral inside. And this little bit of Cabral is a luminous place in our lives.

This interview was conducted in French and Portuguese, and transcribed and translated by Molly Kane.

16. THE SIGNIFICANCE TODAY OF THE CHARISMATIC FIGURE, AMÍLCAR CABRAL

Filomeno Lopes

> *I vow that I shall give my life, all my energy, all my courage, all the ability that I have as a man to the service of my people in Guinea and Cape Verde until the day I die. I shall make my contribution, as far as possible, to the service of humanity, for the improvement in the lives of people in the world. This is my task.*[118]

These words pronounced by Amílcar Cabral in 1969 are the unequivocal response to the question, "Why evoke today this poet, intellectual, politician, and fighter for the freedom of African countries, as well as his atrocious death?" Hence, today, our tribute to Amílcar Lopes Cabral, the charismatic role model of African political leadership.

The Charismatic Figure of Amílcar Cabral in the World Geopolitics Today

As Gérard Chaliand put it, Amílcar Lopes Cabral is "the most beautiful revolutionary figure, together with Nelson Mandela, produced by Africa."[119] He is even more significant for the Lusophone African countries (PALOP, where Portuguese is an official language) and particularly for the countries and peoples of Guinea-Bissau and Cape Verde. However, forty years have passed since Cabral ceased to be physically amongst

118 See Andrade, Mario de, *Obras escolhidas de Amílcar Cabral,* Ed. Seara Nova, Lisbon, 1977

119 See Chaliand, Gérard, *Mythes révolutionnaires du Tiers Monde,* Ed. Seuil, Paris, 1976

us. In fact, in these forty years, both in the PALOP countries and in the rest of the African continent, as well as in Europe, the Americas and Oceania, life has moved on.

Cabral and other historic African and non-African leaders are no longer with us but they are *in* us, they have remained inside each one of us to the extent that each tragic moment of our lives, of our history, becomes an occasion for us to feel how their regard occupies our minds, our hearts, our dreams for a future that is less bad than the present one that has been given us to live in Africa and in the world. This is why, thanks to his charisma as a political leader and what it represents to the whole political and intellectual world of today, we can proudly affirm that *semper aliquid novi ex Africa* (Africa always brings us something new).

As African states, we have become independent, and there have been quite important historical, political, and cultural changes, both for the better and for the worse. New "leaders" have emerged and new generations have grown up and, above all, Africa has celebrated fifty years of the independence of many of its states. We have seen the end of apartheid, with Nelson Mandela installed as the first president of post-apartheid South Africa. We have seen the birth of the African Union and, despite the difficult situations in the Democratic Republic of the Congo, in Mali and in Guinea-Bissau itself, the land of Cabral, the life of the continent continues, advancing slowly, amongst the many tribulations. We see a vertiginous economic growth for many states (Mozambique, Angola, and Cape Verde amongst the PALOP countries), even though we are still in the grip of "growth without development," to use an expression of Samir Amin.[120] And hence the deep significance of the question of leadership, the tragedy of this issue today in the world in general and its evil effects, particularly on the African continent, render Amílcar Cabral alive again in our minds and in our hearts.

120 See Amin, Samir, *La déconnexion. Pour sortir du systeme mondial* (Delinking: towards a polycentric world), Ed. La Découverte, Paris, 1986

Amílcar Cabral as an Icon for our Times?

The philosopher Severino Elias Ngoenha[121] calls iconography a figure of art. Icons, historically speaking, are great personalities who have left an indelible mark or a strong and lasting legacy. Thus, for example, in philosophy we speak of the epoch of Imhotep, Akhenaten, Anton Guillaume Amo, Edward Wilmot Blyden, and Pericles—to mention just a few; in history we refer to Pharaonic Egypt, the Alexandrian period, the era of the great empires (Gao, Ghana, Songhai, Mali). We can talk of the Portugal of Salazar and Marcelo Caetano, of the France of Napoleon, even the Germany of Hitler and the Italy of Mussolini. Is that what Africa and above all the international community meant for Amílcar Cabral?

He was not only a revolutionary chief but also a real leader, in the sense that he was a brilliant intellectual and politician with a broad vision, who mobilized people. Above all he was aware of the mission that history had assigned him, which was to open up the way to the redemption of the countries and peoples of Africa. As he said, "I am a simple African who is carrying out his duty for his country, in the context of our time. A simple African who wants to pay his debt to his people and to live his epoch."[122] Amílcar Cabral was very important in the mobilization of the country for the struggle for the freedom and dignity of people, for promoting the idea of unity and the understanding the end of politics and geopolitics of self protection as people, the end of single destines, and the consequent need to walk together in the direction of the common home of a "family of nations," and towards a vision that goes beyond tribes, ethnicities, races, cultures, religions, nations, and continents. Amílcar Cabral's leadership was not limited to the PALOP countries, but addressed to the historical unity of these five countries and their peoples with all Africans. Amílcar Cabral inspired personalities such as Nelson Mandela and Desmond Mpilo Tutu. It also inspired the various South African liberation movements, helping them to understand clearly that the struggles of the African peoples can not be directed against a race, a

121 See Lopes, Filomeno on Severino Elias Ngoenha, Radio Vaticana, 2006
122 See Andrade, Mario de, op. cit.

group of individuals, or a group of nations, but they should be struggles against the political and geopolitical systems of death—imperialist forms of slavery, colonialism, apartheid, and the other forms of destruction that we have known. In this sense, we can talk of Cabral as an icon of leadership for Africa and the world as a whole.

Nevertheless, icons can be problematic in that they reveal problems and contradictions. Alain, the French philosopher, said that what we need is not great men and great women, but great peoples. Cabral himself insisted on the need for *"direção colectiva"* and " *dirigir em grupo"*(collective leadership and governing as a group), while thinkers like Aimé Césaire, Senghor, Cheikh Anta Diop, and Paulin Hountondji believed that this task belonged to the intellectuals. Does this mean that Amílcar Cabral as an icon was necessary because our peoples were not sufficiently mature and conscious to take up their own historical destiny and therefore needed someone to carry them on their shoulders, or unnecessary, for the popular will he enjoined himself to? In fact, the African Party for the Independence of Guinea and the Cape Verde Islands (PAIGC) is the political liberation movement in a long history of popular resistance in Guinea-Bissau, which started thousands of years before Amílcar Cabral.

In fact, when icons are too strong, they run the risk of preventing the emergence of a broader popular will, which one could call more "democratic." The writer Karlheinz, reflecting on the great personages in the nineteenth century, rightly wondered whether we should continue to exalt these men and women—whether such eulogy does not in the end diminish the general populace, as an integral part of a broad social debate—the "movement" of the times. But, at the same time, these great personalities can wake up people and make them realize that they themselves have the dimension of greatness and change.

In sum, who was Amílcar Cabral, and what kind of icon do we need today? Men and women with great charisma who risk diminishing the emergence of the people, or great peoples who do not need great charismatic personalities to lead them?

*****

Amílcar Lopes Cabral was assassinated on January 20, 1973. His serene face in the profound sleep of death in Guinea-Conakry showed his greatness as a political leader. "When, following his infamous assassination as the leader of the PAIGC in Conakry on 20 January, I went to Guinea Conakry to pay the ultimate tribute," says Joseph Ki-Zerbo, "I saw the impact of the bullet as a hole in the temple and the blood as the sweat of heroes.... But the shot had a boomerang effect: It is a fact that to liberate himself the slave must liberate his master.... But who is to guard the guardians themselves? Still today, Africa awaits a leader with the stature and calibre of Amílcar Cabral." [123]

Amílcar Cabral is thus a model of a poet, writer, political intellectual, and fighter—in sum, a leader. It is true that we continue to laud the figure of Cabral; nevertheless, it seems that we have buried him as they used to bury pharoahs. We have buried a hero, but he has been hermetically closed off from us. Thus the value of unity that Cabral always professed no longer exists, either within Africa or in the African diaspora. What we see instead increasingly is the culture of the egoism of those who govern, the politics of division, and the incitement to racial hatred based on realities that Cabral would not have hesitated to call countervalues. I therefore wonder if the man who died and whom we now remember would recognise himself in our countries today.

The testimony of the leader and political intellectual that Amílcar Cabral bequeaths to the world, to the new African generation, is that he was ready to die for the good of his own people and for the whole of humanity. He refused every offer of personal privilege made to him by the government in Lisbon, because it would not have benefited his people. He thus gave the fascist government to understand that the problem was a question of restoring dignity to a people who had the divine right and duty to be the protagonists of their own history and historicity. For Cabral this need was priceless and in no way negotiable. Thus he put into practice unambiguously what Frantz Fanon once said: "We are nothing

123 Ki-Zerbo, Joseph, "Prologo," in Aristides Pereira, *O meu Testemunho,* Ed. Noticias, Lisbon, 2003

in this land unless we are slaves to a cause, that of our peoples, of justice, and of freedom." [124] Today, unfortunately, in Guinea-Bissau, everything has a price, everything can be bought in Africa and in its diaspora, including our consciences, by the highest bidder.

124 Fanon, Frantz, *Scritti politici,* Ed. Derive Approdi srl, Rome, 2006

17. ON SHOOTING THE BODY AND NOT THE SHADOW

HONOURING AND LEARNING FROM CABRAL FORTY YEARS LATER

Wangui Kimari

The essay below is an exploration of Cabral's words and actions, while acknowledging that the revolutionary impact of the PAIGC, in Guinea and beyond, was not the result of one man's actions, but rather due to the courage, beliefs, and determination of many Afrikan communities. These words come at a time when this subject increasingly occupies our minds and our lands, when Coca-Cola is easier to find than clean water in many Afrikan communities, and when neocolonial governments and institutions such as AFRICOM, NATO, the World Bank, and mining companies work hard to negate the independence struggles that were watershed moments in our histories. At the same time, even in light of the present moment, these humble words are inspired by those who came before—named and nameless—who have always known that Afrikan self-determination is more than just a dream.

Returning to the Source in the Diaspora[125]

Se wo were fi na wosankofa a yenkyi
(It is not wrong to go back for that which you have forgotten.)
—Ghanaian Proverb.

125 For Nanny of the Maroons, Anastasia, Palenque, Bahia, Jacob Odipo, Ota Benga, Sara Baartman, and for all the youth of Africa who know she will always live.

Culture is simultaneously the fruit of a people's history and a determinant of their history.

—Amílcar Cabral.

The main strategy—inheritance of our mother Africa, the only thing they couldn't steal

—Juri Racional, Mano Brown, Brazilian MC.

For Africans born abroad, whether in Brazil, Colombia, Trinidad, the United States, or elsewhere, "returning to the source" has been seen as a viable means of rooting struggles for dignity and self-determination. What do I mean by returning to the source? I do not mean having an Afro or participating in events such as "Black History Month"; these events, while well intentioned, have their limits. Rather, as Cabral said, returning to the source is the "denial of the pretended supremacy of the culture of the dominant power over that of the dominated people with which it must identify itself" (Cabral 1973, p. 63), and a key vehicle for this is Pan-Afrikanism (Cabral 1973, p. 91).

It is in this this way that remembering cultural elements and histories that involve resistance to oppression are utilized to rebuild culture, and consequently form part of our fight for the freedom of our people "to free our people." Such pursuits allow Afrikans to ground and solidify our identities farther away from those of the oppressor and also to create a powerful situation where we learn from history—in particular the strategies and symbols for rebellion waged by those before us.

In Salvador da Bahia Brazil, Afrikan descendants are mobilizing to do just this as part of a comprehensive bid to organise against widespread and institutionalized anti-Black racism. This Pan-Afrikan organising has increased since the late '60s and early '70s. The *Instituto Cultural Steve Biko* (ICSB) emerged from these Afrika centred mobilizations and tasks itself with preparing Afro-Brazilian students, often from poor urban communities, for university education. Certainly, these actions holistically work to challenge the conventionally (violent) white spaces in the city. Above all, the Afrocentric and traditional Afro-Brazilian worldviews that undergird these initiatives allow Black youth to begin/continue the decolonization of their minds, taking back what Biko asserted is the most powerful weapon in the hands of the oppressor.

Similarly, the Afri-Can Food Basket (AFB) in Toronto, Canada, mobilizes Afrikans from the continent and the diaspora to grow organic foods (some of which are from the continent and were taken with the diaspora) which they often do not have access to, because of the cost as well as a lack of space to grow them. In this way the AFB endeavours to reinforce the importance of food in our communities, works towards self-reliance, and simultaneously brings about greater food security and justice for people who often have no access to healthy food.

While they may have different targets and objectives, both these initiatives emphasize the importance of (Pan) Afrikan customs and knowledge in a bid to survive, contest, and overthrow the white supremacist capitalist system that seeks to recolonise our lives.

The challenge as always is to "return to the source," even amidst our contradictions, in a manner that recognizes that returning to the source is a political process, as well as a cultural event; one that involves, tacitly or explicitly, "participation in the mass struggle against foreign political and economic domination."

Essentially, it is to look within ourselves—us who have been colonised and excluded—and the other selves that have historically constituted us, our mothers and fathers, grandmothers, ancestors and spirits, no matter how fractured these connectionss may be. It is to uphold older knowledge, feelings, and practices—and some that are not so old—that are outside of the brutal boundaries that seek to define our state(s), in order to find solutions to our ongoing problems.

In this regard Cabral stated:

> But the people are only able to create and develop the liberation movement because they keep their culture alive despite continual and organized repression of their cultural life and because they continue to resist culturally even when their politico-military

> resistance is destroyed. And it is a cultural resistance which at a given moment can take on new forms, i.e. political and economic, armed to fight foreign domination (Cabral 1973, p. 60)

I am part of the generation who can't speak the language of their grandmothers. While some words resound and are understood, for the most part we are, save for the warmth of an embrace, mute in each other's company. I am also part of the generation born when both the ways in which we traditionally come into and leave the world had been denied. As a result we contend (and unfortunately are sometimes content) with the fantasies created about and for "Queen" Elizabeth in our educational, religious, and polical institutions.

At the same time, we recognize, undoubtedly, that what remains of a lot of our ways of being is fractured and distant, and it is okay for us to move away from those best left behind. Nevertheless, let us hold in cupped hands those that we still have; feel them, study them, remember them, and, to the extent that they advance the liberation of all Afrikan people, bring them to the fore, so that our bodies and spirits can no longer be killed and so that we can stop, as Bantu Mwaura said, raising ourselves and our children to be foreigners in our lands. And it is in this way that we can, on multiple rooted and routed fronts, fight the domination that seeks to extinguish us.

De-NGOizing our Struggles and Committing Class Suicide[126].

> *In an underdeveloped country an authentic national middle class ought to consider as its bounden duty to betray the calling that fate has marked out for it, and to put itself to school with the people: in other words to put at the people's disposal the intellectual and technical capital that it has snatched when going through colonial universities*
>
> —Franz Fanon.

126 *For Mekatilili, Muthoni Nyanjiru, Mwaganu Kaggia, Kimathi and Pio Gama Pinto - asante*

> *We are fighting so that insults may no longer rule our countries, martyred and scorned for centuries, so that our peoples may never more be exploited by imperialists not only by people with white skin, because we do not confuse exploitation or exploiters with the colour of men's skins; we do not want any exploitation in our countries, not even by Black people.*
>
> —Amílcar Cabral.

Cabral said once, in an informal discussion with Afrikans in the United States, that if a thief comes into your house, it is important not to shoot at their shadow but instead to target, discerningly, the body of the intruder. He used this metaphor to illustrate and emphasize the need to look at the origins of the problems we face rather than dissecting their surface manifestations—a phenomenon that many of us in the Kenyan "civil society" have been engaging in.

In many Afrikan countries, Civil society's immersions in surface and neoliberal agendas continues, while many of those less fortunate than the demographic I fit into (middle class, over-educated in foreign lands Afrikan) risk their lives on a day-to-day basis just to survive. Members of the Afrikan working class and peasantry put their lives in jeopardy, using a varied number of scripts, and understand the connections between the oppressions that they face. And, in these their perceptive ways, make the association between lack of water in their neighborhoods and the government/ruling class servility to foreign institutions.

Meanwhile, betraying our revolutionary mission and fulfilling the fate marked out for us by colonial forces, we over-educated intellectuals keep shooting the shadows; merely exploring the surface of both our predicament and our missions through the myriad seminars/workshops/handshakes with ambassadors that often endanger genuine liberatory struggle.

This is not a bid to romanticize the masses who live in conditions and contradictions that are very unjust and complex. Rather, it is a message to us, the privileged in our society, to get engaged in more than "proposal writing warfare" and come down and sit and sacrifice comfort, ego and, above all, (willful?) ignorance, so that we may be part of the self-determination and justice required.

I too, fitting (while hopefully fighting) this demographic, need to make sure that I am doing just this: questioning my actions and position and seeking ways (often filled with unnerving and revealing mistakes about the true extent of the coloniality we live under and that we have internalized) to make sure that my mode of living (and perhaps liberation) does not further entrench oppression and neocolonialism. My class suicide needs to be more then rhetoric; it needs to be a determined decolonial action, not a job.

Now a confession.

When I was maybe seventeen and captivated by the romance of first-year social justice activism within a university in a very cold North American outpost (one that, like its neighbor, was stolen from its indigenous people through genocidal warfare), while on an early morning phone call with my father, I mustered the courage and perhaps also the audacity to declare: "Daddy, I am a communist."

To which, my middle-aged progressive/postcolonial/Nairobi-based traditional father responded, as expected, with silence.

This exchange came to mind when I was thinking about what to write here—where words need to be sparse and actions central. I decided to share this memory because it made me remember the importance of de-colonising and de-NGOizing our work and consciousness. This is because, for many in Kenya who are subject to sinister and arbitrary violence under neocolonialism, fervent declarations of unexplained, inaccessible foreign ideologies and neoliberal tenets indicate a freedom that is not free –and that are often secondary concerns, when the majority still lacks *unga* (maize meal), clean water, land, and justice.

Due to the precarious existence of the majority, they do not need us to engage in excessively abstract, subsidized and donor-funded theories that shoot at shadows. As Cabral said, to have ideology is merely to know what conditions we want to exist under, and to be honest about the situations we are forced to endure. While it is clear that the majority know what conditions they would like to live under, and demand these conditions, for the most part, NGOs and the industrial complex that supports them continue to attend to only the most superficial needs, and in this process engage in a dramatic defence of (some) civil liberties while masking and tempering the urgency of redress in the face of unrelenting injustice.

Therefore, dear over-educated, privileged Afrikan civil society activist/academic/ politician/ "proposal-writing warrior" (are you still with me?): these words act as a behest that we de-NGOize the way we live and work with our people. I recognise the material conditions that we live under require that we find ways to make an income, and often it is in NGOs that we find security. Nonetheless, often, while carrying out the work of these organisations, we fail to genuinely identify with the real strife and the real triumphs that are going on in the spaces where merely surviving is truly resistance. We cannot, however continue to, approach and observe our people through microscopes, Pajero/SUV windows or through the capacity-building terms of our donor-funded reports....

Enough.

Now, forty years after the death of Cabral, almost a century and a half after the cutting up of the continent,and the continuous intentional genocide of our communities, I insist that we stop implicating ourselves in binds that, instead of working for freedom for all of our people and an internationalism for oppressed people everywhere, are re-establishing dominion over them.

Please let USAID/SIDA/CIDA etc. not be the intermediaries between us and the masses. Let us de-NGOize our struggles, question our privilege, and (if we are employed within them) have a long-term goal to work for their demise, for Monitoring and Evaluation (M &E) and more flashy pamphlets with starving Afrikan women and children will not alter the material conditions of the majority.

We should hope that their passing (hopefully soon) will signal and occur in conjunction with an environment of genuine social and economic justice, devoid of an NGOizing of our consciousness that makes us foreign to our land and to our people and that betrays the fates that historically we should be engaged in.

And in these people-centred and people-motivated processes and liberatory fronts (which do not involve shaking hands with Hilary Clinton), we will be moving forward and questioning and undoing our conditions of poverty, imperialism, self-denial and rendition to white supremacy; taking the time (and a real good look at the target) to shoot the body (the colonial, imperialist, white supremacist, capitalist comprador body) and not the shadow. We cannot afford to miss.

References

Cabral, Amílcar. (1973), *Return to the Source: Selected Speeches by Amílcar Cabral.* New York and London, Africa Information Service.

Fanon, Frantz. (200 , 1962). *Wretched of the Earth.* New York, Grove Press.

18. AMÍLCAR CABRAL: WITH US TODAY

Adrian Harewood

I believe that I was first introduced to Amílcar Cabral in the mid-1970s, probably in the pages of *Contrast,* the Black newspaper with the largest circulation and most influence in Canada at the time. *Contrast* was a paper for which my parents, John and Hyacinth Harewood, were columnists. Suffice it to say that at the age of six or seven, I was an avid reader. Some of the other people who appeared in the pages of *Contrast* included Rosie Douglas, one of the student leaders involved in the famous Sir George Williams Affair of 1969 and later prime minister of the Caribbean island of Dominica; Pan-African scholar and author of *Rasta and Resistance*: *From Marcus Garvey to Walter Rodney,* Horace Campbell; Max Stanford (aka Muhammad Ahmad), member of the Revolutionary Action Movement and chairman of the African People's Party; Guyanese historian, Walter Rodney, author of *How Europe Underdeveloped Africa*; and the leader of the New Jewel Movement and later prime minister of Grenada, Maurice Bishop. Every year in late May, beginning in 1972, the paper would mark African Liberation Day. I can remember distinctly seeing pictures of and articles about Amílcar Cabral along with the likes of Angela Davis, Stokeley Carmichael, and Steven Biko.

I next encountered Cabral in my second or third year at McGill university in Montreal in the early 1990s. I was a member of the McGill Black Students Network (BSN) and the Southern African Committee (SAC), the main anti-apartheid grouping on campus. In fact, I was the designated librarian for the BSN and so I was fortunate to meet Cabral in text form in our fledgling library,—books like *Return to the Source* and *Unity and Struggle.* Cabral was a revelation. Reading him grounded us. He made us recognise the weapon that was theory and the necessity of marrying it to our practice.

> Always bear in mind that the people are not fighting for ideas, for the things in anyone's head. They are fighting to win material benefits, to live better and in peace, to see their lives go forward, to guarantee the future of their children.[127]

We in the BSN took our roles as student activists seriously. In fact, we saw ourselves as having a role to play in making a change on the McGill campus, within the greater Montreal community and in the world. We imagined ourselves to be young organic intellectuals in the tradition of a Walter Rodney, veritable extensions of the Montreal community on campus. There was no separation between the so-called community and us. We were inextricably linked. We strived to forge bonds with the people by bringing the community to the campus, hosting events for young school children, running various tutoring and mentoring programmes, hosting cultural events, inviting speakers like Jan Carew, Ivan Van Sertima and John Henrik Clarke, establishing a dynamic library and organising against acts of police brutality. We felt that as students it was critical that we not lose ourselves in the ivory tower that was McGill University and that we make a concerted effort to become fully implicated and integrated in the Montreal community. We brought the campus to that community.

When we read the phrase, "Tell No Lies Claim No Easy Victories," we found it both insightful and inspiring, because it suggested that how one struggled for freedom mattered. The freedom road contained numerous obstacles and a plethora of pitfalls. But there were no short cuts. There would always be setbacks and reversals. The possibility for transformation, for making history, existed in every moment each and every day. The journey, as long and arduous as it may be, was a fundamental part of achieving that freedom. To us, Amílcar Cabral was displaying a deep and genuine humanity by acknowledging that as human beings we were fallible and that in recognizing and admitting that fallibility we could, as the Asian—American activist and former member of the Johnson Forest

127 Amílcar Cabral: From "Tell No Lies, Claim No Easy Victories" (1965)

Tendency along with CLR James, Grace Lee Boggs once told me in an interview in her Detroit home "we could enlarge our humanity."

> Here and there, even among responsible workers there has been a marked tendency to let things slide…[128]
>
> —Amílcar Cabral, *Tell No Lies Claim No Easy Victories*

We regarded Cabral as a veritable standard bearer for accountability and transparency, both of which were important lessons for us as individuals and members of a political grouping. In revealing one's faults, one's errors, one was enabling the possibility for learning and transformation. No one, regardless of their station, regardless of their pedigree or prominence, was above criticism. In fact, not to criticize was to do a disservice to the collective and to the individual.

The "struggle against our own weaknesses" was, as Cabral argued, fundamental. As he put it in *The Weapon of Theory*, "this battle against ourselves—no matter what difficulties the enemy might create- is the most difficult of all, whether for the present or the future of our peoples." This idea resonated with us because it spoke to our own agency as individuals and members of a community. This was in no way to discount or diminish the depredations of imperialism. Imperialism pervaded our reality; it was a constant factor that could only be extirpated through a determined and dedicated struggle. Regardless of imperialism's configuration, those internal contradictions would remain.

Cabral would add in *The Weapon of Theory*, "We are convinced that any national or social revolution which is not based on knowledge of this fundamental reality runs the grave risk of being condemned to failure." We took this to mean that we needed to understand our grouping's internal geography; we needed to mine our interior if we wanted to achieve genuine liberation. And the only way to address those contradictions was through, as Cabral put it, "detailed knowledge of it." One had to be fully cognizant of the specificity of one's condition. Cabral's renowned

128 Cabral (1965): op cit

universalism was a product of his being grounded in the very particular human experience that was Guinea-Bissau.

We often made note of the fact that as an agronomist Cabral had travelled to all corners of Guinea-Bissau, conducting a comprehensive agricultural census. He was thus intimately familiar with the geography, the economy, the social structure and the cultural diversity of the communities that comprised his nation. He had an appreciation for the productive capacity of the soil and indeed the people of his country. Thanks to Cabral's example we learned that, as aspiring revolutionaries, we too needed to become much more familiar with our own local histories. We needed to become much more acquainted with our own surroundings. As Cabral argued … "Our own reality—however fine and attractive the reality of others may be—can only be transformed by detailed knowledge of it, by our own sacrifices and efforts."

> Demand from responsible party members that they dedicate themselves seriously to study, that they interest themselves in the things and problems of our daily life and struggle in their fundamental and essential aspect and not simply in their appearance, Learn from life. Learn from other people. Learn from books. Learn from the experience of others. Never stop learning…. Responsible members must take life seriously conscious of their responsibilities, thoughtful about carrying them out with a comradeship based on work and duty done.
> —Amílcar Cabral, *Tell No Lies, Claim No Easy Victories* (1965)

Cabral's commitment to education and self-improvement was one that we shared and took seriously. This was not some abstract notion. Our studies outside the classroom were as important to us as the assignments we were given inside. We did not reify the knowledge gained at our university as being any more valuable or fundamental than other knowledge, whether acquired from the Black high school students who told us about the particular challenges that they faced within the education system, the broken Congolese immigrant teacher who told us about the humiliations he'd suffered in his class and staff room, **or** from the elders in our community, like the Vincentian politico and former West Indian test cricketer Alfie Roberts. He alerted us to the vital role that Montreal played in the freedom struggles of the 1960s, particularly as the host city for the famed Congress of Black Writers of 1968, and the role that his former group, the Montreal-based Conference Committee on West Indian Affairs, which included the likes of scholar Robert "Bobby" Hill—UCLA professor and future editor in Chief of the Marcus Garvey and UNIA Papers-, Franklyn Harvey, Tim Hector -Antiguan journalist and founder of the Antiguan Caribbean Liberation Movement, and the future Canadian Senator Anne Cools, played in reviving the career of Trinidadian intellectual CLR James—author of such seminal texts as *The Black Jacobins* and *Beyond A Boundary.*

We always made a point of trying to share rather than hoard knowledge. We took it as our mission to democratise information, make it accessible to the masses. It was why we opened the Black Students Network library to our fellow students, but also to members of Montreal's Black community. In the days before the Internet we would always be carrying books by Frantz Fanon, Aime Cesaire, Manning Marable, Alberto Memmi, Audre Lorde, Cheikh Anta Diop, Eduardo Galeano, James Baldwin, Paolo Freire and Patricia Williams. We also carried pamphlets and articles that we had photocopied from journals, newspapers and magazines, like *Race and Class, Radical History, Race Today, NACLA Report on the Americas*, *The Guardian, Signs: Journal of Women in Culture and Society, The Black Scholar, Z Magazine, The Monthly Review, Africa Confidential, The Nation, The Progressive, In These Times*, the anti-apartheid *Journal of the South African Communist Party* and pass them on to anyone we felt might be interested. We distributed reading lists and would bring our fellow students up to the periodical section on the second floor of McGill's McLennan library and alert them to the wealth of information that was in their midst.

We would also share cassette tapes of lectures and speeches by the likes of CLR James, Walter Rodney, Edward Said and David Barsamian, films by Marlon Riggs, Haile Gerima, Isaac Julien, Julie Dash, Dionne Brand, Jennifer Hodge Da Silva, Claire Prieto, Roger McTair, John Akomfrah and the Black Audio Collective, and the music of Linton Kwesi Johnson, Young Disciples, Mutabaruka, Thomas Mapfumo, Steel Pulse, Living Colour, Public Enemy, Tribe Called Quest, Arrested Development, Soul II Soul.

To quote Cabral from a party directive from 1965 entitled *Tell No Lies, Claim No Easy Victories*,

> Every responsible member must have the courage of his responsibilities, exacting from others a proper respect for his work and properly respecting the work of others.

At one point I began encountering difficulties as an organiser within our grouping. I was making a lot of commitments, a lot of promises and not always following through. It was becoming a problem. Indeed, my ability to fulfill my duties was being hampered by my faltering reputation. One of my closest comrades, my best friend in BSN, soon pulled me aside and essentially read me the riot act. He understood the need for all of us within our grouping to be accountable and responsible. He took it upon himself to call me out and alert me to my errors but also to the possibilities that existed for transformation. His solution for my organisational issues was for me to purchase an agenda. I was, of course, mortified by the situation. It was a painful but necessary scolding. My "brother" was alerting me to my deficiencies and failure because he believed that I was capable of better. He understood, like Cabral, that we all must be accountable both for our actions and our inaction. Almost a quarter century on he is the godfather of my son and I am the godfather of his daughter. Today, I understand his intervention today as an act of love.

> We are not fighting simply in order to hoist a flag in our countries and to have a national anthem... We are fighting so that the insults no longer rule our countries, martyred and scorned for centuries, so that our people may never more be exploited by imperialists- not only by Europeans, not only by people with

> white skin because we do not confuse exploitation or exploiters with the colour of men's skin. We do not want any exploitation in our countries not even by Black people.[129]

For Cabral, national revolution was but the first step. It was a step whereby the anticolonial forces gained independence. National liberation was truly about wresting control of the productive forces of society. The goal was to create a new man and a new woman. Indirect control of productive forces by external interests served as the last barrier to genuine national liberation. He insisted that national liberation had to be more than being able to display the rather trivial trappings or symbols of political independence.

> National liberation must put an end not only to suffering but to backwardness. It must enable Africans to rejoin the mainstream of human history and human evolution from which they have been excluded by imperialism. The struggle for national liberation must transform the masses from their present passivity and dependence on others. It must develop in them and through them the power, the will, the capacity, and the structures to govern their own accelerated development....Only through this fundamental transformation in attitudes, and through the creation of new infrastructures by the people themselves, can the social productive forces of the people be liberated.

When Cabral talked about "returning to the source," he was urging Africans to draw from the well of their own traditions to create their own national culture. There was a lucidity and flexibility in Cabral's thought. He seemed, in a word, free. A wholly independent actor; one can see this in his refusal to be boxed in to any ideological corner or political corner. Not only did he seem to us to be intellectually free but he also exhibited

---

129 Amílcar Cabral: From the "Nationalist Movements of the Portuguese Colonies" (1965)

a kind of freedom of the person, a freedom of the spirit that was as refreshing as it was revealing. He wasn't wedded to fundamentalist racialist attitudes, a phenomenon that re-emerged in the 1990s in much of North America at the same time as a reawakening of Black consciousness on campuses and in communities, manifested by an explosion of interest in the life and teachings of Malcolm X.

> We are fighting for the freedom of our people—to free our people and to allow them to be able to love any kind of human being. You cannot love when you are a slave. It is very difficult.[130]

Somehow Cabral escaped the racialist straitjacket that often prevented some of us from fully expressing our humanity. This does not mean that he did not see aspects of the world through the prism of race, but he did not allow race to become his prison.

Finally, we were attracted to Cabral's internationalism. Cabral lived his Pan-Africanism through his practice. He worked in solidarity with his comrades in Angola, Mozambique, South Africa, and the United States—anywhere people were engaged in the righteous pursuit of freedom.

Amílcar Cabral may have been from a small place, yet forty years after his most untimely death, his struggle and the struggle of the people of his tiny West African nation for genuine liberation continues to inspire many beyond their borders.

---

130 Amílcar Cabral: From "Connecting the Struggles: An Informal Chat with Black Americans" (1972)

19. REVOLUTIONARY DEMOCRACY, CLASS-CONSCIOUSNESS, AND CROSS-CLASS MOVEMENT BUILDING

LESSONS FROM AMÍLCAR CABRAL

Maria Poblet

As a Left community organiser in the United States, working with oppressed and exploited people in the San Francisco Bay Area of California, I have benefitted greatly from Amílcar Cabral's work and thought. I am part of a broader growing political tendency that is building a working class base for the Left in urban centres inside the United States, innovating with organising fights for housing and transportation, immigrant's rights, and women's rights, building race-conscious class unity, particularly between oppressed communities of colour who are pitted against each other at the bottom of the economy in the US, and have a strong basis for solidarity with working class and poor people throughout the world.

Like a lot of radical political organising in the 21st century, our tendency, in part, comes out of critiques of the twentieth century socialist models. From rejecting the authoritarianism of Stalin, to broadening the concept of the revolutionary subject to include a broader set of marginalised groups not limited to the industrial working class, to rejecting race-blind class reductionism, to lifting up the liberatory aspects of cultural traditions amongst oppressed people.

Amílcar Cabral's work has been profoundly influential to the development of this political tendency, amongst many others around the world. His theory provides a way to engage with the shortfalls of twentieth century models of radical change that do not throw the class struggle baby out with the Soviet bathwater. Cabral is a luminary amongst the broader set of Third World Marxists who, from Nicaragua to Kenya, led successful national liberation movements. He formed and led the PAIGC, and was instrumental in strategizing the successful overthrow of Portuguese colonialism, not only in his home of Cape Verde & Guinea-Bissau, but also throughout the continent of Africa. He was core to the development of a broader Pan-Africanist tendency, which built strong links to liberation movements in Asia and Latin America, and had inspiring, global impact.

Even in the United States, the belly of the beast, in such a markedly different time, place and set of conditions than the ones Cabral operated in, we have a lot to learn from his work. He grappled with theoretical questions that have parallels to the ones we face today. And, he reached a level of depth and sophistication regarding movement strategy that we have yet to achieve in the 21st century.

Revolutionary Democracy

Today's emerging movements in the West hold democracy to be a core value. They have have emphasized collective decision-making as an attempt to increase engagement, inclusion, and community control. This approach, heavily influenced by Anarchism and Zapatísmo, attempts to remedy problems attributed to top-down approaches by Left political parties of the twentieth century. The vast majority of the people involved in those movements have little knowledge of Cabral's insights on the question of what he called "Revolutionary Democracy."

Cabral's work presents a different approach, in a very different context, with some of the same values. His advice to militants in his organisation reflected a commitment to revolutionary democracy: 'Do not be afraid of the people and persuade the people to take part in all the decisions which concern them—this is the basic condition of revolutionary democracy, which little by little we must achieve in accordance with the development of our struggle and our life.'[131] He addresses this question in a dialectical way, acknowledging what our movements have been

131 Cabral, A. "General Watchwords" speech to PAIGC militants, from *Unity and Struggle*, 1979

beginning to understand: that oppression and exploitation rob people of the capacity to self-govern, both structurally and psychologically, and that building that capacity is a core task within the revolutionary struggle, and not after. This very same assessment is built into radical community organising that seeks to develop working class leaders who can advance the social justice movement as a whole. Structures of support, capacity-building, and decision making that we have built in the community organising sector prioritize people directly impacted by the problems of capitalism, and are attempts to build that kind of revolutionary democracy within our progressive movements.

Cabral called for both collective and individual leadership, and theorized the role of individual leadership as part of a collective whole. He said 'The leader must be the faithful interpreter of the will and the aspirations of the revolutionary majority and not the lord of power'[132]. This approach affirms the role of leaders in and developing the vision emerging from the people, while not putting leaders on a pedestal of unchecked power. To that end he called on militants to 'Tell no lies, claim no easy victories,' and encouraged a practice of profound humility, honest [133]evaluation, and integrity throughout his organisation.

He also theorized collective leadership:

> To lead collectively, in a group, is to study questions jointly, to find their best solution, and to take decisions jointly, it is to benefit from experience and intelligence of each and all so as to lead, order and command better. In collective leadership, each person in the leadership must have his own clearly defined duties and is responsible for the carrying out of decisions taken by the group in regard to his duties... But to lead collectively is not and cannot be, as some suppose, to give to all and everyone the right of uncontrolled views and initiatives, to create anarchy (lack of government), disorder, contradiction between leaders, empty

132 Ibid.
133 Ibid

> arguments, a passion for meetings without results. Still less is it to give vent to incompetence, ignorance, intellectual foolhardiness…In the framework of the collective leadership, we must respect the opinion of more experienced comrades who for their part must help the others with less experience to learn and to improve their work. In the framework of the collective leadership there is always one or other comrade who has a higher standing as party leader and who for this reason has more individual responsibility…We must allow prestige to these comrades, help them to have constantly higher standing, but not allow them to monopolise (take over) the work and responsibility of the group. We must, on the other hand, struggle against the spirit of slackness, and disinterest, the fear of responsibilities, the tendency to agree with everything, to obey blindly without thinking.[134]

The PAIGC was so committed to being an instrument of the people, that, in 1973, after more than a decade of armed struggle, when they finally defeated Portugal militarily, they did not storm the palace of power. Rather, they returned to the people, conducting a vote of confidence amongst the population, affirming their approval through a popular vote before officially taking up governance. This referendum is a powerful example of revolutionary democracy.

What would today's movements look like if we had highly effective, collectively controlled instruments of political struggle? What would organisations look like if we held individuals to high standards of integrity, provided structured developmental support, and consciously built our capacities towards governance?

Reimagining political power is a central challenge to today's twenty-first century generation of freedom fighters. I have been part of experiments in structure that sought to uphold the value of collective leadership, from flat collectives to ultra-democratic centralism, to developmental hierarchies that focused on in-depth training and mentorship for emerging leaders. These approaches, none of them perfect, have re-enforced the

134 Ibid.

core lessons that Cabral offers: the need for clarity on the outcomes you seek, the necessity for alignment and accountability, and the value of collective leadership amongst people who share a political goal.

Class Analysis & Class Consciousness

Cabral argued that no revolution could be truly successful without leadership from the working and peasant classes whose work produced the wealth of the country and of its colonisers, and whose strategic position was powerful enough to turn the tables on economic injustice. And that a revolutionary vision of liberation would not be satisfied by simply replacing Portuguese political and economic control, putting the national bourgeoisie at the top of the exploitative structure created by colonialism.

Gaining political representation or even political control would not be sufficient to truly change the economic structure that colonialism put in place. Neither would it be possible or ideal to return to the way indigenous societies were organised before colonialism. So, Cabral argued, the task of revolutionaries was to make possible the development of national productive forces (the capacity of Cape Verde & Guinea-Bissau to sustain an economy independent of Portugal), while laying the ideological foundations and movement infrastructure to fight against exploitation that would emerge under the rule of the national bourgeoisie.

This sophisticated strategy came from a deep conviction in the fundamental right of his people to live free of exploitation of any kind. He described the national liberation movement in this way: 'We are fighting so that…our peoples may never more be exploited by imperialists not only by people with white skin, because we do not confuse exploitation or exploiters with the colour of men's skins; we do not want any exploitation in our countries, not even by Black people.' [135]

Today's reality is one where the exploiting class is no longer made up only of European colonial rulers. There are plenty of political and corporate leaders from oppressed nationalities, some of whom use their

135 Cabral, A., *African Communist*, No. 53, second quarter 1973

oppressed identity as an excuse to not only exploit others, but to celebrate that exploitation as if it were a hallmark of progress.

The question of class exploitation was core to Cabral's strategy, and is just as important for freedom fighters today. Without organising working class people from oppressed nationalities, our movements lack the strategic base of power that can challenge capitalism's core. Without organising working class and peasant communities, our movements can easily remain focused on social issues without tackling the underlying economic structure of capitalism. That is why organising working class people is so important to building a successful movement towards economic democracy.

He also detailed the role of privileged layers of society in the revolutionary project. The fact that the national petit bourgeoisie live the contrast between the world of the coloniser and the world of the colonised, he said, could be a catalyst for revolutionary consciousness. In fact, he theorized, these layers of society who were privileged in some ways but still not owners of the means of production were likely to see the need for national liberation sooner, given their role in society and in the economy:

> The colonial situation, which does not permit the development of a native pseudo-bourgeoisie and in which the popular masses do not generally reach the necessary level of political consciousness before the advent of the phenomenon of national liberation, offers the petit bourgeoisie the historical opportunity of leading the struggle against foreign domination, since by nature of its objective and subjective position (higher standard of living than that of the masses, more frequent contact with the agents of colonialism, and hence more chances of being humiliated, higher level of education and political awareness, etc.) it is the stratum which most rapidly becomes aware of the need to free itself from foreign domination. This historical responsibility is assumed by the sector of the petty bourgeoisie which, in the colonial context, can be called revolutionary, while other sectors retain the doubts

> characteristic of these classes or ally themselves to colonialism so as to defend, albeit illusorily, their social situation. [136]

Organisers in the twenty-first century can learn from this type of detailed assessment based on the time, place and conditions, and should be asking ourselves these same questions. What is the most strategic role for privileged layers of society in social movements today?

The economic crisis has pushed more and more racially privileged and self-identified middle class people into precariousness and even poverty. Foreclosures, unemployment, loss of pensions, and lack of basic resources like healthcare are no longer problems unique to the self-identified working classes. While it is true that these privileged sectors have not felt the brunt of the burden of the failures of neoliberalism, denying their experiences, or writing them off as irrelevant to the movement is a self-marginalising mistake. Unless we can leverage this opportunity to provide new entry points into the movement, and engage the falling "middle class" in the project of fighting for economic justice for the working class as a whole, our movement will not be able to grow to the scale we need to win. Nor will we be able to capture the imagination of society as a whole.

How to best engage privileged sectors is a complicated question. Just as capitalism has robbed oppressed and exploited people of leadership capacities, it has ingrained privileged people with a complex of superiority that undercuts our collective capacity for revolutionary democracy. A more nuanced understanding that recognises that we all have experiences of privilege and oppression allows us to build a more intersectional analysis. Just as Cabral theorized the unique potential of a sector of the petit bourgeoisie, while positioning the working class as the motive force of change, our movement should also get clear on the role of particular sectors of the falling "middle class," in a broad multiracial, multiclass, multigender movement led by working class people.

---

136 Cabral, A. "The Weapon of Theory" Address delivered to the First Tricontinental Conference of the Peoples of Asia, Africa and Latin America in Havana. January 1966

Class Suicide and Cross-Class Movement Building

This type of cross-class movement building requires a particular framework. Freedom fighters from privileged backgrounds, whom Cabral identified as an important force within the broader front against imperialism, would need to gain a new kind of consciousness and develop a core sense of revolutionary ethics if they were to make real contributions to the movement.

He called for a profound transformation, "in order to truly fulfill the role in the national liberation struggle, the revolutionary petit bourgeoisie must be capable of committing suicide as a class in order to be reborn as revolutionary workers, completely identified with the deepest aspirations of the people to which they belong. This alternative—to betray the revolution or to commit suicide as a class—constitutes the dilemma of the petit bourgeoisie in the general framework of the national liberation struggle."

Class suicide is an amazing concept; a vision of profound transformation and alignment with the revolutionary project, on a collective level that breaks open the next stage of development for the movement.

This is particularly relevant in the face of the ongoing crisis in the capitalist economy and in the world's ecology, as more and more people are downwardly mobile or experiencing ecological collapse and are mobilized to join emerging movements. Not only is there an opportunity for class-consciousness as wealth becomes more and more polarized, there is also an opportunity for privileged sectors of society to develop the moral consciousness that can help create the conditions for the development of twenty-first century liberation movements.

Conclusion

Theory, according to Cabral, was a crucial weapon in the struggle. He agitated for militants to engage in intellectual work, saying, "The ideological deficiency, not to say the total lack of ideology, within the national liberation movements—which is basically due to ignorance of the historical reality which these movements claim to transform—constitutes one of the greatest weaknesses of our struggle against imperialism, if not the greatest weakness of all."[137]

He challenged militants to engage critically, but also advised, "Do not confuse the reality you live in with the ideas you have in your head,"[138] and warned them, "We are not going to eliminate imperialism by shouting insults at it."[139] He challenged freedom fighters to train themselves ideologically, and to simultaneously ground their efforts in the aspirations of everyday people.

> Always bear in mind that the people are not fighting for ideas, for the things in anyone's head. They are fighting to win material benefits, to live better and in peace, to see their lives go forward, to guarantee the future of their children… [140]

This dialectical approach that intertwined theory and practice made Amílcar Cabral one of the greatest visionaries of the twentieth century. Even though his theories are deeply rooted in the movement for national independence in Cape Verde and Guinea-Bissau decades ago, they have a much broader reach and meaning. From the groundbreaking concept of class suicide, to the imagination and application of revolutionary democracy, Cabral's contributions have the potential to support a successful re-emergence of social movements in the twenty-first century.

---

137 Ibid.

138 Cabral, A. "General Watchwords" speech to PAIGC militants, from *Unity and Struggle*,_1979

139 Ibid.

140 Cabral, A. *Semin rio de quadros*, Conakry, 1969

20. TELLING NO LIES IS NOT EASY

A REFLECTION ON FOLLOWING CABRAL'S WATCHWORDS

William Minter

Although I was engaged with liberation struggles in Mozambique and Angola from the mid-1960s, I never had the opportunity to meet Amílcar Cabral. Nor have I ever visited the countries for whose freedom he lived and died. But like countless others in Africa and around the world, I have taken inspiration from the clear-minded guidance and analysis he provided while leading the African Party for the Independence of Guinea-Bissau and Cape Verde.

For me the watchwords from Cabral that have meant the most are the call to "tell no lies, claim no easy victories." There are many characteristics required for effective participation in struggles for social justice. But one is surely the determination to base one's actions on an analysis of concrete realties, be honest with ourselves about difficulties we face, and, as Cabral noted in another context, "Always bear in mind that the people are not fighting for ideas, for the things in anyone's head. They are fighting to win material benefits, to live better and in peace, to see their lives go forward…to preserve the future of their children."[141]

While I have often cited these words, the request for this article prompted me to look a bit deeper into the context and to seek out the Portuguese-language original of the "General Watchwords" for the party from which they were taken. Both the Portuguese and my translation

141 *Guinea-Bissau: Towards Final Victory!: Selected Speeches and Documents from PAIGC* (Richmond, Canada: Liberation Support Movement, 1974), 32. Although appearing in the collection in the same text as "tell no lies," this is in fact from another document, the Portuguese original of which I have been unable to locate.

into English are included at the end of this article. It is clear "tell no lies" was not an isolated slogan, but part of a complex reflection on the need for criticism and self-criticism amongst members of the movement.

In trying to apply those guidelines today, in a context almost fifty years removed, we must, as Cabral insisted take concrete realities into account. We are far from the era of disciplined and apparently unified liberation movements (with both their strengths and weaknesses). While the goal of national political freedom has been attained, the broader goals for which Cabral fought are far from achieved, not least in Guinea-Bissau, which was the terrain of his party's armed struggle.

With globalised communications, his further admonitions, such as "Do not hide anything from the masses of the people" and "Practice and defend the truth, always the truth, to militants, leaders, and the people, whatever the difficulties the knowledge of the truth can create" are just as hard to implement as in his time, and perhaps even more so. While PAIGC militants may have been able to address "the people" in gatherings in the bush, the constituencies for today's social justice movements are almost always dispersed and diverse enough that they can hardly be gathered in one place. Messages through multiple technologies to "militants" and "the people" are inevitably seen, heard, and interpreted or misinterpreted by multiple other audiences as well.

That said I am convinced that the fundamental principles of Cabral's guidance on criticism and self-criticism still apply. And these watchwords fit within the broader context of his determination to base strategy and action on sober analysis of realities.[142] It is an eminently "scientific" approach, where theory is used not as a lazy substitute for empirical investigation but as a guide to it. It is an approach which recognised that the same formula could not be applied to situations as different as Guinea-Bissau and Cape Verde, or even to different regions within Guinea-Bissau. It is one in which fighting against an "enemy" never obscured the recognition that enemy forces were composed of human beings, many of

142 See also "Start out from the reality of our land to be realists," in Amílcar Cabral, *Unity and Struggle* (New York: Monthly Review Press, 1979) 44-63).

whom might become friends under other circumstances. In this, Cabral shared the conviction of leaders such as Eduardo Mondlane and Samora Machel of Mozambique, that distinguishing friends and enemies on the basis of race, nationality, institutional affiliation, or other generic characteristics was a fundamental mistake. And that assuming individuals and political structures could not change was a recipe for failure in the struggle. "Know well our own strength and the enemy strength" was also a mandate to know how to win new allies, including amongst the enemy forces themselves.

This short essay can hardly be adequate for an extensive discussion of the application of Cabral's principles to specific situations facing us today. But it would be incomplete without at least some mention of areas in which, in my opinion, progressive forces have been particularly weak in recent years, evading Cabral's imperatives to investigate concrete realities and to speak the truth.

Let me very briefly address two areas, as examples. One concerns the international debates about political conflicts in Africa, including recent or forthcoming military interventions. The second is the sensitive issue of whether progressive as well as mainstream nongovernmental organisations are willing to live up to Cabral's directives about truth-telling; or, in other words, to practice for themselves the accountability and transparency they freely demand of African and Western governments.

Every internal conflict on the continent features different narratives from parties to the conflict, which are taken up and propagated by international allies. It would be presumptuous for anyone to assume that there is one easy "truth" in the conflicts in Zimbabwe, Libya, or Mali—to cite only a few prominent examples. The only country of the three I know enough about and have enough personal trusted contacts in to write about at any length is Zimbabwe (see, for example, my 2010 article with Briggs Bomba: http://www.africafocus.org/docs10/zim1004.php). But in reposting material from other sources in *AfricaFocus Bulletin*, and providing brief introductory editor's notes, I have to distinguish between analyses I regard as worth reading and those which are so dubious they should rank as "lies," or at least, using a term also cited by Cabral, as based on superficial "appearances."[143] Perhaps I am remiss in not naming names falling amongst the latter. But they include those who, decades after ZANU-PF ceased to be a liberation movement to become the enforcer of a new repressive and oligarchical system, insist on supporting the incumbent regime in Zimbabwe simply because its critics include Western governments. It includes those who see developments in Libya as primarily the outcome of a Western plot and disregard the agency of Libyans themselves in his overthrow of Qaddafi, or dismiss his opponents as Western dupes. And it includes those who think there is any easy answer to the current question of whether to intervene and who should intervene against the Islamic extremists who have devastated Northern Mali.

Rejecting such interpretations as "lies," or based on "appearances," does not imply that there are not also real questions about the motives and strategies of other opposing forces, both internal and international. It is not a blanket endorsement of those who now oppose ZANJ-PF or the Islamists in Northern Mali, or those who contributed to the overthrow of the Qaddafi regime. It is simply to say that in none of these situations, or in other conflicts on the continent, is simply opposing what the United States does or what the West does a substitute for analysis of the concrete realities of each country, its surrounding region, and changing international power balances. Progressives may and will reach different conclusions about the best course of action after making such analyses. But the ideological shortcut of making judgments based on "ideas in people's heads" rather than analysis of complex realities, is clearly one that Amílcar Cabral would have rejected.

Finally, a few incomplete and admittedly inadequate words about nongovernmental organisations and the pressures that work against transparency and accountability to broader constituencies. A high proportion of such groups, both mainstream and progressive, are governed by self-perpetuating boards of directors. For funding they depend either on a small number of large institutional donors (foundations or indirect

143 You can see what I decided I thought worth reading, amongst sources available to me, at http://www.africafocus.org/country/countries.php, and clicking on the relevant country name for the AfricaFocus Bulletins on the country.

government support) or fundraising appeals to a large number of individual donors, most of whom have no role apart from sending in their donations. In most cases, membership dues from a engaged and active membership are only a small proportion of income at best, and the role of such stakeholders in governance is most often token at best and commonly none at all. The boards of directors therefore may have little sense of accountability to their activist supporters or feel any real obligation to keep them informed.

It would be a mistake to interpret accountability and transparency as a dogmatic mandate to never have private internal discussions or to "tell everything," regardless of the consequences. Despite his call below to tell the truth, regardless of the difficulties it may cause, Cabral was well aware of the need for discretion in public discussion of sensitive issues, such as the difficulties his party faced from host countries such as Senegal and Guinea (Conakry), or the support the struggle received from Cuba. Nevertheless, I think many nongovernmental organisations, including progressive ones, most often err on the side of secrecy in speaking with their supporters about difficulties faced.

For much of the history of the organisations with which I have been most involved over my time as an activist, most notably the predecessor organisations of Africa Action (Africa Fund, American Committee on Africa, Washington Office on Africa, and the Africa Policy Information Centre), this structural flaw was balanced by the fact that foundation income was minimal and government income nonexistent. The bulk of individual donations, both large and small, came from engaged activists who expected and received accountability from those governing the organisations, including regular reports on programme and financial status.

Yet all progressive activists are well aware of crises in multiple organisations run by progressive people whose good intentions we respect, in which the constituencies who have helped build the organisation are kept in the dark about current developments reflecting weaknesses. It would not be appropriate to go into details, so as not to violate Cabral's companion insistence in the text below that criticism should not edge over into "intrigues." But it is surely no secret to anyone concerned, for example, that those who contributed their writing skills to Pambazuka News over more than a decade have had no report from the governing board of Fahamu on the crisis which led to the resignation of the founding editor.

Most painful to many of us involved in Africa solidarity work in the United States has been the prolonged crisis at Africa Action. In August 2010 staff unexpectedly failed to receive their salaries. It was subsequently discovered that a reserved endowment had been fully drained, in part by fraud by an office manager and in part by use of endowment funds for operating expenses. Since then, the organisation's board has managed to keep a shell of the organisation in existence. Yet more than two years later there has still been no coherent accounting to the organisation's constituency of what happened nor a strategy for the future which could address the crisis of confidence among former staff, board, and supporters of the organisation. Despite the good intentions of the board members, it is likely that the failure to follow Cabral's advice by confronting hard realities and "telling the truth" will have done as much or more damage to the organisation as did the original financial crisis.

I am well aware that these brief remarks fall far short of any "full truth" or even a comprehensive analysis of any of the issues raised. But hopefully they may serve at least as a call to follow Cabral's example in analyzing concrete realities more deeply rather than relying on appearances, and in using criticism constructively to learn from our own and other's mistakes.

Excerpts from Chapter VIII, "Apply Party Principles in Practice," in *General Watchwords*, November 1965.

Portuguese original from "Palavras de Ordem Gerais," in P.A.I.G.C.: unidade e luta / Amílcar Cabral (Lisbon: Nova Aurora, 1974), 9-66.

English translation below by William Minter

[Alternate English translation of full text of "General Watchwords" is available in Amílcar Cabral, *Unity and Struggle* (New York: Monthly Review Press, 1979), pages 246-249.]

1. Develop the spirit of criticism among activists and officials.

Give everyone at each level, the opportunity to criticize, give their opinion about the work and the behaviour or actions of others. Accept criticism, wherever it comes from, as a contribution to improving the work of the Party, as an expression of active interest in the internal life of our organisation. Remember always that to criticize is not to speak ill or engage in intrigues. Criticism is and must be the act of expressing one's frank opinion openly, in front of those concerned, based on the facts and in the spirit of justice, in order to evaluate the thought and action of others, with the aim of improving that thought and action. Criticism is to build, to help build, to show genuine interest in the work of others and the improvement of that work.

Combat severely evil tongues, intrigues, 'so-and-so says,' unfair and unfounded criticism. To evaluate the thought and action of a comrade does not necessarily mean to speak ill of them. To speak highly, praise, encourage, or stimulate is also part of a critique. Always be vigilant against personal vanity and pride, but don't stint on praise for those who deserve it. Offer praise gladly and frankly to all those whose thought and action serves well the progress of the party. ...

Learn from the mistakes we make or that others make, to avoid making new mistakes, to not fall into the traps that others have fallen in. Criticizing someone does not mean setting yourself against them or victimizing them. It is showing that we are all interested in their work, that we are part of one corporate body, that one person's mistakes affect us all, and that we are vigilant, as friends and comrades, to help them overcome their shortcomings and increasingly contribute to the improvement of the Party.

But critique (proof of the willingness of others to help us or our willingness to help others) should be supplemented by self-criticism (proof of our own willingness to help ourselves improve our thinking and our action).

Develop in all militants, leaders, and combatants, the spirit of self-criticism: the ability of each to make a concrete analysis of their own work, to distinguish good from bad, to recognise their own mistakes and to discover the causes and consequences of these errors. Making a self-criticism is not just to say "yes, I admit my fault, my mistake, and I apologize," while getting ready to commit new faults and new errors. It is not to pretend to repent, while still being convinced that the other person just doesn't understand. Nor should self-criticism be performed as a ritual, while continuing to make mistakes.

Self-criticism is not doing penance. It is an act of honesty, courage, camaraderie, and awareness of our responsibilities, a proof of our willingness to do our duty and do it well, a manifestation of our determination to be better every day and give our best contribution to the advancement of our Party. An honest self-criticism does not require absolution: it is a commitment we make to our conscience not to commit more errors, to accept our responsibilities to others, and to mobilize all our capabilities to do more and better. Self-criticism is to rebuild oneself to better serve.

4. Practice revolutionary democracy in all aspects of the life of the party.

Everyone responsible for leadership must assume their responsibilities with courage, should demand the respect of others for their activity, and should respect the work of others. Do not hide anything from the masses of the people. Don't tell lies. fight lies when they are told. Don't disguise difficulties, errors, and failures. Do not trust in easy victories nor in appearances.

Revolutionary democracy demands that we fight opportunism and not tolerate errors, baseless excuses, friendships and camaraderie based on interests contrary to the interests of the Party and the people, or the conviction that any leader is irreplaceable.

Practice and defend the truth, always the truth, to militants, leaders, and the people, whatever the difficulties the knowledge of the truth can create.

Portuguese original:

1. Desenvolver o espirito da crítica entre os militantes e responsáveis.

Dar a todos, em cada nivel, a oportunidade de críticar, de dar a sua opinião sobre o trabalho e o comportamento ou a acção dos outros. Aceitar a crítica, donde quer qua ela venha, como uma contribuição para melhorar o trabalho do Partido, como uma manifestação de interesse active pela vida interna da nossa organização. Lembrar-se sempre que críticar não é dizer mal nem fazer intrigas. Críticar é e deve ser o acto de exprimir uma. opinião franca, aberta, diante dos interessados, com base nos factos e com espírito de justiça, para apreciar o pensamento e a acção dos outros, com o objectivo de melhorar esse pensamento e essa acção. Críticar é construir, ajudar a construir, fazer prova de interesse sincero pelo trabalho dos outros, pela melhoria desse trabalho.

Combater severamente a má lingua, a mania das intrigas, o 'diz-que-diz,' as críticas injustas e sem fundamento. Apreciar o pensamento e a acção dum camarada não é necessariamente dizer mal. Dizer bem, elogiar, encorajar, estimuar—também é críticar. Sempre vigilantes contra as vaidades e orgulhos pessoais, devemos no entanto poupar elogios a quem os merece. Elogiar com alegria, com franqueza. diante dos outros, todo aquele cujo pensamento e acção servem bem o progresso do Partido. Devemos igualmente aplicar uma crítica justa, denunciar francamente, censurar, condenar e exigir a condenação de todos aqueles que praticam actos contrários ao progresso e aos interesses do Partido; combater cara a cara os erros e faltas, ajudar os outros a melhorar o seu trabalho. Tirar lição de cada erro que cometemos ou que os outros cometem, para evitar cometer novos erros, para cairmos nas asneiras em que os outros cairam. críticar um camarada não quer dizer pôr-se contra o camarada, fazer um sacrificio em que o camarada é a vïtima: é mostrar-lhe que estamos todos interessados no seu trabalho, que somos um e um só corpo, que os erros dele prejudicam a nós todos, e que estamos vigilantes, como amigos e camaradas, para ajudé-lo a vencer as suas deficiências e a contribuir cada vez mais para que o Partido seja cada vez melhor.

...

Mas a crítica (prova da vontade dos outros de nos ajudar ou da nossa vontade de ajudar os outros) deve ser completada pela autocrítica (prova da. nossa própria vontade de nos ajudarmos a nós mesmos a melhorar o nosso pensamento e a nossa acção).

Desenvolver em todos os militantes, responséveis e combatentes, o espirito da autocrítica: a. capacidade de cada um fazer uma análise concreta do seu pr6prio trabalho, de distinguir nele o que está bem do que está mal, de reconhecer os seus próprios erros e de descobrir as causas e as consequências desses erros. Fazer uma autocrítica. néo é apenas dizer sim, reconheço a minha falta, o meu erro—e peço perdão, ficando logo pronto para cometer novas faltas, novos erros. Não é fingir-se arrependido do mal que fez, e ficar, no fundo, convencido de que os outros é que n~ao o compreendem. Nem tão-pouco fazer autocrítica e fazer uma cerimónia para depois poder ficar com a. consciéncia tranquila e continuar a cometer erros.

Autocríticar-se não é pagar um responso ou uma bula nem é fazer penitência. A autocrítica é um acto de franqueza, de coragem, de camaradagem e de consciência das nossas responsabilidades, uma. prova. da nossa vontade de cumprir e de cumprir bem, uma manifestação da nossa. determinação de ser cada dia melhor e dar uma. melhor contribuição para o progresso do nosso Partido. Uma autocrítica sincera não exige necessariamente uma absolvição: é um compromisso que fazemos com a nossa consciência. para não cometermos mais erros; é fazer aceitar as nossas responsabilidades diante dos outros e mobilizar todas as nossas capacidades para. fazer mais e melhor. Autocríticar-se é reconstruir-se a si mesmo, para melhor servir.

...

4. Praticar, em todos os aspectos da vida do Partido, a democracia revolucionária.

Cada responsável deve assumir com coragem as suas responsabilidades, deve exigir dos outros o respeito pela sua actividade e deve respeitar a actividade dos outros. Não esconder nada às massas populares, não mentir, combater a mentira, não disfarçar as dificuldades, os erros e insucessos, não acreditar em vitárias fáceis, nem nas aparêcias.

A democracia revolucionária exige que devemos combater o oportunismo, a. tolerância diante dos erros, as desculpas sem fundamento, as amizades e a camaradagem com base em interesses contrários aos do Partido e do povo, a mania de que um ou outro responszivel é insubstituivel no seu posto.

Praticar e defender a verdade, sempre a verdade, diante dos militantes, dos responséveis, do povo, sejam quais forem as dificuldades que o conhecimento da verdade possa criar.

21. AMÍLCAR CABRAL

TRIBUTE TO AN ORIGINAL AND REVOLUTIONARY THINKER

Demba Moussa Dembélé

Introduction

Amílcar Cabral, the founder of the PAIGC,[144] the Liberation movement that led the armed struggle against Portuguese colonialism in Guinea-Bissau and Cape Verde, is probably one the finest thinkers among the liberation movement leaders in Africa. In fact, Amílcar Cabral was an authentic revolutionary intellectual in the tradition of Frantz Fanon.

His assassination by agents of the fascist Portuguese colonial state on January 20, 1973 deprived Africa of one of its foremost visionary and charismatic leaders. This tribute on the occasion of the 40th anniversary of his assassination aims to honor the memory of a man who dedicated his life to the liberation of his country and Africa and to examine the relevance of his life and actions for today's struggles.

Ideological and Political Background

Growing up in a colonised country, Amílcar Cabral witnessed firsthand the oppression and humiliations inflicted on his people by the Portuguese colonial state. During his high-school years, Cabral observed not only the humiliations of his people by the colonial power but also the devastations caused by a series of famines that killed thousands of his

144 PAIGC is the French acronym for « Parti Africain pour l'Indépendance de la Guinée et du Cap-Vert » (African Party for the Independence of Guinea and the Cape Verde Islands)

countrymen and women between 1941 and 1948. It seems that these tragedies prompted him to undertake agricultural studies at the University, with the aim of using his skills to improve agricultural policies in his country. This context is the general background that contributed to shaping his early social and political consciousness.

But Amílcar Cabral's opposition to colonialism and commitment to the struggle for the liberation of his people were also the result of several political and ideological influences that shaped his thought and strengthened his resolve. During his student years in Lisbon, Cabral was involved in anticolonial student associations and met several future leaders of the liberation movements of the Portuguese colonies of Angola and Mozambique. The anticolonial sentiment was strengthened by echoes of the struggles against colonialism and domination waged by colonies in Africa and elsewhere in the world, exemplified by the war of liberation in Algeria and the Vietnamese victorious resistance against French colonialism. These struggles had had immense echoes in all the colonised and oppressed nations of the world. They had given hope to colonised countries and oppressed people that foreign domination and oppression can be overcome if people are ready and willing to pay the price for their freedom.

Those struggles against colonialism and imperialism were largely inspired by progressive ideologies, such as Pan-Africanism and Marxism, among others.

Pan-Africanism

There is no doubt that the independence of Ghana in 1957 and the War of Liberation in Algeria had given great hope to Cabral and his colleagues from other Portuguese colonies and exposed them to ideology of Pan-Africanism and the ideas and activities of its most prominent representatives, such as Kwame Nkrumah, W.E.B. Du Bois, and C.L.R. James.

Therefore, the influence of Pan-Africanism very likely led Cabral to understand that the liberation of his country could not be separated from that of the rest of the African continent, and that the success of the revolution in his country should be seen as another step towards the liberation of the whole continent. In that context, the solidarity of independent African countries was seen as a natural thing and essential for the success of the armed struggle in his country. This explains why the PAIGC headquarters were located in Conakry, capital of Guinea, a former French colony, which was the only one that rejected, in a referendum, the French neocolonial scheme of "Franco-African Community" proposed by then French President Charles de Gaulle in 1958.

Moreover, from the Pan-Africanist perspective, the struggle against domination and oppression in Africa cannot be separated from the struggles waged by people of African descent around the world, especially in the imperialist centres and their remaining colonies. In fact, the leading figures of Pan-Africanism, except Nkrumah, were all from the diaspora. And the best illustration of the unbreakable link between Africa and its diaspora is given by W.E.B. Du Bois, the revolutionary and foremost African American intellectual of his time, who followed Nkrumah to Ghana, where he died and is buried.

Frantz Fanon and the Algerian Revolution

Another towering figure of Pan-Africanism and revolutionary intellectual of the first order, who certainly had a great influence on Cabral, was Frantz Fanon, one of the fiercest critics of the colonial system. Fanon's total commitment to the Algerian Revolution and his close observation of the colonial system from within led him to write one of the most insightful analyses of the colonial society. It is almost certain that Cabral, like most African progressives of his time, had heard about, or read, Fanon's famous book, "The Wretched of the Earth," which opened the eyes of millions to the tyrannical nature of the colonial system.

Fanon's influence can be seen in Cabral's approach to the revolution in his country. Like Fanon, Cabral viewed decolonisation as a radical process of political, economic, social and cultural emancipation and transformation at all levels in order to create a new society, with a new culture and a new citizen. He put this vision into practice in the liberated areas, in which there were attempts at a radical break from the colonial legacy at the economic, social and cultural levels. In Cabral's mind, the end of imperialist domination, to be complete, must involve uprooting the culture of the colonial power and the rehabilitation of the national culture. Cabral, like Fanon, was uncompromising,

Marxism and Revolutionary Theory

The prominent figures of Pan-Africanism mentioned above also happened to be avowed Marxists. Therefore, the Pan-Africanist ideology and the strong support for the decolonisation process by the former Soviet bloc had reinforced the influence of Marxism in progressive circles and liberation movements in Africa. During that period, almost all progressive intellectuals were exposed to Marxism, and most leaders of the liberation movements, like Cabral, were either Marxist or sympathetic to Marxism.

In his famous speech made in Havana, Cuba, during the celebration of the seventh anniversary of the Cuban Revolution in 1966, Cabral showed a remarkable command of Marxist theory. In that speech he touched on a variety of subjects, including the resistance to imperialist domination, Marxism, the motive force of history, the role of the revolutionary petit bourgeoisie and the role of culture in the struggle for liberation. But Cabral was not a dogmatic Marxist. On the contrary, he adapted Marxist analysis to the specific situation of his country. In the speech he made an original class analysis of his society and of African societies in general that are relevant today.

For Cabral, no revolution can be duplicated by others, because each struggle is specific to each country and depends on the history and culture of that country:

> It is useful to recall…that however great the similarity between our various cases and however identical our enemies, national liberation and social revolution are not exportable commodities…they are essentially determined and formed by the historical reality of each people…

This is why he was able to put together an effective strategy against colonial domination based on a correct analysis of the class contradictions of his society. Cabral concluded that the contradiction between the colonial oppressor and the oppressed people overshadows the contradictions between ethnic groups. Therefore, the mission of the revolutionary movement is to bring the different ethnic groups into a patriotic front against the common enemy, which is the colonial state. This strategy proved correct and led to victory and the independence of Guinea-Bissau and Cape Verde, even after Cabral's assassination.

As a Marxist, Cabral understood the power of ideas, the value of theory in the revolutionary process. In fact, faithful to Lenin's famous claim that "there is no revolutionary movement without revolutionary theory." Cabral observed that "... if is true that a revolution can fail even though it is based on a perfectly conceived theory, nobody has yet made a successful revolution without a revolutionary theory."

This is why for him the absence of a revolutionary theory for a liberation movement will almost inevitably lead to failure of the struggle.

It is this ideological and intellectual background that influenced Cabral's thought, shaped his vision and strengthened his commitment to the struggle against colonial domination.

Cabral's Relevance to Today's Struggles

After forty years of his cowardly assassination, and despite the split between Cape Verde and Guinea-Bissau and the problems experienced by the latter, Cabral has left an indelible imprint in Africa as a revolutionary, an intellectual and a leader Cabral's life and actions contain several messages for today's struggles, especially at a time when the danger of recolonization is becoming a reality, with the imperialist aggression against Libya and French intervention in Ivory Coast. The first message from Cabral's experience is that it is essential to have a good knowledge, an intimate knowledge of his society through a careful investigation. This allowed him to get a clear vision of the objectives to be achieved by the Revolution and draw up a correct strategy based on the concrete economic and social realities of his country. It also enabled him to set up an effective organisational structure bringing together petit bourgeois intellectuals and peasants.

The second and probably most important aspect of Cabral's message is his conviction that to be truly a revolutionary, an intellectual should get rid of his bourgeois tendencies and identify with the interests of the masses and the working classes. In his opinion, this is a fundamental requisite to avoid the betrayal of the revolution. To achieve this crucial transformation, Cabral said that "... the revolutionary petit bourgeoisie must be capable of committing suicide as a class in order to be reborn as revolutionary workers, completely identified with the deepest aspirations of the people to which they belong."

This is the condition for not succumbing to his bourgeois tendencies, which would inevitably lead him to betray the masses and the revolution. Cabral was able to make that transformation himself and identify with the masses, peasants and working classes of his country. In this regard he taught a fundamental lesson of leadership, because, unlike many intellectuals, who take themselves as the "saviors" of the masses, Cabral behaved as a leader who always sought and respected the views of the masses. This is why he was so much respected and even revered by his close comrades and the masses. But this transformation is one of the most difficult things to do for the petty bourgeois intellectuals. In many cases, the bourgeois tendencies end up taking over the revolutionary spirit. This is why several revolutionary attempts failed because the petit bourgeois leadership was not able to identify with the interests of the masses, without whose trust and support no revolution can triumph.

Another key message to retain from Cabral's legacy is that revolutionary theory is absolutely indispensable to conduct a correct analysis and a successful revolution. However, in his writings and conduct of the struggle, Cabral has shown that faith in the theory does not mean making it a dogma. The theory has to be adapted to the specific situation of each country, of each society. In this regard, one may say that Cabral has followed a path similar to the one taken by Chairman Mao Zedong, who used Marxism in an original way to conduct a successful revolution in the most populous country on earth. Cabral always also made the link between theory and practice, because the theory should serve to guide practice and be validated by the latter.

Another important legacy of Cabral's thought is the importance he gave to culture in the process of national liberation. First of all, Cabral was immersed in his country's culture. His widow, Mrs. Ana Maria Cabral, recalled how the respect for his culture shaped his behaviour and influenced his leadership role during the struggle for liberation. He spoke the language of the masses, knew their customs and relied on their wisdom and knowledge of their localities

Like Frantz Fanon, Cabral understood the importance of culture in the imperialist strategy of conquest and domination. In a speech made in 1970 at Syracuse University in the United States as a tribute to the memory of Eduardo Mondlane, Cabral made this observation:

> History teaches us that in certain circumstances it is very easy for the foreigner to impose his domination. But history also teaches us that whatever may be the material aspects of that domination, it can be maintained only by the permanent and organized repression of the cultural life of the people concerned.

Therefore, understanding the role and importance of culture in the strategy of domination and exploitation is a critical element in formulating a strategy of liberation. This is why Cabral emphasized the importance of culture in the resistance to imperialist domination:

> The value of culture as an element of resistance to foreign domination lies in the fact that culture is the vigorous manifestation on the ideological or idealist plane of the physical and historical reality of the society that is dominated or to be dominated.

From this conception, culture should be an integral part of the overall strategy of national liberation and social transformation aimed at building a new society.

Nowadays, we witness the formidable role culture, in the form of music (rap, reggae, traditional music), theater and cinema, is playing in the resistance to global capitalism and imperialist domination. Several progressive musicians have made significant contributions to the African social movement within the African Social Forum and through many other movements.

Conclusion

The assassination of Cabral deprived the African revolutionary movement of one of the most original and creative Marxist thinkers. As said earlier, Cabral was a revolutionary intellectual of the first order. Three key lessons can be drawn from Cabral's revolutionary work as a theoretician and an actor. The first lesson is that the success of the revolution depends on the fusion between leadership and the masses. This means an identification of the leadership with the popular culture and the use of a language understood by the masses. In that sense he was faithful to Fanon's teachings, as already indicated. The second lesson is that the dialectic of theory and practice is essential in the process of liberation, because things keep changing constantly and therefore there needs to be constant reassessment and adaptation between practice and theory.

The importance given by Cabral to theory should be meditated by emerging revolutionary movements. As he correctly observed, so far, "there has been no successful revolution" without being guided by a revolutionary theory. The best illustration of the soundness of this claim is the hard and bitter lesson learned by the youth and progressive forces in the so-called "Arab Spring."The sacrifices made by these forces came to almost nothing, and now, the "Spring" has been transformed into a very cold "Winter"!

Cabral was the embodiment of a visionary and enlightened leadership close to the masses, the kind of leadership that Africa is sorely lacking today, in these troubled times. At a time of so much disappointment with Africa's leadership and cynicism about its political and intellectual "elites," it is refreshing to be reminded that the continent has produced one of the finest revolutionary intellectuals and political leaders of Cabral's stature.

If Cabral remains an icon in progressive intellectual circles in Africa, he is much less known by the youth and ordinary citizens. Yet, such a towering figure deserves to be better known. For this to happen, his thought and example need to be taught in African schools and universities, along with the thought and examples of other prominent revolutionaries and Pan-Africanists who inspired him, like Nkrumah, Lumumba and others, as well as the ideas of those he inspired, like Thomas Sankara.

This is a struggle that progressive political and social forces and intellectuals should take up in order to strengthen the process of decolonising the African mind and reclaiming our true history.

References

Bockel, Alain, "Amílcar Cabral, Marxiste Africain," *Ethiopiques*, no.5, Dakar, January, 1976

Cabral, Amílcar, "The Weapon of Theory," Speech delivered in Havana, Cuba, during the first Tri-continental Conference of the peoples of Africa, Asia, and Latin America, held in January,1966

Cabral, Amílcar, "National Liberation and Culture," A Tribute to Eduardo Mondlane, Syracuse University, February 20, 1970

Cabral, Ana Maria, "Amílcar Cabral," address delivered at the commemoration of the twentieth Anniversary of the Independence of Cape Verde, July 1995

Lo, Ameth, "Amílcar Cabral et la Révolution Panafricaine," Thomas Sankara website, November 2008

SECTION 4:

CABRAL, WOMEN, AND EMANCIPATION

22. "BUT WE HAVE TO FIGHT TWICE"

REFLECTIONS ON THE CONTRIBUTION OF AMÍLCAR CABRAL TO THE LIBERATION OF WOMEN

Stephanie Urdang

"In Guinea-Bissau we say we are fighting two colonialisms, one of the Portuguese and the other of men." This phrase, attributed to Cabral, was quoted repeatedly to me while travelling inside the liberated zones with PAIGC in April and May 1974—a time when solidarity with the anti-Portuguese colonial struggles had peaked. This was also a time when the women's movement—not homogenous by any means—was gaining strength in the United States and Europe. There were intense debates and lines drawn, often exclusionary, as to whether patriarchy was the primary source of women's oppression, and, so to be free, women would have to liberate themselves from men, or whether the liberation of women and the realization of our autonomy could only happen as part of a process of systemic transformation. Those of us who considered ourselves socialists as well as feminists found reaffirmation in the reports about the way in which women were participating in the national liberation struggles—in Africa, Asia and Central America. And those of us whose activism straddled feminism and support for the armed struggles in Africa found that the call for the liberation of women in Guinea-Bissau, Mozambique and Angola both relevant and motivating. It gave us ammunition to argue our cause and lent impetus to the international women's movement.

From listening to Amílcar Cabral talk about his revolution at informal meetings when he came to New York at the beginning of the 1970s, we took away messages of a profound commitment to changing the status and role of women. We believed in his uncompromising honesty and in the clarity of his political position. He would consistently stress the need for women to be liberated in the process of revolution, explaining that women were playing a critical role in the national struggle. We hung onto the declaration by Samora Machel at the Third Party Congress in 1973: "The liberation of women is a fundamental necessity for the revolution, a guarantee of its continuity and a precondition for victory."

I remember a particular meeting with Cabral in New York in late 1972. After he spoke, a friend and I went up to him to ask him for more specifics about women's role in the struggle which he had referred to in his talk. His face lit up and he responded by removing a batch of 8" by 10" photographs from his brief case. He went through them, one by one, pointing out the women in each. This woman is a political commissar for the south front. That woman teaches in a boarding school. Yet another is in charge of the radio broadcasts. Many are health workers; others are in the army. We were taken with the pride in his voice. Three months later, Cabral was dead.

Cabral's speeches and writings were less explicit than his public statements on this particular aspect of his theory and analysis. I would find more in the reports of journalists such as Gerard Chaliand that spoke to that practice. As early as 1966, Chaliand recorded an address by Cabral to a mass meeting of peasants:

> Comrades, we are going to place women in high-ranking posts, and we want them at every level, from the village committees up to the party leadership. What for? To administer our schools and clinics, to take an equal share in production and to go into combat against the Portuguese when necessary.
>
> .... The women and girls will go into the villages as nurses or teachers, or they will work in production, or in the village militias. We want the women of our country to have guns in their hands.

> ...Comrades, young girls are going to be coming into the villages from our bases. But don't anybody think that these girls are up for sale as brides. They will get married if they wish, but there will be no forced marriages. Anyone who does that is worse than the Portuguese. These young girls are going to work in the villages, go to school, be in the militia and the party will exercise complete control. ...The women must hold their heads high and know that our party is also their party. Our party repeats to every one of you that the road we have taken is like the Farim River: it never returns to its source, but flows towards the sea. Likewise the PAIGC will reach its goal, which is the true independence of our people.[146]

While travelling in south and the eastern fronts of Guinea-Bissau, I interviewed women and heard what they had to say about Cabral's call for their participation and how much they felt his loss. Among them were political cadres, health workers, teachers, peasants, members of regional and village tribunals, regional and village councils, peasant women. A quota system was in place for the tribunals and councils, in an effort to ensure that at least two of the five elected members were women. I could not verify how widely this was adhered to, but the women I spoke to insisted that it was. I was aware that where I went and who I spoke to was selective. It was a war zone and I did not speak the local languages. Nonetheless, the women I interviewed, mostly in positions of local leadership, were eloquent about how their lives had changed for the people and for women. Among them were Bwetna Ndubi and Kumba Kolubali.

Bwetna Ndubi, a member of the regional council, met me at a base in the south front. She was Balanta, a dominant ethnic group, who were predominantly animist at the time. She explained:

> We were exploited by the Portuguese. They stole everything from the people of Guinea for centuries. They massacred our people.

146 Gérard Chaliand, *Armed Struggle in Africa: With the Guerrillas in "Portuguese" Guinea* (New York, London: Monthly Review Press, 1971) p. 93

> They stole all our products. They took our people as prisoners... Before our eyes were closed, and we could not see the world. It is the Comrade Cabral who opened our eyes and showed us a new world, so that we could stop this Portuguese domination, so that we could stop all this exploitation. Cabral has cleared the road where we must walk. Cabral has cleared our minds to help us understand...And now we are able to see how important the work of Cabral is. We are in a new world. For this comrade Cabral gave his life. They killed Cabral, but Cabral is not dead. His work continues ...This war is very important. It is not for one day. If it was for one day, we could not learn our story. This war must go slowly for the people to learn how important they are...We know why we are fighting. We don't want to fight, but the Portuguese came to our country and started the war. We did not go to Portugal to fight a war. We have a reason to be free. We are fighting in our own country...Today I work together with men, having more responsibility than many men. This is not only true for me. I understand that I have to fight together with other women against the domination of women by men. But we have to fight twice –once to convince women and the second time to convince men that women have to have the same rights as men...Sometimes I have to leave my home for up to three days on a party mission, and my husband stays home and takes care of everything...Before life was very difficult for women. The party has brought new ways and a new life for women. But we must continue to define our rights ourselves.

Kumba Kolubali, Fula, and Muslim lived in the east front two weeks after the coup in Portugal (hearing the news with a group of militants on a small shortwave radio deep in the *mato)* that brought independence to Portugal's colonies. She told me:

> When the first comrade came here to mobilize us, we were very afraid. We did not know him so we did not trust him. We thought he was dangerous and he would take our things and not pay for

> them. But he talked about all the bad things that the Portuguese were doing, which we understood very well. He said that the party believes that everybody is equal and that we are all one people... Later the party organized a committee in the village to take care of matters that related to the party and to the village. It was elected by the people in our village, and we elected two women as well. Before, it had not been possible to even imagine that things like this could happen. But now life is very different. Now I see more light and now I know that everybody is my brother and my sister. Now we don't talk about colour or ethnic group the way we did before. We know that everybody is from Guinea-Bissau ... We have forced the Portuguese out by the war, and we are able to live much better than before... The difference between my life as a woman before and my life now is very, very big. How could I have ever thought that it would be possible for me to be vice president of a village council one day. Before this was always man's work. When the elections were held, both women and men voted for me and for the other woman on the council. I know they accepted us as members of the council, otherwise they wouldn't have voted for us...You see, before, you were brought up to be a boy or to be a girl. Now things are different. For the party says everybody is the same and we understand this. A boy can be a girl and a girl can be a boy. In other words, each can do what the other can do.

The tone of my writing on Guinea-Bissau in the late 1970s was very hopeful. Too hopeful. Years of work on feminism and gender inequality has shown that transformation is far more complex than we wanted to believe at that time, and just how deeply rooted are power relations in the context of culture. Decades later, a sharpened feminist economic, political and gender analysis recognizes that both men and women are socialized into the roles, attitudes and behaviours that contribute to gender inequality, discrimination and violence against women. It is encouraging to see that men are increasingly joining this struggle, and are examining and confronting their role in perpetuating these power relations.

On returning to Guinea-Bissau in 1976, I found the seeds of a very different process. The women's organisation had become little more than a mouthpiece of the party. A downward spiral had become evident once Guinea-Bissau was independent. Women leaders at the national level, who had been stridently and articulately espousing the need for the liberation of women during the armed struggle, now promoted courses for women hairdressers so that they could look attractive to men, organised embroidery lessons offered by convent nuns rather than carving a space for their own advancement in a heavily male dominated political environment. On that same visit I encountered Bwetna Ndubi. She was a shadow of her former self, not only physically, but also in her personality. My interpreter, disturbed by what she was saying, would only translate the gist of it: that she was disillusioned and poorer; that those who had not been part of the struggle in her region were now in charge and had the power. She had been failed.

Was Cabral proverbially turning in his grave? One can only hope. How many times have we indulged in a game of "What if....?" As it was, his theory and practice had been well ahead of his times. He was an inspiration not only to women in his country but to women in many parts of the world at a time when feminist thinking about the nature of transformation was beginning to take off. Our inspiration was not misplaced.

23. FROM THEORY TO PRACTICE

AMÍLCAR CABRAL AND GUINEAN WOMEN IN THE FIGHT FOR EMANCIPATION

Patrícia Godinho Gomes

The Global Context

The twentieth Century was the century of women's emancipation and the gaining of basic rights such as freedom of expression and the right to vote. In general terms, these victories allowed women the progressive "abandonment" of the strictly private dimension in which their lives unfolded, to affirm themselves gradually in the public sphere[147]. In this way, the political and economic integration of women was characterized by a slow and sometimes contradictory process that presupposed profound changes in the social models and traditional cultural norms as defined by a masculine perspective. It was these norms that contributed to the establishment of the "glass ceiling," an expression that explains the apparently invisible—but real—mechanisms that exclude women from effective participation in public institutions at the top of the pyramid. (Capuzzi, 2004: 12).

The political mobilization of women represents, therefore, an important challenge for the contemporary world in general and the African

147 For more on the condition of women (in the Western world), see Juliet Mitchell, *La condizione della donna,* Torino, Einaudi, 1972 (6ª edizione)

continent in particular[148]. In the period between colonisation and the formation of independent states in Africa, the condition of women underwent extraordinary changes, despite differences from country to country and from region to region. During the processes of decolonisation that occurred in the decade of 1950 to 1960, (but which would go on until the 1990s[149]) the African continent presented to the world more than fifty new states, with diverse political forms—from monarchies to dictatorships, military regimes to civil governments, revolutionary and democratic systems to administrations of populists or authoritarian types. Despite having followed, in a general way, the Marxist or capitalist models in the context of the politics of the Cold War (until the 1990s), power in Africa tended to concentrate in one-party systems, and in most cases was personalized in the figure of the "nation's president" who had freed the country. The centralization of power was followed by bureaucratized and highly inefficient administrative systems and by the elimination or intolerance of the bourgeoning political opposition. This situation led to the emergence of other factors such as: the increase of class and gender inequality; increase of ethnic inequalities; increase of rural-urban migration—often feminine—mainly due to prior movement restrictions

148 Regarding women's role in the societies of sub-Saharan Africa and their relation with politics, trade and culture, see Catherine Coquery-Vidrovitch, *Les africaines. Histoire des femmes d'Afrique noir du XIX au XX siècle*, Paris, Editions Désjonquéres, 1994; Margaret Jean Hay e Sharon Stitcher, *African women south of the Sahara*, London/New York, Longman, 1984, in particular, the chapter on the participation of the women in the armed struggle and their contribution to the nationalisms, pp.140-182.

149 *Os países de língua oficial portuguesa* (PALOP)/Countries with Portuguese as Official Language or Portuguese speaking countries—Guinea-Bissau, Cape-Verde, Angola, Mozambique, São-Tomé and Príncipe, together with others, are countries historically known as countries of "second decolonisation," that is, countries that had reached independence between the years 1970 and 1990 and not in the years 1960 as most African States. Some of these countries (Guinea-Bissau, Angola and Mozambique) had faced violent armed struggles and others (South Africa and Zimbabwe) had been confronted with hard policies of apartheid, and others still would come to achieve independence in the late 1980s and the beginning of 1990s through armed struggles (Namíbia and Eritrea).

(during the colonial period) and of "modernizing" ideas of the 1950s and 1960s; the low level of training and education for the majority of the Africans, especially women, among whom the illiteracy rate was very high.

After the national liberation struggles in which African women participated directly and actively, economic and political development models were adopted based on the state nationalism, leading to the democratisation of societies. These processes contemplated relevant women's emancipation projects by means of the elimination (or at least the attempt at the elimination) of customary practices considered harmful for women (precocious matrimony, inheritance discrimination, rights over children, etc.). Feminine and feminist mobilizations were incorporated into the national reconstruction projects. This practice presupposes the previously unsuccessful association between feminism and nationalism in Africa[150].

In "socialist" states there was an important participation of feminine mass organisations. Angola, Guinea-Bissau, Mozambique and Cape Verde, basically the "second generation" of governments of Marxist inspiration that became independent during the 1970s, experienced this kind of active mobilization. At the international level this conjuncture was favorable to the protection of women's rights. The growing world interest for feminine questions led the United Nations, during the Mexico Conference, to declare 1975 as "International Woman's Year." In this world forum, gender inequalities at the educational and economic levels in less advanced countries were addressed and, for the first time, the African countries made their voice heard as free countries with regards to the situation of women.

But it would especially be the decade 1975-1985, that would see a surge in gender policies at the global level, culminating in the Nairobi Conference. Important studies appeared on the condition of African women and gave emphasis to projects with the objective of reinforcing the role of women in development, among them: Rosaldo and Lamphere 1974; Etienne and Leacok, 1980; Hay and Sticher, 1984; Boserup, 1970; Amadiume, 1987. It is in this context that discussion about the

150 These thematics had been profoundly analyzed by scholars, amongst them the political scientist Cynthia Enloe in her work *Bananas, beaches and bases. Making feminist sense of international politics*, 1990.

women's emancipation in Guinea-Bissau is framed, emphasizing the political, cultural, and social revolution promoted by Amílcar Cabral and the PAIGC. This process would contribute to the progressive change of mentalities regarding the role of woman in society.

Cabral, the PAIGC, and women in the reconstruction process

To talk about Guinean women and the process of national reconstruction implies revisiting the history of the struggle for independence and also the legacy, even of precolonial times. Although it does not constitute the objective of the present analysis, it is important to underscore the fact that the approach to the theme of the condition of women in Guinea-Bissau implies necessarily a study of the period that preceded the Portuguese colonisation in this area, since the region that today corresponds geographically to the Republic of Guiné-Bissau was, in the pre-colonial era, politically organised in kingdoms (that constituted independent nations) and populated by diverse sociolinguistic groups such as the Felupes, the Banhuns, the Cassangas, the Balantas, the Bijagós, the Nalus and the Brames—that embrace today's Brâmes, Pepel and Manjaco—besides Fulas and Mandingas, who would later arrive in this area through migrations. In this complex frame, women had a status that varied in accordance with the social organisation that they belonged (more or less stratified societies) and that determined their role in the family, the economy and in the exercise of sociopolitical authority. [151]

151 For a more complete reading on the paper of Guinean women before the armed struggle see: *Comissão Nacional das Mulheres da Guiné* (CNMG)/National Commission of Guinea Women, *1º Congresso das Mulheres, Caderno nº 1 "Mulher antes da luta,"* Bissau, 3-7 November 1982, Abril 1982, Lisbon, Centre of Information and Development Amílcar Cabral-CIDAC, cota GW-M I-2 to dossier; Philip Havik et al (Orgs), *Caminhos cruzados em antropologia e história*, Lisbon, the Press of Social Sciences – ICS, 2010; Philip Havik, "Women and trade in the Guinea Bissau region: the role of African and luso-African women in trade networks from the early sixteenth to mid-nineteenth century," Africana Studia, vol.52 (1994), pp.84-120.

The struggle for political and civil rights for women in Guiné-Bissau gained momentum after the formation of the African Party for the Independence of Guinea and Cape Verde (PAIGC), the liberation movement created in 1956 that would lead the liberation struggle which culminated in the unilateral declaration of the independence of Guiné-Bissau, on 24 September 1973, in Madina do Boé[152]. In its programme of action it established the equality of men and women, stating that "men and women enjoy the same rights in the family, at the work and in public activities (PAIGC, 1965:2). These words translate into a veritable revolution and innovation regarding the status of the woman in the public sphere. In the context of armed struggle, the liberation movement appealed to the rights of women, to their integrity and their respect. But this result would only be possible with the realization among women that emancipation and freedom depended, first of all, on themselves and their will to struggle against all obstacles of their own culture—precocious marriage, procreation in adolescence, female circumcision, rights over children, right to inheritance—of their subordination to men.

Theorizing on the armed struggle in Guinea-Bissau, Amílcar Cabral[153] evidenced from the onset the fundamental role of women in the revolution and in the national reconstruction process. The success of any type of social transformation, according to Cabral, consisted "of proofing in which form a woman participates at the most ample process of liberation of the society (...) our revolution will never be victorious if we do not achieve the full participation of women (Cabral, 1972)."

---

152 For a more complete reading on this subject, see Patricia Godinho Gomes, *Os fundamentos de uma nova sociedade. O PAIGC e a luta armada na Guiné-Bissau* (1963-1973), Torino, l'Harmattan Italia, 2010, in particular chapter 2 - Os fundamentos do futuro Estado da Guiné-Bissau, pp.29-82; Leopoldo Amado, *Guerra colonia e guerra de libertação nacional (1950-1974): o caso da Guiné-Bissau*, Lisboa, IPAD-Instituto Português de Apoio ao Desenvolvimento, 2012.

153 . Regarding the biography and political trajectory of Amílcar Cabral, see Julião Sousa Soares, *Amílcar Cabral, vida e obra de um revolucionário*, Lisboa, Vega, 2011.

It was necessary to start from the concrete reality of Guinea-Bissau, from the sociocultural situation and from the then existing gender[154] relations. Since women's position is well differentiated, but fundamentally one of dependence, a profound work of changing mentalities without creating conflicts or fractures was the challenge. As Cabral stated,

> [A]t the beginning men didn't want meetings with women. Step by step, we did not force, while in other areas women attended the meetings immediately, without problems. We have to have consciousness of the general reality of our country, but of the particular realities of each thing, to be able to guide the struggle correctly (Cabral, 1976: 132).

The Guinean women joined the struggle even at the phase of clandestine organisation. In the urban centres they carried out connection tasks, ceding their houses many times for meetings of the party, preparing and distributing propaganda material, cooking for many militants who found themselves in hiding in their houses—pursued politicians

---

154 In general, societies through their institutions (ideological devices) of culture, beliefs and traditions, system of education, civil laws, and sexual and social division of labor, construct women and men as bipolar subjects, opposite and asymmetrical citizens: feminine and masculine involved in a relationship of domination and subjugation. In this case gender relations translate themselves into the subordinate status of women, fruit of their gender role (see Mónica Ferro, "Emancipação da Mulher africana. A participação no seu próprio desenvolvimento,"in Oscar Soares Barata e Sónia Infante Girão Frias Piepoli (Eds), *África. Género, educação e poder*, Lisboa, Centro de Estudos Africanos-Instituto Superior de Ciências Sociais e Políticas, 2005, pp.85-129; Naila Kabeer, "Empoderamiento desde abajo: qué podemos aprender de las organizaciones de base?," in Madalena Leon (Org), *Poder y empoderamento de las mujeres*, Bogotá, MT Editores, 1997; Ana Alice Costa, *As donas do poder. Mulher e política na Bahia*, Salvador, NEIM/UFBA e Assembleia Legislativa da Bahia, 1998 (Colecção Bahianas, vol.2).

who tried to evade the PIDE[155]. They were the matrix, serving as a link between the diverse clandestine "cells" spread throughout the territory, participating directly in political activities. Carmen Pereira, one of the PAIGC's most dynamic women who assumed various political posts during and after the armed struggle, stated the following:

> ... the position of women was very backward. To greet her husband, for example, a woman would have to kneel and put her forehead on the floor. She went to work and the husband stayed home. She worked till sundown, came home, greeted her husband, prepared the meal, got some water for him to wash with, brought him food and knelt before giving it to him. The Party has struggled against such negative traditions and done away with most of that. Now men work with women in the fields. In the past, Muslim man never wanted a woman to go to a meeting. There were many meetings during the struggle and women were very interested to hear what was going on. The men would refuse to let them go for three or four times, but women would keep insisting. Finally the men were obliged to accept. Now women are on the village committees and are sometimes elected president. Men now accept women leading meetings, because it is a Party directive and they see why it is correct (Pereira, 1978: 63).

The narratives of the struggle contain several examples of women's determination, not only to join the process, but also to show the decisive influence they exercised over the men/husbands and children, holding them to the ideals of the struggle. It should be pointed out that the liberation struggle caused

155 *Polícia Internacional de Defesa do Estado* (PIDE)/International Police for the Defense of the State was created in 1954 in Lisbon (Portugal) with the principal objective of repressing all possible forms of demonstrations by the Africans against the colonial power, in the colonies as in the metropolis. As of 1957 delegations of the PIDE had been opened in all African colonies, becoming a true instrument of control of the information. On the activities of the PIDE, see Instituto dos Arquivos Nacionais/Torre do Tombo, Direcção Geral dos Serviços de Censura, 1 livro, 337 maços, auxiliares de pesquisa: L602/5.

enthusiasm among young girls, for whom new perspectives of life were opening, far from the logic of colonialism and of some customs that tradition had imposed on them. However, in spite of the successes gained in the military field, the party structure of the PAIGC presented evident weaknesses, which led, at a given moment during the process, to the inevitable overlapping of some traditional structures, in particular, modes of some "retrograde" practices and customs that went on to constitute the line of action of certain leaders in certain liberated regions. These deviations were reflected in various domains, particularly with regards to the women's participation in political questions.

Despite various obstacles, Guinean women made irreversible gains. As of 1972, women began to be part of the political organs[156] of the PAIGC and in people's courts as jury members. They knew the struggle should be something more than national liberation. It was necessary to realize, in a permanent form, a double struggle: against colonialism and against the obstacles that hindered their advance within society.

There have been various other areas where women had distinguished themselves: in military operations with the intensification of the war from 1966 and as militia and integral part of the military units in the war fronts (Gomes, 2010a). On the other hand, the education system that then evolved in liberated zones of Guinea-Bissau counted on the fundamental support of women in all its aspects and levels. In schools' management committees and among students' representatives (the case of *Escola Piloto*), girls were represented equally with boys (3 girls and 3 boys), beside the teachers' representative and the political representative[157] (PAIGC, 1971). At the same time, the schools' control group, the organ responsible for the coordination of school activities (programmes, budget, students' management), comprised 4 members, among them 2 men and 2 women. Also in the health sector, women played an extremely important role—as

nurses and laboratory technicians—with several of them pursuing higher

156 . This was the case of Carmen Pereira, first elected Political Commissioner and first vice-president woman of the *Assembleia Nacional Popular* (ANP)/Popular National Assembly.

157 . PAIGC, Regulamento interno dos internatos das regiões libertadas, Conacry, 1971, Fundação Amílcar Cabral, Praia (Cabo-Verde).

education studies in foreign countries[158]. All this despite women's social roles still being limited to the domestic dimension.

The Udemu: In Search of a Women's Political Organisation

Besides defining the major objectives—national liberation and construction of a model of society well defined in its programme—the PAIGC was concerned about the feminine question from the onset. It was in virtue of reinforcing this component that in 1961, in Conakry, the *União Democrática das Mulheres da Guiné e Cabo-Verde* (UDEMU)/ Democratic Union of the Women of Guinea and Cape Verde appeared, having as main task the mobilization of women for better integration in the process of the armed struggle. During its existence, besides its internal work, the UDEMU launched itself onto the international arena through its activities, making an important contribution to the struggle in the diplomatic field. The gender perspective outlined by the PAIGC was an extremely important element for the prestige it acquired at the international level. Meanwhile, the evolution of the armed struggle and the need it created for the integration of women cadres in various sectors—at the time seeking recruits—would lead to the extinction of the UDEMU in 1966, only five years after its creation.[159] Regarding this, Carmen Pereira stated,

158 . The percentage of women with middle level training and university education increased from 6 in 1964 to 132 in 1972. Women were gradually achieving important positions in the management of newly established sanitary services. See Patricia Godinho Gomes, 2010b: 106-121.

159 . Comissão Nacional das Mulheres da Guiné-CNMG, *1º Congresso das Mulheres, Bissau-Congresso da organização para o enquadramento da mulher no desenvolvimento*, 3 a 7 de Novembro de 1982, Centro de Informação e Desenvolvimento Amílcar Cabral-CIDAC, Lisboa, cota-GW MI-2 dossier. Sobre a UDEMU vejam-se também: CNMG, *Iº Congresso das Mulheres-Mulher guineense e a luta*, Bissau, 3 a 7 de Novembro de 1982, CIDAC, Lisboa,cota- GW M I-2 dossier; UDEMU, *IIº Congresso-A mulher na família*, Bissau, 4 a 8 de Dezembro de 1988, CIDAC, Lisboa, cota-GW M I-7 dossier; UDEMU, *IIº Congresso-A mulher na luta para o desenvolvimento*, CIDAC, Lisboa, cota-GW-M I-7 dossier; CNMG, Iº Congresso das Mulheres- mulher e a reconstrução nacional, Bissau, 3 a 7 de Novembro de 1982, CIDAC, Lisboa, cota-GW-M I-2 dossier.

> [A]t the beginning of the struggle the Party created the Democratic Union of Women of Guinea, but we lacked cadre for this. All the experienced women were at the front, participating in the armed struggle, doing the political work, so they could not take part in the organisation. Now that the war is over the Party has created a committee composed of ten leaders, cadres and militants of the Party. The committee is now preparing to organise the women of the Party (Pereira, 1978: 66).

The Feminine Commission, created in the aftermath of a meeting held in Bissau in January 1975 and presided by PAIGC Secretary General Aristides Pereira, had, as a mission, to analyze attentively the condition of Guinean women and their interests in order to elaborate programmes for the improvement of the condition of the woman throughout the national territory. An important campaign of sensitization and political mobilization of Guinean women was undertaken, explaining and clarifying the objectives for the creation of a female organisation. The struggle for emancipation continued within the existing sociopolitical structures in liberated regions and outside the country, where the PAIGC Feminine Commission (and later the National Commission of the Women of Guinea) always represented itself, actively participating in international encounters and acquiring great visibility. [160]

The creation of the National Commission of the Women of Guinea in June 1979, with the main objective of contributing to the work initiated

160 Diverse women's organisations had visited Guinea-Bissau in the context of exchange relationship, amongst them, the Committee of Soviet Women, a delegation of Cuban women in February 1978, a delegation of the Organisation of Pan-African Women in March 1978. The National Commission of Guinea-Bissau Women participated in various meetings and international seminars: the 10th Congress of the FDIF in Berlin, in 1975; Seminar realized in the Republic of Guinea; international seminar on the integration of women in development, realized in Madagascar. *Comissão Nacional das Mulheres da Guiné* (CNMG)/National Commission of Women of Guinea, *Iº Congresso das Mulheres - Congresso da Organização para o Enquadramento da Mulher no Desenvolvimento*, Bissau, 3 to 7 November 1982, p.19, Amílcar Cabral Centre for Information and Development, Lisbon, cota-GW-M I-2 dossier).

by the PAIGC Feminine Commission, led to a profound restructuring of the UDEMU, culminating in the decision to hold the first National Congress of Women in 1982. This first congress of Guinean women had as fundamental objective the redefinition of the structure of UDEMU, which since the mid-1960s had stopped functioning, as was earlier stated. The UDEMU should contribute "to the construction of a democratic society, in which all citizens have the same rights and duties, without discrimination of colour, sex, religion, or social origin, a society where it is guaranteed the exercise of fundamental freedoms and rights." [161]

In the new organisation's programme of action, various obstacles and difficulties that Guinean women faced were underscored, and the related aspects for which it was fundamental to intervene:

- Conscientization of women about the importance of their role in the national productive effort;
- Recognition, by society, of the importance of their role in this sector, as creators producers of national wealth;
- Promotion of a better and equal distribution of national wealth on the basis of the individual's productive capacity and not on criteria based on sex;
- Capacitation of women to engage in work in a responsible way, favoring the struggle to curb discrimination against women regarding job access;
- Promotion of the participation of women in the leadership superstructure in order to guarantee their inclusion in the decision-making process;
- Promotion of women in political, cultural and literary terms;
- Provide incentives for the technical-scientific and professional training of women;
- Facilitation of the participation of women in the party structures.

---

161 *Comissão Nacional das Mulheres da Guiné* (CNMG)/National Commission of Women of Guinea, *Iº Congresso das Mulheres - Congresso da Organização para o Enquadramento da Mulher no Desenvolvimento*, Bissau, 3 to 7 November 1982, p.25.

The promotion and integration of women in development was already a concern dating back to the period of the armed struggle, resulting in the creation of UDEMU, which was worried about issues directly related to women's promotion . However, this organisation, by virtue of its fundamentally partisan character, remained limited in its capacity of response to the new demands of the independent state.

The Legacy of Cabral: Which Perspectives for Guinean Women?

The process of female emancipation in Guinea-Bissau was unquestionably favored by the armed liberation struggle. The concern for educating women and transforming them into one of the key elements in the fight for independence was mainly due to the vision of Amílcar Cabral and the perseverance of Guinean women.

Since independence, the Guinean government has ratified various international accords for the protection of the rights of women, amongst them the 1979 Convention for the Elimination of all Forms of Discrimination against Women (CEDAW) whose facultative protocol was adopted in the national juridical order in 2000. Many gains were achieved in the thirty-nine years that followed independence, especially in terms of the education and training of women in urban and, to a lesser extent, rural areas. But if, on the one hand, the Constitution of the Republic of Guinea-Bissau guarantees equal rights between men and women in the various public and private domains of life, on the other hand, various obstacles still persist today that continue to prevent the achievement of gender parity. Regarding the political trajectory and the victories in terms of women's rights, Teodora Inácia Gomes[162] affirmed that in the

162 For the biography of Teodora Inácia Gomes, one of more significant female figures in the struggle for the rights of Guinean woman, the author is currently conducting research on the story of her life that will be published in the next months in Italy, in a collection entitled "«Le altre storie»: Donne nei processi politici e di sviluppo in Africa. Il caso dei PALOP-Paesi Africani di Lingua Ufficiale Portoghese," a project jointly coordinated with Luca Bussotti of the Centre of African Studies of the ISCTE of Lisbon and Severino Ngoenha of the *Universidade São Tomás de Moçambique.*

past women didn't have enough freedom to participate in meetings to be chosen for political activities. But a lot of work was already made in that direction. Already there is consciousness by women to present their candidacies. The candidacies are normally presented by the organisations themselves or by the party structures in which women work. Since many of our women work at the level of the structures of the parties, it is from there that they are chosen. But what it is fundamental is to understand that we are making an important work of sensitization of women in order to integrate them in the structures of the parties, for them to be ready and to be chosen whenever the possibility prevails, whether in the parliament, the government, the regional structures, the institutes, or the courts, because it is not only the parliament that exists; there are other structures. There are already many women who, at this moment, are sensitized and conscious of the fact that they voluntarily want to be chosen to work in one of the structures that I just referred to.[163]

These were the legacies left by Amílcar Cabral to women: education, political participation, and economic and cultural emancipation.

However, in spite of the positive results, Guinean women still face various difficulties in terms of participation in political and leadership positions: lack of financial means to support their own candidacies to political offices or decision-making positions; the lack of unity amongst women in supporting a female candidate; finally, a lack of engagement and involvement in the political structures that oftentimes translates into lack of initiative and the resulting absence of women in the selection processes of candidates of the parties and of the other political organisations.

At the parliamentary level, many "battles" were won by women—namely, approval of laws regarding reproductive health, family planning, and female genital mutilation (FGM)—in 2011. A lot remains to be done, especially with regards to the struggle against gender violence (sexual, economic, and domestic). As long as legal mechanisms that can serve as the basis are not created, there will not be any means to fight these crimes. Women themselves must, above all, be the ones to fight, in unity, against violence.

163 Interview with Teodora Inacia Gomes conducted by the author, Lisbon, 25/10/2012.

Bibliography

Amílcar Cabral, "Os princípios do Partido e a prática política," in Mário de Andrade (Ed), *A arma da teoria-Unidade e luta*, vol.I, Lisboa, Seara Nova, 1976. pp. 117-188;

Catherine Coquery-Vidrovitch, *Les africaines. Histoire des femmes d'Afrique noir du XIX au XX siècle*, Paris, Editions Désjonquéres, 1994;

Lucia Capuzzi, "Il volto femminile del potere," in Bianca Maria Carcangiu (a cura di), *Donne e potere nel continente africano*, Torino, L'Harmattan Italia, 2004, pp.12-56;

Margaret Jean Hay e Sharon Stitcher, *African women south os the Sahara*, London/New York, Longman, 1984;

"Carmen Pereira: woman revolutionary," in *Sowing the first harvest. National reconstruction in Guinea-Bissau*, Oakland, CA, LSM Information Centre, 1978, pp.61-66 (Centro de Informação e Desenvolvimento Amílcar Cabral, Lisboa, cota-GW-H I-10;

Patrícia Gomes, "A importância das Forças Armadas Revlucionarias do Povo (F.A.R.P.) na luta pela libertação da Guiné-Bissau," Poiésis (issn: 21792534), 2010a, vol.3, n.6, pp.121-139 (disponível em http://www.doaj.org/doaj?func=openurl&issn=21792534&genre=journal);

Patrícia Godinho Gomes, *Os fundamentos de uma nova sociedade: o PAIGC e a luta armada na Guiné-Bissau (1963-1973)*, Torino, L'Harmattan Italia, 2010b;

Patrícia Gomes, Muleka Mwewa, Gleiciani Fernandes (Eds.), *Sociedades desiguais: género, cidadania e identidade*, São Leopoldo/RS, Nova Harmonia, 2009;

Naila Kabeer, "Empoderamiento desde abajo: qué podemos aprender de las organizaciones de base?," in Madalena Leon (Org), *Poder y empoderamento de las mujeres*, Bogotá, MT Editores, 1997;

Ana Alice Costa, *As donas do poder. Mulher e política na Bahia*, Salvador, NEIM/UFBA e Assembleia Legislativa da Bahia, 1998 (Colecção Bahianas, vol.2)

Mónica Ferro, "Emancipação da Mulher africana. A participação no seu próprio desenvolvimento," in Oscar Soares Barata e Sónia Infante Girão Frias Piepoli (Eds), *África. Género, educação e poder*, Lisboa, Centro de Estudos Africanos-Instituto Superior de Ciências Sociais e Políticas, 2005, pp.85-129

Documents

Comissão Nacional das Mulheres da Guiné-CNMG, *1º Congresso das Mulheres, Bissau-Congresso da organização para o enquadramento da mulher no desenvolvimento*, 3 a 7 de Novembro de 1982, Centro de Informação e Desenvolvimento Amílcar Cabral-CIDAC, Lisboa, cota-GW MI-2 dossier;

Comissão Nacional das Mulheres da Guiné-CNMG, *Iº Congresso das Mulheres-Mulher guineense e a luta*, Bissau, 3 a 7 de Novembro de 1982, CIDAC, Lisboa, cota- GW M I-2 dossier;

UDEMU, *IIº Congresso-A mulher na família*, Bissau, 4 a 8 de Dezembro de 1988, CIDAC, Lisboa, cota-GW M I-7 dossier;

UDEMU, *IIº Congresso-A mulher na luta para o desenvolvimento*, CIDAC, Lisboa, cota-GW-M I-7 dossier;

CNMG, Iº Congresso das Mulheres- mulher e a reconstrução nacional, Bissau, 3 a 7 de Novembro de 1982, CIDAC, Lisboa, cota-GW-M I-2 dossier;

PAIGC, *Regulamento Interno das regiões libertadas*, Conacry, 1971, Fundação Amícar Cabral, Praia (Cabo verde);

PAIGC, *Programa do PAIGC-Programa Maior*, Conacry, 1965, Fundação Amícar Cabral, Praia (Cabo verde);

PAIGC, Rapport sur le role politique-social et économique de la femme en guinée et aux iles du cap vert, Conacry, 1972, Fundação Amícar Cabral, Praia (Cabo verde);

ALTERNAG, *Estudo/Inquérito. A participação da mulher nas esferas de decisão*, estudo realizado sob a orientação das consultoras Maria Cecília Ramos da Fonseca e Maria da Conceição Moura, Bissau, Agosto de 1996, CIDAC, Lisboa, cota-GW-M I-8

SECTION 5:

CABRAL AND THE PAN-AFRICANISTS

24. WALTER RODNEY AND AMÍLCAR CABRAL

COMMON COMMITMENTS AND CONNECTED PRAXIS

Patricia Rodney, Asha Rodney, Jesse Benjamin, Hashim Gibril, and Senai Abraha

Walter Rodney and Amílcar Cabral were martyred sons of Africa in the arduous yet unfinished struggle to liberate Africans and all colonised peoples from foreign domination. Born in 1924, Cabral was 18 years older than Rodney, who was born in 1942. If we were fortunate enough to see both living today (2012), Cabral would be 88 and Rodney 70 years old. The assassination of these leaders in their prime was tragic and the consequences linger on. The struggles for liberation and transformation that Cabral and Rodney led and inspired in, respectively, Guinea-Bissau and Guyana, are still very far from being realized. Today's pressing need for progressive leadership on the African continent, in the African diaspora states, and beyond, makes the study of Cabral and Rodney of continuing relevance.

Most of Cabral's intellectual and activist work was done in the 1960s, whereas the bulk of Rodney's work was done in the late 1960s and throughout the 1970s. Rodney's most important work, *How Europe Underdeveloped Africa,* came out in 1972, the year before Cabral was assassinated, and two years before Guinea-Bissau's independence in 1974. The late 1960s through the early 1970s was the period when their work and activity overlapped, intertwined, influenced each other, and was shaped by the local and global movements of which they were both integral parts. In 1966, for example, Cabral wrote *Weapons of Theory* while Rodney published *Masses in Action* and completed his PhD in African History, which was subsequently published as *History of the Upper Guinea Coast 1545-1800*.[164] Both Cabral and Rodney recognised the reinstatement of colonialism as neocolonialism in postindependence Africa and the Caribbean, and adopted Marxist theory as a tool for interpreting and overcoming neocolonialism. For them, theory was valuable as an analytical weapon in so far as it could be utilized in practical struggles for freedom.

Education and Political Engagement

Cabral and Rodney both received Western-oriented education. They could readily have become members of the local petit bourgeoisie. They refused, however, to accept the status quo and chose instead the complex path of leading their people towards freedom—eventually, paying the ultimate price. But what led Cabral and Rodney to choose the life of a revolutionary?

Cabral left home after completing his secondary education in Cape Verde to study in Lisbon, Portugal where he qualified as an agricultural engineer in 1950. During his student days in Lisbon he was introduced by friends to the Portuguese Communist Party. He returned home during the holidays and educated the population about soil erosion and its effects on the environment, using this forum to do political education by analyzing how destruction of the environment affected social and political conditions within the country. The Portuguese authorities were quick to respond forbidding him access to the radio airwaves and blocking the teaching of his night course.

On the completion of his studies in 1952, Cabral returned home and under contract with the Agricultural and Forestry Services of Portuguese Guinea worked in the countryside where he was exposed to the harsh daily realities of the lives of the peasantry. In 1955, the Governor demanded that he leave Bissau, although he gave him permission to return annually for family related matters. Cabral took up a position in Angola,

164 *History of the Upper Guinea Coast 1545-1800.* Oxford: Clarendon Press, 1970.

and joined the Movement for the Liberation of Angola (MPLA). During one of his visits to Bissau in September 1959, he and other progressive elements founded the African Party for the Independence and Union of Guinea and Cape Verde (PAIGC).

After completing his secondary education, Rodney studied at the University of the West Indies, in Mona, Jamaica, for the next three years where he obtained first class honors in History. During his stay in Jamaica Rodney was involved in debating, and both student and party politics. In 1963, after graduating from UWI, he proceeded to London to complete a PhD at the School of Oriental and African Studies (SOAS). While a student in London, Rodney was involved in student and community political activity. He was a regular speaker at the West Indies Student Centre and at Speakers' Corner, Hyde Park on Sunday afternoons. Rodney shared a similar experience with Cabral when the government of the Republic of Guyana under the leadership of President Forbes Burnham refused to allow Rodney's voice to be heard on the radio and forbade the government-owned radio station from allowing him to read his children's stories. The stories are based on historical accounts of how different peoples came to Guyana, and were aimed at educating Guyanese children on their complex and inter-connected heritage. Initially, a popular and respected radio personality was allowed to read the stories, but then the government completely banned the reading of the stories. The government also prevented Rodney from taking up an academic appointment at the University of Guyana, before escalating its persecution.

Cabral cofounded, with Dr. Agostinho Neto, the Popular Movement for the Liberation of Angola (MPLA) in 1956.[165] Cabral was also one of the founders of the African Party of Independence of Guinea-Bissau and Cape Verde Islands in 1956 and was its leader at the time of his assassination on January 20, 1973. On his return to Guyana in 1974, Rodney became involved with progressive movements and joined the Working Peoples Alliance (WPA), which declared itself a political party on July 27, 1979. (Lewis 1998: 228) This party was unusual in its formation; it

165 Cabral biography, on CODESRIA website: http://www.codesria.org/spip.php?article572, accessed 12/18/12.

opted for a provisional executive and a rotating chairmanship. The executive was predominantly made-up of Afro-Guyanese and Indo-Guyanese middle-class intellectuals. (Ibid) The rotating leadership meant that there was no one leader but a shared leadership. However, Walter Rodney was the person most recognised as the leader by the Guyanese people, the Burnham regime and the international community.

Philosophy, Leadership, and the Role of the Intellectual

Both Cabral and Rodney advocated an intellectual leadership that was dedicated to the revolutionary aspirations and empowerment of the people. This style of leadership results from the commission of "class suicide." In the words of Rodney, such leadership must be "grounded" with the people. This "grounding" would educate Black intellectuals and prepare them to function as revolutionaries. Walter Rodney described this leadership as guerilla intellectualism (GI). He portrayed the Black intellectual as a guerilla embedded within a hegemonic colonial/neocolonial order against which he/she had to mobilize his/her intellectual resources.

Rodney and Cabral exemplified this leadership typology in the context of African and broader neocolonial struggles. Rodney urged Black intellectuals to embrace the "first and major struggle," that is, the struggle over ideas, by using their positions within the academy to challenge Eurocentric ideas. Furthermore, as a product of a bourgeois environment, the Black intellectual must first be emancipated from the entrapment of bourgeois culture, indeed from what Rodney characterized as the "Babylonian captivity" of bourgeois society.[166] He suggested two ways of accomplishing this—by vigorously attacking negative Eurocentric and hegemonic ideas and theories, and by fully identifying and grounding with the people—thereby undergoing, in the process, what Cabral called, "A spiritual reconversion of mentalities." This commission of class suicide,

166 Tunde Adeleke, "Theoretical Discourse on the Challenges of Black Intellectuals in Post-Modern America," in: Nikita Basov, et al (eds.), *The Intellectual: A Phenomenon in Multidimensional Perspective*, Oxford, UK: Inter-Disciplinary Press, p. 22.

which Rodney and Cabral prioritized, entailed the cultural reeducation of the intellectual "in the native 'mass character,'" and his/her "spiritual reconversion of mentalities."[167]

Both Rodney and Cabral fully embraced the two sides of the intellectual—a theoretician as well as a revolutionary, someone who was not just an armchair scholar but also a fully engaged practitioner. The latter disposition came from the commission of class suicide. Through "grounding" with the masses and learning from them, the guerilla intellectual acquires understanding of the peoples' needs, and thus is better able to lead the struggle.

Rodney used his intellectual resources to challenge and deconstruct both what he perceived as the prevailing hegemonic and bourgeois theories of his times, and the colonial and neocolonial structures of exploitation and domination. He abandoned what would have been a lucrative and successful academic path to fully immerse himself in the working class struggles in his native Guyana; a commitment that eventually took his life. Cabral, on the other hand, lost his life in the vanguard of his native Guinean revolutionary struggles against Portuguese colonialism. Like Rodney, Cabral could have retreated to the safety and comfort of ivory tower intellectualism, but chose the path of the people and their struggle.

Scholarship can be a weapon if it exposes the misconceptions and falsehoods of competing "understandings," provides surer knowledge, seeks to determine the strategies for focused change, and identifies the agencies of liberation. This, in sum, is what the theoretically and ideologically grounded analyses of social realities by Cabral and Rodney have contributed to the political, economic, and cultural struggles of African peoples worldwide. Cabral's seminal statement regarding the indispensability of correct analytical understanding argues: "if it is true that a revolution can fail even though it is based on perfectly conceived theories, nobody has yet made a successful revolution without a revolutionary theory."[168] This declaration

167 Ibid.

168 Amílcar Cabral, "The Weapon of Theory," in *Revolution in Guinea: Selected Texts by Amílcar Cabral*, trans. and ed. by Richard Handyside (New York, New York: Monthly Review Press, 1969), 93.

derives from the theoretical recognition gained by practice that national liberation consists of the struggle of a people to regain the ability to create and recreate their history,[169] and that "ignorance of the historical reality which these [national liberation] movements claim to transform—constitutes one of the greatest weaknesses of our struggle against imperialism."[170] In related vein Rodney affirmed: "The purpose [of his scholarship] has been to try and reach Africans who wish to explore further the nature of their exploitation;"[171] and that sure knowledge of African history is a "weapon"[172] in the "struggle of the level of ideas"[173] engaged in by the "guerrilla intellectual."[174] Both Cabral and Rodney made clear that the struggle against imperialism involves applying strategies and policies derived from thorough, engaged analyses of complex, conflictual conditions.

Marxist Theory, Culture, and Class Struggle in Political Practice

Both Cabral and Rodney utilized Marxist political economy as a contingent explanatory tool that needed to be adapted to local conditions. Both saw political economy as inherently rooted in specific local cultural conditions, and therefore questioned whether culture was epiphenomenal, as some classical and doctrinaire Marxists have maintained. Culture was seen as the necessary medium through which real people, in real social conditions, and with real historical contexts, engaged specific dynamics of inequality, oppression, and social transformation. In their hands, neither race nor class became abstractions, with universal applicability; but were important variables to be calculated and understood.

---

169 Ibid. 101-102.

170 Ibid. 92.

171 Walter Rodney, *How Europe Underdeveloped Africa* (Dar es Salaam, Tanzania: Tanzania Publishing House, 1976), 8.

172 Walter Rodney, *The Groundings with My Brothers* (Trenton, New Jersey: Africa World Press, Inc., 1990) 51.

173 Walter Rodney, *Walter Rodney Speaks: The Making of an African Intellectual* (London, United Kingdom: Bogle-L'Ouverture Publications, 1996) 39.

174 Ibid. 111-114.

Twentieth century anticolonial struggles were important proving grounds in the long battle to break Marxist theory and praxis free from its linear, unilineal evolutionist mold, in which it was first assumed that only fully capitalist proletarians could lead a socialist revolution. After the Bolshevik revolution, which we know from unpublished manuscripts[175] that Rodney studied extensively, the Maoist and Cuban Rebellions demonstrated the possibility and efficacy of peasant insurrections, and inspired similar actions in anticolonial struggles throughout Africa and its diaspora, as well as in other colonial territories. Now that additional sectors could be understood as potentially revolutionary, their cultures and ways of knowing became important to mobilizing that consciousness into action, and also became important for making the revolution relevant to the people undertaking it. While infrastructure (political economy) was originally understood to determine superstructure (the place of culture and identity), it was in lived practice during anticolonial struggles like those that Cabral and Rodney studied and engaged in, that this theoretical and practical relationship was rethought, and culture began to take on much greater significance. While the Frankfurt School and other theoretical tendencies like it are often credited in the academy with the emergence of cultural analysis in the service of revolution, it is far more attributable to the always theorized anticolonial insurrections and agitations that comprised Pan-Africanism and similar tendencies throughout the Twentieth Century, and of which Rodney and Cabral were heirs and leading practitioners.

Today, there is still intense debate about the role and importance of identity in revolutions, whether or not class is the primary unit of analysis, and what role race plays in relation to class and gender. Rodney and Cabral both challenged our understandings of culture, and refused reductionist conceptualization of the critical categories of race and class, and their role in revolutionary praxis, which is one of the main reasons

175 This unfinished book, with extensive notes and several completed chapters, is available in the Walter Rodney Papers, Archives Research Centre, at the Atlanta University Centre's Robert W. Woodruff Library, which Rodney's family deposited there in 2003.

they remain important touchstones for anyone interested in true social transformation.

Prominent in Cabral's and Rodney's extensive legacies are their emphases on precisely understanding the socio-economic and cultural realities of their peoples as a necessary basis for successful political struggle to bring about national liberation. In pursuing this understanding, class relations and class struggle feature pointedly in their analyses of social structure and the possibilities for radical political transformation.

Class struggle is an incisive vantage point from which to examine contemporary politics in Africa. It is the vantage point of, fundamentally, political economy—the struggle to defend or advance conflicting (contradictory) material interests emanating from the economic relations imbedded in African social formations. The class dimension of African politics is part of the dynamic interplay amongst dominant and subordinate social forces on the continent. Cabral's and Rodney's analyses focus on 1) the character of the African ruling class in terms of historical and dialectical development, composition, ideology, material interests, political practices, and alliances; 2) the array of allied and subordinate classes, class fractions and other social solidarities that compete with the African ruling class in shaping the character, tasks and possibilities of the post-colonial state; and 3) the need for revolutionary praxis ("class suicide") on the part of petit bourgeois militants.[176]

Cabral's and Rodney's joint emphases on the prominence of class struggle again emerge from their engagement in and systematic reflection on the anti-hegemonic, national liberation struggles of their peoples.

---

176 See for example: Amílcar Cabral, "Brief Analysis of the Social Structure in Guinea" in *Revolution in Guinea*). Walter Rodney, "The Politics of the African Ruling Class," lecture, Institute of the Black World, Atlanta, summer, 1974; "Towards the Sixth Pan-African Congress: Aspects of the International Class Struggle in Africa, the Caribbean and America," in *Pan-Africanism: Struggle against Neo-colonialism and Imperialism - Documents of the Sixth Pan-African Congress*, Horace Campbell, ed. Toronto: Afro-Carib Publications, 1975.

Race and the Race/Class Nexus in Practice: Diasporic Specificities

Like Cabral, Rodney understood clearly that race was a social construction, as opposed to conferring inherent biological or essential characteristics, as was claimed and used as a justification during the rise and duration of the colonial world order. In so doing, he followed a long tradition in the Pan-African world, which saw race pride and consciousness as critical to resistance to white supremacy, even while knowing it was a contingent social construction. Variants of this view can be seen in leading Diaspora Marxists, such as W.E.B. Du Bois, C.L.R. James, or Claudia Jones, long before social constructionism became *de jure* in the academy. Rodney, and this tradition generally, deserve far more credit in the genealogy of knowledge of contemporary critical theory than he has yet received.

To illuminate Rodney's thinking on race, we cite two spatially disparate examples in his illustrious career, both from 1974. The first is from his work in Guyana, where he and the WPA sought to unite the Afro-Guyanese and Indo-Guyanese communities. His solidarity with and analysis of Arnold Rampersaud is one window into this process.[177] The other example comes from Rodney's grounding with the Institute of the Black World (IBW), in Atlanta, at the height of the race/class debate in the Black Power movement in the United States.

Rodney's involvement with the Arnold Rampersaud case in 1974 indicated that his ideological commitment to multiculturalism was backed up by practical involvement in defense of Indian political activists who were victims of Afro-Guyanese intimidation and violence. Rampersaud was an activist of the PPP who had been charged with the murder of a police constable, James Henry, who was killed while guarding the toll station at the #3 Village on the Corentyne. Rampersaud was arrested while going to take food for his brother who had been held on the previous

177 This case, and all his work with the WPA, reveal Rodney's practical application of the goal of racial unification, whereas his posthumously published volume, *A History of the Guyanese Working People, 1881-1905* (1981), locates this goal in his (re) writing of history. This incredible balancing of his praxis, even during the intensely difficult conditions he lived under in Guyana, remain an inspiration to this day.

day in connection with the toll gate shooting. Arnold Rampersaud was a well-known PPP activist in the Corentyne and his supporters contended that he was being framed by the government. In one of his speeches on behalf of Rampersaud, Rodney dealt with the issue of race and politics in Guyana. (Lewis: 221) He felt that,

> More than one political party has been responsible for the crisis of race relations in this country. I think our leadership has failed us on that score. I think external intervention was important in bringing the races against each other from the fifties and particularly in the early 1960s. But I am concerned with the present. If we made that mistake once, we cannot afford to be misled on that score today. No ordinary Afro-Guyanese, no ordinary Indo-Guyanese can today afford to be misled by the myth of race. Time and time again it has been our undoing. (Rodney 1982:8)

Rodney opposed racial (or race-only) politics from the standpoint of the need to reduce the socially and politically constructed and manipulated divisions amongst the Guyanese working people. He came out against the transfer of the case from the predominantly Indian area of the Corentyne to the predominantly Afro-Guyanese area of the capital, Georgetown, where the jury was made up mainly of Afro-Guyanese men. Instead, Rodney suggested that the target of attack in the struggle for justice for Rampersaud was the Afro-Guyanese middle class and the leadership of the ruling party.

Denied by the Burnham dictatorship the salary of his academic post in Guyana, Rodney traveled occasionally to the United States to lecture and raise funds for his family, and this included a leading role in the IBW's Summer Research Symposium, 1974. Derrick White's important new history of the IBW (2011) reveals yet another Rodney/Cabral link: the six week research project was shaped around testing the applicability of the development theories of Rodney's *How Europe Underdeveloped Africa* and Cabral's *Return to the Source* (149). The IBW, as a think tank in support of United States and global Black social movements, sought answers to the increasingly contentious and doctrinaire race/class debate. Rodney suggested parallels between the neocolonialism in Guyana, the Caribbean and Africa, and the cooptation of the growing Black middle class in the US. (151)

Utilizing what he and the IBW associates called a "racialized political economy" approach, Rodney suggested that both race and class were flexible, contingent, socially constructed categories that were "historically interchangeable,"[178] and specifically that,

> ...each [race and class category] [has] a validity of its own. In other words, one is not just purely derivative of the other. There may be at one particular point in history the racial contradiction may have derived from the basic class contradiction. At another point the class contradictions reinforce or react upon the race contradictions and so that what I'm getting away from is a sort of simplistic analysis which takes one of these factors, either one, and ascribes to them the sole or preponderating determining historical influence in a society like this [America]. (153-154)

This is an important new window into the subtlety of Rodney's thinking on race and class. We have long known about Rodney's powerful racial affirmations in *Groundings with My Brothers*,[179] and that throughout his career Rodney thought history should not be written neutrally, but in the service of the race/the oppressed. His sophisticated, particularist, racialized political economy is less well known, and can also be seen in action in his reaction to the Sixth Pan-African Congress, where intense debates between Black nationalists and Marxists threatened to divide the

178 To illustrate, Rodney said: "What is a white man today may not be a white man tomorrow." This places Rodney in the company of James Baldwin and far ahead of "whiteness studies," in both his analysis of whiteness and the fluidity and socially constructed nature of identity.

179 Rodney was a crucial voice in the rise of global Black Power movements and articulations, in response to the dehumanization of global white supremacy; what Paget Henry called "the ontological appearance of their [Black peoples'] humanness." (2009: 146)

movements of that era: "I think we must beware of being trapped into generalizations that are supposed to be valid for the whole of the Pan-African world… it does not help to generalize." Rodney argued that the nationalist and Marxist perspectives are "unnecessarily antagonistic," and that "race and class are not absolutes," but instead concepts that arose historically. (157)

In summation of this perspective, one cannot do better than the resonant prose of Wole Soyinka:

> In an intellectual world rendered increasingly turgid by ideological mouthers and phrase-mongers, Walter Rodney stood out for lucidity, relevance, for a preference for actuality, its analysis and prescription over and above slavish cant… He was clearly one of the most solidly ideologically situated intellectuals ever to look colonialism and its contemporary heir—Black opportunism and exploitation—in the eye, and where necessary, spit in it. (1980)

Conclusions

There are many reasons why comparison of the lives and works of Rodney and Cabral remains salient, and this short essay has examined a few of them. It is meant more as a reflection and a contribution to a larger conversation than as anything final or definitive.

In the years since both gave their lives in the service of revolution and social justice, the world has changed in many ways. The long 1980s and their aftermath left the Non Aligned Movement and other revolutionary forces in disarray, and it remains to be seen what the current juncture provides by way of resumption and reinvigoration of those same energies in new and refined forms in various parts of the world, from Latin America and the Caribbean to the Arab/African Spring. At the same time, critical advances in theory and its engaged practice have continued to accumulate, and to build on the work of Cabral, Rodney, and our other ancestors, so that whatever social movements emerge now, they will not be the same as those that came before.

Some continue to try to pigeonhole Rodney and Cabral into neat categories that suit their agendas. Some have advanced readings of Rodney, for example, that stress his class analysis over his racial consciousness, or see the former as giving way to the more mature perspectives of the latter.[180] However, like Cabral, Rodney's theory was never just abstract, but always grounded in historically and socially situated analysis and engagement, and therefore always reflected the lived complexities of the world being studied and transformed. Just as comprador members of the oppressed races were often recruited to the forces of neocolonial rule, so too were members of oppressed classes coopted ideologically and even individually. Just as the concept of "class suicide" identified allegiance against one's own inherited privileges and with the oppressed, similar racial formulations that rely more on political commitment than phenotype were identified and can be extended into the present.

Critical political economy perspectives continue to have salience in our modern world, which has seen the Zapatista uprising, the second Bolivarian Revolution in South America, the Occupy Movement in the US, and the Arab/African Springs currently under way in Africa and the Middle East. While the academic fad of post-colonial theory never resonated with those grounded in Rodney's neocolonial analysis (and its anti-neocolonial consciousness) new theories like Subaltern Studies in South Asia, and Coloniality in the America's build on and extend the corrective historiographic interventions of Rodney and Cabral, and the dependency theory origins of Rodney's *How Europe Underdeveloped Africa*.

One can only wonder what contributions Rodney and Cabral would have made to these and other debates if their lives had not been cut short. It remains our collective task to carry forward this work as well as we can. Much work remains to be done. For example, this essay did not engage the questions of education that these great thinkers devoted significant

180 Alex Dupuy's, "Race and Class in the Postcolonial Caribbean: The Views of Walter Rodney," (*Latin American Perspectives* 107, Spring 1996), is a good example of this. For more detailed critiques, one can site several student presenters at the Engaging Walter Rodney's Legacies Conference, Binghamton NY, 1998; and more extensively: Young (2008).

time to, such as the intersections of Freirian praxis in both of their work, or their links and disjunctures with Nyerere.

Writing this in Atlanta at the close of 2012, we share a hope in the continued scholarly and political engagement of the works of Rodney, Cabral and their generation, to better inform the current generation and its ongoing task to make the world better than they found it. It is our hope that as it did during the Civil Rights period, and during the 1970s around the Institute of the Black World, Atlanta will continue to play a leading role in the study and practice of social change and revolutionary transformation. To this end, we hope the presence here of the Walter Rodney Foundation, the Walter Rodney Papers housed at the AUC Woodruff Library,[181] and the annual Walter Rodney Symposium[182] also held at the Woodruff Library, will provide material and space for some of the necessary groundings we face in our time. Much work remains to be done. We hope this essay points in the direction that some of this conversation might continue.

Select Bibliography

Adeleke, Tunde (2010). "Theoretical Discourse on the Challenges of Black Intellectuals in Post-Modern America." In: Nikita Basov, et al (eds.), *The Intellectual: A Phenomenon in Multidimensional Perspective.* Oxford, UK: Inter-Disciplinary Press, pp. 21-32.

Bogues, A. (2009). "Black Power, Decolonization, and Caribbean Politics: Walter Rodney and the Politics of the Groundings with My Brothers." *Boundary*, 127-147.

181 The Atlanta University Centre Woodruff Library's Archives Research Centre is open by appointment only: archives@auctr.edu or (404) 978-2052, and for a link to the Walter Rodney Papers finding aid: http://www.auctr.edu/rwwl/FindingAids/WalterRodneyPapers.pdf.

182 The 10th Annual Walter Rodney Symposium will be held on March 22-23, 2013, at the AUC Woodruff Library.

Cabral, A. (1965). *Tell no lies, Claim no easy victories...* Retrieved November 10, 2012, from: http://www.marxists.org/subject/africa/cabral/1965/tnlcnev.htm

Cabral, A. (1966, January). *The Weapon of Theory.* In *Revolution in Guinea: Selected Texts by Amílcar Cabral*, trans. and ed. by Richard Handyside. New York, New York: Monthly Review Press, 1969.

Cabral, A. (1966, January). "Brief Analysis of the Social Structure in Guinea." In *Revolution in Guinea: Selected Texts by Amílcar Cabral*, trans. and ed. by Richard Handyside. New York, New York: Monthly Review Press, 1969.

Cabral, A. (1969). *Towards final victory.* Retrieved November 10, 2012, from: http://www.marxists.org/subject/africa/cabral/1969/tfv.htm.

Freire, P. (1969). *Pedagogy of the Oppressed.* New York: Continuum.

Gibbons, A. (2011). *The Legacy of Walter Rodney in Guyana and the Caribbean.* Maryland: University Press of America.

History. (2012). *Historical Events for Year 1966.* Retrieved October 23, 2012, from History Orb: http://www.historyorb.com/events/date/1966?p=5.

James, C. (1981). *Walter Rodney and the Question of Power.* Retrieved October 2012, 2012, from: http://www.marxists.org/archive/james-clr/works/1981/01/rodney.htm.

Lewis, Rupert Charles. Walter Rodney's Intellectual and Political Thought. Jamaica: The University of the West Indies Press, 1998.

Lopes, C. (2006). Amílcar Cabral: a contemporary inspiration. *African Identities*, 1-5.

Mendy, P. K. (2006). Amílcar Cabral and Liberation of Guinea-Bissau: context, challenges and lesson for effective leadership. *African Identities*, 7-21.

Rodney, W. (1966). *Masses in Action. New World Quartely.*

Rodney, Walter (1969). *The Groundings with My Brothers.* London: Bogle-L'Ouverture Publications.

Rodney, Walter (1972). *How Europe Underdeveloped Africa.* London: Bogle-L'Ouverture Publications, and Dar es Salaam, Tanzania: Tanzania Publishing House, 1972.

Rodney, W. (1972). "Education in Africa and Contemporary Tanzania." *W.E.B. Du Bois Department of Afro-American Studies, University of Massachusets Amherst* (pp. 82-99). Boston: University of Massachusets Amherst.

Rodney, W. (1972). *Problems of Third World Development: A Discussion of Imperialism and Underdevelopment.* Los Angeles: UCLA.

Rodney, W. (1972b). *The African Revolution.* Retrieved November 10, 2012, from: http://www.marxists.org/subject/africa/rodney-walter/works/africanrevolution.htm.

Rodney, W. (1974). "The Politics of the African Ruling Class," lecture, Institute of the Black World, Atlanta, summer.

Rodney, W. (1975). "Towards the Sixth Pan African Congress: Aspects of the International Class Struggle in Africa, the Caribbean and America." In: *Pan-Africanism: Struggle against Neo-colonialism and Imperialism—Documents of the Sixth Pan-African Congress*, Horace Campbell, ed. Toronto: Afro-Carib Publications.

Rodney, Walter (1981). *A History of the Guyanese Working People, 1881-1905*. Baltimore: Johns Hopkins University Press.

Rodney, Walter (1982). "In Defense of Arnold Rampersaud." Guyana: Working People's Alliance.

Rodney, Walter (1990). *Walter Rodney Speaks: The Making of an African Intellectual.* Trenton, New Jersey: Africa World Press, Inc.

Soyinka, Wole (1980). "The Man Who Was Absent." *And Finally They Killed Him: Speeches and Poems at a Memorial Rally for Walter Rodney, 1942-80*, Oduduwa Hall, University of Ife, Nigeria, Friday, June 27, 1980.

UNSC. (2012, May 4). *Update Report on Guinea-Bissau.* Retrieved November 9, 2012, from UN Security Council: http://www.securitycouncilreport.org/update-report/lookup-c-glKWLeMTIsG-b-8079461.php.

White, Derrick (2011). *The Challenge of Blackness: The Institute of the Black World and Political Activism in the 1970s.* Gainesville: University Press of Florida.

Wick, A. (2006). Manifestations of Nationhood in the Writings of Amílcar Cabral. *African Identities*, 45-71.

Young, K. B. (2008). Walter Rodney's Pan Africanism. *Peace Review: A Journal of Social Justice* (20), 487-495.

25. CLASS AND STRUGGLE

CABRAL, RODNEY, AND THE COMPLEXITIES OF CULTURE IN AFRICA

David Austin

> *...They say that the countryside has turned verdant, a most beautiful colour, because it is the colour of hope...*
> —*Amílcar Cabral (1946)*

Some time in the late 1990s, I had a series of discussions with a friend from Senegal that helped to crystallize for me some of the challenges related to Caribbean political-intellectuals who wrote and thought about African politics. At the time I had inherited the recordings of several lectures by C.L.R. James that had been delivered in Montreal in the late 1960s. The lectures covered a range of topics, including one presentation titled "Policy and Program for Developing Countries." In the lecture James described the dismal social and political state in Africa—corruption, poor governance, illiteracy—and then, drawing on his deep knowledge of European history, acknowledged the inevitability of military coups in much the same way that they had historically occurred in Europe during Cromwell's Revolution in Britain and during the French Revolution. Then, drawing on Lenin's analysis of Russia in 1920-21, James called for a literacy campaign in African societies as, he argued, those who are illiterate are "outside of politics." He also called upon African politicians to "change those governments which they inherited from former colonial powers" and introduce cooperative systems that would "involve the population in the development of the economic and social life of the country."[183] That James did not suggest how his ideas would be carried through does not detract from his analysis as, in the final prognosis, he called for process that would actively engage Africans in politics, or more appropriately, would allow Africans to actively engage in the political process.

As I read James account, it was difficult to ignore the sense of despair that undergirded his reasoning. While his pragmatic approach made sense on one level, I was left with the sense that he saw the African continent as existing outside the boundaries of modern history and, despite his hopes for change, hopelessly sinking into a political abyss. And while his analysis reflected his understanding of current trends in African politics, it lacked the nuance and depth of understanding of the deep structures of African cultures and societies that had characterized his work in other areas. In other words, unlike so much of his other work, and despite his understanding of conventional African politicians—many of whom he had been associated in London in the 1930s—when it came to the African continent, James was writing from the outside.

I shared James's lecture with Ameth Lo who at the time had recently moved to Montreal and was an active member of GRILA (the Group for Research and Initiative for the Liberation of Africa). And while I dithered and attempted to make sense, and even justify James's analysis—despite my unease—Ameth's response was swift, clear, and to the point—in a manner that was reminiscent of Amílcar Cabral. Ameth simply pointed out that James's limited understanding of the African continent— the nuances of its diverse politics, cultural dynamics, and social structures—had prevented him from developing a full appreciation of the challenges confronting the continent and the prospects for social change within it. As I would later conclude after listening to Ameth, James was applying Western, and West Indian, sensibilities to a continent and terrain that he could not possibly have understood from his limited contact with Africa and despite—or perhaps as a result of—his close contact with

183 C.L.R. James, "Policy and Program for Developing Countries," (Montreal: unpublished, circ. 1967).

African leaders such as Kwame Nkrumah, Jomo Kenyatta, Namdi Azikiwe, amongst others.

In retrospect, Ameth helped to save me from what, in his own way, V.Y. Mudimbe has described as the African diaspora's invention of Africa. While Mudimbe was speaking about a different kind of invention to that of James, the end result was the same: James's invention or imagining ultimately hovered above the lived experience of the majority of Africans, so-called ordinary people for whom in other contexts James had often described in terms of their ability to do the extraordinary.

James was part of a long history of Caribbean engagement with the African continent that loosely fits under the broad banner of Pan-Africanism. In the nineteenth and early twentieth centuries, African emancipation was the central preoccupation of West Indian Pan-Africanists such as Edward Wilmot Blyden, Henry Sylvester Williams, and Marcus Garvey. The African continent was a beacon of hope, the figurative motherland, and Caribbean Pan-Africanists believed that their freedom was intricately tied to the fate of the African continent.

But the West Indian road to Africa, to borrow a term from James, was not without its share of controversy. Not only did West Indians often "invent" Africa, creating an imaginary continent, replete with often romanticized notions of ancient African societies and kingdoms on the one hand and an image of contemporary Africa as a dark continent in decline from this illustrious past, on the other; implicit, and often explicit, in this reasoning was the idea that "scattered Ethiopians" of the Americas would rescue Africa and restore it to its former glory.[184] Seen as a component part of the West Indian's recovery from the legacy of slavery and the colonial degradation, this idealized perception of Africa is understandable. The road to Caribbean rehabilitation passed through Africa and, if West Indians were to humanize their own existence, the continent itself would have to be rehabilitated, even if this meant re-imagining it in ways that were not in keeping with the lived experience of continental Africans.

184 See V.I. Mudimbe, *The Invention of Africa: Gnosis, Philosophy, and the Order of Knowledge* (Bloomington and Indianapolis: Indiana University Press, 1988), and particularly pages 98-134 on Blyden.

By the 1930s, however, a new and highly politicized Caribbean conception of Africa emerged as exiled West Indians and Africans came into close contact with one another in European metropolitan centres.[185] It was while in exile that a second wave of West Indians "rediscovered" the continent, as they sought to reclaim their humanity in the face of colonialism at home and racism abroad. In the process, West Indian paternalism partially gave way to genuine collaboration and solidarity amongst West Indians and Africans. In London in the 1930s, West Indians George Padmore and James of Trinidad, Amy Ashwood Garvey of Jamaica and Ras Makonnen (formerly George T.N. Griffith) of British Guyana agitated for African liberation alongside several future African leaders, including Nnamdi Azikiwe of Nigeria, I.T.A. Wallace Johnson of Sierra Leone, Jomo Kenyatta of Kenya and later Kwame Nkrumah of the Gold Coast (later Ghana). Their work in exile culminated in the Fifth Pan-African Congress in Manchester in 1945, laying the foundation for the independence of Ghana and other colonial territories on the continent. During this same period in Paris, Aimé Césaire and Suzanne Lacascade of Martinique, Léon Damas of French Guyana and Leopold Senghor of Senegal, amongst others, established the literary-philosophical Negritude movement. Along with the emergence of the journal *Présence Africaine* and a publishing house of the same name founded by Alioune Diop,

185 For an analysis of the role of exiled intellectuals and politicos in anticolonial struggles, and on C.L.R. James in particular, see Edward Said's *Representations of the Intellectual* (New York: Vintage Books, 1996), pp. 47-64 and *Culture and Imperialism*, (New York: Vintage Books, 1993), 336 and Bill Schwartz (ed.) *West Indians in Britain* (Manchester: Manchester University Press, 2003). For references to Caribbean exiles in Canada see David Austin, "In Search of A Caribbean Identity: C.L.R. James and the Promise of the Caribbean" in David Austin (ed.), *You Don't Play with Revolution: The Montreal Lectures of C.L.R. James* (Oakland, CA: AK Press, 2009), Alfie Roberts, *A View for Freedom: Alfie Roberts Speaks on the Caribbean, Cricket, Montreal, and C.L.R. James* (Montreal: Alfie Roberts Institute, 2005), Paul Buhle, *Tim Hector: A Caribbean Radical's Story* (Jackson: The Press of University of Mississippi, 2006), and David Austin, "All Roads Led to Montreal: Black Power, the Caribbean, and the Black Radical Tradition in Canada," *in Journal of African American History*, vol. 92, no. 4 (Fall 2007), 516-539.

Negritude inspired a cultural renaissance in Africa and the Caribbean as France's colonies agitated for independence and self-determination.

In the1960s, the focus of the Caribbean exiles shifted from Africa to the Caribbean as a new generation of West Indians, in part inspired by independence and liberation movements in Ghana and other parts of Africa, set about transforming the Caribbean. Building on the foundation of their predecessors, they embraced a combination of Caribbean nationalism, Third World internationalism and socialism. These exiles played a crucial role in the emergence of the Caribbean New Left, which began, in a sense, with the "Rodney Riots" in Jamaica following Walter Rodney's expulsion from that country after his participation in the Montreal Congress of Black Writers and culminated with the rise and subsequent fall of the Grenada Revolution (1979-1983).[186]

But Africa remained central to the work of West Indians such as Frantz Fanon and later Rodney, and many other Caribbean political-intellectuals of the post-World War II period, and continued to inform those who were now primarily concerned with the Caribbean. But of the Caribbean women and men that attempted to engage the African continent, it was Rodney, even more than Fanon, who developed a complex understanding of African societies and attempted to understand those societies on their own terms, not through the lens of modernist notions of progress.

In *A History of Upper the Guinea Coast: 1545 to 1800*, Walter Rodney examines trade and social relations between primarily Portuguese merchants and West Africans. As we learn from him in *Walter Rodney Speaks: The Making of an African Intellectual,* the book represents an effort to bring to bear a kind of proto-class analysis of the history of slavery and colonisation in Africa.[187] *A History of Upper Guinea Coast* is centred

---

186 Brian Meeks, *Radical Caribbean: From Black Power to Abu Bakr* (Kingston, Jamaica: The Press of the University of the West Indies, 1996), 1–2 and David Austin, "Vanguards and Masses: Global Lessons from the Grenada Revolution," in Aziz Choudry and Dip Kapoor, *Learning from the Ground Up: Global Perspectives on Social Movements and Knowledge Production* (New York: Palgrave Macmillan, 2010), 173-189.

187 Rodney, *Walter Rodney Speaks: The Making of an African Intellectual* (Trenton, NJ: African World Press, 1990), 27.

on the sociology and economic history of the West African coast prior to and during the slave trade, and the impact of the trade on African societies. And in this painstakingly researched study, Rodney provides the reader with insight into the inner-workings and dynamics of West African societies during this period. In the process he raises similar issues to those raised by Amílcar Cabral in relation to twentieth century Guinea-Bissau under Portuguese rule. In many ways, Cabral's analysis of Guinea-Bissau makes explicit in a the twentieth century context what Rodney projects in his analysis of sixteenth to eighteenth century West African history.

Walter Rodney was a close associate of James. He read James's classic work on the Haitian Revolution as a university student in Jamaica and participated in a study group with C.L.R. and Selma James as he pursued a PhD. in history in London. These study sessions at the Jameses' home included a number of Caribbean nationals, several of whom would go on to play active political roles in the post-independent Caribbean. From Rodney's account, the study group had a tremendous impact on him. Grappling with his own ideas and approach to history, and finding nothing "in the English political scene that was helpful,"[188] Rodney found the study group indispensable to his political development. "Getting together in London and meeting over a period of two to three years on a fairly regular basis," says Rodney, "afforded me the opportunity…to acquire a knowledge of Marxism, a more precise understanding of the Russian Revolution and of historical formulation."[189] "One things is certain about C.L.R. James," adds Rodney: "he has mastered a whole range of theory and historical data and analysis. This explains why he was very good at focusing in [on the subject matter]"[190] and "as many people know, C.L.R. had that habit of really incisively dismissing bourgeois foolishness. And I think that his wife, Selma James, in her own right had a complimentary if different style that tended in that same direction."[191] For Rodney,

188 Ibid.

189 Ibid.

190 Ibid., 28-29.

191 Ibid., 29.

both C.L.R. and Selma James "exemplify the power of Marxist thought. That's what one got—a sense that a bourgeois argument could never really stand a chance against a Marxist argument, provided one was clear about it."[192] But despite his admiration for the Jameses, it was Rodney who made a unique contribution to our understanding of Marxist theory and class struggle during this period, and not by drawing on European history, but by turning to a troubled part of the history of the African continent.

In 1970, a revised version of Rodney's PhD thesis was published as *A History of Upper Guinea Coast.* The book is the least known of his major publications and it is fair to say that it has been generally ignored by Rodney scholars, particularly American scholars, according to Rodney,[193] although, perhaps for different reasons, Pan-Africanists have also tended to shy away from it. *A History of Upper Guinea Coast* is unique for its nuanced description of the relationship between Africans and Europeans during the period of the European slave trade of Africans. It also illustrates the role of Africans in the slave trade, as Rodney distinguishes between the aims and aspirations of the African ruling class, on the one hand, and those of the majority population, on the other. Somewhat empirical in its approach, the book outlines the way in which the African elite were both used and manipulated by Europeans during the slave trade, and the way in which African elites also consciously manipulated their European counterparts in order to profit from the enslavement of other Africans. Rodney never loses sight of the fact that it was Europeans who orchestrated and were the primary beneficiaries of the slave trade. But, referring to the existence of social classes in the Upper Guinea Coast and the phenomenon of slavery, Rodney informs us: "the kings were just as likely to rob their own people as to attack their neighbours."[194] He also suggests "it could scarcely have been simple coincidence that the Djolas and the Balantas, who produced the least slaves either by raiding or by

192 Ibid.

193 Ibid., 27.

194 Walter Rodney, *A History of Upper the Guinea Coast: 1545 to 1800* (1970; New York: Monthly Review Press, 1980), 117.

preying upon each other, were the very tribes with an amorphous state structure, from which a well-defined ruling class was absent."[195] Rodney also suggests that "Tribal divisions were not, then, the most important." "When the line of demarcation is clearly drawn between the agents and the victims of slaving as it was carried on among the littoral peoples," he adds, "that line coincides with the distinction between the privileged and the unprivileged in the society as a whole."[196] "The Atlantic slave trade was deliberately selective in its impact on the society of the Upper Guinea Coast," according to Rodney, "with the ruling class protecting itself, while helping the Europeans to exploit the common people. This is of course the widespread pattern of modern neocolonialism."[197]

Several major points stand out in Rodney's arguments, points that illustrate his unique traits as an historian and Pan-African figure. First, Rodney had no qualms about implicating African rulers in the Atlantic slave trade, a critique that he would later extend to contemporary African and Caribbean rulers. Yet he did so without absolving Europe of its pivotal role in the trade of Africans and without overlooking the fact that those who most benefited from the trade were Europeans and white North Americans. Hence his mention of neocolonialism, which suggests that the book was animated by political and economic developments in "postcolonial" Africa.

Second, in identifying class differences in Africa, Rodney was able to separate the "common" people from the elite who acted in accordance with their own interests as opposed to those of the entire population. This too is an analysis that he would draw upon in his assessments of contemporary African and Caribbean developments in his later work.

Third, in reflecting on class in Africa during the early days of the slave trade, Rodney contributed to our understanding of class struggle and capitalism. Perhaps more than anyone else, C.L.R. James understood the central role that slave labor played in the emergence of global capitalism. As James remarked in *The Black Jacobins: Toussaint L'Ouverture and the San Domingo*

---

195 Ibid.

196 Ibid.

197 Ibid.

Revolution, slave plantations in the Caribbean housed the first factories of global capitalism. These factories carried out the complicated process of turning raw sugar cane into sugar and, situated on the North Plain of Haiti, they were the jewel of colonial trade.[198] For James, the concentrated presence of large numbers of slaves laboring in these proto-capitalist factories was closer to the modern proletariat than its counterparts anywhere in the world at the time.[199] This point has yet to be fully appreciated.

African slave labor was central to inaugurating the modern capitalist era. This was the most economically advanced (and socially backward) system in the world. And James argued that Black slaves were being socialized in the production process in a manner that, as Marx argued, would lead to the overthrow of the system that dominated workers as they developed class-consciousness. Despite the fact that Marx was not thinking about Black or African laborers when he described the working-class, the Haitian Revolution not only struck a blow against slavery but was also important because it struck at the heart of French and European capital and capitalist production. In reflecting on class struggle and the slave trade in West Africa, Rodney provides insight into a process that would lead to amongst the first acts of resistance to the enslavement of Africans, and thus amongst the first acts of resistance against what would become capitalism. In the process, Rodney, like James, challenges us to shift our understanding of capitalist development and the primacy of labor from Europe to Africa, laying the seeds for his later work in *How Europe Underdeveloped Africa*.

Rodney's description of the Djola and Balanta is reminiscent of the writing of Amílcar Cabral. While Rodney's analysis was informed by historical research, Cabral was an agronomist by training who surveyed the rural areas of Guinea-Bissau and, in the process, drew conclusions about the social structures of diverse African ethnic groups within the region. His intimate and very detailed understanding of the territory of

198 C.L.R. James, *The Black Jacobins: Toussaint L'Ouverture and the San Domingo Revolution* (London: Allison & Busby, 1980 [1938]), 47-48.
199 James, *The Black Jacobins*, 86, James, "The Haitian Revolution in the Making of the Modern World," in David Austin (ed.), *You Don't Play with Revolution: The Montreal Lectures of C.L.R. James* (Oakland: AK Press, 2009), 54.

Guinea-Bissau, coupled with his penetrating insights, brought him to conclusions that complement Rodney's: "In societies with a horizontal structure, like the Balanta society…the distribution of cultural levels is more or less uniform, variations being linked solely to individual characteristics and to age groups. In the societies with a vertical structure," Cabral informs, "like that of the Fula…there are important variations from the top to the bottom of the social pyramid. This shows…the close connections between the cultural factor and the economic factor, and also explains the differences in the overall or sectoral behaviour of these two ethnic groups towards the liberation movement."[200] Moreover, the "class character is still more noticeable in the behaviour of privileged groups in the rural environment, notably where ethnic groups with a vertical structure are concerned, where nevertheless the influences of assimilation or cultural alienation are nil, or virtually nil.

This is the case of the Fula ruling class, for example. "Under colonial domination," adds Cabral, "the political authority of this class (traditional chiefs, noble families, religious leaders) is purely nominal, and the mass of the people are aware of the fact that the real authority lies with and is wielded by the colonial administrators. However, the ruling class retains in essence its cultural authority over the mass of the people in the group, with very important political implications."[201] The colonial authorities, knowing this reality, "install chiefs whom it trusts and who are more or less accepted by the population, gives them various material privileges including education for their eldest children, creates chiefdoms where they did not exist, establishes and develops cordial relations with religious leaders."[202] This system, we are told, "by means of the repressive organs of colonial administration…ensures the economic and social privileges of the ruling class in relation to the mass of the people," though "this does not remove the possibility that, among these ruling

200 Amílcar Cabral, "National Liberation and Culture," in *Unity and Struggle* (London: Heinemann Educational Books Ltd., 1980), 144

201 Ibid., 145.

202 Ibid., 145-6.

classes, there may be individuals or groups of individuals who join the liberation movement."[203]

Cabral's ideas not only resonate with Rodney's, but also with the work of Mahmood Mamdani. In *Citizen and Subject: Contemporary Africa and the Legacy of Colonialism*, Mamdani argues that[204] until the problems of the urban-rural dilemma—the dichotomy between urban civil rule and rural or customary law—is resolved, factionalism will continue to prevail and political governance will remain, at the very least, a major challenge and, at its worse, continue to manifest itself in bloodletting and inter-ethnic conflicts. The similarities between Cabral and Mamdani rest less in their overall analyses and more in the fact they both point to the dilemma that the hierarchical and centralized urban rule and customary law has posed for the African continent. For Mamdani, in order to get beyond the present state of political despair in Africa, the nature of rule in both the rural and urban regions must be simultaneously transformed and democratised, creating the conditions for the active participation of both citizens in the city and subjects under customary rule in the country while attempting to reconcile the differences in these forms of social organisation.[205]

Perhaps like no other African political leader, Cabral spoke frankly and openly about class and the dangers of the ruling elite betraying the aspirations of their people. (It is perhaps time that we reconsider the word "betrayal" in this context. Betrayal implies that common interests have been compromised, when in actual fact, what both Rodney and Cabral suggest is that the interests of the ruling elite are often closer to those of the colonisers than they are to their subjects.) Like Rodney and Fanon, Cabral understood the importance of class differentiation in the shaping of African societies and was fully conscious of the role these differences could play in post-colonial Africa. But unlike Fanon's modernism, and like Rodney, Cabral's analysis was rooted in an understanding

---

203 Ibid., 146.

204 Mamdani, M (1996): *Citizen and Subject: Contemporary Africa and the Legacy of Late Colonialism*. Princton, Princeton University Press.

205 Ibid., 301.

of the peculiar features of Guinea-Bissau which he then, as great theorists do, generalized in his analysis of Africa, but without over-generalizing.

It is remarkable that Cabral's analytical contributions are not more widely acknowledged and studied in greater detail. He was certainly one of the last century's brilliant political minds and theorists who lent clarity to the complex interplay of forces that define the African continent. Cabral was one of the major influences on Walter Rodney's thought, and it is not surprising that, through different means, they would come to similar conclusions about the nature of class struggle in Africa. In writing about the Atlantic slave trade at this early stage in his political life, Rodney was conscious of the prevailing socio-economic climate in Africa and the Caribbean and used history as a means of contextualizing and assessing contemporary events in the much the same way that Cabral arrived at theoretical-political conclusions through his intimate understanding of social and economic structure of Guinea-Bissauan society. Both challenged the dominant narrative of Marxism and the primacy of European (white) labor, a history that has historically omitted the centrality of slavery and Black labor and the significance of colonialism to the formation of capitalism. Both, in their own ways, point to the importance of conducting assiduous research—one as a historian and the other as an agronomist and revolutionary leader and theorist. For them, theory is not abstract, but drawn from social relations and specific historical contexts; this is what makes ideas potentially universal and part of the universal human experience—providing that we don't attempt to impose purported universals upon particular human experiences.

Of course, culture and history are not only experienced through class, but also through gender and various kinds of human experiences, and clearly women did not experience class differentiation, slavery, or colonialism in precisely the same way that men did. These are obvious omissions in Cabral and Rodney's work. With this in mind, there is much that we can learn from their analyses as we attempt to disentangle the contemporary dynamics of struggle on the African continent, its diaspora, and in other social and political contexts around the world.

26. REMEMBERING CABRAL TODAY

Amrit Wilson

It is perhaps a sign of the neoliberal erasure of history that Cabral's writings are no longer as widely known as they once were. In the seventies and eighties, his ideas influenced a whole generation of progressive and radical Africans, and across the world in the United States and Europe they inspired a generation of activists who had come from 'Third World' countries. His descriptions of colonial violence spoke directly to us, mirroring our experiences and histories not only across Africa but in Asia, the Caribbean and Latin America.

> The political and armed resistance of the people of the Portuguese colonies, as of other countries and regions of Africa, was crushed by the technical superiority of the imperialist, with the complicity of or betrayal by some indigenous ruling classes. Those elites who were loyal to the history of and to the culture of the people were destroyed. Entire populations were massacred. The colonial kingdom was established with all the crimes and exploitation which characterize it… Repressed, persecuted, betrayed by some social groups who were in league with the colonialists, African culture survived all the storms, taking refuge in the villages, in the forests, and in the spirit of generations who were the victims of colonialism. Cabral, A. [1973] (1970) p49.

We were struck by his critical approach and his dazzling commitment to truth. What we got from him was not the fairly routine glorification of anticolonial movements by their often white liberal cheerleaders but a highly nuanced analysis of the way forward, with all its myriad pitfalls. These critical writings struck a chord with everyone from a 'Third

World' background and had a special relevance to others like myself, who, as women, were often acutely aware of the patriarchal ideologies inherent in many movements.

In his *Weapon of Theory*, an address delivered to the first Tri-Continental Conference of the Peoples of Asia, Africa and Latin America in Havana in 1966, for example, Cabral argued that the 'battle against ourselves [which]— no matter what difficulties the enemy may create — is the most difficult of all... This battle is the expression of the internal contradictions in the economic, social, cultural (and therefore historical) reality of each of our countries. We are convinced that any national or social revolution which is not based on knowledge of this fundamental reality runs grave risk of being condemned to failure. (Cabral, A 1966 p 2).

While in his essay, "Tell No Lies, Claim No Easy Victories," he spoke out against what is essentially the inherent machismo of militarism:

> Some people get used to the war, and once you get used to a thing it's the end: you get a bullet up the spout of your gun and you walk around.... there has appeared a certain attitude of 'militarism', which has caused some fighters and even some leaders to forget the fact that we are armed militants and not militarists. This tendency must be urgently fought and eliminated within the army. (Cabral 1965 p2).

But perhaps it was Cabral's seminal writings on culture which inspired us most. His poetic and dialectical metaphor of culture as 'simultaneously the fruit of a people's history and a determinant of history' (Cabral, A. [1973] (1970) p 41), or his argument that 'no culture is a finished whole. Culture, like history, is an expanding and developing phenomenon ... [with] highly dependent and reciprocal... linkages with the social and economic reality of the environment, with the level of productive forces and the mode of production of the society which created it' (Cabral, A. [1973] (1970) p50), made it clear to us then that culture was the dynamic, ever-changing product of struggle, not an static entity interchangeable with circumscribed notions of 'tradition' as defined by colonial anthropology (and also more recently by British multiculturalism).

His language, permeated with his agronomist's knowledge of and dedication to plants, had a unique impact on us. He wrote,

> Culture is an essential element of the history of a people. Culture is, perhaps, the product of this history, just as a flower is the product of a plant. Like history, or because it is history, culture has as its material base the level of its productive forces and the mode of production. Culture plunges its roots into the physical reality of the environmental humus in which it develops, and it reflects the organic nature of the society, which may be more or less influenced by external factors … Just as happens with the flower in a plant, in culture there lies the capacity (or the responsibility) for forming and fertilizing the seedling, which will assure the continuity of history, at the same time assuring the prospects for evolution and progress of the society in question (Cabral, A. [1973] (1970) p 41-42).

Revisiting these passages today, one wishes that Cabral had had more time to elaborate on these ideas and explain them further. Was the 'seedling' the movement itself and what did 'forming and fertilizing the seedling' mean in political terms? Was it the development of a movement, which would be the vehicle to carry forward the struggle and lead to victory?

But of course these were writings from the heart of the struggle—jotted down in course of a protracted war of liberation against one of the most violent and racist colonial powers in Europe. A war in which some 75 percent of the countryside was liberated in less than ten years of struggle and during which schools and health care were established to serve a population where 99 percent had not been able to read and write and 60 percent of babies had died before they were one year old.

Portuguese colonialism was presided over by such semi-feudal, fascist dictators as Salazar, who commented famously, 'Africa does not exist', and Caetano, with his tactics of 'smiling and bloodshed'. It was also actively supported by the growing might of US imperialism and by the major European powers—France, Germany and, of course, Britain, which had for centuries dominated Portugal. As Cabral had put it, "[Britain] adopted a tactic. It said: Portugal is my colony—if it preserves colonies, they are also my colonies—and England defended the interests of Portugal by force."

The liberation movements of the three African countries ruled by Portugal, the PAIGC in Guinea-Bissau, the MPLA in Angola and FRELIMO in Mozambique were closely linked, but of these three countries only Guinea-Bissau, the poorest of the three, was a Portuguese colony in an economic sense. The resources of Angola and Mozambique were siphoned off by the more powerful European countries, while, as Cabral said, Portugal 'remained the policeman and receiver of taxes'.

"Portugal," Cabral had told his audience at an informal meeting with Black organisations in the United States held by the Africa Information Service, "would never be able to launch three colonial wars without the help of NATO, the weapons of NATO, the planes of NATO, the bombs of NATO: The Americans know it, the British, the French, the West Germans know it, and the Portuguese also know it very well. We cannot talk of American participation in NATO, because NATO is the creation of the United States." (Cabral [1973] (1972) p 82).

The '60s and '70s were the tumultuous years of the Cold War, when America was trying to take control of European colonies, or ex-colonies, and, in a striking parallel with today, using informers, carrying out assassinations, engineering regime change and bolstering pro-Western governments. It is against this background that a remarkable generation of African revolutionaries—Cabral, his close comrade Agostinho Neto, leader of the MPLA, Abdulrahman Babu from Zanzibar and Patrice Lumumba from Congo, amongst others, not only fought colonialism and US imperialism but sought to build a socialist Africa. They knew and interacted with each other and there are many similarities (and a few interesting differences) in their strategies and theoretical approaches.

Babu and Cabral are also two theoreticians of the period whose writings and speeches are still easily available to us. Both saw unity across ethnic differences as crucial to any movement for national liberation. Cabral and the PAIGCC struggled from the mid-1960s until his death in 1973 to unify the multiethnic population and variety of interests of Guinea-Bissau and to "preserve," as he wrote, "the positive cultural values of every well-defined social group, of every category, and to achieve the confluence of these values in the service of the struggle, giving it a new dimension—the national dimension." A decade earlier, Babu and his comrades in Zanzibar had struggled similarly, but in different circumstances. They had aimed to unite the people in Zanzibar and build a mass party, the Zanzibar Nationalist Party (ZNP), which would mobilize the people from all racial groupings in a struggle against colonialism, highlighting, at the same time, the need to unite the working class and poor peasants. To an extent this was successful, but eventually the colonial divide and rule policies exacerbated the latent Arab-African tensions in Zanzibar. At this point the ZNP capitulated and became the party of the Arab elite. Babu and other progressives left it to set up the revolutionary Umma Party, dedicated to working for Pan-Africanism and a socialist Zanzibar and transcending the Arab-African divide.[206]

All the leaders of this generation of revolutionaries rejected the racist division of Africa between countries 'North of Sahara' and 'South of Sahara'. Pan-Africanism, in Cabral's words (p. 91) had to be worked for, and clearly it was futile to expect it to be pursued by the pro-imperialist rulers who had come to power in many African states: "It is not for me to accuse Houphouet- Boigny or Mobutu, because they do not want it. They cannot want it! It is... difficult for some heads of state in Africa

206 In December 1963, the British handed over power to the Arab Sultan of Zanzibar. The Zanzibar revolution happened shortly afterwards. That the US succeeded in 'neutralising' Zanzibar and joining it to Tanganyika under the pro-Western leadership of Julius Nyerere is one of the lasting tragedies of East Africa. After the CIA engineered the creation of Tanzania, to place Zanzibar under the control of the pro-Western leadership of Julius Nyerere, Babu was briefly a cabinet minister in the Nyerere government, only to be imprisoned for six years and condemned to death. Released after an international campaign, but with the death penalty still hanging over him, he left Tanzania and lived in the US and UK from where he continued to write and speak about and actively engage in African politics.

to accept African unity as defined by Nkrumah" (Cabral [1973] (1972) p 91)[207]. As Babu wrote in an article commemorating Agostinho Neto, some fifteen years later,

> Africa's post-colonial states as instituted by the departing colonialists were not the proper instruments for bringing about unity. On the contrary, they were meant to intensify divisions and competition among themselves for the benefit of imperialist forces and for international finance capital. Not only have the leaders developed a vested interest in the status quo, but also the very nature of their colonial economies is not conducive to unity; it is conducive to disunity and competition.

Pan-Africanism in the vision of Cabral, Babu, Neto, and other revolutionaries of their generation "was not to be created by a 'union of African states' but from the united will and solidarity of the revolutionary people of Africa." (Babu, A.M. [1993] (1988) p 73.

Related to these analyses of Pan-Africanism and centrally important to the struggles of the era was the nature of the colonial state and what to do about it. "We are not interested in the preservation of any of the structures of the colonial state." Cabral told his listeners at a speech in America, "It is our opinion that it is necessary to totally destroy, to break, to reduce to ash all aspects of the colonial state in our country…" Cabral [1973] (1972) p 83.

---

207 In December 1963, the British handed over power to the Arab Sultan of Zanzibar. The Zanzibar revolution happened shortly afterwards. That the United States succeeded in 'neutralising 'Zanzibar and joining it to Tanganyika under the pro-Western leadership of Julius Nyerere is one of the lasting tragedies of East Africa. After the CIA engineered the creation of Tanzania, to place Zanzibar under the control of the pro-Western leadership of Julius Nyerere, Babu was briefly a cabinet minister in the Nyerere government, only to be imprisoned for six years and condemned to death. Released after an international campaign, but with the death penalty still hanging over him, he left Tanzania and lived in the United States and United Kingdom from where he continued to write and speak about and actively engage in African politics.

Babu's ideas complemented and extended this, "The colonial state" he wrote, "was designed to suppress the entire people and it was based on the use of violence. That kind of state was not intended to develop the people but to undermine their self-respect so as to make it easier to rule them. Its economic activity was limited to the production and export of agricultural commodities for the consumption and production needs of the metropolitan countries. Needs of the people were ignored…" (Babu, A.M. [1993] (1981) p. 20. In fact, as Cabral pointed out, "Some African countries preserved the structures of the colonial state. In some countries they only replaced a white man with a Black man, but for the people it is the same." Cabral [1973] (1972)

Cabral reminded us that "the people are not fighting for ideas, for the things in anyone's head. They are fighting to win material benefits, to live better and in peace, to see their lives go forward, to guarantee the future of their children." Cabral (1965).

Babu, writing of the next stage (i.e. economic development in a newly independent country) sketched a blueprint for self-reliant development, which would provide these benefits. "It cannot be over-emphasized that people are our most precious capital, and therefore, they must eat well, be housed and clothed well. This then is our starting point. The economy must be so structured to provide adequate food, good housing and cheap but good clothing. In the course of providing these, the economy will also develop a good agricultural foundation, together with engineering and extensive textile industries. All of these will create vast employment opportunities for people currently un- or under-employed, who in turn will help expand the home market—essential for further industrial and agricultural development." (Babu, A.M. [1993] (1980) p. 12.

Today we are witnessing a new scramble for Africa's resources, preceded by military conquest. Imperialist armies have proliferated across Africa—French and British forces, NATO, and the US army's new incarnations and surrogates, AFRICOM, and 'peacekeepers' such as ECOWAS in addition to the armies of African countries, whom imperialism has coerced into fighting on its behalf. These are new colonial wars which clear the way for the corporate loot of Africa's oil, gas, uranium and much else, and as before this plunder is justified with self-righteous arrogance, this time in the name of democracy, humanitarianism and the often Kafkaesque logic of the 'War on Terror'.

Meanwhile, in America and in Europe the experiences of one recession after another, always accompanied by escalating racism, bring home the reality that capitalism is in severe crisis. As we read Cabral's last New Year's message of 1973, we are struck once again by his relevance to our struggles today. What he said about Guinea-Bissau and dying Portuguese colonialism is now true on a much wider scale: "The enemy tries vainly to make the Corubal river return to Fouta Djalou instead of flowing towards Goba and the sea. This attempt, like that of tricking our people with the mirage of 'the better Guine,' à la Portugal, and that of making African fight African, is doomed to failure…Without a doubt they will take shameless aggressive action... But all in vain. For no crime, no use of force, no manoeuver, of word or deed, of the criminal colonial Portuguese aggressor will be able to stop the march of history, the irreversible march of our own African people…." (Cabral, A.[1973] (1973).p 99-105).

References

Babu, A.M. [1993] (1980) 'Open Latter to Prime Minister Mugabe' in Babu, Salma and Wilson, Amrit (eds.) *The Future that Works, selected writings of A.M.Babu,* Trenton: Africa World Press

Babu, A.M. [1993] (1981) 'The Tanzania that might have been' in Babu, Salma and Wilson, Amrit (eds.) *The Future that Works, selected writings of A.M.Babu,* Trenton: Africa World Press.

Babu, A.M. [1993] (1988) 'The Visionary Neto' in Babu, Salma and Wilson, Amrit (eds.) *The Future that Works, selected writings of A.M.Babu,* Trenton: Africa World Press.

Cabral, A (1965) Tell no lies, claim no easy victories http://newritings.wordpress.com/2009/02/11/cabral-tell-no-lies-claim-no-easy-victories/

Cabral , A (1966) 'The Weapon of theory', Address delivered to the first Tricontinental Conference of the Peoples of Asia, Africa and Latin America held in Havana in January, 1966. http://www.marxists.org/subject/africa/cabral/1966/weapon-theory.htm .

Cabral, A. [1973] (1970) 'National Liberation and Culture', in Africa Information Service,(ed) *Return to Source: The Selected Speeches of Amílcar Cabral*, New York: Monthly Review Press.

Cabral [1973] (1972) 'Connecting the Struggles: an informal talk with Black Americans' in Africa Information Service,(ed) *Return to Source: The Selected Speeches of Amílcar Cabral*, New York: Monthly Review Press.

Cabral, A.[1973] (1973) 'New Year's Message' in Africa Information Service,(ed) *Return to Source: The Selected Speeches of Amílcar Cabral*, New York: Monthly Review Press.

27. CABRAL'S THEORY OF STRUGGLE AND CARIBBEAN REVOLUTIONARY PARALLELS

Perry Mars

What is most remarkable about Amílcar Cabral's thesis on revolutionary struggle is his insistence that cultural practices are pivotal to successful revolutionary transformation, The major challenge in this regard was to construct a particular methodology of struggle relevant to both colonial and post-colonial conditions. The primary objective was to mold an organic force of revolutionary political leadership capable of combatting colonial oppression and transforming neocolonial relationships and practices. Cabral's ideas on this theme paralleled and reinforced similar revolutionary perspectives of Caribbean intellectual activists, in particular the thoughts and practices of Frantz Fanon and Walter Rodney. Together, their intellectual and organisational efforts influenced revolutionary developments in the Caribbean, mainly in the form of Leftist upsurges and socialist experiments during the 1970s and 1980s.

Attributing significance to cultural practices in revolutionary struggle has affinities also with the earlier efforts amongst Caribbean activist intellectuals residing in the United States during the 1920s and 1930s, particularly the works of CLR James, members of the African Blood Brotherhood (ABB) and the Pan-Africanist movement at the time. The novelty or significance of this cultural centred approach resides in its contrasting and complementary relationship with the deep structuralism of the orthodox Marxism that influenced most revolutionary activists and theorists of the twentieth century. Apart from armed struggle, Cabral and his Caribbean counterparts regarded theory, ideology and history itself as weapons or tools in the realization of revolutionary change.

Theory as Weapon

Briefly, Cabral's main thrust in his 1965 speech on "Theory as Weapon" is about what could be termed decolonising the mind of the colonised or oppressed subjects, particularly of those he termed the national bourgeoisie, or those in the Caribbean context that could be identified as the privileged middle class elite. Here Cabral regarded struggle against internal contradictions and ideological deficiency as absolutely necessary for revolutionary successes against European colonisers and modern imperialism. In essence, revolutionary theory is primarily about combatting Eurocentric thought, ideology and education. The weapon of theory, according to Cabral, should necessarily be linked with armed struggle. This means that the more politically conscious of the Western educated domestic elite or national bourgeoisie must be prepared to "commit class suicide" as Cabral put it, to become capable of leading the working classes in national liberation and revolutionary struggles.

Similarly, Fanon contended that the primary motor in the struggle against colonial and neocolonial oppression is self-liberation., Rodney later suggested that a sense of history itself is a major instrument in the struggle against imperialism and the neocolonial political elite. What these theorists have in common is the high value they place in the organic sources of revolutionary leadership and the pivotal role of self-perception and knowledge of one's own history in bringing about successful revolutionary outcomes. Much like Gramsci, they championed the significant role of organic-activist intellectuals in conducting successful working class revolution. Thus the link between theory and practice is indispensable in revolutionary struggle.

Decolonisation and National Liberation

Whereas the contributions of Cabral and Fanon were historically effective as challenges against colonialism and imperialism, Rodney's contributions were more directly pointed at autocratic elites of neocolonial regimes in politically independent African and Caribbean states. These challenges to colonial or post-colonial oppression were more specifically directed against both white imperialism and Black dictatorial rulers in Africa and the Caribbean. But above all, for these revolutionary theorists, the fundamental struggle towards national liberation and revolutionary change was against one's own weaknesses. By this self-assertive approach, the colonised and oppressed people whose history has been suppressed by imperialism will be able ultimately to regain their true historical personality and identity.

Cabral and Fanon openly advocated armed or violent struggle towards national liberation. Rodney, however, was largely silent on, although not necessarily opposed to, the need for violence in confronting dictatorial post-colonial regimes in the Caribbean—although many in the leadership of his party in Guyana, the Working People's Alliance, including Rodney himself, died violently via police or military interventions. The differences here might be due to the operational distinctions between the colonialism that preoccupied Cabral and Fanon and the imperialism that was the more immediate target of Rodney. European colonialism maintained its political dominance basically through the direct use of force and violence, while US imperialism in the Caribbean tended to be more subtle and indirect and centred mainly on foreign economic exploitation rather than political domination, which made strategies of counter violence feasible in the former case and nonviolent strategies thinkable or optional in the latter case.

These theorists also agreed that in Africa and in the Caribbean the nationalist elite facilitated foreign hegemonic control, and consequently played a rather ambivalent role as a class in the struggles towards decolonisation, national liberation, and political independence since the latter half of the twentieth century. The irony of this Westernized elite rule in Africa and the Caribbean is that while members of this class are a conduit for the persistence of Western imperialism within these territories, it is usually from this very class that the main opposition and challenges to colonial rule and imperialist control are derived.

Class Relations: Feasibility of Class Suicide

Cabral's contention was that sections of the national political elite could become instrumental in the national liberation and revolutionary struggles only to the extent they are prepared to commit "class suicide" by abandoning their traditional class privileges and preferences. Similarly, Rodney advocated the need for members of this elite to shed what he called their "Babylonian captivity"; while Fanon agreed that these must abandon their Eurocentric orientations to become relevant for revolutionary struggles. Fanon further suggested that European racism against members of this national elite also propels the latter into resistance against colonial and imperialist domination. Meanwhile, this racism divides the population into warring racial camps over which the national leadership class has little or no control. At the same time, according to Fanon, the nationalism professed by this class soon degenerates into chauvinism and tribalism.

For Cabral, however, the contradictions between classes are far more significant than those between tribes or races. In this equation, the working classes (broadly defined by Cabral to include the peasantry and the national petit bourgeoisie) become the true revolutionary vanguard. Similarly, Caribbean theorists like Fanon and Rodney, regard the racial/ethnic dimension as subordinate to class forces in the revolutionary process, even if only under certain historically specific conditions. Fanon, in writing of the West Indian, contended, for example, that "a Negro worker in the West Indies will be on the side of the mulatto worker against the middle class Negro,"and further argued that the enemy of "the Negro," as he called him, was not so much the white man but "a man of his own colour." Fanon further concluded that an even more intensive opposition existed between the West Indian and the African than against the European. Rodney, however, was more nuanced in his contention that under some conditions, like in Cuba, Black and white working people collaborate (because white Cuban workers have also been colonised), unlike America, where white workers tend to be "more imperialistic" and therefore more racist against Black workers.

While the superior organisational capability of the Caribbean middle classes puts members of these classes in positions of leadership of working class movements, the typically foreign orientation and outlook of these leaders allow for flaws in this inter-class relationship. Leadership betrayals, as in the cases of foreign instigated splits and purges in the Leftist movements, ranged from the internal divisiveness that led to the breakup of the Caribbean Labor Congress (CLC) in the 1940s, to similar factionalism leading to the defeat of the Caribbean socialist momentum of the 1970s and 1980s. The Caribbean, therefore, is generally devoid of initiatives towards class suicide in Cabral's sense of the term. In Rodney's terms, political intellectuals need to abandon their Babylonian captivity and class privileges and become properly grounded with the urban and rural working classes if revolutionary changes are to be realized.

The few labor or political leaders in the Caribbean who were prepared for such a self-sacrificial task, like Richard Hart, Cheddi Jagan, Walter Rodney, and Maurice Bishop, have had mixed results in bringing about the immediate revolutionary changes they envisaged. Yet over time their common revolutionary goals, such as greater democracy in the 1950s, political independence in the 1960s, socialist programmes in the 1970s and bargaining power for the working classes since the 1960s, were met with the support of the masses and working people across the region, notwithstanding the consistently massive and violent retaliations by foreign hegemonic powers against these developments.

For a long time, the historical dominance of the privileged middle class elites kept the working classes at bay for leadership positions in the political and revolutionary movements in the Caribbean. However, since the emergence of the organised Left in the 1940s, working class militants have gradually been propelled to the forefront of political activism across the region. Alliances between political organisations and working class supports, such as in the formation of the National Joint Action Committee (NJAC) in Trinidad and the Working People's Alliance (WPA) in Guyana, emerged in the 1970s with the specific mission of bridging the gaps that divided the working classes along racial, ethnic, and ideological lines. Unfortunately, the problem of ethnic divisiveness proved to be too entrenched for any single political vanguard to readily resolve.

A most recent example of organic leadership at the grass roots level was the labor- cum-community protest that erupted in August 2012 in Linden, Guyana, against government impositions and neglect of communal demands. This Linden struggle holds a lesson about grass roots leadership of working class struggles, which has the potential for successful political and policy changes. What compares the NJAC struggle in Trinidad with the bauxite community struggle in Guyana is the largely successful effort to replace traditional top-down leadership arrangements with the more community generated leaders and representatives, and labor-political collaboration and solidarity at the mass and communal levels. What, however, is different about the Guyana bauxite workers struggle is their consistent resistance to the vanguardist type of leadership imposed from the outside by political parties and interest groups that are part of the typically divisive power politics at the national level.

Prospects for Revolutionary Change

The relevance of Cabral's theory of liberation for Caribbean revolutionary thought and practice relates mainly to questions about (a) the relationship between armed struggle and cultural level initiatives towards change, (b) prospects about reversing or transforming Eurocentric thought and patterns of behaviour, and (c) the very feasibility of class suicide as revolutionary strategy.

Regarding violence in approaches to change, the context or conditions of engagement must be taken into account. That Cabral and Fanon operated under conditions where the violence and brutality of colonial regimes were unyielding makes a strategy of counter violence thinkable, or inevitable. Historically, Caribbean revolutionary politics tended to be largely nonviolent protest and agitation on the part of the underdog and disadvantaged classes. Whenever violence erupted in Caribbean political and labor resistance, it usually followed violent police or state interventions in peaceful protests. Yet significant and fundamental political changes, including democratisation, independence, and socialist experiments, came through mass agitation and pressures, notwithstanding the relative absence of armed struggle. But the battle continues against the neocolonialist outlook that is clearly evident amongst the Caribbean political elite.

The second issue regarding Cabral's recommendation for battle against neocolonialism calls up the irony that focusing combat on Eurocentric thought tends to reinforce the leadership status of the middle classes, who are usually the most advanced repositories of Eurocentric education in Africa and the Caribbean. There is not yet much traction in this direction of decolonising elitist education in the English-speaking Caribbean, notwithstanding recent strenuous efforts at recognising the creolisation of the English language in schools and the increasing use of the vernacular in popular Caribbean music and song, as exemplified in the calypsos of the Mighty Sparrow and the reggae expressions of Bob Marley. The problem or challenge so far is to devise an adequate Caribbean or Afrocentric educational curriculum that at the same time is capable of accessing advancements in knowledge made possible by increasing technological globalisation.

Finally, the applicability of Cabral's proposal on class suicide comes up against the very entrenchment and intransigence of middle class rule in the Caribbean. Indeed, the historical dominance of the middle classes across the region proved hard to dilute. But there were some contradictions here too, since those prepared to commit class suicide in the interest of the working classes were not similarly prepared to dress down from their leadership role in preference for the cultivation of leadership directly from the grass roots and working classes themselves. Efforts to train the working classes to take over leadership of revolutionary struggles were limited at best, while leadership remained in the hands of the reformed or soon resurrected national political elite. Alas, since the advent of economic globalisation policies imposed by the IMF following the debacle of the Caribbean Left in the 1980s, most of the political leadership even of the once-revolutionary Left across the region have become neoliberals now.

28. AMÍLCAR CABRAL AND PAN-AFRICANISM

Explo Nani-Kofi

Introducing Pan-Africanism

I will define Pan-Africanism as the ideas and efforts made by people of African descent and/or the present population of Africa to reverse the unfair relationships that exists between Africa, Africans, and the rest of the world. Despite Africa's richness in natural wealth, the continent is incredibly marginalised economically and doesn't have political weight in relation to the rest of the world. People of African descent worldwide are disproportionately represented in the most downtrodden sections of society throughout the various countries in which they reside.

There is a diaspora older than the recent migration. The original diaspora arose mainly from enslavement, and those in it have borne the brunt of this marginalisation. In fact, the Eastern Older Diaspora in the Middle East, Caspian Sea, and Europe has not been as remembered as the one in the Americas and Europe. The organisation and mobilisation for the restoration of fairness and equity in humanity as a united African people has become known as Pan-Africanism, and the movement that has grown alongside it is the Pan-Africanist movement.

Amílcar Lopes da Costa Cabral

In the precolonial era, the question of unity against occupying forces was simple and quite easy to deal with. However, the postcolonial era, with Black people holding government office and supposedly running affairs, Black people as representatives for the multinational companies and Blackplaying all manner of roles, including the president of the United States of America, things have become more complicated with regards to the strategy for

Pan-Africanism. It is in this complexity that Amílcar Lopes da Costa Cabral towers as a theoretician and a strategist for the Pan-Africanist cause. Amílcar Cabral was the leader of the African Party for the Independence of Guinea and Cape Verde (PAIGC) before his assassination on January 20, 1973.

Amílcar Cabral avoided the use of terminology and slogans, so whilst his theoretical influences, especially the uncompromising position on class, are very clear, those who have prejudices based on terminology find it impossible to attack Cabral, as they do others who may be coming from the same angle as Cabral. His approach helps unite the movement in a progressive and radical direction. It also helps explain many of the questions which are raised around the postcolonial state in Africa and its failures. He made the case for centrality of the postcolonial state for the African crisis in his statement, "The problem of the nature of the state created after independence is perhaps the secret of the failure of African independence."[208]

Importance of Theory

Amílcar Cabral emphasised the importance of theory in building the movement for a successful revolution. He pointed out that ideological deficit, which arises from the ignorance of the historical reality that liberation wants to transform, was a serious weakness of the movements. For him, it was important for the African liberation movements and others to pay attention to the problem of a common struggle. It was his position that enough experiences have been accumulated to help define a general line of thought and action to eliminate ideological deficiency. He drew attention to the fact that these conclusions came out of experiences of the African liberation struggle and that of others. He said, "To those who see in it a theoretical character, we would recall that every practice produces a theory, and that if it is true that a revolution can fail even though it be based on perfectly conceived theories, nobody has yet made a successful revolution without a revolutionary theory." [209]

208 Amílcar Cabral, Cabral, *Connecting The Struggles – An Informal chat With Black Americans*; New York, October 20, 1972

209 Amílcar Cabral, Cabral, Connecting The Struggles – An Informal chat With Black Americans; New York, October 20, 1972

Brothers, Sisters, or Comrades?

When Amílcar Cabral met the African Americans in 1972 during his visit to the United States, he took the opportunity to lay down part of his vision, tactics, and strategy for the Pan-African struggle, as it was the occasion to discuss issues of struggle on the continent and in the diaspora. He introduced the question of merely being blood relations—like brothers and sisters. He felt that was not enough in to unite the struggle and that people should develop their relationships as comrades; camaraderie marks the relationship of political engagement, making the stakes higher. He held the position that the contribution of African Americans towards solving problems in the United States assisted the advancement of the African struggle, and it was unnecessary for all African Americans to pack luggage to come to struggle in Africa. He told his United States audience that racism is a product of certain circumstances, but that racism cannot be fought with racism. He stressed the reality that when you suffer racism, you cannot love the ones who cause you the suffering, but for him it wasn't a fight of white people against Black people. Whilst they fought against Portuguese colonial rule, they were not against the Portuguese people as a whole. "We are fighting for the freedom of our people—to free our people and to allow them to be able to love any kind of human being." [210]

He advised that you have to combat the causes of racism. He said when you have a problem you have to change the light and that will affect the shadow. He let people know that in struggle, you have to consider the conditions of the terrain you fight in, and people you organise in different places have different conditions. He felt that there should be proper analysis, as opposed to taking things which seem alike as the same. He stressed that this will avoid wasting time. He argued that the point was not to do the correct thing now, but to do it as soon as it becomes possible.[211]

---

210 Amílcar Cabral, Connecting The Struggles – An Informal Chat With Black Americans, New York, October 20, 1972

211 Amílcar Cabral, Homage To Kwame Nkrumah, Conakry, Guinea, May 1972

Tribute to Kwame Nkrumah

He acknowledged Kwame Nkrumah as a leader, and in fact as his leader, in the Pan-Africanist movement and paid one of the highest tributes on the occasion of his death. Touching on Kwame Nkrumah's greatness and his achievements, Cabral, in his usual way, asked a number of questions;

> We must however draw the lesson from all events. Even at this moment of grief, we must ask ourselves some questions the better to understand the past, live the present and prepare for the future... For example, what economic and political factors made the success of the betrayal of Ghana possible, despite Nkrumah's personality, courage and positive action?...True, imperialism is cruel and unscrupulous, but we must not lay all the blame on its broad back. For, as the African people say: `Rice only cooks inside the pot'...Just how far would the success of the betrayal of Ghana have been linked or not to the questions of class struggle, contradictions in the social structure, the role of the Party and other institutions, including the armed forces, in the framework of a newly independent state'. Just how far, we wonder, would the success of the betrayal of Ghana have been linked or not linked to the question of a correct definition of that historical entity, that craftsman of history, the people, and to their daily action in defense of their own conquests in independence? Or then, just how far might not the success of the betrayal be linked to the key question of choice of men in the revolution? [212]

He explained that in finding answers to these questions, we throw more light on Kwame Nkrumah's greatness. He also drew attention in the tribute to the fact that Nkrumah himself understood all these difficulties and pointed this out to them (other freedom fighters) from time to time. This was evident in Nkrumah's own reflections after the coup,

212 Kwame Nkrumah Dark Days In Ghana, London, 1966; Africa And The World, London, March 1966; June Milne, Kwame Nkrumah – The Conakry Years (His Life And Letters), London, 1990

as he pointed out how his own party, the Convention People's Party, was not an appropriate vehicle for carrying the Pan-African struggle, and how many within the leadership were found wanting. Kwame Nkrumah has detailed this in his book *Dark Days in Ghana* during his interview with Douglas Rogers in the March 1966 issue of "Africa And The World," as well as in his various letters in *Kwame Nkrumah—The Conakry Years: His Life and Letters*, compiled by June Milne.[213]

Amílcar Cabral, in addressing the questions he posed, concluded that,

> The African peoples and particularly the freedom fighters cannot be fooled. Let no one come and tell us that Nkrumah died from cancer of the throat or any other sickness. No, Nkrumah was killed by the cancer of betrayal, which we must tear out by the roots in Africa, if we really want to liquidate imperialist domination definitively on this continent.

He also warned that, so long as imperialism exists in an independent African state, there must be a liberation movement in government, or else it will not be truly independent.[214] As Cabral analysed the cancer of betrayal which killed, he couldn't predict what awaited him. In his case the cancer of betrayal was not subtle, as he was dragged at three in the morning on January 20, 1973 and shot to death like a goat by his own comrades, with whom he was fighting in the trenches against Portuguese colonialism.

Class Struggle

Cabral was clear on the point that class struggle is a motivating force for revolution and social change. He explained the difficulties that the African struggle faces with the role of the African petit bourgeois in the postcolonial era. Cabral pointed out that,

---

213 Amílcar Cabral, Homage To Kwame Nkrumah, Conakry, Guinea, May 1972

214 Amílcar Cabral, "Brief Analysis of Social Structure in Guinea," a seminar held in the Frantz Fanon Centre in Treviglio, Milan, from May 1 to 3, 1964.

> As for the Africans, the petit bourgeoisie can be divided into three sub-groups as regards the national liberation struggle. First, there is the petit bourgeoisie which is heavily committed and compromised with colonialism: this includes most of the higher officials and some members of the liberal professions. Second, there is the group which we perhaps incorrectly call the revolutionary petit bourgeoisie: this is part of the petit bourgeoisie which is nationalist and was the source of the idea of a national liberation struggle in Guinea. In between lies the part of the petit bourgeoisie which has never been able to make up its mind between the national liberation struggle and the Portuguese. Next come the wage-earners, which you can compare roughly to the proletariat in European societies, although they are not exactly the same thing: here, too, many members of this group were not easy to mobilise—wage-earners who had an extremely petit bourgeois mentality and whose only aim was to defend the little they had already acquired. [215]

African Petit Bourgeoisie

Cabral pointed out that the African petit bourgeoisie is the class which will take control of the state in the postcolonial era. He noted that, since it is a service class, it doesn't even have the capacity to act as a national bourgeoisie. It is left with the option to either side with the imperialist or with the working class. This is a very important question of the Pan-Africanist movement in the postcolonial era. This question was being addressed by the All African People's Conferences, in which Cabral was one of the steering group members.

> In order not to betray these objectives, the petit bourgeoisie has only one road: to strengthen its revolutionary consciousness, to repudiate the temptations to become "bourgeois" and the natural pretensions of its class mentality; to identify with the classes of

215 Amílcar Cabral, Unity And Struggle – Speeches And Writings Of Amílcar Cabral, New York, 1979

> workers, not to oppose the normal development of the process of the revolution. This means that in order to play completely the part that falls to it in the national liberation struggle, the revolutionary petit bourgeoisie must be capable of committing class suicide as a class, to be restored to life in the condition of a revolutionary worker completely identified with the deepest aspirations of the people to which he (she) belongs.[216]

Cabral sees the importance of international solidarity. He felt, however, that our international friends would do well to understand the circumstances within which we work, so that this can inform them of how to effectively assist us. He drew attention to some of the weaknesses in the European Left approach to solidarity. The European Left sometimes assumes or even demands that the African petit bourgeoisie that comes into government advance the path of revolution, ignoring the path through which the petit bourgeoisie ascended to power.

National Liberation and Culture.

Some acclaimed Pan-Africanists haven't come to terms yet about how culture can be a facilitator for achieving African unity instead of being divisive. In a lecture on national liberation and culture, Cabral started by informing the gathering that, "When Goebbels, the brain behind Nazi propaganda, heard culture being discussed, he brought out his revolver." Cabral explained that history teaches us that any form of foreign domination can be maintained by a permanent and organised repression of the cultural life of the people concerned. He said,

> The ideal for foreign domination, whether imperialist or not, would be to choose: either to liquidate practically all the population of the dominated country, thereby eliminating the possibilities for cultural resistance; or to succeed in imposing itself without

216 Amílcar Cabral, National Liberation And Culture, Speech At Eduardo Mondlane memorial Lectures, Syracuse University, New York, February 20, 1970

> damage to the culture of the dominated people--that is, to harmonize economic and political domination of these people with their cultural personality. [217]

Pan-African unity will be facilitated by ending the suppression of the cultural life of Africans.

Conclusion

As stated earlier, Cabral is not one of those who use a lot of terminology to address Pan-Africanism or socialism, but when you go back to what Pan-Africanism or socialism are about, and then return to the contents of Cabral's speeches and writings, you will find that he has been one of the most articulate on both these issues. Cabral, guided by his understanding of the issues, communicates effectively with his audience. He is, therefore, the indispensable source when it comes to addressing the theory, tactics, and strategy of Pan-Africanism in the postcolonial era, especially when it comes to the reality of Africa as it is today. Despite the fact that he was killed forty years ago, Cabral's positions describe what we are going through today as if he were describing them now.

217 Amílcar Cabral, National Liberation And Culture, Speech At Eduardo Mondlane memorial Lectures, Syracuse University, New York, February 20, 1970

SECTION 6:

CABRAL, CULTURE, AND EDUCATION

29. CABRAL, CULTURE, PROGRESS, AND THE METAPHYSICS OF DIFFERENCE

Olúfémi Táíwò

Were we to take seriously Cabral's injunctions respecting culture, its place in national liberation, and its role in progress, a lot of what is done in the name of scholarship on Africa, by both African and Africanist scholars, would not pass muster. This is because we have embraced the racism-inflected metaphysics of difference that was originally used to deny our humanity and our place at the summit of civilizations. Progress requires that we eschew this metaphysical paradigm in rebuilding our culture towards the completion of national liberation.

Amílcar Cabral's ideas and writings reward continual revisits. The occasion of the fortieth anniversary of his assassination by agents of the Portuguese secret service is a welcome opportunity to take another look at his writings and assess them, not only for their cogency, internal consistency, political relevance, or philosophical sophistication, but also, and more importantly, for their uncanny prescience. My focus in this reflection turns on a singular prescient warning respecting the dialectic of identity and culture in Africa and in Africa's relations with the rest of the world.

Cabral was very exercised by the matter of culture. Colonialism did a lot of damage to the culture of the colonised. Indeed, part of the strategy of the coloniser to ensure the subjugation of the colonised was to deny the humanity of the latter. And given that one of the singular manifestations of our humanity is the culture that we create and transmit through successive generations to our progeny, it is obvious that to deny our humanity is to deny that Africans have any legacy of monuments, ideological and physical institutions, processes and practices that can justifiably be regarded as our contribution to the world's summit of civilizations. To our colonisers, our music was noise, our dance was obscenity, our religion was fetish, we did not have literature, philosophy was beyond our ken, and, most of all, we were a people without history. In short, it was at the behest of our conquerors that we became a part of humanity's history march.

When the colonisers—French, Portuguese, and British—denied that Africans are human and are, therefore, culture bearers and history-makers, they did not single out any particular African group. They made no distinctions amongst African groups or cultures. Of course, it stands to reason that they did not think that Africans could be treated as individuals, an attitude which, in the peculiar context of our historical epoch—the modern age—with its singular concern with the principle of subjectivity, is almost absurd. In light of this collective indignity, it comes as no surprise that in their response to this denial, Africans, during the national liberation struggle and in the aftermath of independence, have repeatedly affirmed a collective identity and a corresponding African culture. Here is the danger: in responding to a collective denial with a collective affirmation, one has not really transcended the limits imposed by the denier. Quite the contrary, in so doing, one has conceded, however unwittingly, the truth of the denial.

When colonialism and its operators and ideologists denied that Africans are human, they were proceeding from a metaphysical standpoint defined by radical Otherness. Africans are radically different from human beings, and if they may be considered human, their humanity was of such a different temper that they may be treated as inferior beings. Thus was inaugurated what I now call the *metaphysics of difference*. The metaphysics of difference predate colonisation; it was originally created to justify the enslavement of Africans and expiate any guilt or moral culpability in the execution of the transatlantic slave trade and the New World slavery that was built on it.

In the modern age, the dignity attached to the sheer personhood of a human individual is inviolate, and the modern age is the only one in history that has made the promotion and protection of the dignity of the individual the metaphysical template from which all other philosophic and practical ideas, institutions, practices, and processes are fashioned. The ideologists of modernity could not at one and the same time proclaim the universal entitlement to dignity of all humans while enslaving a significant section of the human race. The solution is simple: Africans *are* different; therefore, no sin or crime is committed in enslaving them.

Certainly we do not talk of dog culture or the culture of other lower animals or inanimate objects. Only humans create culture, and by so doing leave for posterity a record of their creativity, their genius, and, for good measure, their follies. As bad as this racism-inflected denial of our humanity is, it is worse that, in negating it, we have, in the main, adopted its dubious starting point and made it our own. That is, many African scholars have embraced the metaphysics of difference, and it now informs a large part of scholarship by both African and Africanist scholars. There is a high degree of essentialisation that characterises discussions of African phenomena from the criteria of what it is to be African—in its many forms and manifestations—to how one ought to conduct oneself, one's social relations, or with whom one may have relations and in what depth. From reacting to the ravages of difference-denominated denial of our humanity, we have become earnest apostles of the metaphysics of difference and censorious guardians against its transgressors. In our earnestness to affirm African difference, we have forgotten or chosen to ignore the racist provenance of this ahistorical, false metric.

Frantz Fanon long ago realized this and made clear a similar logical connection between denial and its negation. Fanon wrote that, "following the unconditional affirmation of European culture came the unconditional affirmation of African culture."[218] Neither "unconditional affirmation" is likely to be insightful or hold much promise of illumination for our understanding of its substantive focus. At the same time, Fanon unhesitatingly traced the genealogy of this orientation. According to him, "it is all too true that the major responsibility for this racialisation of thought, or at least the way it is applied, lies with the Europeans who have never stopped placing white culture in opposition to the other noncultures."[219]

---

218 Frantz Fanon, *The Wretched of the Earth*, trans. Richard Philcox, New York, Grove Press, 2004, p. 151

219 Fanon, p. 150

I would like to suggest that we owe Cabral a debt of gratitude for apprehending, even if he did not so name it, what I have called the metaphysics of difference, and warning all and sundry of the pitfalls attached to it. We can all use a reminder of this dimension of Cabral's humanism.

> We talk a lot about Africa, but we in our Party must remember that before being Africans we are men, human beings, who belong to the whole world. We cannot therefore allow any interest of our people to be restricted or thwarted because of our condition as Africans. We must put the interests of our people higher, in the context of the interests of mankind in general, and then we can put them in the context of the interests of Africa in general.[220]

In insisting that the world and general humanity be the framework for the unfolding of national liberation and the rebuilding of African culture that would emblematise that liberation, Cabral forewarned against the crude generalisations that now frame some of the discourse on Africa and things African. Contrary to his forebodings, the metaphysics of difference now defines much of African self-definition and the conceptualisations of Africa in scholarship. The failure of liberal democracy and the rule of law to take root in many parts of Africa was for so long attributed to the inherent incompatibility of a nebulous African culture with the tenets of modern political philosophy. Witchcraft continues to exercise African and Africanist scholars alike because of the persistent influence of the metaphysics of difference in the scholarly imaginary concerning Africa.

African phenomena continue to be designated differently because the African experience is adjudged to be irremediably different from those of other peoples in other parts of the world. Only recently have scholars begun, ever so timidly, to allow that the problem of creating supranational identities from the motley traditions of particularism that populate the continent is not different from what obtains in the overwhelming percentage of the world's countries. For so long, scholars were led on a wild

220 Amílcar Cabral, *Unity and Struggle: Speeches and Writings*, trans. Michael Wolfers, London, Heinemann, 1980, p. 80.

goose chase conveniently labeled "nation-building" as the primary lens through which to see the problem of creating supranational identities, as if this were a peculiarity of African polities. Whereas the truth of the matter is that the business of manufacturing a modern citizenship to overlay the multiple nationalities and ethnicities that typify most countries in the world is *exactly* what African countries were required to do in the aftermath of independence. But African scholars allowed themselves to be led down theoretical blind alleys once they accepted that theirs was a special problem conveniently dubbed "tribalism" and the challenge it poses to the pseudo-problematic of "nation-building."

Cabral knew that separating Africa and Africans from the general flow of common human experience could only lead to the retardation of social processes on the continent. Cabral knew well the danger of confronting the denial of African culture with the affirmation of some unique, one-of-a-kind African culture. He cautioned against selecting any number of behavioural traits as being essentially African and unlike anything to be found amongst other peoples of the world. He feared that such affirmations would not allow Africans to embrace and enact the rapid changes that the continent would need if it were to march again in tandem with the rest of common humanity.

Cabral's theory of culture and its place in national liberation merits extra attention. National liberation occurs when a people reassume their capacity for history-making, epitomized by "the liberation of productive forces" and "the ability freely to determine the mode of production most appropriate to [their] evolution" and which "necessarily opens up new prospects for the cultural process of the society in question, by returning to it all its capacity to create progress."[221] There are many pitfalls on the path to this attainment. First, he warns us to abjure,

> [T]he supposition that there can be *continental* or *racial* cultures. This is because, as with history, culture develops in an uneven process, at the level of a continent, a "race" or even a society. The coordinates of culture, like those of any developing

221 Cabral, p. 143.

> phenomenon, vary in space and time, whether they be material (physical) or human (biological and social). The fact of recognizing the existence of common and special traits in the cultures of African peoples, independently of the colour of their skin, does not necessarily imply that one and only one culture exists on the continent. In the same way that from the economic and political point of view one can note the existence of *various Africas*, so there are also *various African cultures.*[222]

When our moral and political philosophers affirm, caveats notwithstanding, the idea of communalism as emblematic of what they designate as African culture, they run afoul of this caution from Cabral. When they affirm "Ubuntu" or some version of it, as the centrepiece of a so-called African metaphysics, they run afoul of Cabral's caution. When scholars write as if Africans are marked by an "intense religiosity," they also run afoul of this caution.

Worst of all, when things that we should have gotten rid of a long time ago amongst our cultural practices—belief in witchcraft, for instance, and institutions that should have no place in our modern setting, such as rule based on ascription rather than merit and on selection rather than the consent of the governed—are turned into constitutive elements of a putative African culture, we likewise fail to pay heed to Cabral's admonition. He could not have been more direct in the following:

> There are many folk who think that being African is being able to sit on the ground and eat with one's hand. Yes, this is certainly African, but all the peoples of the world have gone through the stage of sitting on the ground and eating with one's hand. There are many folk who think that it is only Africans who eat with their hands. No, all the Arabs in North Africa do it. But even before they were Africans, before they came to Africa (they came from the East to Africa), they used to eat with their hands and seated on the ground.[223]

222 Cabral, p. 149. My italics.
223 Cabral p. 57

He later added for flourish,

> If you see a film about the Vikings of olden days, you can see them with great horns on their heads and amulets on their arms, setting off for war. And they would not set off for war without their great horns on the head. No one should think that to be African one must wear horns on one's chest and an amulet around one's waist. Such persons are individuals who have not yet properly understood the relationship between man and nature. The Portuguese did the same, the French did it when they were Franks, Normans, etc. The English did it when they were Angles and Saxons, voyaging across the sea in canoes, great canoes like those of the Bijagos.[224]

Cabral was not ready to regard as definitive of African identity traits and practices that were mere contingencies in the historical evolution of humankind. By turning, say, witchcraft and its diffusion amongst Africans into anything other than a sign that "such persons are individuals who have not yet properly understood the relationship between man and nature," scholars are turning Africans into permanent equivalents of the Vikings of olden days and their great horns and amulets. Such may titillate, but I doubt that they illuminate our understanding of African processes.

Cabral calls on us to eschew the metaphysics of difference and, instead, treat African phenomena as they really are: examples of the general human experience denominated by specific histories and nothing more. We need critically to engage with and seek always to understand in the most complex ways the historical evolution of humankind as this unfolds within specific cultures. For Cabral, this is the only route to progress, to the kind of culture that would do justice to the very goal of national liberation: the restoration and efflorescence of the human dignity of ordinary Africans. To do this, our appreciation of the different cultures in Africa must be characterised by honesty and frankness. We must not embroider our weakness nor exaggerate our strengths. We must, in all ways,

224 Cabral, p. 57

be willing to rid our cultures of anachronisms, while borrowing what we lack but is present in other cultures with which we are familiar, regardless of the latter's racial or geographical provenance.

> We must have the courage to state this clearly. No one should think that the culture of Africa, what is really African and so must be preserved for all time, for us to be Africans, is our weakness in the face of nature. Any people in the world, of whatever status, has gone through the stage of these weaknesses, or has to go through them. There are folk who have not reached it: they spend their lives climbing trees, eating and sleeping, nothing more yet. And then, what myths they still believe! We should not persuade ourselves that to be African is believing that lightning is the fury of the deity (God is feeling angry). We cannot believe that to be African is to think that man has no mastery over the flooding of rivers. [225]

Any observer of the contemporary African scene at the present time cannot fail to see that the weaknesses that Cabral highlighted now dominate the continent, probably to a worse degree than when he wrote. The continent has become one vast theater of religious fundamentalisms, dueling for supremacy over who has the most following in numbers and the most intensity in zealotry. Saddest of all, our universities are themselves wallowing in this supernaturalist cauldron. Cabral was quite prescient in his insistence on the centrality of culture to true national liberation. And it is why he was concerned to take a critical scalpel to our indigenous culture. Nor was he afraid to acknowledge the obvious: "Our struggle is based on our culture, because culture is the fruit of history and it is a strength. But our culture is filled with weakness in the face of nature. *It is essential to know this.*"[226]

That his warning is relevant at the present time is the best indicator of how poorly African intellectuals have internalised the lessons from Cabral's

225 Cabral, pp. 57-8.
226 Cabral, p. 58. My italics.

writings. They do bear reiteration; it is what progress enjoins. Yes, we must affirm, even celebrate, "the cultural values of African peoples."

> But in the face of the vital need for progress, the following factors or behaviour would be no less harmful to [Africa]: unselective praise, systematic exaltation of values without condemning defects; blind acceptance of the values of the culture without considering what is actually or potentially negative, reactionary or regressive; confusion between what is the expression of an objective and historical material reality and what appears to be a spiritual creation or the result of a special nature; absurd connexion of artistic creations, whether valid or not, to supposed racial characteristics; and finally nonscientific or ascientific critical appreciation of the cultural phenomenon.[227]

Were we to take seriously Cabral's injunctions respecting culture, its place in national liberation, and its role in progress, a lot of what is done in the name of scholarship on Africa by both African and Africanist scholars would not pass muster. And I have no doubt that Cabral would take a dim view of much that is passed off these days as African culture, especially in the humanities and social sciences. Africa's continuing failure to embrace the scientific revolution is the ultimate reason for the relevance of Cabral's disquisition on culture and progress. A significant step towards remedying this defect is the extirpation of the metaphysics of difference.

227 Cabral, p. 150.

30. CABRAL AND FREIRE

THE IMPORTANCE OF CULTURAL CAPITAL IN REBUILDING A SUCCESSFUL EDUCATION SYSTEM IN GUINEA-BISSAU

Brandon Lundy

This chapter revisits two attempts to institutionalise a radical approach to teaching in Guinea-Bissau put forward by Paulo Freire and his predecessor Amílcar Cabral. This chapter analyses how cultural capital influenced each man's educational initiatives in the country. Throughout this chapter, *cultural capital* refers to a social lubricant within a cultural landscape or "habitus" that includes accumulated, "embodied" cultural understanding that confers power to the bearer to effect real change (Bourdieu 1986).

As leader of the African Party for the Independence of Guinea and Cape Verde (PAIGC), Cabral worked to revise the inherited colonial educational system by relying on his strong cultural ties to the country. Most scholars agree that he was quite successful in generating a revolution amongst the people of Guinea-Bissau that a majority could support. After his assassination, the PAIGC leadership continued Cabral's commitment to education by enlisting the Brazilian exile, educator, and radical thinker, Paulo Freire, to help them develop an adult literacy programme beginning in 1975. From the outset, Freire advocated for a collaborative and engaged educational style, what he called "authentic help" (1978:8) built on the *people's reality*. Freire participated in the adult literacy programme from May, 1975, to October, 1976. He attempted to understand the national milieu of Guinea-Bissau by visiting the country several times and reading the works of the nation's architect,

Amílcar Cabral. For Freire, however, his task to develop a viable adult literacy programme would prove to be daunting as an outsider in the face of grinding poverty, a largely uneducated population, little usable infrastructure, political disagreements over the country's direction, and a fractured educational legacy that favored the country's elite.

Cabral's Vision for Education in Guinea-Bissau

The Portuguese government under the fascist Estado Novo of António de Oliveira Salazar invested little in its African colonies in terms of developing infrastructure or promoting their ideology of *assimilação* (assimilation).[228] Patrick Chabal (2003:16-17) showed that in the 1950 colonial census, there were only 1,478 (0.39 percent) *assimilados* in Portuguese Guinea (present day Guinea-Bissau) from a total population of 502,457, the lowest percentage in all of Portugal's African colonies. In more than five centuries, Guinea-Bissau remained one of Portugal's "least penetrated and least developed" African colonies (Harasim 1983:82).

The limited formal education that was taking place in West Africa was cautiously brought about by colonial regimes to develop good workers and low-level administrators "without running the risk of creating critical and thinking people" (Harasim 1983:96). According to Eduardo de Sousa Ferreira, "a very limited African elite was educated for one purpose only: to support Portuguese hegemony and act as an intermediary between the colonial machinery and the African population" (1974:55).

Amílcar Cabral himself noted that there were only 43 Catholic mission schools operating in Portuguese Guinea by 1962, serving a population of just 800 students (1979:25). In addition, there were no universities and only one secondary school. Cabral himself, along with his

228 "In order to become assimilated, the *indigena* had to be 18 years old and to speak Portuguese correctly. He had to earn a sufficient income for himself and his family and to produce two testimonies of good character. He must have attained a sufficient level of education. He was required to submit a birth certificate, a certificate of residence, a certificate of good health, and a declaration of loyalty; and to have paid the appropriate taxes and fees" (Chabal 2003:16).

few contemporaries, had to go to Portugal for postsecondary education. This is where he and several other expatriate Africans from Portuguese colonies began to develop a unified philosophy of "re-Africanization" (an assertion of African self-identity) to counter the colonial attempts at "de-Africanization" (Chabal 2003:42) in which "culture belonged only to the colonisers" (Freire 1978:14). It was this idea of a shared critical consciousness that Cabral promoted amongst not only the small proletariat but even more so amongst the rural masses of Guinea-Bissau through formal and informal educational initiatives.

For Amílcar Cabral, the revolutionary power of education was central to the continuation and success of the independence movement and future of the country. In a 1968 interview, he explained:

> The difficulties of our struggle were mainly those inherent in our situation as an underdeveloped—practically nondeveloped—people whose history was held back by colonialist and imperialist domination. A people that started with nothing, a people with a 99 percent illiteracy rate—you have already seen the effort that we have to make now to teach our people to read and write, to create schools—a people that had only 14 university-trained men—this people was surely going to have difficulties in carrying out its armed struggle...It is a struggle for schools, for hospitals, so that children won't suffer. That is our struggle...And, if you had the opportunity to speak to the children, you would see that even our schoolchildren are already politically and patriotically aware and desire the independence of our country. They have an awareness of mutual understanding, of national unity and of unity on the African continent. [1969b:143, 145-146]

The fledgling nationalist education system during Guinea-Bissau's liberation struggle focused on both ideology and practicality. It was a driving force behind PAIGC's campaign for state formation. Cabral realized, "The people do not fight for ideas or anything that is simply in men's heads. They accept the sacrifices required by the struggle in order to be able to live better and in peace. They want to guarantee the future and progress for their children" (1969a:23).

PAIGC's "Major Programme" of 1963 highlighted five educational initiatives. (1) Education reform including the expansion of secondary, postsecondary, scientific, and technical capacity was needed. (2) Free and universal education along with the eradication of illiteracy was necessary. (3) Dismantling of the colonial educational system had to take place to break free from Portuguese hegemony. (4) Writing and preserving indigenous and Creole languages as well as protecting and promoting national literature and arts were critical for educational advancement. Moreover, (5) striking a balance between preserving tradition and modernizing was the only way to achieve mass acceptance of the latter through culturally accepted mechanisms (Harasim 1983:111).

Cabral's leadership of the independence movement inspired a revolutionary ideology amongst its citizenry, as demonstrated through their successful collective actions (Forrest 1992; Galli & Jones 1987) and emergent mutual respect for diverse cultural groups within the country (Davidson 2002; Pattee 1973). Cabral, using critical theory and grounded practice, succeeded in building cultural capital amongst the oppressed Bissau-Guineans.

For example, Cabral maintained a political strategy of nonalignment to ensure international support from both the East and the West during the Cold War years, while using socialist language throughout the liberated education system. Cabral tasked three trusted PAIGC leaders, including his half brother and the eventual first president of Guinea-Bissau, Luís Cabral, with designing a progressive and *culturally sensitive* curriculum. Syllabi for five primary-school years were created, including subjects like conversational Creole and civics, which was "designed to instill nationalist fervor in first-year children" and eventually covered in-depth study of the PAIGC (Dhada 1993:98). "To minimize brain drain, an advanced course on the history of the PAIGC in the context of world politics was introduced, as was a new interdisciplinary course, nationalist themes in the performing, dramatic, and visual arts" (Dhada 1993:105; see also, Rudebeck 1974).

Unfortunately, while attempts were made to create a comprehensive yet culturally sensitive educational system, what eventually emerged was a two-tier system, one for the civilian public sector that was severely underfunded and understaffed, and a second set of boarding schools that catered to the needs of the liberation movement. At the same time, after 1966, when the Portuguese intensified their campaign, PAIGC school administrators were coping with decreasing enrollment due to parents' refusal to let their children leave home because of increased bombings.

> To overcome parental resistance, the PAIGC leaders established a string of coaxers who went to villages near day primary schools with a view to overcoming resistance—or what the party called "detrimental traditions." … "The men and women who refused to send their children to school are enemies of our struggle," said Cabral. [Dhada 1993:108-109]

In some regards, the PAIGC educational initiatives worked too well. Eventually, the PAIGC boarding schools "helped breed and perpetuate a new proto-military class— a class that subsequently came to dominate postcolonial independence politics" (Dhada 1993:112). Their biggest hurdle to comprehensive education was the fact that they were unable to reach enough of the population in the midst of armed rebellion. Between 1965 and 1972, PAIGC was only able to educate a yearly average of 10,989 students, about a quarter of which were female (Urdang 1979:175). Due to this inadequate capacity, no adult education and literacy took place during the liberation struggle (Harasim 1983:117). After independence, Mario Cabral, the commissioner of State Education and Culture (note his title linking *education* and *culture*), tried to resolve this deficiency by contacting Paulo Freire, an acquaintance and supporter of Cabral and the resistance. Freire's postcolonial contributions to Guinea-Bissau's educational system will be explored next.

After Cabral: Freire and Guinea-Bissau

Writing about the vision for Guinea-Bissau at the start of the new nation, journalist Stephanie Urdang suggested,

> The very process of education was itself helping to develop a new society. The students were being prepared for a future that did not yet exist, and in this way were themselves molding the future. Their education was an insurance that the revolutionary direction of the society into which they would pass would be carried forward. "Our type of education," said Cabral, "has to be conditioned in each phase of the struggle by *the life and the history we experience* at a given moment." [Urdang 1979:171, italics mine]

Similarly, Freire notes, "To the extent that we become capable of transforming the world, of naming our own surroundings, of apprehending, of making sense of things, of deciding, of choosing, of valuing, and finally, of *ethicizing* the world, our mobility within it and through history necessarily comes to involve *dreams* towards whose realization we struggle" (2004:6-7, italics in original). Freire advocates here for what he calls a "counter-hegemonic" approach in the classroom through the establishment of a dialogic relationship between students' and teachers' shared culture. Freire was successful in exposing forms of domination through education found in all societies by helping to expose the political nature of such institutions.

Linda M. Harasim, in her 1983 doctoral thesis, *Literacy and National Reconstruction in Guinea-Bissau: A Critique of the Freirean Literacy Campaign*, notes how shared ideological congruencies attracted the PAIGC-led Guinean government to pursue the Freirean method. Freire recognised the high levels of political literacy of the Bissau-Guinean people. He worked hard to develop a *context-specific* literacy model that assumed particular social relations and motivations: a desire to acquire literacy; develop an educational infrastructure; train competent teachers; provide the necessary resources to support these endeavors; and politically develop, support, and maintain a long-term literacy campaign (Harasim 1983). Between 1976 and 1980, when Harasim's evaluation took place, however, these social, economic, and political relations and motivations were slow in materializing throughout the countryside of Guinea-Bissau.

Freire himself recognised the pitfalls of what he was invited to do. Reflecting two decades later, Freire recalls, "The challenge for me in Africa, as I pointed out in *Letters to Guinea-Bissau: Pedagogy in Process*, was to be cautious always and aware of my role as an outsider who had been invited to provide some help with the transformation of the inherited colonial educational structure" (Freire and Macedo 1995:399). He continued, "I always stressed the importance of a thorough analysis of culture in the development of a liberatory educational plan. In fact, *the importance of culture* was not my idea, since their leader Amílcar Cabral understood extremely well the role of culture in the struggle for liberation" (Freire and Macedo 1995:399, italics mine). Freire, along with his French counterpart, Pierre Bourdieu, viewed culture as something more than a reproduction of social or national character and heritage (Bourdieu and Passeron 1977).[229] Culture was central to their approach, because they believed that "Liberation begins with the recognition that knowledge at its root, is ideological and political, inextricably tied to human interests and norms" (Giroux 1979:261).

Despite Freire's emphasis on culture as a foundation for education, he was only able to partially grasp the cultural *realities* affecting Guinea-Bissau during his brief encounter. Amílcar Cabral, on the other hand, was fully engaged with the ground-level cultural conditions and worked within them to maximize a nationalist sentimentality without denying unique cultural practices and activities amongst disparate groups. Cabral's multicultural approach sought unity in diversity. As such, Cabral is a prime example of a radical educator, who used "the *cultural capital*—language and life style of the oppressed—in an effort to promote amongst them an interest and critical reading of reality on both the local and larger levels" (Giroux 1979:265, emphasis mine). With the 1980

229 "Culture provides a society with the symbolic language for interpreting the boundaries of individual and social existence" (Giroux 1979:260).

coup and subsequent political unrest over three decades, however, neither Cabral nor Freire's initiatives were given adequate time to develop into successful cultural institutions. Interestingly, a more contemporary study (Cissoko and Daun 1989; Daun 1997) of the educational system in Guinea-Bissau shows that both men's approaches emphasizing cultural capital and competency continue to have great potential and should not be overlooked in future educational initiatives.

Daun (1997) systematically demonstrates the problems with Guinea-Bissau's primary educational system by presenting the findings from a large survey of more than 2,400 students and 125 teachers from 24 lower primary schools. To start, it was determined that the least successful students, based on pass and drop-out rates, were rural Balanta girls whose primary form of communication was their own ethnic language (Ahlenhed et al. 1991). Daun's study showed that the primary factor in higher pass rates and lower drop-out rates was the common use of a similar language between the student and the teacher, in this case, the Portuguese Creole lingua franca. Daun goes on to interpret this finding as indicating the importance of socio-cultural and economic similarities between instructor and pupil (Daun 1997:67).

Next, culturally-oriented factors for the teacher were found to be important in determining the success rates of students, including the teacher's gender, identity, religious participation, and participation in local activities, which supports the argument presented thus far (Daun 1993, 1997; Daun and Gomes 1993). Unfortunately, contrary to this finding, the teachers were frequently transferred by the Ministry of Education in a deliberate attempt to prevent tribalism. In so doing, many of the teachers had no family, local support, or adequate cultural capital in the communities they served. This led to a deprioritization of classroom instruction by the teacher and poor academic performances by the students (Daun 1997:60; Cissoko and Daun 1989).

Daun concluded her research by identifying additional problems and potential solutions to the educational dilemma plaguing Guinea-Bissau. For example, school and community agendas are often in opposition, educated youth have no professional outlets, agrarian and cultural obligations are time consuming and viewed as more necessary than formal education particularly in rural communities, and communication barriers are largely disregarded. To help overcome these obstacles, Daun suggested that new teachers should be trained to adapt to local culture, be provided enough economic compensation to concentrate on pedagogy, and understand linguistic issues affecting the classroom where Portuguese is spoken by less than 1 percent of the enrolled student body (Daun 1997:69).

Conclusion

Daun's findings show that the Cabral-Freirean educational legacy in Guinea-Bissau has continued merit. Now, more than ever, policy makers in Guinea-Bissau need to consider cultural capital as an effective strategy to providing a meaningful service to the country's population in the face of resource inadequacies. Education starts with a shared understanding and empathy between administration, teachers, parents, and pupils. By knowing and understanding their students, they can help position them to succeed in the Bissau-Guinean context and challenge the unequal global system.

Guinea-Bissau's Ministry of Economy, Planning, and Regional Integration released their "Second National Poverty Reduction Strategy Paper" (PRSP) in June, 2011. In alignment with the United Nation's Millennium Development Goals (MDGs) for education (universal enrollment and gender parity in schools by 2015), much of the PRSP's focus was on developing education. In that same year, however, education and health expenditures combined made up only 20.7 percent of the country's budget, while the international recommendation is 40 percent (2011:19). The PRSP demonstrates that both the educational track record remains poor (e.g., 2010 saw a national literacy rate for women of 39.3 percent, and fewer than half the students enrolled in school will complete their sixth year) and the educational initiatives are largely being dictated from outside the country. Unfortunately, none of the five action plans or six government commitments outlined in the report recognise the importance of culture in education paramount to both Cabral and Freire's approaches (2011:37).

Only when discussing the implementation of "Measure V" of the PRSP, aimed at developing and improving the quality of the education system in Guinea-Bissau, is the importance of cultural capital, as argued in this chapter, even broached—"prepare and adopt new school programmes appropriate for the country's *economic and social realities*" (2011:88, italics mine). This chapter suggests that working within cultural realities fosters trust and will lead to achievable, context-sensitive programmes of study that can advance Guinea-Bissau's human capacities. Without the acknowledgement of the importance of culture in education, the status quo remains.

References

Ahlenhed, B., G. Callewaert, M. Cissko, and H. Daun

(1991) *School career in lower primary education in Guinea-Bissau. The pupils and their socio-economic and cultural background.* SIDA Education Division Document No. 54, Stockholm.

Bourdieu, Pierre

(1986) "The Forms of Capital". In *Handbook of Theory and Research for the Sociology of Education.* J. Richardson, ed. Pp. 241-258. New York: Greenwood.

Bourdieu, Pierre, and Jean Claude Passeron

(1977) *Reproduction in education, society, and culture.* Thousand Oaks, CA: Sage Publications.

Cabral, Amílcar

(1969a) *Palavras de ordem gerais do Camarada Amílcar Cabral aos responsaveis do partido* (Novembro de 1965). Conakry: PAIGC (September).

Cabral, Amílcar
(1969b) *Revolution in Guinea: Selected Texts by Amílcar Cabral.* R. Handyside, transl. New York: Monthly Review Press.

Cabral, Amílcar
(1979) *Unity and Struggle, Speeches and Writings of Amílcar Cabral.* M. Wolfers, transl. New York: Monthly Review Press.

Chabal, Patrick
(2003) *Amílcar Cabral: Revolutionary Leadership and People's War.* Trenton, NJ: African World Press.

Cissoko, M., and H. Daun
(1989) *A Vida Profissional e Social dos Professors do EBE.* (The professional and social life of the teachers in lower primary). Ministry of Education/INDE, Bissau.

Daun, Holger
1993 *O Professor e Sucesso Escolar dos Alunos do Ensino Basico Elementar na Guinea-Bissau.* (The teacher and pupils school success in lower primary in Guinea-Bissau). Institute of International Education, Stockholm University/ SIDA, Stockholm.

Daun, Holger
(1997) "Teachers Needs, Culturally-Significant Teacher Education and Educational Achievement in an African Context—The Case of Guinea-Bissau." *International Journal of Educational Development* 17(1):59-71.

Daun, H., and A. Gomes
(1993) *O Papel do Professor e As Caracteristicas dos Alunos no Sucesso Escolar na Guinea-Bissau.* (The role of the teacher

and the characteristics of the pupils in school success in Guinea-Bissau). Institute of International Education, Stockholm University and SIDA/Ministry of Education, Stockholm/Bissau.

Davidson, Joanna
(2002) Plural Society and Interethnic Relations in Guinea-Bissau. In *Engaging Cultural Differences: The Multicultural Challenge in Liberal Democracies*. R. A. Shweder, M. Minow, and H. R. Markus, eds. Pp. 417-431. New York: Russell Sage Foundation.

Dhada, Mustafah
(1993) *Warriors at Work: How Guinea Was Really Set Free*. Niwot, CO: University of Colorado Press.

Ferreira, Eduardo de Sousa
(1974) *Portuguese Colonialism in Africa: The End of an Era*. Paris: UNESCO Press.

Forrest, Joshua B.
(1992) *Guinea-Bissau: Power, Conflict, and Renewal in a West African Nation*. Boulder, CO: Westview Press.

Freire, Paulo
(1978) *Pedagogy in Process: The Letters to Guinea-Bissau*. C. S. J. Hunter, transl. New York: The Seabury Press.

Freire, Paulo
(2004) *Pedagogy of Indignation*. Boulder, CO: Paradigm Publishers.

Freire, Paulo, and Donaldo P. Macedo
1995 *A Dialogue: Culture, Language, and Race*. Harvard Educational Review 65(3):377-402.

Galli, Rosemary E., and Jocelyn Jones
(1987) *Guinea-Bissau: Politics, Economics and Society.* Boulder, CO: Lynne Rienner.

Giroux, Henry A.
(1979) Review: Paulo Freire's Approach to Radical Education Reform. *Curriculum Inquiry* 9(3):257-272.

Harasim, Linda M.
(1983) *Literacy and National* Reconstruction in Guinea-Bissau: A Critique of the Freirean Literacy Campaign. Ph.D. Diss. Toronto, Canada: Department of Educational Theory, University of Toronto.

Pattee, Richard
(1973) Portuguese Guinea: A Microcosm of Plural Society on Africa. *Plural Societies* 4 (4): 57-64.

Republic of Guinea-Bissau Ministry of Economy, Planning, and Regional Integration
(2011) *Second National Poverty Reduction Strategy Paper. DENARP/PRSP II (2011–2015)*, Bissau, June 2011. Washington, DC: International Monetary Fund.

Rudebeck, Lars
(1974) *Guinea-Bissau: A Study of Poltical Mobilisation.* Uppsala, Sweden: Scandinavian Institute of African Studies [Nordiska Afrikainstitutet].

Urdang, Stephanie
(1979) *Fighting Two Colonialisms: Women in Guinea-Bissau.* New York: Monthly Review Press.

31. CABRAL, CULTURE, AND EDUCATION

N. Barney Pityana

How shall we measure Progress there where the dark-faced Josie lies? How many heartfuls of sorrow shall balance a bushel of wheat? How hard a thing is life to the lowly, and yet how human and real! And all this life and love and strife and failure— is it the twilight of nightfall or the flush of some faint-dawning of the day?

Thus mused W.E.B. Du Bois, one of the early Pan-Africanist intellectuals, who ended his life in Ghana, on the Continent where he knew his forebears once dwelt. In this essay, *On the Meaning of Progress*[230], Du Bois was recalling his early years in the rural Deep South, where he first toiled to bring learning to the eager and opportunity to those whom destiny sought to consign to the fate of the unknown. Whatever the challenges and contradictions, he could still perceive, in the darkness, the "flush of some faint-dawning of the day." Such are those who are to make a difference to our world, many of them unheralded but present and faithful, driven by an inner spark of genius and inspiration. Today these are the educators and academics, the intellectuals in all walks of life, who are shaping a future for our nations.

Culture and education are words that are often placed side by side. The sequence of the words belies the truth that these are interchangeable and mutually reinforcing expressions of meaning. There is therefore the recognition that "education" and "culture" are interlinked, and it is truly not possible to have one without the other. One presumes that this topic is of pertinent interest to the African Union and its programs for the advancement of the Objectives set out in the Constitutive Act of the

230 *The Souls Of Black Folk*; New York; Dover Publications, 1903.

African Union, 2000. In particular that the AU should achieve greater unity and solidarity amongst African nations and peoples, accelerate socio-economic and political integration, promote sustainable development, and advance research, especially in science and technology (Article 3). The purpose of this address is to explore the linkages between culture and education and examine the processes of knowledge formation and developments from an African perspective.

It is noticeable that the view of culture in many international instruments, especially UNESCO, posits a view of culture that is formalist and denuded of its radical character. For example the UNESCO Declaration on Cultural Diversity (2001) refers to culture as the "distinctive spiritual, material, intellectual, and emotional features of society or social group, and that it encompasses, in addition to art and literature, lifestyles, ways of living together, value systems, tradition, and beliefs." The value of the declaration, I submit, lies in the extent to which it makes the connections between culture and education explicit, that it is "at the heart of contemporary debates about identity, social cohesion, and the development of a knowledge-based economy."

There is also the developmental approach to culture that the declaration espouses: "Cultural diversity widens the range of options open to everyone; it is one of the roots of development, understood not simply in terms of economic growth, but also as a means to achieve a more satisfactory intellectual, emotional, moral and spiritual existence" (Article 3). UNESCO has gone further. In its latest convention on the Protection and Promotion of the Diversity of Cultural Expressions, adopted by the General Assembly of UNESCO at the thirty-third session in Paris in October, 2005, UNESCO emphasizes the interrelationship between education and culture as preconditions for sustainable development.

It has been suggested that Antonio Gramsci, Franz Fanon, and Amílcar Cabral write from the perspective of revolutionary cultural theory as they assert the transformative character of culture rather than the conservative impulses of some culture practitioners. Fanon sees the role of culture as the "awakener of the people … to speak to the nation, to compose the sentence which expresses the heart of the people, and to become the mouthpiece of a new reality in action." Antonio Gramsci states that "every revolution has been preceded by an intense labor of social criticism, of cultural penetration and diffusion...." Finally, for Amílcar Cabral, culture "enables us to know what dynamic syntheses have been formed and set by social awareness in order to resolve these conflicts at each stage of evolution of that society in search of survival and progress...." The essence of these reflections is to note that culture is a necessary tool for discovery, advancement, and change.[231] It best expresses itself and has lasting value when it transcends the past and the presence while building on them in order to better understand the present and shape (or take responsibility for) the future.

There has been a resurgence of scholarship on Amílcar Cabral, not least amongst African scholars both in Africa and in the diaspora. For Cabral cannot be confined to the achievements of the liberation struggle in Guinea-Bissau and the Ilha Cabo Verde. Largely during the course of that struggle, he has bequeathed to critical scholarship in Africa and the world social and political theories that can now be applied to analyze and model social transformation. It was after all Cabral who perceived and articulated the link between revolutions and theory when he stated that "nobody has yet made a successful revolution without a revolutionary theory." [232] Speaking in the context of national liberation movements, he drew attention to the evolution of societies and their distinctive features in the production cycle, to the dynamism and mutative character of classes:

> In fact in the general evolution of humanity and of each of the peoples of which it is composed, classes appear neither as a generalised and simultaneous phenomenon throughout the totality of these groups, nor as finished, perfect, uniform, and spontaneous

231 A full discussion of the various theories of culture can be found in my "Beyond Transition: The Evolution of Theological Method in South Africa – A Cultural Approach," an unpublished doctoral thesis submitted to the University of Cape Town (1995); pp67 ff.

232 *The Weapon of Theory*, an address delivered to the First Tri-Continental Conference of the Peoples of Asia, Africa and Latin America held in Havana, Cuba, January 1966 –http://www.marxists.org/subject/africa/cabral/1966/weapon-theory.htm

> whole. The definition of classes within one or several human groups is a fundamental consequence of the progressive development of the productive forces and of the characteristics of the distribution of wealth produced by the group or usurped from others.... (1966:3).

In this way he developed a more nuanced and fluid theory of the class structure in African society which was not as deterministic as that in Marxist orthodoxy at that time. In this way the responsibility for revolution could be owned by a wider set of social forces, who would be responding to their social circumstances. And so he concluded: "... the level of productive forces, the essential determining element in the content and form of class struggle, is the true and permanent motive force of history." For him the abiding history of peoples will outlive any class determinants, and man will "continue to produce and make history, since he can never free himself from the burden of his needs, both of mind and body, which are the basis of the development of the forces of production."

That is an extract from Cabral's celebrated essay, *National Liberation and Culture* (1970), in which he opens up the possibility of societies creating their own culture with each generation:

> The liberation of productive forces and consequently the ability to determine the mode of production most appropriate to the evolution of liberated people. Necessarily opens up new prospects for the cultural development of the society in question, by returning to that society all its capacity to create progress (1970:5).

Surely such a cognitive openness to new styles of living, new and different understandings of one's world, and new instruments of aesthetic and intellectual engagement opens up the possibility of culture being a helpmate of education rather than merely a hindrance.

Amongst the more significant Cabral scholars one must count Carlos Lopes and Carlos Cardoso, but new work is emerging from younger scholars like PLE Idahosa, and I cite his seminal essay, *Going to the People:*

Amílcar Cabral's Materialist Theory and Practice of Culture and Ethnicity (Lusotopie 2002/2: 29-58). The essence of Cabral for our topic today is stated by Idahosa as "knowledge in the service of liberation." At issue was his recognition of sound theory and of culture for revolution. Of essential import in Idahosa's view is that Cabral sought to "develop people's self- consciousness and an awareness of their power to make their own history...." He had a unique trajectory towards development and revolutionary change, and that was a set of values based on theory and social context, and on a moral calculus that would be an abiding compass for the postindependence conditions.

I have dwelt on Cabral and his theories because I wish to make a point he may never have made, and that is that culture is the means for prying open the sources of knowledge; education will lead to a deeper appreciation and value of culture. I therefore now turn to the relationship between culture and education.

Education, it is now widely acknowledged, is a necessary resource for human existence by which nature endows us with the power of inquisitiveness, with a desire to expand our knowledge base and to discover the new, to exercise our intellectual capacity to extract meaning from our world, to expand one's social and intellectual horizons, and to gain insight, skills, and knowledge, which in turn can add value to our surroundings as we find them. Education is the beneficent factor in human relations and in humanity's relationship with its natural environment. So understood, education, formal and informal, is a fundamental human right, the irreducible essence of human nature. Education therefore must be exploited, nurtured, valued, advanced, developed, shared, and disseminated freely as a common good.

Scholars now gradually acknowledge diversities in science. We can no longer speak of a homogenous science, any more than we can speak of the prince of the sciences. What has emerged, says Hans N Weiler[233], is a "conception of knowledge that is at once more differentiated (in the

233 Hans N Weiler: *Challenging the Orthodoxies of Knowledge: Epistemological, Structural, and Political Implications of Higher Education*; Unesco Forum on research and Higher Education Policy, 1-3 December 2004.

sense that it differs by the objects of knowledge and the circumstances of generating it) and more contingent (in the sense of statements that are valid only under certain conditions)." Weiler then talks about the casualties of this development; but I prefer to refer to the benefits. Under this rubric now, ethics, moral understanding, and artistic expression can no longer be dismissed as "unscientific." Social scientists can now acknowledge the "cultural" attributes of knowledge. There is recognition that societies have culturally sensitive ways of knowing and understanding, something which historically has been denied. That has meant that there are also culture-specific notions of epistemology. This has made it possible for indigenous knowledge systems and other culture-oriented knowledge systems to be affirmed as valid systems of knowledge.

The Beninoise philosopher Paulin J Hountondji[234] can therefore confidently conclude that,

> The Third World today has structures of scientific and intellectual production where an extremely important work is done, a work the results of which sometimes have a resounding impact world-wide. It is out of question here to minimise that production or to ignore its value. The only problem is to know how it functions, how, by whom and in whose service it is exploited, what position it holds in the general knowledge economics world-wide, in other words, are those structures henceforth truly autonomous?

Hountondji makes the case for the legitimacy of knowledge produced in the South in noncartesian models of knowing and being. He observes that the creation of knowledge was always perceived to be the preserve of Western academies; the rest of us mere consumers.

The interrogative character of culture, as Cabral presents it, means that society may have to live with uncertainties, because, as Hans Weiler is quoted as saying, "New ways of knowing bring with them a profound

234 *Globalised Knowledge: Imbalances and Current Tasks*; Unesco Forum Colloquium on Research and Higher Education Policy, Paris, December 2004.

doubt about established conventions in the production of knowledge and an exhilarating sense of a new beginning."[235] Armed with Cabral's view of culture, I believe that the stage is now set for us to examine how a culture-oriented education system can deliver a liberatory system of education. Cabral sought to develop people's self-consciousness and an awareness of their power to make their own history. He also provided for us an abiding compass informed by values based on theory and social context, as well as a moral calculus. Liberation, Franz Fanon observes, is always preceded by the "renewing of forms of expression and the rebirth of the imagination."

In a similar vein, other great African minds have since exhorted Africans to take up that power of which Cabral speaks. Most of the strategies, tactics, aims, and goals are formulated and expressed in the plethora of policies, declarations, frameworks, and partnerships, such as Education For All, UNESCO instruments and programs, the OAU/AU initiatives, especially NEPAD and the APRM, to name but a few. These articulate quite poignantly a very lucid understanding of what such power should and indeed must achieve. It remains one of the mysteries and tragedies of our time that despite this understanding, and despite one well-intentioned educational initiative after another, launched by one august body after another, the intellectual capital seems to remain trapped in the vacuum of the debate so generated, unable to ignite effectively that spark that will galvanize Africa to committed and concerted action *en masse.* We need to intensify our efforts if we are to bring to fruition the wonderful plans for this continent and do justice to its enormous potential. And so it would be remiss of me were I to neglect the urgency and importance of our educational mission in Africa, and the important role that governments can and must play in this regard.

On a more positive note, what has emanated from recent years of debate and interrogation of African issues is an increasing awareness and acceptance of the need to work together as a continent and an African

235 In Homi K Bhabha: *Global Pathways to Knowledge: Narration and Translation*; Unesco Forum Colloquium on Research and Higher Education Policy; Paris, December 2004.

community in addressing our education needs. It also makes good sense to use this strategy when dealing with the international community. One strong articulate voice articulating a very clearly defined message will surely be heard more clearly than a chorus of discordant noises.

Franz Fanon, a native of Martinique in the Caribbean, adopted Africa as his own native land. He became to many of us the voice of the liberation struggle of Algeria and a critic of the postindependence lethargy and antirevolutionary malaise that set in, as it often happens to many of our countries. In his speech, *The Reciprocal Bases of National Culture and the Fight for Freedom,* published in his celebrated book of essays, the *Wretched of the Earth*, Fanon ends his address with these words:

> If man is known by his acts, then we will say that the most urgent thing today for the intellectual is to build up his nation. If this building up is true, that is to say, if it interprets the manifest will of the people and reveals the eager African peoples, then the building of a nation is of necessity accompanied by the discovery and encouragement of universalising values.

That, I submit, is the challenge of education and culture, properly understood.

32. RAP KRIOL(U) [236]

THE PAN-AFRICANISM OF CABRAL IN THE MUSIC OF THE YOUTH

Miguel de Barros and Redy Wilson Lima

> *... Cabral ka môri... Cabral e mi Cabral e bô Cabral e tudu kauberdianus e guineenses...*
>
> *(Cabral is not dead ...Cabral is me Cabral is you Cabral is all Cape Verdeans and Guineans.)*

In the 1990s, with the wave of democratisation in Guinea-Bissau and Cape Verde, the PAIGC as well as the PAICV, being both political parties and considered as the "strength, light, and guidance of the people," lost their status. As a result, the youth reinvented new forms of interactions with their peers in a context marked by globalisation and Afro-Americanization of the world, where hip-hop culture, through its oral element, rap, appears as a vehicle for freedom of expression and protest amongst the most precarious urban groups. This article analyzes

236 Kriol(u) = Creole: It refers to an emergent Creole language at the beginning of the 16th century from a mixture of mainly Portuguese vocabulary and structural elements of mandinka, wolof, fula and other West African languages. The Guinean and Cape Verdean creole are part of the oldest Upper-Guinea group of creole languages. For more profound examination, see the following authors: Coelho, A. (1868), *Os dialectos românicos ou neo-latinos na África, Ásia e América*, Coimbra: Imprensa da Universidade; Carreira, A. (1982), *O crioulo de Cabo Verde - surto e expansão*, Lisboa: Gráfica Europam; Veiga, M. (2002), *O Cabo-verdiano em 45 Lições*, Praia: INIC; Pereira, D. (2006), *Crioulos de base portuguesa*, Lisboa: Caminho.

how the young Guinean and Cape Verdean provided, through rap, a renewed context for the Pan-Africanist and nationalist discourse of Amílcar Cabral, taking into account the challenge of preventing the erasure of collective memory and history, the alleged betrayal of his ideals by today's political leaders, and the need to recover Cabral as the guide of the people, representing him as an emcee (messenger of truth).

Since its beginnings, the appeal of rap seems to reside in its accessibility and easy use by the youthful majority with scarce economic and cultural resources (Bennett, 2001). Through the analysis of documents and speeches of Amílcar Cabral, the narratives of rap music espoused Guinean and Cape-Verdean youth, the participant observation in concerts and recording studios, and the informal conversation with the rappers, we can see Creole language [here designated as *kriol(u)*] as an instrument of the (re)mapping and construction of a new nation that, from Augel's (2007) perspective, transforms into an act of freedom through the conquest of emotional, affective, and identified territory. Thus the rapper (re)introduces an ideological and militant function, using the linguistic patrimony of Guinea and Cape-Verde.

This article critically illustrates the discussions of youth about the political and governmental practices of the contemporaries of Cabral, about their own protests against marginalisation, and social oppression, assuming for themselves the role of protagonists of their civic actions, looking for new emancipatory mechanisms through rap music.

Rap is used as an instrument of negotiating and/or reclaiming public space, displacing traditional rhythms such as *Gumbé* [237] and *Batuku* [238] (*Finason*), with the capacity to use radio and the Internet for a new form of youthful protagonism—the conscious rap.

From Youth of the "Party" to Uncertain Transitions

In Guinea-Bissau and Cape Verde, the need to control the youth has been a concern since the colonial period. Under colonialism, this was

237 Musical style of Guinea-Bissau.
238 Musical style of Guinea-Bissau.

carried out mainly by the Catholic Church, whose function was "to civilize" behaviours and attitudes. This process gained political impetus with the creation of political organisations such as the *Mocidade Portuguesa* (Portuguese Youth).

During the PAIGC mobilization for the armed struggle, the youth question had a particular resonance, especially in the creation of the spaces for the formation of the "New Man" in the liberated zones in the forests of Guinea-Bissau, where the "Pilot Schools" [239] models had been replicated in the final phase of the armed struggle.

In the post-independence period, a one-party regime was established in Guinea-Bissau and Cape Verde, governed by the PAIGC as a party-state, which strengthened the coordination of mass organisations with socialist/communist inspiration. The *Juventude Africana Amílcar Cabral* (JAAC), or Amílcar Cabral African Youth, was created with a view to the construction of a nation-State to guarantee the unity between Guinea-Bissau and Cape-Verde. The 1980 military coup in Guinea-Bissau ended the project of unity with Cape-Verde. The *Partido Africano para a Independência de Cabo-Verde* (PAICV), or African Party for the Independence of Cape Verde, had little influence on the youth.

In 1991, with the wave of democratisation in the two countries, both the PAIGC and the PAICV lost their stature as the "force, light, and guide of the people," which simultaneously implied the end of the chain of "domestication" of spirits (Barros, 2010: 7). However, the regimes in the two countries related differently to youth organisations. In Guinea-Bissau the PAIGC regarded the JAAC as its partisan youth organisation, later creating the *Conselho Nacional da Juventude* (CNJ), or National Youth Council, which had a national structure (under government control). In Cape Verde the reorganisation implied the transformation of the

---

239 Inaugurated in February 1965, in Conakry (Republic of Guinea), had for purpose to give shelter, protection and education in boarding school regimen to the children victims of bombardments and the practical and ideological formation of quadres of the liberation movement. For deeper understanding, see: Godinho Gomes, P. (2010: 91-104).

OPAD-CV[240] into a nongovernmental organisation, retaining the same name, whereas the JAAC became extinct (Lima, 2012: 203).

It was during this period, when the existence of one form of youth organisation was being extinguished, that rap music started to penetrate the Guinean and Cape Verdean societies through American productions. In the case of Guinea-Bissau, it was mainly through music from Portugal, while in the case of Cape Verde, it was through the growing influence of North American "gangsta" rap .

On the streets, rap plays a crucial role in the mobilization for protest (through music, the body, and clothing) of urban youth. It is in this way that *kriol(u) RAPpers* seek to use the "ideology of the word" (Morgan, 2009) so that they can present themselves as "MC"—*os mensageiros da verdade* (the messengers of the truth).

In Guinea-Bissau and in Cape Verde, *Cabral ka muri/mori* (Cabral is not dead) is a slogan that immortalizes the spirit of sacrifice and struggle that Cabral himself made.

Of the conscious/political rap that mention Cabral, four basic aspects stand out:

1. A preoccupation with maintaining Cabral as reference against the risk of collective and historical whitewashing of memory;
2. Criticism of the "comrades" and current politicians vis-à-vis practices of alien to the political thoughts expressed by Cabral;
3. Utilization of Cabral as "guide" and bearer of hope;
4. Cabral as messenger of the truth, that is to say, as MC.

Thus, for example:

> ...poku poku guentis sta ta skeci / bu sta mori manenti na mimoria di nos povu / bu storia / ta duvidadu pa gerason mas nobu / nem bu imagem ka sta mas na livru primaria / na dinheru / djes trau / ... bu bai bu dexa puema pa nôs kriança ki e flor di

240 Abel Djassi Pioneer Organisation – Amílcar Cabral's *nom-de-guerre* – structure created during the national liberation struggle.

> revoluson i di sperança / mas mesmu si ka sta xinti bu prizensa / kriança sta nasi e ka konxi storia di ses eróis / alguem / ki da si vida pa liberta si povo se foi / es ta trokau pa eróis virtuais / homem-arranha, super-homem
>
> —POMBA PRETO, Abel Djassi, 2010

> ... little by little people start forgetting / you are dying permanently in the memory of our people / your story is doubted by the younger generation / neither your image is present in primary school books / your image was removed from money notes / ... you left leaving behind a poem for our children who are the flowers of the revolution and of hope / but even if your presence is not felt / children are born without knowing the story of their heroes / gone is somebody who gave his life to free his people / you have been turned into virtual heroes / spider-man, super-man
>
> —Pomba Preto (Black Dove), Abel Djassi, 2010

In general, the preoccupation with the maintenance and actualization of the live memory of Cabral is more present in the narratives of Cape Verdean rappers than amongst Guineans.

> ...Disgrasa d'es tera kunsa desdi mortu di Cabral / Chefi di guera matadu / Objetivu di luta mudadu / En vez di concordia nacional i bin concordia criminal
>
> —Torres Gemeos, Culpadus, 2008

> ...The disgrace of this land started with the death of Cabral / The war chief was assassinated / The objective of the struggle was changed / Instead of national concordance / Came criminal concordance.
>
> —Torres Gemeos, Culpadus, 2008

> ...Ma n punta, será ki anos ku na paga díbida di n ba luta? NAU! / Ei abós ke Amílcar falaba bos es? NAU! / Ke Amílcar falaba bos ora ku luta kaba pa nterga povu fatura? / Bo mata Amílcar bo nteral djuntu ku si konbersas / Konbersas ki pusível i pasa sedu impusível
>
> —FBMJ, Guiné ka na fika sin, 2008
>
> ...But I ask, are we to pay the debt for them having fought? NO! / Hey did Amílcar tell you this? No! /Amílcar told you to deliver the invoice to the people after the struggle? /NO! / You killed Amílcar and buried him together with his conversations / Conversations that were possible turn impossible
>
> ...Bardadi situason sta gravi / Kampu kinti / Amílcar Cabral erói mas garandi / Aonti bu matadu aós bu fidju na sufri kansera garandi / Kin ku pudi imajinaba kuma anós no na abandona no tera / Nde ku no firma ku arma na mon no nganha ki guera / Kontra no toma independensia no pensa kuma tudu na sedu mindjor / Ma son kansera vida di djintis na tiradu suma flor
>
> —N`PANS, Fidjus di Guiné, 2006
>
> ...Truth is, the situation has worsened / The heat is on / The greatest hero Amílcar Cabral / Assassinated yesterday, your children suffer much today / Who could have imagined that we will abandon our land / Where we stood and defended with arms in our hands and won that war / When we took independence we thought that everything would be better / But only suffering, the lives of our people are being taken away as if they were flowers

In this part, there is a feeling of revolt and disenchantment with the lack of opportunities, social justice, peace, and unity for these youths.

...Na nha tera ka tem so morna ku koladera / Tem monti asnera kes ta bari pa baxu stera / Gosi e dibaxu meza ki nigosius sta fitxadu / ... Monti makakisi i monti makaku di fatu, gordu i tudu fartu / Otus ta furta k apa farta ma sin pa mata fomi / Ami n sta odja monti mininu ta sufri na lugar di omi / ...Thugs sta ta aumenta tudu dia pa alimenta skina / Alvés n ta pensa si tudu kel stôria di thugs li e ka un bodi espiatóriu ba tudu es prublema di susiadadi li / Juventudi ka sta dadu oportunidade / Monti sta ta termina lise upa inisia na mundu di marginalidade / Monti Zé-ninguen sta ta fazi so maldadi pamô es dadu puder pa ser autoridade

—Buddha, Na Nha Tera, 2008

In my country there is not only morna and koladera / There are many foolishness that is swept under the mat / Now it is under the table that deals are closed / ...many monkey businesses and many monkeys wearing suits, fat and all fed up / Others steal not to be well fed but to kill hunger / I watch many children instead of men suffering / ...Thugs increase every day to support loiters /their day starts when yours ends / and I go about thinking if all this history of thugs is not a scapegoat for all the problems of the society / The youth is not given opportunity / Many are about to finish high school to enter in the course of marginality /Many nobodies make only wickedness because they were given power to be the authority

E sufrimentu i garandi dimás / Te gosi no fika tras / Di nos i pena / Di nos i tristi / Nha ermons até kuandu? / Tera di Amílcar Cabral / Ex-colónia di Portugal / Nunde ku 80% di povu ta vivi mal / Vizinhu di Conakry ku Senegal / Situadu na kosta osidental / sukundidu na kintal ... Tera di no eroína mama Titina Silá / Djintis ku luta / pa serka António Spínola / Independensia tomadu prejuízu kunsa ten / Povu ta vivi mal pa un grupusinhu vivi ben ... Chefi bati rendimentu / Povu entra na sufoku / No

> sai di país mas limpu / Pa país mas porku / 7 di junhu komplikanu situason / Balas di kanhons matanu populason
>
> —Mc Mário, Don Pina E Patche Di Rima, Relatório 1973-2012, 2012

> This suffering is too much / Up till now we lag behind / ... My brothers until when? / Land of Amílcar Cabral / Ex-colony of Portugal / Where 80% of the people live badly / Neighbor of Conakry and Senegal / Situated in the west coast / Hidden in the backyard … land of the heroine Titina Sila / People who fought / to expel Antonio Spinola / Independence achieved injuries began to appear / People live badly for a small group to live well … Chief reduced incomes / People began to suffocate / we leave the most cleanest country / To the most dirtiest / June seventh complicated the situation /cannon balls killed our population

When the narratives that present Cabral as "guide" are presented in direct speech, the references carry the appeal to the struggle, and resistance, re-appropriating the slogan *Cabral Não Morreu* (Cabral is not dead).

> …Cabral kaba ku sufrimento kulonial / Ma luta ka kaba e dexanu pa nu kontinual / Inton kuzê nu sta spera? / Nu jura bandera / ka tem tenpu pa brinkadera / … Nu ten ki luta oji i sempri
>
> —FARP, Antis Barku Skravu, 2007

> …Cabral ended colonial suffering / But the struggle is not finished and he left it for us to continue / So what are we waiting for? / We swear allegiance to the flag /There is no time for games / … We have to fight today and always.

> ...Cabral ka môri / Cabral tinha razon / E ka môri / E fika na nôs kurason / El e nôs erói /... Si bu pensa ma Cabral sta mortu bu sta enganadu pamô Cabral e mi Cabral e bô Cabral e tudu kauberdianus e guineensis ...
>
> —Kaya, Lbc Minao Soldjah E Chullage, Amílcar Cabral, 2010
>
> Cabral is not dead / Cabral was right / He did not die / He remains in our hearts / He is our hero ... And if you think that Cabral is dead you are wrong because Cabral is me Cabral is you Cabral is all Cape Verdeans and Guineans ...

In this part, the rappers invoke Cabral, between the dream and the hope, with a concern for mobilizing a new generation to be able "run behind the damage." Moreover, Cabral is presented as a factor of pride and identity for the future:

> ...Amílcar Cabral / Omi ku ta pensaba futuru di no tera...Bu nomi ku n ta ronka / I bu bandera na nha testa / Bu inu na nha boka...nha identidadi nunka n ka na disisti del
>
> —FBMJ, Guiné ka na fika sin, 2008
>
> ... Amílcar Cabral / The man who used to think about the future of our country ... / Your name I show off with / And your flag on my forehead / Your anthem in my mouth / I will never give up my identity.

Many rappers use Cabral's own speeches in their music. That is the case of the *Sindykatto de Guetto* (Golpe de Stadu [coup d'état], 2011), *Rhyman* (Bissau, 2007), and 4ARTK (Strela Negra [Black Star], Abel Djassi, 2010).

Today, in the major cities of Cape Verde (Praia, Mindelo, and Assomada) and in the Guinean and Cape Verdean diaspora, we encounter many youth hungry for knowledge about their African origin. They look to the nationalists, especially Cabral, but also Malcolm X and others figures of the North American antiracist struggle. In Guinea-Bissau the orientation is more Afrocentric, with the trajectory of Nelson Mandela as the model. However, it is through Cabral, the revolutionary, that this spirit is today incorporated, especially by rappers, street poets, and new "warriors of freedom."

In Guinea-Bissau the deliberate search for the organisation of a movement was initiated after the realization of the first rap music festival in 2000, through the Association *Guiné RAP* under the leadership of the producer and radio entertainer, Cícero Gomes Spencer.[251] In practice, this process has been enhanced through radio, especially *Radio Jovem.*[252] In the last four years, the weekly two-hour interactive program, *Ondas Culturais* (Cultural Waves), has, besides promoting new talents originating from *bairros* of the Bissau and the interior of the country, contributed to the promotion of cultural identity of those who claim to be the true *fidjus di tchon* (children of the land) because they tell the "tchoss" [truth]. This radio station has been organising freestyle rap competitions every Friday on the veranda of the station building, serving as a stage for live performance and also allowing the listeners to call to vote for the music presented during the week and choosing the month's top hits.

In Cape Verde, the conscious hip-hop movement, reclaimed by radio announcer and presenter Jorge "Djodje" Andrade,[253] once again seeks the Cape Verdean identity (now the African root) in exogenous movements and anchored in the nativist idea of the Egyptian, constituting a type of creole neonativism, with the difference of marking itself by a radical

---

251 Figure previously connected with local traditional cultural groups (songs, dances and poetry) of local, producer and presenter of the first programme of *RAP* on radio in Guinea-Bissau, in 1996, on *Radio "Pindjiguiti,"* and one of the co-coordinators of the first *RAP* music festival, in 2000.

252 Belonging to the National Network of Youth Association – RENAJ

253 Former university student in the United States of America, country where he converted himself into an africanist in contact with the North American africanist movement, mentor of various programmes of radio about RAP and others afro music, that aim to divulge the culture of the African man, in his own words - the true man, and of some RAPpers in the city of Praia, Mindelo and in the Diaspora.

break with the Lusitanism, but also with the patriotism, such that the Cape Verdean man/woman is viewed as a descendant of the African expatriated in his/her native land.

The representation of Cabral in the politicized youth music of Guinea-Bissau and Cape Verde, with a pan-Africanist perspective, as reflected in his statement, "I am a simple African," not only dislodges or "liberates" the inheritance of Cabral from his "comrades," but especially gives a sense of appropriation of the causes defended by this revolutionary, updating them and empowering the actors on the stage, thus reinventing a new nation—*RAP krioul(u)*.

Conclusion: Contest and Conquer the Public Space

In the two last decades, the social and civic consciousness of youth has gained impetus—mainly through the use of music as public space for social, cultural, and political protests, and through the redefinition of youth identities. One of the principal elements that contributes to the visibility of this action is the appropriation of the street, contributing simultaneously to reclaiming free space for protest, creation, affirmation, and the transformation of youth into incontestable agents of public life.

It was through rap, with its contentious character and explicit aversion to the dominant culture, that the alienated youth found a way to call the attention of society to the situation that they lived in the townships, revolting against propaganda and incentives to violence, promoting Afro-Centrism and Pan-Africanism. In 2010, the *Movimentu di Luta pa Libertasom* Kultural (Movement of Struggle for Cultural Liberation), during the year of *hip-hop kriolu* in Cape Verde, created the catchphrase "*Cabral pega na arma noz nu sta pega na mikrofoni ke noz arma,*" or "Cabral took the gun, we take the microphone, that is our gun."

The use of radio enabled the popularisation of their messages and to the spread of kirol(u). Cabral remains the principal reference for youth and, according to the Guinean historian Peter Mendy (2005: 759), a source of inspiration for the progressive forces of meaningful change in all of Africa.

The social conditions in which the rappers live constitute the basis of unity of their action of protest to conquer the public space and to carry the public outcry:

"When we took independence, we thought that everything would be better… the lives of our people are being taken away as if they were flowers."

Bibliography

ABBINK, J. (2005), "Being young in Africa: The politics of despair and renewal" in Abbink, Jon.; I. van Kessel (ed), *Vanguard or Vandals. Youth, Politics and Conflict in Africa*, Leiden: BRILL.

ALIM, H. S. (2003). "We are the Streets: African American and the strategic construction of a street conscious identity." In: Sinfree Makoni, Geneva Smitherman, Arnetha F. Ball, and Arthur K. Spears, Eds. *Black Linguistics: Language, society and politics in Africa and the Americas*. New York: Routledge, 2003, p. 40-59.

APPADURAI, A. (2004), "The Capacity to Aspire: Culture and the Terms of Recognition," in Rao, V. and Walton, M. (Eds), *Culture and Public Action*, Stanford, CA: Stanford University Press, pp. 59–84.

AUGEL, J. & CARDOSO, C. (1996), *Transição Democrática na Guiné-Bissau e Outros Ensaios*. Bissau: INEP.

AUGEL, M. (2007), "Cantopoema do Disassossego—posfácio à obra poética."In SEMEDO, O. *No Fundo do Canto*. Belo Horizonte: Nadyala;

BANKS, M. *et All* (1992), *Careers & Identities*, Milton Keynes, Open University Press.

BARROS, M. (in press), "From the radios to the stage: juvenile political participation and dissention through RAP," in MARTINS, R. & CANEVACCI, M. (Eds), *"Who we are"—"Where we are": identities, urban culture and languages of belongings in the Lusophone hip-hop*, Oxford: Sean Kingston Publishing.

BARROS, M. (2012), "*Civil Society in the process of democratization and development in Guinea-Bissau (1991-2011),*" in OLAGBOYE, B. (Eds), *Civil Society and Development in West Africa*, WACSI.

BARROS, M. (2010), "Associativismo Juvenil Enquanto Estratégia de Integração Social: O caso da Guiné-Bissau," In: Centro de Estudos Africanos/ISCTE- Instituto Universitário de Lisboa e Centro de Estudos Africanos/Universidade do Porto (Org.) *50 anos das independências africanas: desafios para a modernidade.* ISCTE/IUL, Lisboa, 9-11 September. Portugal: ISCTE/CEAUP. [Online], Available in: http://repositorio.iscte.pt/bitstream/10071/2271/1/CIEA7_7_BARROS_Associativismo%20juvenil%20enquanto%20estrat%C3%A9gia%20de%20integra%C3%A7%C3%A3o%20social.pdf [Accessed on 08 January 2012].
BECK, U. (2000), *The Brave New World of Work*, Cambridge, Polity Press.

BENNETT, A. (2001), *Cultures of Popular Music*, Buckingham: Open University Press.

BENNETT, A. (2001), *Popular Music and Youth Culture: Music, Identity and Place*, London: Macmillam.
BRITO-SEMEDO, M. (2006), *A construção da identidade nacional: análise da imprensa entre 1877 e 1975*, Praia: IBNL.

BORDONARO, L. (2007), *Living at the Margins. Youth and Modernity in the Bijagó Islands (Guinea-Bissau)*, Ph.D. Diss. ISCTE, Lisbon.

CABRAL, A. (1973), "National Liberation and Culture," in CABRAL, A., *Return in the Source: Selected Speeches of Amílcar Cabral*, New York: Monthly Review Press.

CARDOSO, K. (2008), "Violência grupal urbana em Cabo Verde: um exemplo de globalismo localizado?," Comunicação apresentada no Workshop Pré-congresso: *Os jovens e os caminhos de futuro: novos mapas para as ciências sociais e humanas*. Centro de Estudos Sociais da Universidade de Coimbra (CES-UC) 18 de Junho de 2008.

CHIGUNTA, F. (2002), "The Socio-Economic Situation of Youth in Africa: Problems, Prospects and Options," Working Paper, SSA;

COMAROFF, J. & COMAROFF, J. (2000), "Réfléxions sur la Jeunesse - Du passé à la postcolonie," in Politique Africaine, N.° 80, Université du Chicago.

CONTADOR, A.C and FERREIRA, E.L. (1997). *Ritmo & Poesia: os caminhos do RAP*. Lisboa: Assírio & Alvim.

FERNANDES, G. (2006) *Em busca da Nação: notas para uma reinterpretação do Cabo Verde crioulo*. Florianópolis: UFSC.

FORMAN, M. (2002), *The Hood Comes First*: Race, Space and Place in RAP and Hip-Hop. Middletown, Conn.: Wesleyan University Press.

FORTES, C.M. (2011). *Estudo diagnóstico sobre a juventude, inovação e inserção sócio-económica*. Praia: MJEDRH.

FRADIQUE, T. (2003), *Fixar o movimento: representações da música RAP em Portugal,* Lisboa: D. Quixote.

GODINHO GOMES, P. (2010), *Os Fundamentos de uma Nova Sociedade: o PAIGC e a luta Armada na Guiné-Bissau (1963-1973)*, Torino: L`Harmattan.

GUERREIRO, M. & ABRANTES, P. (2007), *Transições Incertas. Os jovens perante o trabalho e a família.* Comissão para Igualdade no Trabalho e no Emprego, Lisboa: Editorial do Ministério da Educação.

HOBSBAWM, E. (2002), Nações e Nacionalismos desde 1780, Rio de Janeiro: Paz e Terra.

HONWANA, A. & De Boeck, F. (Eds) (2005), *Makers and Breakers: Children & Youth in Postcolonial Africa*, James Currey: Oxford, Africa World Press: Trenton; Codesria: Dakar.

INE, (2011). *Apresentação IV Recenseamento Geral da População e Habitação 2010.* Praia: INE.

LIMA, R.W. (in press), "RAP e representação do espaço público na cidade da Praia," in MARTINS, R. & CANEVACCI, M. (Eds), *"Who we are"—"Where we are": identities, urban culture and languages of belongings in the Lusophone hip-hop*, Oxford: Sean Kingston Publishing.

LIMA, R.W. (2012), "tribos urbanas da Praia: os casos dos thugs e dos RAPpers," in p. 43-50. In ÉVORA, I. & FRIAS, S. (Orgs.) *In Progress: 1º Seminário sobre Ciências Sociais e Desenvolvimento em África.* CEsA-ISEG, Lisboa, 27-28 de Outubro de 2011. Portugal: CEsA-ISEG. [Online], disponível em: http://pascal.iseg.utl.pt/~cesa/files/Doc_trabalho/3-RedyWilsonLima.pdf [Acessed January 08, 2012].

LIMA, R.W. (2010), "Thugs: Vítimas e/ou Agentes da Violência?," in *Revista Direito e Cidadania, (Edição Especial—Política Social e Cidadania)*, nº 30, CES-UC.

LOPES, C. (1989), "*A historicidade da construção nacional na Guiné-Bissau,*" in *A Construção da Nação em África. Os exemplos de Angola, Cabo-Verde, Guiné-Bissau, Moçambique e S. Tomé e Príncipe,* Colóquio Internacional, Bissau, 7-9 January 1986, Bissau: INEP/CODESRIA/UNITAR, p. 243-266.

MARTINS, F. (2010), "O paradoxo das oportunidades: jovens, relações geracionais e transformações sociais—notas sobre Cabo Verde," *Working Paper CRIA 4*, Lisbon.

MBEMBE, A. (1985). *Les jeunes et l'ordre politique en Afrique noire.* Paris: L'Harmattan.

MENDY, P. (2005), "Cabral na Guiné-Bissau Colonial: contexto, desafios e conquistas," in FAC/CODESRIA/FMS (Orgs.), *Cabral no Cruzamento de Épocas. Comunicações e discursos produzidos no II Simpósio Internacional Amílcar Cabral.* FAC/CODESRIA/FMS, Praia: Alfa Comunicações.

MEPIR, (2011). *Documento de Estratégia Nacional de Redução da Pobreza/DENARP II.* Bissau: MEPIR.

MONTEIRO, F. (2008), "Cabo Verde na encruzilhada atlântica," in *ebookbrowse,* http://ebookbrowse.com/cabo-verde-encruzilhada-atlantica-fatima-monteiro-pdf-d76946024 [Acessado June 6, 2012].

MORGAN, M. (2009). *The Real Hip Hop: Battling for Knowledge, Power and Respect in the L.A. Underground.* Durham: Duke University Press.

PAIS, J.M. (2005). *Ganchos, tachos e biscates: jovens, trabalho e futuro.* 2nd ed. Porto: Ambar.

PARDUE, D. (in the press), "Chronotope Identification in Kriolu RAP," in MARTINS, R. & CANEVACCI, M. (Eds), *"Who we are"—"Where we are": identities, urban culture and languages of belongings in the Lusophone hip-hop*, Oxford: Sean Kingston Publishing.

REIS, J. (2001), "A globalização como metáfora da perplexidade? Os processos geo-económicos e o simples funcionamento dos sistemas complexos," em Boaventura Sousa Santos (org.), *Globalização: Fatalidade ou Utopia?*, Porto, Edições Afrontamento, cap. 2, pp. 109- 134.

SIMÕES, J.A. (2010). *Entre a rua e a internet: um estudo sobre o hip hop português*. Lisbon: ICS.

SOARES SOUSA, J. (2011), *Amílcar Cabral (1924-1973). Vida e morte de um revolucionário* africano, Lisboa: Nova Veja.

VIGH, H. (2006), *Navigating Terrains of War: Youth and Soldiering in Guinea-Bissau*. New York: Berghahn.

WUTHNOW, R. (1989), *Communities of Discourse*, Harvard University Press, Cambridge.

XAVIER DE PAULA, B. (2011), "*Das teorias racistas às diásporas africanas: o negro na sociedade brasileira*," paper presented at the *XI Congresso Luso Afro Brasileiro de Ciências Sociais*, 07/10 August, Salvador: UFBA.

SECTION 7:

CABRAL AND AFRICAN AMERICAN STRUGGLES

33. AMÍLCAR CABRAL AND THE TRANSFORMATION OF THE AFRICAN AMERICAN LEFT IN THE UNITED STATES

Bill Fletcher, Jr.

Before the break of dawn on October 15, 1972, I set off on a pilgrimage to see Amílcar Cabral receive an honorary doctorate and speak at Lincoln University in Pennsylvania. Riding in a Volkswagen Bug with a man who would become one of my best friends (the present Dr. Steven C. Pitts), we were instructed by his father that the car, handed down to Steve, had a tendency to overheat. As a result, we stopped roughly every hour on a trip that started at Harvard College in Cambridge, Massachusetts, and ended at Lincoln. After the programme was over, we turned right around and drove back.

Steve and several other Black radicals at Harvard had heard that Cabral was to speak. We were originally all going to get in a VW bus and drive, but one after another, my colleagues dropped away until it was just Steve and me. A college freshman and a radical activist since my early days in high school, I was familiar with Cabral's name and the struggle for the independence of Guinea-Bissau and the Cape Verde islands from Portuguese colonialism. That said, I knew little about his approach to revolutionary theory, which had been a hallmark of his work for quite some time.

With great anticipation, Steve and I waited for Cabral to speak on that very warm Sunday in October in a poorly ventilated building on campus. Cabral was introduced and addressed the audience. In all honesty, I do not remember any of the content of the speech. The speech was actually not a speech at all but rather a paper that he was delivering. There were no rhetorical devices and little excitement. I faded out, literally and figuratively, as I tried to stay awake after having driven for so many hours. I later found out that the paper was published as "Identity and Dignity in Struggle," and contained his famous reference to the need to "return to the source."

Cabral's speech was followed by an electrifying oration by the then Owusu Sadauki (Howard Fuller), one of the chief organisers of the May, 1972, African Liberation Day demonstrations and head of Malcolm X Liberation University in North Carolina. Sadauki/Fuller—who would over time move from being a left-wing Pan-Africanist, to a Marxist-Leninist, to an advocate for school choice, and, ultimately, to becoming a friend of George W. Bush—rocked the house that day and brought everyone to their feet.

But we were there to see Cabral and to honor his life and work. Few of us would guess that within three months he would be dead as a result of a conspiracy between factionalists within his own party and Portuguese agents.

That Moment for the Black Left

Although Cabral had been active since the 1950s, he began to have an impact on the Black Left in the United States by the late 1960s. By that time, the broad left wing of the Black Freedom Movement was undergoing important changes. Influenced by Malcolm X, what came to be known as the Black Power Movement had myriad tendencies, each with its own recipe for Black freedom. Many Pan-Africanists and cultural nationalists suggested that the struggle for Black freedom had to be conducted either on our own or, at best, with other people of colour. In some cases, there was no particular route of struggle suggested at all, but rather the cultivation of an alternative culture, businesses, and space, while awaiting some sort of apocalypse or undefined socio-political transformation. Countering this were two tendencies. One was the revolutionary nationalism represented by groups like the Revolutionary Action Movement, the Black Panther Party, and the Republic of New Africa, which, while having significant differences, nevertheless advanced the need for mass organising, political action, and the fight for power. The Panthers, in particular as they came to be influenced by Marxism, were attacked by some Black nationalists for adopting an approach that was allegedly alien to the Black experience. The other tendency was more amorphous but included some within the Black Left who did not identify with nationalism at all, either having been influenced by the Communist Party of the Unites States, or other currents on the Left. These forces were, for a host of reasons, often discounted by many forces in the Black Power Movement as allegedly residing outside of the experience of Black America. This was an unfair and inaccurate criticism given the role that many of these activists played in the Black Freedom Movement and in other social movements where they advanced the antiracist struggle.

By the early 1970s, there was some rethinking underway in many Pan-Africanist and nationalist circles in the United States. Influenced by the then ousted President of Ghana, Dr. Kwame Nkrumah, elements of the Pan-Africanist movement in the United States began moving left and considering whether socialism served as a credible and principled goal. This move reflected a broader search in the left wing of the Black Freedom Movement for a response to the strategic plateau that had been attained by the movement in the years following the civil rights victories and the later murder of Dr. Martin Luther King Jr.

Cabral as an Independent Marxist Thinker

It was at that moment that Amílcar Cabral became a significant figure in the evolving Black Left. In order to appreciate this, it is worth drawing a distinction between Nkrumah and Cabral. Nkrumah was and forever shall be a hero for Pan-Africanists and anti-imperialists. Having led the struggle for the independence of what came to be known as Ghana, he sought a nonaligned role in the world, while at the same time taking assistance from the USSR, China, and, indeed, the United States. His ideas regarding the development of Ghana were influenced by Marxism and his assessment of the successes of the countries that flew the banner of socialism. After his overthrow in 1966, he moved even further to the left.

Cabral, on the other hand, was a Marxist theoretician. I have never seen anything that Cabral wrote where he self-identified as such, but any reading of his work demonstrates that his analytical tools were consistently derived from the methodology elaborated by Karl Marx and Frederich Engels.

In addition to serving as a theoretician, he was the leader of one of the most important and advanced national liberation struggles in Africa at the time. Under his leadership, the African Party for the Independence of Guinea-Bissau and Cape Verde (PAIGC) liberated much of the territory of the Portuguese colony and was preparing to declare its independence when Cabral was murdered.

That Cabral was both a theoretician in the Marxist tradition and the leader of a successful African national liberation movement presented problems for those Black activists who viewed, incorrectly, the Marxist tradition as simply a European approach to social transformation. Cabral, and increasing numbers of African freedom fighters, saw no such inconsistency and did not hesitate to say so.

Three Theoretical Contributions

Three theoretical contributions, in particular, had an impact on much of the Black Left in the United States.

Cabral's famous essay, "National Liberation and Culture," held note as a response to a narrow, largely economic deterministic approach to social transformation, on the one hand, and on the other, cultural determinism and mythology. In the famous clashes between revolutionary Black nationalists led by the Black Panther Party and cultural Black nationalists led by Ron Karenga (and until 1974, by Amiri Baraka), the question of culture was seriously mishandled. Because forces aligned with Karenga saw Black freedom as rooted in a cultural movement, forces around the Panthers tended to ignore real cultural issues within Black America or treated them as sideshows.

Cabral's analysis emphasized the importance for any revolutionary movement of understanding the actual culture of the oppressed within which one seeks to base oneself. In doing so, one must look dialectically at the *actual* culture, both in its positive and negative features. Thus,

Cabral repudiated radicals who denigrated cultural work (or created cultural caricatures) as well as those who privileged it above all else.

A second contribution by Cabral was the notion of "class suicide." Though the term was original, the underlying concept was deeply rooted in the experience of revolutionary Marxists. In the case of Guinea-Bissau, Cabral saw elements of the middle strata, specifically the nationalist wing of the petit bourgeoisie, as playing a leading role in the struggle for national liberation, but only if they successfully abandoned the aspirations of their class of origin and placed themselves firmly within the working class and peasantry of the country.

When the concept of class suicide was introduced to the Black Left in the United States it took on a complicated reality. It coincided with the growing recognition by the Black Left of the critical importance of basing a radical movement within the oppressed classes of Black America (and ultimately other oppressed segments in the United States). This meant moving away from a hierarchical relationship with the masses—for instance, serving as lawyers, doctors, professors, and other typical roles in the middle strata—and rooting radical practice amongst the oppressed by organising side-by-side.

As was typical of much radical activity in the 1970s, class suicide was frequently interpreted in very linear and dogmatic terms. Any radical who did not go into workplaces to organise, for instance, was suspect as not being truly revolutionary. At the same time, those who went into workplaces to organise side-by-side with workers (as opposed to serving as paid organisers for unions or community-based organisations) frequently assumed that the mere act of getting such jobs was evidence of having abandoned the aspirations of one's class origin.

Cabral suggested that class suicide was not a specific or one-time act; it was actually a process and practice. One does not eliminate all vestiges of one's class aspirations by engaging in armed struggle for freedom or, for that matter, taking this or that job or turning down specific opportunities (that might be made available as a result of one's class background). Rather, class suicide must be linked to building a movement for social transformation in which the oppressed are the direct instruments of their own liberation. In that sense, class suicide is not irreversible, a point that Cabral does not address but which can be deduced from the trajectory of many liberation struggles and other revolutionary movements (where one-time revolutionaries have morphed into a new elite or bourgeoisie).

A third contribution focused on Cabral's notion of national liberation struggles being a process of a people "returning to history." This was an invaluable insight in that it suggested that colonialism had taken the oppressed outside of what would have been their normal path of development and deformed their evolution. National liberation, then, was not only a matter of freeing a people from external domination and national oppression, but was an emancipatory process at a more fundamental level. It was about colonised people regaining their humanity and self-determination—a self-determination that went far beyond a national flag and borders to chart their own trajectory.

Returning to history was not only valuable for traditionally colonised people but equally for considering the question of African Americans under the boot of white supremacist national oppression. African Americans, whose ancestors were largely (with the exception of Cape Verdeans) ripped out of history and implanted in the United States as slaves, were central as a workforce in the development of North American capitalism. They have been treated as a people without a history. As a result, the struggle for African American liberation becomes not only a struggle for rights, but a struggle to rediscover our own history and place on this planet, including our relationship to and with the rest of the African world.

Cabral's "returning to history" transcends a cultural nationalist obsession with a mythological past or an academic understanding of history. It links history to the future and to the need of a people to recreate itself in a contemporary context. To put it differently, understanding history is insufficient in the absence of a popular revolutionary project.

Central to Cabral's thinking and practice was the reaffirmation of the dignity and humanity of those who have been subject to colonialism and national oppression. He reminded the Left that history preceded the class struggle and would continue well after the end of antagonistic classes.

Cabral and Cape Verdeans

Cabral held great significance for a segment of Black America that for years was not recognised as being part of Black America, and for that matter often saw itself as something other than part of Black America: Cape Verdean Americans.

Cabral's father was Cape Verdean, and Amílcar's early schooling took place on the Cape Verde Islands (five hundred miles off the coast of Senegal). Though Cape Verde and Guinea-Bissau were jointly colonised by Portugal, they had very different, though overlapping, histories. Ethnic differences would, after independence, contribute to some of the tensions that ultimately led to Cape Verde and Guinea-Bissau separating and forming independent nation-states.

During the nineteenth century, Portuguese whalers and fishermen sailed with Cape Verdean crews throughout the North Atlantic. Many Portuguese and Cape Verdeans came to settle in North America, particularly in southern New England. The nature of Portuguese colonialism was such that, ideologically, it provided a mechanism for the colonised to often believe that they had been accepted into Portuguese society. Thus, the fact that Cape Verdeans came to North America not as slaves but as seamen (and later with their families) led them to self-identify as "Portuguese" and sometimes as "white" but not as "Negro," "Black," "Afro-American," or "African American."

Cabral and the national liberation struggle in Guinea-Bissau and Cape Verde had a transformative impact not only on those respective colonies, but on Cape Verdeans in the United States. The combination of the civil rights and later Black Power phases of the Black Freedom Movement in the United States with the national liberation struggle in Guinea-Bissau and the Cape Verde resulted in a major rethinking amongst Cape Verdean Americans of their status both domestically and internationally. The consciousness change involved both a reaffirmation of the Cape Verdean identity, heritage, and pride, as well as a "Black consciousness" and the beginnings of a break with Portuguese colonial mentality. Organisations developed amongst Cape Verdean Americans, including the PAIGC Support Committee, and later annual celebrations of Cape Verde's independence from Portugal (July 5, 1975), which in places like New Bedford, Massachusetts, became major events. Through all of this, Cabral and his image loomed large.

Legacy

The murder of Amílcar Cabral was a tremendous loss not only to the national liberation movement of Guinea-Bissau and Cape Verde, as well as Africa as a whole, but to the international Left. Thinkers of the quality of Amílcar Cabral simply do not come along every day.

Cabral became legendary in the Black Left and broader Left in the United States. He legitimized the idea of a person of African descent not only being a Marxist but a Marxist theoretician integrally linked to a national liberation struggle. Cabral's legitimacy helped to demythologize Africa and African cultures, while at the same time serving as a source of immense pride in what Africa produced. It cannot be overstated that the fact that Cabral could not be perceived as a creature of any other nation or political force lent an unusual level of credibility to him personally and the politics he elaborated.

Cabral, then, assisted in the evolution of many African American militants and radicals who were proponents of cultural nationalism as well as various forms of cultural and economic determinism to take a *path* towards Marxism. Few international figures played such a role. It was not just the courage of Cabral and the PAIGC against all odds—which would itself be a sufficient basis to hold him and his movement in high esteem—but Cabral's concrete, provocative and illuminating analyses on the challenges associated with actual anti-imperialism and anti-colonialism that made him especially unique. He sought to grapple with revolutionary Marxist theory appropriate to his country and indeed the world in the latter part of the twentieth century.

Cabral's legacy is complicated. While the PAIGC survived his assassination and went on to successfully secure independence from Portugal for Guinea-Bissau and Cape Verde two years later, the process that had appeared to have been transformational ran into headwinds. In addition to the separation of Cape Verde from Guinea-Bissau, in 1980 a process of revolutionary transformation came to a halt in Guinea-Bissau and regressed to the point that, today, Guinea-Bissau is viewed not as a beacon of socialism or of revolutionary advance, but rather as a weakened nation-state that serves as a major transit point for narcotics destined for Europe.

It is pointless to wonder where Guinea-Bissau and Cape Verde would be today had Cabral lived. What does demand study is what transpired both during his lifetime and immediately afterward that laid the foundation for the regression of a movement and society that seemed to have so much potential to stand tall and play a major role in Africa despite its small geographic size. In that sense, Cabral's work is far from complete.

The African American Left owes Cabral a special note of gratitude and honour, for he opened the eyes of so many of us to the multidimensional process of social transformation. And that this was done by an African made the message so much more compelling.

34. LINKING THE STRUGGLES

AMÍLCAR CABRAL AND HIS IMPACT AND LEGACY IN THE BLACK LIBERATION MOVEMENT

Kali Akuno

Since the close of the fifth Pan-African Congress in Manchester, England, and the end of the second great inter-imperialist war (better known as World War II) in 1945, the radical wing of the Black Liberation Movement in the United States has been inspired by and drawn many lessons from its reciprocal interactions with the national and social liberation movements of Africa (primarily from 1945 through 1994) and the diaspora (particularly those of the Caribbean).

The radical elements of the BLM—composed primarily of revolutionary nationalists, socialists, communists and anarchists—have over the years learned and incorporated many of the critical aspects of the theories and strategies of radical social transformation developed by many of the twentieth-century intellectual and political towers of the African world revolution. Of all of these leaders and theoreticians from Africa, the Caribbean, and Latin America, however, none made more profound theoretical and strategic contributions to the advancement of the BLM than Amílcar Cabral.

What separates Cabral from the others, however, is that his work provided detailed theoretical and strategic clarity on a number of fundamental questions that were critical to understanding the transition from "American colonialism" to neocolonialism following the defeat of legalized white supremacy in the early 1960s. Some of Cabral's particular contributions centred on the following questions:[254]

- The limitations of national liberation within the capitalist world-system
- The internal material basis for neocolonialism within colonised and oppressed nations and the critical dangers associated with this form of capitalist penetration and imperialist rule
- The ideological and theoretical weaknesses and shortcomings of the peoples movements for liberation and the detriments they pose to the success of the movements
- The centrality of culture to anti-imperialist resistance and the need to create a new culture through struggle to restore oppressed people into full agents of their own history and identity
- The imperative of class struggle within the oppressed nation and the necessity of class "suicide" amongst critical segments of the nation (or nation-class, as Cabral himself stated) but most particularly the petit bourgeoisie, who often constitute the leadership of the movements, given their strategic location within the capitalist mode of production and its national/international hierarchies

These are some of the fundamental challenges confronting the movement.

Cabral's theoretical, insightful works did not spring from thin air. Cabral developed his theories—on the motive forces of history, colonialism, imperialism, questions of national liberation, neocolonialism, class, and class struggle within national liberation movements, the transition to socialism, the centrality of culture and identity to resistance and social transformation—from his unique social experiences, his central location

254 There are three key speeches of Cabral that present the clearest articulations of his theories and strategic reflections and which have had the most profound and enduring impact on the BLM. These speeches are: "the Weapon of Theory" (1966), "National Liberation and Culture" (1970), and "Identity and Dignity in the Context of the National Liberation Struggle" (1972).

in the struggle against Portuguese colonialism and his critical study of the numerous challenges and failures of the national liberation movements on the African continent in the 1950s and 60s.

Cabral was born in Guinea-Bissau in 1924 and was reared primarily in Cape Verde, a small island formerly ruled by Portugal. He studied to be an agronomist in Portugal. In the employment of the Portuguese colonial administration in the 1950s Cabral was able to gain extensive knowledge of the cultures and social conditions of the various peoples of Guinea-Bissau and (to a lesser degree) Angola, by performing agricultural census studies. In September 1956, Cabral established the *Partido Africano da Independecia da Guinea e Cabo Verde* or *PAIGC*, which lead Guinea-Bissau and the Cape Verde islands to political independence in the 1970s. While living in Angola, also in 1956, Cabral collaborated with Mario de Andrade and Antonio Agostinho Neto to form the *Movimento Popular Libertacao de Angola* or *MPLA*, which played a leading role in the liberation of Angola.

In 1957, as part of a conference in solidarity with the Algerian anticolonial movement in Paris, Cabral again partnered with Mario de Andrade and Antonio Agostinho Neto to form the *Movimento Anti-Colonista* or *MAC,* to discuss strategies to overthrow Portuguese colonial rule. In 1958, Cabral attended the All-African People's Conference in Accra, Ghana organised by Kwame Nkrumah to coordinate support for the liberation movements from the existing independent nation-states and to unite the liberation movements on a continent-wide basis[255]. In 1960, while in Tunisia, Cabral established the *Frente Revolucionaria Africana para a Independencia Nacional das colonias Portuguesas* or *FRAIN.* FRAIN was established to coordinate the strategies and initiatives of the PAIGC and MPLA against Portuguese colonialism. In 1961, while in Casablanca, Morocco, Cabral helped to establish the *Conferencia das Organizacoes Nacionalistas das Colonias Portuguesas* or *CONCP,* to expand

255 See Mario de Andrade (1979), "Biographical Notes," *Unity and Struggle: Speeches and Writings of Amílcar Cabral.*

upon and replace FRAIN to include FRELIMO from Mozambique and the MLSTP from Sao Tome and Principe, in order to coordinate resistance to Portuguese colonialism on the African continent. In January 1963, Cabral and the PAIGC initiated the armed phase of the resistance movement in Guinea-Bissau, which lead to its formal political independence from Portugal in September 1974[256].

Cabral was a principle architect in the overthrow of Portuguese colonialism and the weakening of imperialist domination of Southern Africa. As the spokesperson for the PAIGC, MPLA, and CONCP, Cabral was able to travel extensively throughout the world. Cabral used the knowledge gained on his travels to judiciously assess the many failures of the first wave of national liberation movements. These experiences shaped his worldview, theory and, most importantly, his practice as a revolutionary nationalist, socialist, and internationalist. It was Cabral's particular ability to systematically and scientifically summarize these experiences in a coherent and concrete fashion that made his work applicable to the ongoing struggle for liberation of people of African descent in the United States.

Uniting with Our "Comrade"

The BLM came to know Cabral and his work through a dynamic set of interlocking organisations and networks linking activists based in the United States with the national liberation movements in Africa and Asia (the Vietnamese in particular) and revolutionary and progressive governments and social movements in Latin America (particularly Cuba), Africa (primarily Ghana, Tanzania, Guinea, and Algeria), Asia (particularly China) and the Eastern Bloc. These links consisted of survivors from the anti-communist repression and purges of the late 1940s and '50s, groups like the Council on African Affairs (CAA) headed by the likes Alphaeus Hunton, Paul

256 Ibid, and Young, Robert J. C. (2001) *Postcolonialism: An Historical Introduction*, pp. 283-292. .(publisher? …for all)

Robeson, and W.E.B. Du Bois[257], liberal organisations like the American Committee on Africa (ACOA)[258]; and a host of religious and academic institutions, Black and white, that had been active, particularly around missionary activities in Africa and in supporting students from Africa to attend academic institutions in Europe and the United States. Through these links, activists engaged in progressive social movements were able to encounter their international counterparts via international conferences, student exchanges, solidarity missions and campaigns.

Another critical link that facilitated the introduction and ongoing communication between revolutionaries from the continent with revolutionaries from the BLM in the United States were Black ex-patriots that lived in Europe or on the African continent, particularly in Ghana and Tanzania[259]. Conversely, African students and political exiles based in the United States and Europe played this critical role in reverse.

The Student Non-Violent Coordinating Committee, or SNCC, was the first major student and youth-oriented organisation to introduce the BLM to the likes of African revolutionaries like Cabral. Over the course of its 9-year existence, from 1960 to 1969, SNCC took several delegations to various parts of Africa to exchange lessons in the struggle and engage in international campaigns. SNCC's first major trip to the continent was in the fall of 1964, when a delegation of 11 members visited the Republic of Guinea, then led by President Ahmed Sekou Toure[260]. The SNCC delegation was exposed to an extensive amount of literature about the national liberation movements on the continent while in Guinea,

---

257 Von Eschen, Penny (1997) *Race Against Empire: Black Americans and Anti-Colonialism 1937-1957.*

258 Minter, William, Hovey, Gail, and Cobb, Charles Jr. (eds) (2008) *No Easy Victories: African Liberation and American Activists over a Half Century 1950 – 2000*, pp 15-22.

259 See Ibid, pp. 59-150, Sherwood, Marika, (2011) *Malcolm X Visits Abroad*, and Gaines, Kevin K. (2008) *African Americans in Ghana: Black Expatriates and the Civil Rights Era.*

260 Ibid, pp 83-112.

some of it invariably from Cabral and the PAIGC, which was operating out of Guinea at that time[261].

The next major SNCC trip to the continent was in the fall of 1965, when several members visited Ghana and attended the Organization of African Unity (OAU) conference being held in the capital, Accra[262]. Cabral and several members of the PAIGC were in attendance at the OAU conference. However, it is unclear to what extent they were able to meet and make exchanges at the conference. They were, nonetheless, definitely exposed to the PAIGC's politics at the conference via presentations made by their representatives.

The first critical introduction of Cabral and his work to the BLM was provided by Immanuel Wallerstein, a renowned academic on African affairs, via an interview he conducted and published in 1965 entitled "Our Solidarities"[263]. This interview was one of the first major pieces on Cabral and the struggle of the PAIGC against Portuguese colonialism to appear in English. It received modest distribution via the left-wing press in the United States, but was read and disseminated by Black activists in the Student Non-Violent Coordinating Committee (SNCC) and the Revolutionary Action Movement (RAM) in New York City, Detroit, Washington, DC, Atlanta, Oakland, and Los Angeles.

The BLM's first major encounter with Cabral and his work occurred in January 1966 in Havana, Cuba, on occasion of the Tri-continental Conference of Solidarity of the Peoples of Africa, Asia, and Latin America[264]. Cuba—like Ghana, Guinea, and Tanzania on the African continent in the 1960s—played a critical role as a revolutionary socialist state engaged in active struggle against United States and European imperialism.

---

261 Wilkins, Fanon Che (2007), *The Making of Black Internationalists: SNCC and Africa before Black Power 1960 – 1965.*

262 Ibid.

263 See reference in Minter, William, et al, (eds) (2008) *No Easy Victories: African Liberation and American Activists over a Half Century 1950 – 2000*, and Braganca, Aquino, Wallterstein, Immanuel (1965) *The African Liberation Reader Volume 1: The Anatomy of Colonialism.*

264 See Young, Robert J. C. (2001) *Postcolonialism: An Historical Introduction*, pp. 204-216.

In this role, Cuba gave shelter, support, and resources to revolutionary organisations from throughout Latin America and the world. In this same vein, Cuba was also home to many BLM exiles. The most prominent BLM exile in Cuba during the 1960s was Robert F. Williams. Williams was a militant from North Carolina who fled into exile to avoid false imprisonment for an act of self-defense against white terror in 1961[265]. He was one of the most outspoken advocates for armed self-defense and the formation of Negro Gun Clubs in the late 1950s and early 1960s.

In support of Williams, the Cuban government provided him with contacts to the various revolutionary organisations that visited or had representatives stationed on the island and with access to printing and broadcast facilities to propagate his message back to forces within the United States[266]. Robert Williams, other BLM exiles, and several members of RAM attended the 1966 Tri-Continental Conference, and, like most in attendance, were highly impressed with Amílcar Cabral and his address to the conference: "*Weapon of Theory*."

Through the *Crusader* journal and his extensive personal correspondence with BLM partisans, Williams, along with the RAM cadre in attendance, introduced Cabral and his works to their first major audience within the movement. Following the Tri-Continental Conference BLM revolutionaries began critically studying Cabral and the national liberation movements against Portuguese colonialism in the pursuit of how they might help advance the struggle for Black national liberation within the territories claimed by the United States.

From 1966 through the 1970s, more and more BLM partisans visited Africa and engaged in regular and sustained contact with African revolutionaries, particularly those individuals and movements that were operating out of progressive states—Algeria, Egypt, Guinea, and Tanzania (Ghana was removed from this equation in 1966 following a military coup that overthrew the Nkrumah government)—such as the PAIGC, MPLA, FRELIMO, the African National Congress (ANC), the South

265 See Mullen, Bill V. (2002) *Transnational Correspondence: Robert F. Williams, Detroit and the Bandung Era*.
266 Ibid.

African Communist Party (SACP) and Pan-Africanist Congress of Azania (PAC). These exchanges facilitated the deeper exposure of the BLM to the ideas and movements of African revolutionary leaders of national liberation movements like Amílcar Cabral, or from states engaged in socialist experiments, like Sekou Toure in Guinea or Julius Nyerere in Tanzania.

In 1969, Basil Davidson, a progressive British Africanist scholar, published one of the most historically important works on Cabral, the PAIGC, and the national liberation movement in Guinea-Bissau, entitled *The Liberation of Guinea: Aspects of an African Revolution.* [267] This work was read extensively by partisans of the BLM, particularly amongst college students in the late 1960s and early 70s in organisations like the Pan-African Union (PAU) in California and the Student Organization for Black Unity (SOBU) in North Carolina.[268] Another critical work also published in 1969 was *Revolution in Guinea: An African People's Struggle,* by a British collective called Stage One. This was one of the first English publications of a collection of Cabral's speeches and writings, and received a decent distribution in the United States amongst BLM forces. It was from this publication that many in the BLM were introduced to the saying most commonly associated with Cabral, "Tell No Lies. Claim No Easy Victories."[269]

By 1969 there were several radical Black and multinational solidarity committees operating throughout the United States that were providing material and political support to the national liberation movements against Portuguese colonialism and white settler colonialism in Southern Africa (Azania, Zimbabwe and Botswana in particular)[270]. The solidarity

267 Davidson, Basil (1969) *The Liberation of Guinea: Aspects of an African Revolution.*

268 Tyehimba, Watani (2012) *A View from the House of Umoja*, and Johnson, Cedric (2007) *Revolutionaries to Race Leaders: Black Power and the Making of African American Politics,* Chapter 4.

269 Cabral, Amílcar (1969) *Revolution in Guinea: An African People's Struggle*. published by STAGE 1, 1969.

270 , Johnson, Cedric (2007) *Revolutionaries to Race Leaders: Black Power and the Making of African American Politics,* Chapter 4, and Minter, William, et al, (eds)

committees played a critical role in spreading Cabral's ideas throughout the BLM. These networks also played a critical role in providing forums for African revolutionaries in the United States to make their case and present their ideas directly. Cabral and the PAIGC directly benefitted from this organising on two occasions. Cabral first visited the United States in 1970, where he gave several lectures throughout the state of New York and held several dialogues and interviews in New York City related to the promotion of the PAIGC's and allied CONCP organisations' advocacy for self-determination and national independence at the United Nations.[271]

In addition to Cabral's first visit to the United States, another critical event occurred in 1970 that had a major impact on the spread of his ideas in the BLM. In February of that year, members from the Afrikan People's Party (APP) and the House of Umoja (HOU), based in Los Angeles, collaborated with Guyanese revolutionary Eusi Kwayana and the African Society for Cultural Relations with Independent Africa (ASCRIA), along with Forum, from St. Vincent, the Afro-Caribbean Movement from Antigua and the PAC from Azania, to develop the Pan-Afrikan Secretariat (PAS) in Georgetown, Guyana[272]. Guyana, then led by Prime Minister Forbes Burnham, was operating as a progressive base for revolutionary international coordination throughout the Caribbean, South America, and Africa, and was home to several BLM exiles and ex-patriots from the late 1960s to the 1990s. The PAS was the first organisation to call for the international launching of African Liberation Day (ALD), originally called World-Wide African Solidarity Day (WWASD), and held the first ALD observances in 1970 and 1971, respectively, in Guyana, Canada, Europe and in several cities in the United States[273]. WWWASD/ALD was specifically intended to promote the African World Revolution, giving

(2008) *No Easy Victories: African Liberation and American Activists over a Half Century 1950 – 2000*, chapters 3 and 4.

271 Minter, William, et al, (eds) (2008) *No Easy Victories: African Liberation and American Activists over a Half Century 1950 – 2000,* Chapter 3, and Cabral, Amílcar (1979) *Unity and Struggle: Speeches and Writings of Amílcar Cabral.*

272 Tyehimba, Watani (2012) *A View from the House of Umoja.*

273 Tyehimba, Watani (2012) *A View from the House of Umoja.*

particular focus to the struggles against Portuguese colonialism in Africa, settler-colonialism in Southern Africa, neocolonialism in Africa and the Caribbean, and the New Afrikan Independence Movement within the confines of the United States.

A connected development occurred on the East Coast through the auspices of SOBU and Malcolm X Liberation University (MXLU). In the fall of 1971 Owusu Sadaukai, one of the founders of SOBU and MXLU, toured the liberated territories of Guinea-Bissau, Angola, and Mozambique. In Mozambique, Sadaukai was implored by Samora Machel, the leader of FRELIMO, to build an international campaign in support of the national liberation movements of Mozambique, Angola, and Guinea-Bissau. Upon his return, Sadaukai released a six-part report on his trip in the movement publication the "*African World*"[274]. This series was widely distributed in the movement and played a pivotal role in helping to launch and guide the formation of the African Liberation Day Coordinating Committee (ALDCC). The ALDCC, a broad coalition of BLM forces representing different tendencies and trends within the movement, called for and organised the groundbreaking May 27, 1972, ALD demonstration that mobilized more than 100,000 participants throughout the United States, including Washington, DC, San Francisco, Los Angeles, and New Orleans. Following the success of ALD, the ALDCC expanded and transformed into a more permanent structure, the African Liberation Support Committee (ALSC), which was the fulcrum of support for the national liberation movements in African through the mid-1970s[275]. ALD and the ALSC were very intentional in their promotion of the works of Amílcar Cabral and other national liberation leaders of the era, such as Eduardo Mondlane and Samora Machel of FRELIMO and Robert Sobukwe of the Pan-Afrikanist Congress (PAC).

---

274 Johnson, Cedric (2007) *Revolutionaries to Race Leaders: Black Power and the Making of African American Politics*, page 138 – 139 and Minter, William, et al, (eds) (2008) *No Easy Victories: African Liberation and American Activists over a Half Century 1950 – 2000*, Chapters 3 and 4.
275 Johnson, Cedric (2007) *Revolutionaries to Race Leaders: Black Power and the Making of African American Politics*, Chapter 4.

Just as critical as the promotion Cabral and the views of other CONCP leaders was the film "*A Luta Continua*," which was produced by Robert Van Lierop and disseminated by the Africa Information Service (AIS) in 1972[276]. AIS was founded by BLM activists Prexy Nesbitt and Van Lierop in 1971, specifically to distribute educational materials about the national liberation struggles against Portuguese colonialism lead by CONCP. The film was shot in 1971 in Mozambique and Tanzania, and focused on the armed struggle being waged by FRELIMO. The film spread like wildfire from 1972 through the mid-1970s, and perhaps more than anything else made the ideas of Cabral and Machel real and concrete to millions of Black folks in the United States. AIS subsequently published "*Return to the Source: Selected Speeches by Amílcar Cabral*," the first major collection of Cabral's writings and speeches published in the United States, in 1973.

The AIS was also instrumental in coordinating Cabral's final visit the United States in 1972. During this visit Cabral asked the Africa Information Service to set up a meeting with various leading forces in the BLM.[277] The meeting was held in New York City on the twentieth of October and involved participants from over thirty BLM organisations. The speech was entitled "Connecting the Struggles: An Informal talk with Black Americans," and had a profound and lasting impact on the BLM in all its diversity, as it clearly affirmed the interconnectedness between the African liberation struggles on the continent with those in the United States, the Caribbean, and beyond.

A Luta Continua!

Agents of the Portuguese colonialists assassinated Amílcar Cabral shortly after his last trip to the United States on January 20, 1973[278]. The ef-

276 Minter, William, et al, (eds.) (2008) *No Easy Victories: African Liberation and American Activists over a Half Century 1950 – 2000*, chapter 4.

277 Minter, William, et al, (eds.) (2008) *No Easy Victories: African Liberation and American Activists over a Half Century 1950 – 2000*, page 93, and Cabral, Amílcar (1979) *Unity and Struggle: Speeches and Writings of Amílcar Cabral.*

278 Cabral, Amílcar (1979) *Unity and Struggle: Speeches and Writings of Amílcar Cabral.*

fectiveness of Cabral's work and leadership in helping to guide a peoples' revolutionary movement proved the "cut off the head and body will whither" theory to be false in this case. Following his assassination, the PAIGC escalated the war against the Portuguese and not only led Guinea-Bissau to political independence in 1974 but also overthrew the fascist Salazar-Cateano regime (that had ruled Portugal since 1932 by a group of Portuguese military officers called the Movimento das Armed Forcas or MAF—which translated into English means Armed Forces Movement) in April 1974, admittedly influenced by the theories and moral example of Amílcar Cabral[279].

Half a world away, Cabral's works had also become common parlance within the BLM by the time of his death. His works greatly aided the political and theoretical development of the BLM in the 1970s. Cabral's work is still being studied and referenced today by revolutionary nationalist and Pan-Africanist organisations like the All African People's Revolutionary Party (AAPRP), the African People's Socialist Party (APSP), the Organization of Black Struggle (OBS), the Pan-African People's Organization (PAPO), the Provisional Government of the Republic of New Afrika (PG –RNA), the Malcolm X Grassroots Movement (MXGM), and the New Afrikan People's Organization (NAPO).

References

Braganca, Aquino de, Wallerstein, Immanuel (1982) *The African Liberation Reader, Three Volumes*, Zed Press, London, England.

Bush, Roderick D. (2000) *We Are Not What We Seem: Black Nationalism and Class Struggle in the American Century*, New York University Press.

Bush, Roderick D. (2009) *The End of White World Supremacy: Black Internationalism and the Problem of the Color Line*, Temple University Press, Philadelphia, Pennsylvania.

279 Cabral, Amílcar (1979) *Unity and Struggle: Speeches and Writings of Amílcar Cabral.*

Cabral, Amílcar (1969) *Revolution in Guinea: An African People's Struggle*, Stage 1, London, England.

Cabral, Amílcar (1973) *Return to the Source: Selected Speeches by Amílcar Cabral*, edited by Africa Information Service, Monthly Review Press, New York, New York.

Cabral, Amílcar (1979) *Unity and Struggle: Speeches and Writings of Amílcar Cabral*, Monthly Review Press, New York, New York.

Chabal, Patrick (2003) *Amílcar Cabral: Revolutionary Leadership and People's War*, Africa World Press, Trenton, New Jersey.

Cruse, Harold (2002) *The Essential Harold Cruse: A Reader*, Palgrave Macmillian.

Davidson, Basil (1969) *The Liberation of Guinea: Aspects of an African Revolution*, Penguin Books, Middlesex, England.

Davidson, Basil (1984) "On Revolutionary Nationalism: The Legacy of Cabral," *Latin American Perspectives*, Issue 41, Volume II, pp. 15-42.
Ferguson, Herman (2011) *An Unlikely Warrior: The Evolution of a Revolutionary*, Black Classic Press.

Gaines, Kevin K. (2008) *African Americans in Ghana: Black Expatriates and the Civil Rights Era*, University of North Carolina Press.

Grady-Willis, Winston A. (2006) *Challenging U.S Apartheid: Atlanta and Black Struggles for Human Rights 1960-1977*, Duke University Press.

Johnson, Cedric (2007) *Revolutionaries to Race Leaders: Black Power and the Making of African American Politics*, University of Minnesota Press, Minneapolis, Minnesota.

Kadalie, Modibo M. (2000) *Internationalism, Pan-Africanism, and the Struggle of Social Classes*, One Quest Press, Savannah, Georgia.

Magubane, Bernard (1983) "Towards a Sociology of National Liberation from Colonialism: Cabral's Legacy," *Contemporary Marxism: Journal of the Institute for the Study of Labor and Economic Crisis*, No. 7.

McCulloch, Jock (1983) *In the Twilight of Revolution: The Political Theory of Amílcar Cabral*, Routledge and Kegan Paul, London, England.
Meriwether, James (2009) *Proudly We can be Africans: Black Americans and Africa 1935-1961*, University of North Carolina Press.

Minter, William, Hovey, Gail, and Cobb, Charles Jr. (eds.) (2008) *No Easy Victories: African Liberation and American Activists over a Half Century 1950 – 2000*, Africa World Press, Trenton, New Jersey.

Mullen, Bill V. (2002) "Transnational Correspondence: Robert F. Williams," Detroit and the Bandung Era, *Works and Days*, 39/40, Volume 20.

Sherwood, Marika (2011) *Malcolm X Visits Abroad*, Tsehai Publishing, Los Angeles, CA.
Tyehimba, Watani Sundai Umoja (2012) "NAPO/MXGM Roots and Timeline: A View from the House of Umoja," Unpublished, Atlanta, Georgia.

Tyson, Timothy B. (2001) *Radio Free Dixie: Robert F. Williams and the Roots of Black Power*, University of North Carolina Press.

Van Deburg, William (1993) *New Day in Babylon: The Black Power Movement and American Culture 1965-1975*, University of Chicago Press.

Von Eschen, Penny (1997) *Race Against Empire: Black Americans and Anti-Colonialism 1937-1957*, Cornell University Press, New York, New York.

Young, Robert J. C. (2001) *Postcolonialism: An Historical Introduction*, Blackwell Publishing, Oxford, England.

35. PRAXIS FROM THE CENTRE BACK TO THE MARGINS

AMÍLCAR CABRAL'S METHOD AS A GUIDE FOR RECONSTRUCTING THE RADICAL BLACK POLITICAL SUBJECT

Ajamu Baraka

The value of Amílcar Cabral's contributions to global Black liberationist praxis are many and are reflected in the various essays in this special volume. But in my view, as an activist whose theater of struggle is in the United States, the contribution that has endured the most over time is his fierce commitment to intellectual freedom. That commitment, as reflected in his theoretical formulations and practice, affirmed a central tenet of the Black radical intellectual tradition. That tenet asserts the absolute necessity for Black radical theories to be freed from any dogmas or doctrines that require the complexities of African people and their socio-historic experiences to conform to frameworks not emanating from and defined by African people themselves. Cabral's rejection of a formulaic Marxism, for example, was not a rejection of Marxism—it was a result of his understanding that a successful struggle for national liberation in Guinea-Bissau could not be built on theories borrowed from other socio-historical experiences; that it was necessary to "see" the realities of the land and people with all their complexities and contradictions.

For Cabral, the epistemological question was no question at all, because it was the people—their experiences, culture, and struggles for personhood—that was the foundation of knowledge. It was this "return to the source," the validation of those voices from the margins, be it from peasants in Latin America or urbanised Black women in the United States, that subsequent radical activists have elaborated on, from Paulo

Freire to Patricia Hill Collins. This is my starting point when I assess the thought and practice of Cabral, and indeed it should be the starting point of any efforts to assess Black theorists, from early abolitionists in the United States through to various forms of Pan-Africanism, and to the latest theories of radical Black feminists. This wide range of thought, which I have collapsed under the broad heading of "Black Radical Tradition," have an underlying link—a desire to develop liberatory theory and practice that constructs a "Black political subject" and advances the struggle for the emancipation of Black humanity and, by extension, oppressed humanity in general.

Bearing this in mind, what are the essential elements of Cabral's approach that are important for contemporary radical political practice in the United States?

1) The commitment to theoretical independence: Cabral's materialist analysis of objective socio-economic conditions was the starting point for his theorizing. While this is familiar as part of a traditional Marxist methodology, Cabral's approach required an intellectual independence that allowed him to see the unique characteristics of Guinean society that was structured by colonial capital. Freed from predetermined dogma, Cabral and his fellow revolutionaries in Guinea-Bissau formulated strategies based on the social realities they faced on the ground and not in someone's imagination or texts from the early twentieth century.
2) Method of criticism, self-criticism, and grounding oneself in the people as the source of legitimacy, knowledge, and guidance: Cabral's approach to criticism and self-criticism serves as a much-needed reminder of an approach to accountability and theoretical and practical assessment that has become a lost practice for many activist organisations. Cabral's method of telling no lies and claiming no easy victories was a revolutionary principle that ensured honesty, accountability, and a never-ending struggle against human weaknesses in the fight for collective and individual transformation. It requires the elimination of any lines

between the revolutionary cadre and the people—something that is a challenge for the residual element of vanguardism still infecting revolutionary theory and practice in the United States.

3) The role of culture and ideology: Cabral's theories on the role of culture and ideology as mechanisms for both liberation and domination are instructive for Black revolutionaries in the United States, who must struggle to overcome some of the most effective methods ever developed for imposing bourgeois cultural and ideological hegemony in the entire capitalist world. For Cabral, it would be impossible to develop effective strategies for social change without a thorough understanding of the cultural and ideological mechanisms of control and manipulation that were being employed against the people.

While some might argue that Cabral's theories are only useful analytical categories for understanding social realities and developing revolutionary practice in the Global South, I will argue in this short essay that Cabral's approach to understanding the dialectics of culture and ideology, grounded in the ongoing changes in the forces of production, provides the methodology for deconstructing the social realities of contemporary US society and developing a Black radical strategic program.

Shifting the Focus Back to the Cultural and Ideological Mechanism of Domination

> *History teaches us that, in certain circumstances, it is very easy for the foreigner to impose his domination on a people. But it also teaches us that, whatever may be the material aspects of this domination, it can be maintained only by the permanent, organized repression of the cultural life of the people concerned.*[280]

280 Amílcar Cabral, National Liberation and Culture speech at Syracuse University, 1970

Post-Marxist analysis has come to understand and better appreciate the role of culture and ideology beyond the simplistic misunderstandings of the superstructure—base dichotomy. Even as many Western Marxists were either unaware of or still struggling with the contributions of theorists like Antonio Gramsci, Cabral pointed us towards the importance of these factors in the struggle for power and during the revolutionary transformation of society. Yet, for many elements of the US Black Left involved in base-building organising, issues of culture and ideology never received the theoretical attention they deserved, and a great deal of the critical work on culture and the role of ideology that was being generated in academia never found its way into the hands of Black activists for several reasons, including the notorious anti-intellectualism of radicals in the United States and the institutional weaknesses of the Left in the United States.

It is my contention that the failure of the Black Left in the United States to develop the theoretical tools to understand and intervene with the rapidly shifting cultural and ideological realities at various critical conjunctures accounts for the Left being completely unaware of the cultural and ideological terrain that had paved the way for the ascendency of a centre-right technocrat in the person of Barack Obama to the highest office in the United States settler State. But even more critically, the insufficient understanding on the part of Black activists on the issue of ideological and cultural hegemony has resulted in a myopic view of the impact of Obama's presidency on the consciousness of Black people in the United States. This failure has had devastating consequences for revolutionary practice in the United States, primarily because of the central role that Black people have played in advancing radical social change in the United States. Cabral's analysis of the role of culture revealed how the dominating group imposes its worldview and values through the mechanism of culture and should have alerted Black theorists in the United States of the need to give more attention to the cultural terrain.

If we would have applied Cabral's critical approach to the cultural and ideological terrain of the United States from the 1940s forward and grounded that analysis in the rapid changes taking place in the material base of capitalist productive relations as they related to African Americans, as his method suggests, we would have seen how the cultural and ideological struggle took form and changed over time.

We would have seen how the convergence of reform liberalism, state actions, and the collaboration of some activists transformed the radical movement for Black human rights in the late '40s and early '50s into a struggle for so-called integration by the 1960s. This reformulation took place at the same time that significant changes were taking place in African American social structures. The reshifting of European imperialist power struggles, known as the Second World War, created new opportunities in Northern wartime industries that served as a magnet for African Americans in the Southern region, who as late as 1940 had a 90 percent poverty rate. This, along with the mechanization of agriculture and the ending of various land tenancy schemes, and of course the constant terror of unrestrained white power, served as the push that began the rapid proletarinization of African American labor in key urban centres in the North and the West. Even with these changes, the segregated character of US society resulted in the creation of Black enclaves that served as centres for the creation and nurturing of a vibrant civil life and specific cultural articulations in both the North and the South. But all of this changed with the development of the political motion broadly referred to as the Black Liberation Movement (BLM), which emerged in the 1960s.

Cabral asserts that it is not possible to harmonize economic and political domination of a people who have maintained a "cultural personality." It can be argued that African Americans were more than just a racial group—they were also a distinct ethnic group that was forged through common historical experiences and cultural practices. In other words, African Americans possessed the characteristics of a "people." A people, however, who were blocked from the full development of their "peoplehood" or nationality, and who were physically separated through a process some referred to as domestic colonisation. While the structures of colonial white supremacy ensured that African Americans were nationally oppressed people, the white colonial power did not feel the necessity to actively undermine the cultural integrity of African Americans in the same way that it did with the surviving members of the various indigenous peoples.

But with the advent of the BLM in its various forms expressing an anticapitalist, anti-imperialist programme of support for revolutionary change in the United States and globally, the response from the US government was as swift as it was predictable. The assault on the Black Liberation Movement was a multipronged military, political, but even more importantly, cultural and ideological attack.

Launched in the '60s and taking different forms in the '70s, it was a programme of containment with the objective to inoculate the African American community from the influences of "militant" Black revolutionaries. The strategy entailed a "soft counterinsurgency" programme to supplement the "hard" counterinsurgency programmes of the Federal Bureau of Investigation's (FBI) COINTELPO, which had as its objective the physical elimination of internal Black opposition. The soft approach was the development of programmes and approaches that would psychologically integrate Black people into an idea of an American national identity that stressed common historical experiences and values. This intentional policy had as its objective the creation of an African American with emphasis on "American"—an individual who, despite pigmentation, would have a worldview, sensibility, consumer taste, religion, and value system indistinguishable from any other American. This policy of integration was accomplished by instituting methods that were used by the state to contain and domesticate the indigenous populations. Methods were not as brutal as the "Indian boarding schools," where colonial authorities physically took indigenous children for forced cultural conversion; for African Americans the cultural assault took the form of forced busing schemes, the identification of our brightest for special "scholarships" at prestigious white institutions far from their communities, support for "Black business development," and the co-optation of oppositional leaders' messages into a narrative of common national destiny—the transformation and deification of Dr. King being the most obvious of these efforts.

Of course there are many who would disagree with this analysis of the structural and ideological changes that have occurred over the last three decades that paved the way for what many of us have seen as the rightward turn of the African American community. But the issues of culture and ideology must become a more central component of analysis and debate in our efforts to rebuild a radical Black opposition in the United States. Tragically, many Black activists have not understood that in terms of culture, the Obama phenomenon—the emotionally charged, nonrational support given to Barak Obama by significant numbers in the Black communities—represents the conjunctural integration of African Americans into an "American" identity and consciousness that is not that dissimilar from the average white America.

While Cabral suggested that cultural resistance was "indestructible" and could take on new forms, he could not have anticipated the overwhelming power of bourgeois culture and ideology to impose itself on a people subjected to its influences on a daily basis.

The Obama phenomenon reveals the depth of the pathology that is created when oppressive culture is internalized by the oppressed. The process of individual and collective repression, which is a function of the ongoing trauma of white supremacist social relationships, is constructed on an ideological and cultural foundation that normalizes a process in which the humanity of Africans is constricted, distorted, and even denied. The result for some Black people has been that instead of resistance, a pathological dependency was created in which proximity to whiteness came to define our/their humanity and human worth. This dependency has played itself out in the public space through the vicarious validation received from white society through the personage of Obama. This phenomenon has a ubiquitous cross-class character that has invaded every aspect of Black life in the United States, from poor inner-city communities to the disparate spaces where the Black bourgeoisie congregate. As a consequence, it has created the most formidable cultural and ideological challenge for the construction of oppositional consciousness and movement in the history of the Black experience in the United States.

An analysis of the impact of the bourgeoisie's cultural "war of position" to create an American out of the African American experience and the Obama phenomenon should not be seen as an ahistorical attempt to reinscribe an essentialist notion of Black culture and what constitutes a "Black community" or people. Political support for Barack Obama should also not be pathologized. Many Obama supporters, including radical Black activists, offer diverse and what they would consider mature and sophisticated arguments for supporting Barak Obama in 2008 and his recent reelection. However, it was precisely a historically-fixed, static, essentialist understanding of what constituted the imagined "Black community," its culture and identity that facilitated a turning away from the study of culture and ideology. And by turning away from culture and ideology to only focus on political economy, Black activists missed the profound cultural and ideological shifts that had occurred amongst Black people that required a counter-hegemonic strategy of cultural and ideological struggle.

It is Cabral's approach—the reading of "our" realities in the territory called the United States—that we must internalize if we are to identify the methods, appropriate organisational forms, and ideological content that will inform and reflect an effective revolutionary praxis. And an essential component of this work requires nothing less than the reconstruction of a new radical Black Subject.

From Cabral to Revolutionary Black Feminism: The Rehabilitation of the Black Subject

The one element that Cabral thought indispensable for the success of any revolutionary process was victory in the struggle against our weaknesses. Whatever the cultural and ideological mechanisms of domination created by an enemy committed to maintaining its power over the oppressed, it is the battle against our own weaknesses that is the most difficult to overcome. Why is that? Because this battle is the expression of the internal contradictions in the economic, social, cultural (and therefore historical) reality of each of our countries' and implies that in order to overcome our weaknesses, we first have to know that they exist.

Cabral reminds us that oppressive social relationships and structures can only be transformed by detailed knowledge of the reality that we are attempting to change. The failure of Black revolutionaries to construct a praxis to counter the neoconservative cultural and ideological inroads made into the Black community, as well as the repressive apparatus of the state, cannot be explained just by the institutional weaknesses of the BLM. While that is certainly a factor, one of the most significant factors that help to explain why Black Left theorists were unable to construct an oppositional programme stems from the marginalisation of the theoretical work of revolutionary Black feminists. It is critically important that we face up to that reality. It has been this marginalisation, when not completely excluded from the Black radical tradition, that has arrested the development of theory that would have grounded the BLM in the emerging realities, understandings, and needs of our people.

It is from radical Black theory that we fully understand culture as a site of strategic contestation, a contradictory terrain of struggle. And it is from revolutionary Black feminist thought that we look at the world differently and more accurately. Black feminist theory provides the framework for understanding the complex, intersectional relationships of class, race, gender, sexuality, etc. that construct identity and shape social experiences. And in better understanding the complex, interrelated, and multiple forms of oppression, we are able to construct a politics of liberation that can recentre the BLM as a force that can ground and unite the broader movements for US decolonization and radical social transformation.

Without the insights and experiences of Black women—working class and poor—systematized theoretically, our collective understanding of Black social reality was partial and, therefore, our ability to construct liberatory practice severly limited. So while Cabral's method is instructive, it is in the margins where new knowledge exists, and it is from those marginal spaces that Black feminism draws its insights and ability to produce a more comprehensive and relevant oppositional and visionary program. It is in those marginal spaces where the suppressed perspectives and experiences of Black working class and poor women provide the corrective to orthodox, male-centred theories of social formation and social change.

The construction of a political subject is a political project. A willful, conscious process created out of specific socio-historical circumstances. It is through the construction of a new Black "political subject"—that process, according to Black radical theorist Bell Hooks, that emerges "as one comes to understand how structures of domination work in one's life"[281]—that we can counter the effects of white supremacist, capitalist, patriarchal ideological and cultural hegemony. And it is a "radical" Black political subject, conscious of its oppositional history and informed by a vision of liberation that is inclusive, that provides the basis for the construction of a new Black radical politics. Cabral's critical approach to apprehending social reality, intellectual independence, and honesty provided valuable first steps towards the development of a collective political subject. But it is the intimate understanding of the historical specificities of race, class, gender, sexuality, national oppression, and the challenges of constructing critical consciousness in the complex realities of the Western metropolis that must serve as the basis for the reconstruction of a radical Black political subject.

The continued expansion of an internationalist African subjectivity is being enriched by the anticolonial, anti-white supremacist, and now antipatriarchal struggles that have emerged from the margins of mainstream cultural dominance. But the tasks before us are still daunting. In this protracted fight for our collective dignity, we cannot afford any self-deceptions; we cannot mask the difficulties we face, the mistakes and failures that we have experienced and will experience; and we certainly will not claim any easy victories. But if we emulate Cabral's honesty and commitment to the belief that people can transform themselves in the process of transforming their realities, we can be certain that we will win in the end.

281 Bell Hooks, Yearning: Race, Gender, and Cultural Politics, p 15

References

Cabral, Amílcar, "The Weapon of Theory," speech at the Tricontinental Conference in Havana, Cuba, 1966

Cabral, Amílcar, "National Liberation and Culture," speech at Syracuse University, 1970

Hooks, Bell, *Yearning: Race, Gender, and Cultural Politics*, Boston, South End Press,1990

36. CABRAL, BLACK LIBERATION, AND CULTURAL STRUGGLE

Makungu M. Akinyela

I became an activist in the Black liberation movement in the United States of America as a young university student in 1972, just one year prior to the death of Amílcar Cabral. It was Cabral, Malcolm X, and Frantz Fanon whose names, images, and ideas were most prominent in shaping my early political development. These three giants were most influential in the development of the revolutionary Black nationalist theory and practice that was the root and grounding of my life and continues to be a tremendous influence, four decades later.

Malcolm was seminally important to linking Black Nationalism and African American people to the burgeoning anticolonial struggles of the time. At the same time, Fanon was key in demonstrating through his writing and his practical commitment what Black internationalism looked like. It was from Cabral, however, that revolutionaries learned how to build a practical revolutionary theory from their own experience and cultural context. It is from Cabral that the Black liberation movement learned that revolutionary struggle must be pragmatic and that it must be ruthlessly self-critical in its assessment of the struggle in the context of real situations. Cabral's (1969) axiom, "tell no lies, claim no easy victories…," became for thousands of young nationalists in the United States both a warning and a guiding principle of how to wage a revolutionary struggle.

These and other ideas of Cabral were very important to the development of revolutionary Black Nationalism as espoused by the Revolutionary Action Movement's House of Umoja (RAM/HOU), which was the movement organisation through which I began my activist career. Cabral's ideas on national liberation, and culture in particular, and the relationship of cultural struggle to the development of a national identity against colonial oppression were very evident in the theory and practice of the revolutionary Black Nationalism of the early 1970s to 1980s. In the United States, this was a particularly significant issue in that within the Black liberation movement there were, on the one hand, contending groups promoting the cultural nationalism espoused by the Us Organization, and on the other, the nonculturalist intercommunalism espoused by the Black Panther Party for Self Defense (BPPSD). *Kawaida*, the primary theory of Black cultural nationalism as developed by Maulana Karenga (2004), posited that cultural revolution must be waged and won by Black people before political revolution was possible. Karenga argued that cultural revolution would be waged through the "rescue and reconstruction" of traditional African history and cultural practices.

Though the BPPSD initially adhered to some ideas of revolutionary Black Nationalism, the party soon rejected both Black Nationalism and internationalism, under the theoretical direction of Huey P. Newton (2006). In his theory of "revolutionary intercommunalism," Newton argued that nations no longer existed, which would have been a surprise to Cabral. An important aspect of Newton's theory is his notion of the vanguard role of the lumpenproletariat. Newton argued that, rather than the working class, the peasantry, or even the petit bourgeoisie being central to building a revolutionary movement, it was in fact the pimps, prostitutes, drug dealers, etc. who were the most revolutionary class in the Black liberation struggle. This argument was made with only marginal thought to the need to challenge the culture and consciousness of this class. Newton (1968) argued that cultural nationalism was reactionary and contributed to the people's oppression. He said,

> Cultural nationalism, or pork-chop nationalism, as I sometimes call it, is basically a problem of having the wrong political perspective. It seems to be a reaction, instead of responding to political oppression. The cultural nationalists are concerned with returning to the old African culture and thereby regaining their identity and freedom. In other words, they feel that the African culture will automatically bring political freedom. Many times cultural nationalists fall into line as reactionary nationalists.

These extremes in cultural analysis, aided by a lack of maturity within the movement, left both of these wings of the Black liberation movement extremely vulnerable to government infiltration, disinformation, and disruption through the FBIs Counter Intelligence Program (COINTELPRO), which left scores of Us members and Panthers dead from intergroup shootouts, emotionally damaged, or languishing in prison and laying the blame on each other.

Different from either the cultural nationalism of the Us Organization or the revolutionary intercommunalism of the Black Panther Party, the revolutionary Black Nationalism of RAM/HOU, influenced by Cabral's analysis, argued that *cultural struggle* is not a distinct stage which precedes the political struggle, as the cultural nationalists argued, nor is culture an issue somehow largely insignificant to how revolution is waged, as the Panthers believed.

Revolutionary Black nationalists agreed with Cabral (1973 p. 43) that, "national liberation is necessarily an act *of* culture." Revolutionary Black Nationalism in the United States, in unity with Cabral, saw this when a movement for liberation was waged in communities around police abuse as was done by the Coalition Against Police Abuse (CAPA) in Los Angeles, or for workers' rights. Similarly, this was also seen in the struggles to challenge the legitimacy of the celebration of the United States Bicentennial as the Afro-American Anti-Bicentennial Committee (AAABC) did from 1974 through 1976. These were in fact a struggle for the minds and hearts of the people. Cabral (1973 p. 45) wrote,

> A reconversion of minds—of mental set—is thus indispensable to the true integration of people into the liberation movement. Such reconversion—re-Africanization, in our case—may take place before the struggle, but it is complete only during the course of the struggle, through daily contact with the popular masses in the communion of sacrifice required by the struggle.

Rather than imagining that cultural analysis was something unimportant to and distinct from political struggle, or that cultural revolution somehow could be waged prior to and again distinct from the political struggle, learning from Cabral, revolutionary Black Nationalism understood that day-to-day political struggle around the important questions and situations of Black, lived experience in fact was a process of re-Africanization and creating a national identity of Black people distinct from the colonising American identity under which they were oppressed. They agreed with Cabral that "[h]istory proves that it is much less difficult to dominate and to continue dominating a people whose culture is similar or analogous to that of the conqueror" (1973 p. 48). When day-to-day political struggle is engaged in, it becomes clear that culture is not about re-creating ancient African traditions from all around the African continent (though these traditions may be helpful in redefining African identity) or about creating rigid definitions of what is or is not African. Cabral, like Fanon, believed that culture, understood as revolutionary action, was a living, dialectical force within society. Cabral (1973 p. 50) writes,

> Culture, like history, is an expanding and developing phenomenon. Even more important, we must take account of the fact that the fundamental characteristic of a culture is the highly dependent and reciprocal nature of its linkages with the social and economic reality of the environment, with the level of productive forces and the mode of production or the society which created it.

In other words, unlike some cultural nationalists, Cabral and the revolutionary Black nationalists of the RAM/HOU understood that culture is under constant reconstruction and recreation and is absolutely linked to social and economic forces in society. Cabral, in an African-centred challenge to traditional Marxist materialist analysis, argued that it was not class struggle which was the motive force of history, but rather the productive forces of a particular society which were the motive force of history, whatever the society's social structure. He argued that this understanding, unlike traditional Marxism, did not leave Africa and Africans outside of history, simply because these societies did not have class structures in the manner understood by Marxists. At the same time, while challenging Marxist ideas, Cabral understood that Africans and other colonised people did not live in some antiseptic bubble outside of the realities of capitalist domination. Cabral's nationalist analysis included an analysis of capitalism and the resultant imperialism and colonialism which impacted Africa and the rest to the third world.

This ability to "eat the fish and spit out the bones" in his criticism of Marxist analysis was a powerful example by Cabral for revolutionary nationalists in the United States struggling to understand the situation of Black people in the United States through the lens of an authentic African-centred world view, which allowed the Black Liberation Movement to maintain a connection with the worldwide anticolonial and anticapitalist struggles of other third-world peoples.

Cabral (1969 p. 102) in fact argues that the great moral contradiction of imperialism and colonialism is that these systems deny oppressed peoples their self-agency, or as revolutionary nationalists argue, self-determination.

> We therefore see that both in colonialism and in neocolonialism the essential characteristic of the imperialist domination remains the same: the negation of the historical process of the dominated people by means of violent usurpation of the freedom of development of the national productive forces.

What Cabral is arguing here is that oppression stunts the colonised people's self-agency (self-determination) by denying them control of their own productive forces, whether it be land, labour, or tools. In effect, colonialism, by exploiting the land, labor, and wealth of the colonised, denies them control of their own historical destiny and development. He says that this is a negation of the oppressed people's historical process. By extension, a revolutionary struggle for national liberation "rejects the negation of its historical process." This is truly what Marxists would call a "negation of the negation."

This leaves us with the question: What can Black activists learn from Amílcar Cabral today, forty years after his untimely death? As of this writing, Barack Obama has just won re-election for a second term as president of the United States. What the first four years exposed was that, despite liberals' and conservatives' wishful thinking that his election would bring in an era of postracial enlightenment, the election of the first African American president has only exposed the still festering white supremacist leanings of a significant section of the American population. As the country struggled to salvage the economy, even as the unemployment rate improved overall, ever so slightly, it remained largely unchanged for African Americans at around 14 percent, twice the national rate. Several high profile deaths of African American youths, like Trayvon Martin, exposed the reality that every thirty-six hours, a Black person is killed by the police or some other representative of the state in the United States of America. On the international front, as the war in Afghanistan has raged on, the US policy of imperial domination through military might has been magnified by the Obama administration, most profoundly demonstrated through assassinations and killing of both foreign- and domestic-born combatants by American drones. Queen Mother Audley Moore, an early revolutionary Black nationalist leader and a mentor of Malcolm X, was known for saying, "you might not think you are *at* war, but whether you like it or not, you are *in* a war." This seems to be the situation, not just with African Americans, but, as the US capitalist system has hardened, with other communities of people in the United States as well. In this light, it is clear to me that many of Cabral's lessons on culture and the revolutionary situation are pertinent and useful today.

Finally, Cabral encouraged a practical approach to national liberation struggle. That practicality also influenced the revolutionary Black Nationalism of the RAM/HOU and other organisations. Through practicality, movements are able to survive even the worst of onslaughts. It was understood that theory is critical to successful national liberation struggles; theory, however, which is not self-critical and open to being tested is simply ideology. While it may seem that revolutionary theory and practice has declined in the United States, especially within the African American communities, there is a front of stiff resistance in urban centres around the United States. Young people, workers, and organisers are rebuilding and learning lessons about organising through these past difficult years. The lessons and legacy of martyrs and heroes like Amílcar Cabral will contribute to the re-emerging liberation movements of the twenty-first century in the United States.

References

Cabral, Amílcar (1973) 'National Liberation & Culture', in Africa Information Services (ed.) *Return to the Source: Selected Speeches of Amílcar Cabral,* New York, Monthly Review Press

Cabral, Amílcar (1969) 'Tell No Lies, Claim No Easy Victories' in Richard Handyside (ed.) *Revolution in Guinea: Selected Texts by Amílcar Cabral*, New York, Monthly Review Press

Karenga, Maulana (2004) *Kawaida Theory: An African Communitarian Philosophy*, Los Angeles, Kawaida Publishers

Newton, Huey P. (2006) 'Intercommunalism', in Gadala, Amy (ed.) *Revolutionary Intercommunalism & The right of nations to self determination*, Newtown, Whales, Cyhoeddwyr y Superscript ltd.

Newton, Huey P. (1968) An interview with Huey P. Newton, http://www.hippy.com/modules.php?name=News&file=article&sid=76 accessed 27 November 2012

37. THE BLACK PANTHER PARTY, AFRICAN LIBERATION, AND AMÍLCAR CABRAL

Walter Turner

I don't believe there is life after death, but if there is, we can be sure that the souls of our forefathers who were taken away to America to be slaves are rejoicing today to see their children re-united and working together to help us be independent and free.

—Amílcar Cabral [282]

At the height of the African liberation movements in the late 1960s, the *Black Panther Party Newspaper* provided extensive news and analysis on the liberation struggles in the Third World. The *Black Panther Party Newspaper* from 1968 to 1971 maintained a regular page on international affairs and utilized news services from Africa, Asia, and the Caribbean to highlight the importance of the African liberation struggles to African Americans and American activists. The BPP newspaper consistently made the connections between the movements for human rights at home and abroad by covering events in Africa, Vietnam, Brazil, Cuba, and Palestine. The treatment of these events and their placement in the Black Panther Newspaper provided readers of the Black Panther Party with a window into the liberation struggles of the 1960s and the 1970s. As a result of the BPP newspaper, African American communities were able to develop an awareness that would be essential for a global view of the world and later struggles against colonialism, imperialism, and apartheid.

The late 1960s were a turning point in the civil rights movement. The urban rebellions throughout the country and the voices of SNCC and

282 Piero Gleijeses, Conflicting Missions: Havana, Washington and Africa 1959-1976 (Chapel Hill: University of North Carolina Press, 2002) p. 198

Malcolm X added a militant dimension to Black Nationalism. The voices were younger and heard by a larger, more discontented mass of African Americans and young activists. Representatives of SNCC had traveled to Africa in the 1960s and had an opportunity to meet with President Sekou Toure of Guinea and Malcolm X in Kenya. During his lifetime, Malcolm X was able to visit Africa on four occasions and addressed the (OAU) Organization of Africa Unity in 1964. Upon his return to the United States in 1964, he spoke on a programme with Ms. Fannie Lou Hamer of the Mississippi Freedom Democratic Party, and noted the need for African Americans to organise a "Mau Mau" similar to that in Kenya. That speech would be one of his last before his assassination two months later, in February of 1965.

The transatlantic connection between Africa and African Americans was far from new. Black Nationalism, Pan-Africanism, and Black Radical Internationalism have always played a significant role in the African American movements for self-determination. The Back-to-Africa movements of the nineteenth and twentieth centuries[283] were a sign that African Americans saw an intimate connection between their fate in the United States and the status of African people worldwide. African Americans played a role in supporting and participating in the Pan-African Congresses of the early twentieth century and catalyzed the Garvey Movement and the Harlem Renaissance in the 1920s. When African American soldiers returned from World War II, the connections between Africa and African Americans became an integral part of the civil rights movement.

> After 1959 the spirit of African nationalism was fanned to a high flame, and we then began to witness the complete collapse of colonialism. France began to get out of French West Africa; Belgium began to make moves to get out of the Congo; Britain began to make moves to get out of Kenya, Tanganyika, Uganda, Nigeria, and some of these other places.
>
> —Malcolm X speaking at the Bandung, Indonesia Conference that was held in April 1955 and set the groundwork for the nonaligned movement.

283 Paul Cuffeee, Martin Delaney, Henry McNeal Turner, and Marcus Garvey

The *Black Panther Party Newspaper* provided a regular source of news and analysis on the wars for liberation in Angola, Mozambique, and Guinea-Bissau. The BPP newspaper offered a regular mix of international affairs, news on African American communities in the United States, and information that highlighted the community survival programmes of the Black Panther Party. It was not unusual to find news on the PAIGC, MPLA, FRELIMO, or the ANC in the regular editions of the BPP newspaper. The paper provided regular coverage on the Vietnam War and encouraged African American soldiers to question their role in the imperial wars in Southeast Asia.

The Bandung conference was a concrete step in building a post-World War II nonaligned movement that included Africa, Asia, and Latin America. After his attendance at the independence celebration of Ghana in 1957, Martin Luther King presented a sermon at his church in Atlanta entitled, "The Birth of A New Nation." Dr. King's congregation at Dexter Avenue Baptist Church had allocated $2,500 for his travel to Africa. Martin Luther King was part of a delegation of dignitaries to Ghana that included Congressman Adam Clayton Powell Jr., labor leader A. Phillip Randolph, Ralph Bunche, and Norman Manley, the future prime minister of Jamaica. The travel of Dr. and Mrs. King took them through stopovers in Dakar, Senegal, and Monrovia, Liberia. While he was in Africa, King met with Ghanaian president, Kwame Nkrumah, and Tanzanian nationalist, Julius Nyrere. His journey concluded with a visit to Nigeria before returning back to the United States. In his speech of April 1957, King said,

> Ghana has something to say to us. It says to us first that the oppressor never voluntarily gives freedom to the oppressed. You have to work for it. And if Nkrumah and the people of the Gold Coast had not stood up persistently, revolting against the system, it would still be a colony of the British Empire. Freedom is never given to anybody, for the oppressor has you in domination because he plans to keep you there, and he never voluntarily gives

> it up. And that is where the strong resistance comes. Privileged classes never give up their privileges without strong resistance.[284]

The next year, President Kwame Nkrumah hosted the Conference of Independent Africa states, which called upon all members of the United Nations to intensify efforts to combat racialism and segregation in South Africa, the Central African Federation, and Kenya. The 1958 All African Peoples Conference endorsed Pan-Africanism and the desire for unity "amongst African peoples." The conference rejected the claim of Portugal that its colonies constituted part of metropolitan Portugal and demanded immediate independence for countries in Africa under Portuguese rule. The conference went further to condemn nuclear testing on the African continent and demand independence for South West Africa.

In 1955 Amílcar Cabral traveled to Angola and joined the MPLA (Popular Movement for the Liberation of Angola). Cabral had attended school in Portugal in the 1950s where he met and befriended Agostinho Neto, who would be the first president of Angola, and Marcelino dos Santos, a founding member of the MPLA and of FRELIMO. After his return from Angola, the PAIGC was formed, and in April of 1961, the PAIGC, together with FRELIMO and MPLA, formed—in Morocco—the Conference of Nationalist Organizations of the Portuguese Colonies. The war in Guinea-Bissau began in 1963 when the PAIGC started concerted attacks on Portuguese installations.

The Black Panther Party for Self Defense had been formed in 1966 and supported not only the African liberation movements but a radical Pan-Africanism that worked to inform its grassroots supporters of the wars being fought worldwide for liberation and self-determination. A survey of the newspapers between 1968 and 1971 reveal extraordinary press coverage on Africa and efforts to make the connection between struggles in Africa and those of African Americans at home. Even after the FBI induced splits in the BPP in 1971, the various newspapers of the

284 Dr. Martin Luther King, "The Birth of a New Nation" in A Call to Conscience: The Landmark Speeches of Dr. Martin Luther King, Jr. , edited by Clayborne Carson and Kris Shepard. 29-30 (New York: Time Warner, 2001)

party factions continued to provide news and information on struggles for liberation in Africa.

The Black Panther Party was politically committed to internationalism when it was formed in 1966. The BPP had strong connections with Cuba from the outset. When George Murray, minister of education of the Black Panther Party, attended a conference in Guantanamo, Cuba, in 1968, he was told by the Cuban representative that "Cuban revolutionaries [were] prepared to give their lives for the cause of Afro-Americans, which is the cause of the people of the world."[285] The presentation was part of the National Campaign of Solidarity with the Afro-American People, and included representatives from the countries of Guinea and Korea. Alfredo Gonzalez, the first secretary of the party in Guantanamo, said that "the time will come when those who have assassinated hundreds of Black citizens and unleashed dogs against them because they have claimed their rights will have to account for their actions."[286]

In 1963 Amílcar Cabral made contact with Cuban representatives in Algeria, and in 1966 he traveled to Cuba for the Tricontinental Conference. Cabral requested military support from Cuba and then returned to Guinea to build support with President Sekou Toure. Cabral asked that the Cubans send mechanics and mortar experts and insure that they would be Blacks or dark mulattoes so they would blend in with the fighters in Guinea-Bissau. This pattern of Cuba sending Blacks and mulattoes to their military efforts in Africa would be a consistent policy throughout the Cuban efforts to assist the Portuguese colonies in their struggle for independence. After the independence of Angola in 1975, Cuba would send more than 30,000 troops over almost fifteen years to repel invasions against Angola by South Africa and its Western allies. The defeat of South Africa and its allies in Angola was a decisive victory that enabled the independence of Zimbabwe, South Africa, and Namibia.

The Black Panther Party publicized their connections with Africa and revolutionary struggles throughout the newspaper. Various editions of the *Black Panther Newspaper* included a page titled, "International

285 The Black Panther , October 19, 1968, pg. 3
286 Ibid

News," with border photos of Che Guevara, Ho Chi Minh, Mao Zedong, and Patrice Lumumba. The November, 1968, edition of the newspaper included a news clipping detailing the efforts of the United Nations General Assembly to strengthen sanctions legislation against Rhodesia and extend them to Portugal and South Africa, because neither of the countries had abided by the United Nations sanctions resolution. The article noted that Portugal and Rhodesia had provided mutual defense for South Africa and that both of the countries were engaged in a bitter struggle with "Black freedom fighters." "Portugal is a country that is doomed to collapse without the life giving raw resource that she steals from Angola and Mozambique."[287]

The November, 1968, issue of the BPP newspaper noted that soldiers and children in Guinea had been attacked with shrapnel and napalm. The victims were shown on Cuban television, as their visit to Havana had been arranged by OSPAAL (Organisation in Solidarity with the People of Africa Asia and Latin America). A report on the same page showed a photo of the completion of the Tanzania section of the Tanzania-Zambia Railway. This railroad, which was completed with the support of China, was essential in providing landlocked Zambia an outlet for exporting goods other than via South African ports. The same issue noted the attempts by South Africa to "jam" radio broadcast on "Radio Hope" that were coming from Tanzania to South Africa. As the wars intensified in Guinea-Bissau and the other Portuguese African territories, the Black Panther Party Newspaper expanded the amount of coverage on Africa.

The coverage of African liberation struggles in the BPP newspaper conveyed a strong message to readers of the paper. The struggles for liberation and self-determination in the United States were intimately connected to the struggles for liberation throughout the world, not only the African continent. The party often devoted several pages or more to the coverage of international affairs. Some of the articles were brief, and had been posted from press services that included news agencies in China and Cuba. The Cuban organisation OSPAAL and its feature magazine Tricontinental were widely used as sources for news on international affairs.

287 The Black Panther, November 1968,

OSPAAAL had been founded in Havana in 1966 as an outgrowth of a conference that included representatives from Guinea, the Congo, South Africa, Angola, Vietnam, the Palestine Liberation Organisation, Puerto Rico, and Chile, amongst others. Amilar Cabral was an attendee at that conference in 1966.

By the end of 1968 the circulation of the Black Panther Newspapers had reached over 100,000, and would reach 250,000 by the 1970s. The BPP newspapers in 1969 covered a variety of international themes, with an emphasis on the African continent. There were articles on Mozambique, Haiti, Thailand, Zimbabwe, Zambia, Guinea, Nigeria, Palestine, the Congo, Vietnam, Al Fath, Chile, Brazil and China. An October issue of the BPP newspaper interviewed six women from the Black Panther Party on solidarity with the struggles of South Africa, China, Vietnam and Palestine. The article, "Al Fath Speaks to Africa," emphasized the solidarity of Palestinians with the struggles in Africa and noted that they had attended the Pan-African Cultural Festival in Algeria because "the same circumstances which created the white regimes in Rhodesia and South Africa created the State of Zionism in Palestine." The same issue of the paper highlighted news on the armed wing of the African National Congress (Umkhonto We Sizwe) and the intensification of the armed conflict in Angola.

The years of the late 1960s were critical turning points for the liberation movements in the Portuguese colonies. By 1969 the PAIGC, under Amilar Cabral, had acquired anti-aircraft weapons and were able to challenge the Portuguese air supremacy. It became clear that for all intents and purposes, Portugal had lost the battle in Guinea and that the government of Portugal was conflicted internally about its ability to retain control of its "overseas territories." By 1971 the PAIGC controlled all of the territory outside of the cities in Guinea-Bissau.

The September 1969 edition of the Black Panther Newspaper featured an article by Amílcar Cabral that was reprinted from the *Tricontinental* magazine of June of 1969, titled "The Power of Arms." Several photos of Cabral were printed in the paper, and the entire speech covered three issues of the BPP newspaper in September and October of 1969.

Cabral made the connection between the war being carried out by the Portuguese and Western interests.

> With regard to the position of the Portuguese in the war, we are of the opinion that they are carrying it out because of the criminal policy of their government, and because they are afraid of decolonization. Portugal is an underdeveloped country, it is a semi-colony of England, the United States, and other countries.... It prefers the role of intermediary to having to withdraw from Angola. It prefers to let Angola be exploited by the United States, Belgium, England, etc. rather than moving out and leaving it only to others.[288]

Inside Portugal, the cost of the war and dissatisfaction within the military would lead to the overthrow of the Caetano government in 1974, leading to independence for Mozambique, Guinea-Bissau, Cape Verde and Angola. The "Portuguese in Guinea" article of June 1970 noted that Portugal was engaged in attacks against Guinea-Conakry (French) to undermine and weaken the successes of the PAIGC. "Like the US in South Vietnam, popular armed struggle has driven Portugal against the wall in its West African colony of Guinea-Bissau. "[289]

While Cabral was in New York in 1972 to speak at the United Nations, he had an opportunity to speak with a group of African Americans at a meeting that had been organised by the African Information Service. He started his talk by saying, "I am bringing to you—our African brothers and sisters of the United States—the fraternal salutation of our people in assuring you we are very conscious that all in this life concerning you also concerns."[290] Cabral was speaking at a moment when the PAIGC was about to declare victory in the long war against Portuguese

288 "The Power of Arms" The Black Panther, Saturday September 27, 1967, pg. 3

289 "Portuguese in Guinea" by Amílcar Cabral, The Black Panther, December 1970 , pg. 15

290 "Connecting the Struggles: an informal talk with Black Americans" in Return to the Source: Selected Speeches of Amílcar Cabral, ed. Africa Information Service, Monthly Review Press, London, 1973, pg. 75

colonialism. "It is also a contribution for you to never forget that you are Africans."[291] Cabral continued:

> You can be sure that we realize the difficulties you face, the problems you have and your feelings, your revolts, and also your hopes. We think that our fighting for Africa against colonialism and imperialism is a proof of understanding of your problem and also a contribution for the solutions of your problems in this continent. Naturally, the inverse is also true. All the achievements towards the solution of your problems here are real contributions to our own struggle. And we are very encouraged in our struggle by the fact that each day more of the African people born in America become conscious of their responsibilities to the struggle in Africa.[292]

The international role of the Black Panther Party must be placed in the larger context of events in the United States and throughout the world in the late 1960s. African Americans and their allies were building a movement to effect social and political change in every arena of society. The objectives of the BPP became a platform for many other activist organisations of that era. The themes of police brutality, poor housing, inadequate education and racism resonated with every African American. Many other organisations, with few changes, adopted the format of the 10 Point Program and Platform of the Black Panther Party. As a result of the success of the Black Panther Party and the larger movement for African American self-determination, the United States government, under the auspices of the FBI and the COINTELPRO program, took every step possible to undermine the party through infiltration, misinformation and assassination. It was frightening to the fulcrums of power that the party could make alliances with liberation movements throughout the world. This same set of interests on a global level would lead to the assassination of Amílcar Lopes da Costa Cabral in January of 1973.

291 Ibid, pg. 76
292 Ibid, pg. 76

The Black Panther Party contributed to the framing of a consciousness based on concrete examples of struggles in the United States and those in Africa and abroad. The BPP newspaper coverage on Africa was included in a larger frame of imperialism and colonialism throughout the world. The same edition of the paper that included a story on police brutality or violations of the rights of African Americans in Chicago, Oakland, New York or Houston included a story on colonial wars being waged against countries around the world that were seeking independence and self-determination. The *Black Panther Party Newspaper*, 1966 to 1972, complemented an international movement that spoke clearly against imperialism and on the side of revolution and independence. The struggles of Amílcar Cabral and the PAIGC mirrored the fights for freedom and self-determination that were the foundation of the Black Panther Party.

38. MEMORIES OF BLACK LIBERATION

AMÍLCAR CABRAL

Angela Davis

For a time during the late 1960s, Amílcar Cabral was as important a figure for the United States Black Liberation Movement and other radical formations as Che Guevara, Stokeley Carmichael, and Rap Brown. We seemed to evoke the national liberation campaign in Guinea-Bissau and Cape Verde with the same ease with which we referred to Black struggles in Los Angeles and South Philadelphia. Of course few of us had ever visited those countries—although Harry Belafonte had arranged a trip for a number of SNCC (Student Nonviolent Coordinating Committee) activists to Conakry, Guinea (the former French colony that abuts Guinea-Bissau to the south), which served as the headquarters for Cabral's liberation movement. The summer of 1964 was Freedom Summer in the United States. In Africa, especially in southern Africa and in Mozambique, Angola, Guinea-Bissau, and Cape Verde, national liberation movements were passionately challenging white supremacy and the Portuguese Empire. In the United States, after the racist murders of Chaney, Goodman, and Schwerner in Mississippi and the Democratic National Convention, where Fannie Lou Hamer demanded that the Mississippi Freedom Democratic Party be seated, Harry Belafonte organised what he called a "recuperative getaway" for Mrs. Hamer, Bob Moses, Julian Bond, James Foreman, and other key members of SNCC. Four years later, when I spent time with Jim Foreman, who was mentoring a small group in Los Angeles who had recently created LA SNCC, I heard him refer frequently to that trip and to Guinea's role in supporting the independence movement in Guinea-Bissau and Cape Verde.

Jim Foreman and my friend Charlene Mitchell, a Black leader of the US Communist Party, were the two people from whom I heard most about Amílcar Cabral during that period. Charlene, who would become the driving force behind the international campaign to free me that was launched after my arrest in October, 1970, had actually met Cabral. Shortly before meeting him, she had had a contentious encounter with Eldridge Cleaver, then headquartered in Algeria, during which he argued that the Cubans and some of the African leaders had "sold out the revolution." Cleaver's position came up during Charlene's meeting with the PAIGC leader in Morocco, who was quick to point out that too many so-called Black revolutionaries assumed that fighting, as opposed to the transformation of popular consciousness, was the essence of revolutionary change. As a leader who had spent many years on the ground using his training in agronomy to organise villagers in Guinea-Bissau into liberated zones, he clearly understood how dangerous it was to romanticize revolutionary practice. In this sense he challenged conventional tendencies to take literally Fanon's argument that violence is a cleansing force.

Eldridge Cleaver was not the only one to romanticize revolution by allowing the fight to overshadow the goal towards which the fighters were striving. In fact, one of the major problems of that era was the tendency to be seduced by masculinist and militarist images of struggle. Cabral consistently challenged those ideas. And despite the fact that too many of us failed to develop more complicated ideas about revolutionary change, radical Black activists of that era did indeed understand how our connections—material and symbolic—with liberation movements on the continent of Africa helped to transform the way we envisioned freedom movements inside the United States. Figures like Amílcar Cabral (and for some of us also Augustinho Neto and Samora Machel) helped us to imagine the horizons of freedom in far broader terms than were available to us through what we now call "civil rights discourse."

Those of us who were Marxists and were inclined to join our African comrades in proclaiming that anticolonial struggles were pivotal arenas of global resistance to capitalism were as wary of provincial and capitalist-inflected definitions of "Black Power" as we were of the assimilationist strategy associated with conservative civil rights advocacy. Thanks to Cabral, we recognised that our very conception of Black liberation, which distinguished our strategies and goals from that of an approach based strictly on civil rights, was closely linked to national liberation struggles in Africa. In other words, we were deeply connected not only with US freedom movements, but also with the post-World War II anti-imperialist efforts in Africa, Asia, and Latin America. Thus, our relationship to Amílcar Cabral and his people in Guinea-Bissau and Cape Verde was not abstract. We depended on the sense of internationalism accorded to us by Cabral in order to develop our own critiques of narrow integrationism and our more capacious visions of "Black liberation."

It may well be that we relied too heavily on iconic leaders: Fidel Castro, Che Guevara, Frantz Fanon, Patrice Lumumba, Amílcar Cabral. However, this pantheon of revolutionary men (some of us discovered women like Haydée Santamaria and Célia Sanchez) did help to sustain our belief in the possibilities of global liberation. When I joined the Communist Party after our SNCC chapter disintegrated (ironically, because one of the New York leaders felt that the women had too much power in LA SNCC), I became a part of a formation within the party called the Che-Lumumba Club. Around the same time, I helped to campaign for a college at the University of California, San Diego, which would serve the needs of Black, Latino, and working-class white students. We chose to call this future college Lumumba-Zapata. We could have just as easily called it Guevara-Cabral. I do know that during that period, many male babies were named after Cabral. Such naming practices—whether of institutions or children—reinforced our affinity with people standing up against colonialism and US imperialism all over the planet.

But Amílcar Cabral was so much more than a symbol. As a revolutionary theorist, he emphasized the importance of tending to the particularities of each liberation struggle—political, economic, and, he emphasized, cultural. In his widely circulated address to the first Tri-continental Conference in Havana (January, 1966) entitled, "The Weapon of Theory," he underscored the fact that revolutions were not formulaic and could not be simply transferred from one site to another. Of course the excitement of the Cuban Revolution, which had triumphed in 1959, was not only what it accomplished ninety miles from the shores to the United States, but rather the potential it announced for future (and hopefully similar) radical transformations. Rather than attempt to reproduce the strategies and tactics that were successful on the island of Cuba, Cabral urged us to develop our theories and strategies by directly engaging with the specific economic, political, and cultural locations of our struggles.

> However great the similarity between our various cases and however identical our enemies, national liberation and social revolution are not exportable commodities; they are, and increasingly so every day, the outcome of local and national elaboration, more or less influenced by external factors (be they favorable or unfavorable) but essentially determined and formed by the historical reality of each people....The success of the Cuban revolution, taking place only ninety miles from the greatest imperialist and antisocialist power of all time, seems to us, in its content and its way of evolution, to be a practical and conclusive illustration of the validity of this principle.[293]

In a meeting with US Black activists several months before his assassination, he further elaborated on the importance of envisioning the struggle in terms that are far more profound than guns and violence.

> In our country we have been fighting for nearly 10 years. If we consider the changes achieved in that time, principally in the relationship between men and women, it has been more than 100 years. If we were only shooting bullets and shells, yes, 10 years is too much. But we were not only doing this. We were forging a nation during these years. [294]

---

293 (http://www.marxists.org/subject/africa/cabral/1966/weapon-theory.htm)
294 "Connecting the struggles: An informal chat with Black Americans Amílcar Cabral" *Pambazuka News* 2010-09-16, Issue 496 http://pambazuka.org/en/category/features/66966

Cabral always emphasized the need to engage in deep analysis. In other words, analyses simplistically based on analogical thinking were unacceptable. In the same meeting with US Black activists, he referred to a conversation he had had with Eldridge Cleaver, with whom he discussed the nature of the colonial condition. Cleaver was set on arguing that Black people in the United States were subject to a form of colonial domination. He pointed out that,

> Many times we are confronted with phenomena that seem to be the same, but political activity demands that we be able to distinguish them. That is not to say that the aims are not the same. And that is not to say that even some of the means cannot be the same. However, we must deeply analyse each situation to avoid loss of time and energy doing things that we are not to do and forgetting things that we have to do.[295]

The lessons we learned from Amílcar Cabral were invaluable. I never met him in person, but I do remember passionate conversations about the imminent collapse of the Portuguese empire with Augustinho Neto in Tanzania in 1973. We spoke about the death of Cabral, which was still fresh in everyone's memory. During that trip to Africa, I also spent time in Conakry, Guinea, and there, on the soil where he was assassinated, I was able to pay tribute to a man who helped to transform the destiny of the planet.

---

295 *Ibid.*

SECTION 8:

SELECT BIBLIOGRAPHY

COMPILED BY CHRIS WEBB, JEAN-PIERRE DIOUF AND FIROZE MANJI

The following bibliography is divided into two parts: a list of selected publications by Amílcar Cabral, and a select bibliography of publications about Cabral.

BY CABRAL

Cabral, Amílcar (1954) "Acerca da Contribuição dos 'Povos' Guineenses Para Produção Agrícola da Guiné," *Boletim Cultural de Guiné Portuguesa*, vol. 9, pp. 771-777

Cabral, Amílcar (1954) "Acera de Utilização da terra na Africa Negra," *Boletim Cultural de Guiné Portuguesa*, vol. 9, no. 34, pp. 401-415

Cabral, Amílcar (1954) "Para O Conhecimento do Problema de Erosão do Solo da Guiné," *Boletin Cultural da Guiné Portuguesa*, vol. 9, no. 33, pp. 163-193

Cabral, Amílcar (1954) "A Proposito de Mecanização da Agricultura na Guinée Portugaise," *Boletin Cultural da Guiné Portuguesa*, vol. 9, no. 34, pp. 389-400

Cabral, Amílcar (1956) "Recenseamento Agricola da Guiné, Estimativa em 1953" *Boletin Cultural da Guiné Portuguesa*, vol. 11, no. 43, pp. 7-243

Cabral, Amílcar (1958) "A Propos du cycle cultural arachide-mils en Guinée Portugaise" *Boletin Cultural da Guiné Portuguesa*, vol. 13, no. 49, pp. 149-156

Cabral, Amílcar (1958) "Feux de brousse et jacheres dans le cycle cultural arachide-mils," *Boletim Cultural de Guiné Portuguesa*, vol. 13, no. 49, pp. 257-268

Cabral, Amílcar (May 1962) "La Guinée Portugaise set les Iles du Cap Vert," *Voice of Africa*, vol. 2, no. 5, p. 37

Cabral, Amílcar (March 1963) "Liberation Movement in Portuguese Guinea," *Voice of Africa*, vol. 2, no. 3, p. 32

Cabral, Amílcar (May 26 1965) "Guinée dite Portugaise et Cap Vert: La lutte du PAIGC," *Remarques Africaines*, no. 243, pp. 19-22

Cabral, Amílcar (June 1965) "Liberating Portuguese Guinea from Within," *The New African*,
vol. 4, no. 4, p. 85

Cabral, Amílcar (October 1965) "Our Solidarities: An Interview with Amilcar Cabral"; *The African Liberation Reader* no. 2, pp.110-11

Cabral, Amílcar (1967) "Mankinds Way To Progress," *World Marxist Review*, vol. 10, no. 11, pp. 48-49

Cabral, Amílcar (Sept.-Oct. 1968) "Determined to Resist", *Tricontinental*, no. 8, pp. 114-126

Cabral, Amílcar (1969) "Guinea (B) Political and Military Situation," *Tricontinental*, vol. 4, no. 37, pp. 25-34

Cabral, Amílcar (May-June 1969) "Guinea: The Power of Arms" *Tricontinental Monthly*, no. 12 pp. 25-34

Cabral, Amílca (Jan. 1970) "Frente al Ultra Colonialismo Português" *Pensamiento Crítico*, no. 36, pp. 186-197

Cabral, Amílcar (July-October 1970) "PAIGC: Optimistic and Fighter," *Tricontinental Bimonthly*, no. 19-20, pp. 167-174

Cabral, Amílcar (1971) *"Our People Are Our Mountains: Amilcar Cabral on Guinean Revolution"* Committee for Freedom in Mozambique, Angola and Guinea, London, pp. 21-22

Cabral, Amílcar (November 1971) "PAIGC Attacks," *Tricontinental*, vol. 6, no. 68

Cabral, Amílcar [1921-1973] (May 13th May 1972) "Cabral On Nkrumah :' Speech Delivered By The Secretary General of PAIGC, Amílcar Cabral, at The *Symposium Organized by the Democratic Party of Guinea [PDG] in Memory of President Dr. Kwame Nkrumah*, People's Palace of Conakry [n.p.], Jihad Productions

Cabral, Amílcar (July-August 1972) "Fruits of a Struggle," *Tricontinental*, 31, pp. 60-77

Cabral, Amílcar (1972) "Identity and Dignity in Struggle" *Southern Africa,* vol. 5, no. 9

Cabral, Amílcar (Fall 1972) "Identity and Dignity in the National Liberation Struggle," *Africa Today*, vol. 19, no. 4, pp. 39-47

Cabral, Amílcar (1972) "On the Contribution of the" Peoples" of Guiné to Agricultural Production in Guiné" *Emerging Nationalism in Portuguese Africa. Documents (Stanford)*,pp. 352-355

Cabral, Amílcar (1972) "PAIGC's Denunciation [of Portuguese Plans to Chemically Destroy Crops in Guine-Bissau before the Coming Harvest]", *Tricontinental bulletin* 71

Cabral, Amílcar (1972) "*Revolution in Guinea: Selected Texts*", Monthly Review Press, New York

Cabral, Amílcar (Spring 1973) "Fruits of Struggle", *Tricontinental,* vol. 5, p.12

Cabral, Amílcar (1973) "Identity and Dignity in the Context of the National Liberation", *Pan-African Journal,* vol. 6, no. 3, pp. 368-378,

Cabral, Amílcar (Winter, 1973) "Report to Our Friends", *Africa Today,* vol. 20, no. 1, pp. 7-13

Cabral, Amílcar (1973) "Realities," *Tricontinental,* 22, pp. 96-109

Cabral, Amílcar (1973) "*Return to the Source: Selected Speeches of Amilcar Cabral.*", Monthly Review Press, New York

Cabral, Amílcar (1973) "A Strategy for Struggle" *The Black Scholar*

Cabral, Amílcar (1973) "The Struggle Has Taken Root," *Tricontinental,* vol. 8, no. 84, pp. 42-48

Cabral, Amílcar (January-March 1973) "Support for the People's Legitimate Aspirations to Freedom, Independence and Progress," *Objective: Justice,* vol. 5, no. 1, pp. 3-7

Cabral, Amílcar (June 1974) "A Cultura e a Combate Pela Independencia", *Seara Nova,* no. 1544, p. 5

Cabral, Amílcar (1974) "*Revolution in Guinea: An African People's Struggle*", Stage 1, London

Cabral, Amílcar (1974) «*Textos Politicos de Amílcar Cabral: Declaracoes Sobre o Assassinato*», Lisboa, Livraria Ler

Cabral, Amílcar (1975) «*La Descolonizacion del Africa Portuguesa: Guinea-Bissau*», Ediciones Periferia, Buenos Aires

Cabral, Amílcar (1975) «La Lutte du P.A.I.G.C. : Chronologie des principaux événements», In *Unité et lutte I, l'armede la théorie*, Maspéro, Paris

Cabral, Amílcar (1975) « Mémorandum du Partido Africano da Independência da Guiné e Cabo Verde au Gouvernement portugais», In *Unité et lutte II, La pratique révolutionnaire,* Maspéro, Paris

Cabral, Amílcar and Andrade de, Mário (1976) "*A Arma da Teoria: Unidade e Luta*", Seara Nova

Cabral, Amílcar (1977) "*A Práctica Revolucionária*", vol. 2, Seara Nova

Cabral, Amílcar and Vale, Michel (1977) "The Role of Culture in the Struggle for Independence", *International Journal of Politics*, pp. 18-43

Cabral, Amílcar (1977) "*Unidade e Luta*", Seara Nova, Lisbon

Cabral, Amílcar (1979) "The Role of Culture in the Liberation Struggle", In Mattelard, Armand and Siegelaud, Seth, *Communication and Class Struggle, vol. 1*, International General, New York, pp. 205-212

Cabral, Amílcar (1979) "*Unity and Struggle: Speeches and Writings of Amilcar Cabral*", Monthly Review Press, New York

Cabral, Amílcar (1980) "*Unity and Struggle*", Heinemenn, London
Cabral, Amílcar (1984) 'The Theory of the National Liberation Struggle.' *Latin American Perspectives, vol.* XI, no. 2, pp. 43-54.

ON CABRAL

Abdullah, Ibrahim (2006) "Culture, Consciousness and Armed Conflict: Cabral's Déclassé/(Lumpenproletariat?) in the Era of Globalization", *African Identities,* vol. 4, no. 1, pp. 99-112.

Ahmed, Feroz (1973) "Amilcar Cabral: An Editorial." *Pakistan Forum,* vol. 3, no. 4

"Amilcar Cabral" (January-March 1973), *Objective Justice,* vol. 5, no. 1, pp. 2-3

Amilcar Cabral - la pratique revolutionnaire (1975), Maspero, France

Andrade Mario de (1973) "Amilcar Cabral: profil d'un révolutionnaire africain," *Présence Africaine,* vol. 86, no. 2

Andrade, Mario de (1980) «*Amilcar Cabral: Essai de Biographie Politique*», Maspero, Paris

Andrade, Mario de (1980) «*Amilcar Cabral*», Maspero, Paris

Andreini, J.C. and Lambert, M.C. (24 janvier 1973) "l'Assassinat d'Amilcar Cabral," *Le Monde*

Andreini, J.C. and Lambert, M.C. (1978) «La Guinée Bissau d'Amilcar Cabral à la reconstruction nationale», Editions l'Harmattan, Paris

Anise, Ladun (1975) "Cultural Revolution and National Liberation", *The Black Scholar,* vol. 6, no. 7, p. 45

Audelman, D. A. (May 1970) "Profile: Cabral, Pragmatic Revolutionary Shows how an African Guerilla War can be Successful", *Africa Report*, 15, pp. 18-19

Araujo, Norman. (1966) *"A Study of Cape Verdean Literature"*, Boston College, Chestnut Hill, MA

Batalha, Luis (2004) *"The Cape Verdean Diaspora in Portugal: Colonial Subjects in a Postcolonial World"*, Lexington Books, Lanham, MD

Benot, Yves (1984) "Amilcar Cabral and the International Working Class Movement", *Latin American Perspectives,* vol. 11, no. 2, p. 81-96

Bienen, Henry (1977) "State and Revolution: The Work of Amilcar Cabral", *Journal of Modern African Studies,* vol. 15, no. 4, pp. 555-568

Bienen, H. (24 Nov. 1980) "Bissau Coup Ousts Portugal," *West Africa*, no. 3305, p. 2345

Biggs-Davison, John (1971) "The Current Situation in Portuguese Guinea" *African affairs,* pp. 385-394

Blackey, Robert (1974) "Fanon and Cabral: A Contrast in Theories of Revolution for Africa" *Journal of Modern African Studies,* vol. 12, no. 2, pp. 191–209

Bockel, Alain (Janvier 1976) «Amilcar Cabral, marxiste africain», *Ethiopiques*, no 5, pp. 35-39

Bragança de, A. (19 Feb. 1973) "Le complot contre Cabral," *Afrique-Asie*, no. 24, pp. 10-11

Bragança de, A. (5 Feb. 1973) "La longue marche d'un révolutionnaire africain", *Afrique-Asie*, no. 23, p. 12-19

Bragança de, A. (1976) «*Amilcar Cabral*», Pontos de Vista, Lisboa

Brittain, Victoria (2006) "They had to die: Assassination against Liberation", *Race & class,* vol. 48, no. 1, pp.60-74

Buijtenhuijs, R. "La Guinée-Bissau Independente Balantas e Brames do Território de Bula," *Kroniek van Afrika* , no. 175/2, pp. 153-166

Cabral, L. (Nov-Dec. 1969) "Portuguese Guinea: United Front against Imperialism", *Tricontinental Bimonthly,* 15, pp. 141-146

Campbell, Horace (2006) "Revisiting the Theories and Practices of Amilcar Cabral in the Context of the Exhaustion of the Patriarchal Model of African Liberation", In John Foban-Jong and Thomas Ranuga (Eds.), *The Life, Thought and Legacy of Cape Verde's Freedom Fighter Amilcar Cabral (1924–1973): Essays on His Liberation Philosophy,* Mellen Press, Lewiston, NY, pp. 79–102

Castanheira, José Pedro (Juin 2003) «Qui a fait tuer Amilcar Cabral ?», Harmattan, Paris

Chabal, Patrick (1980) "Amilcar Cabral as Revolutionary Leader" Ph.D. dissertation, Trinity College, University of Cambridge

Chabal, Patrick (1981) "The Social and Political Thought of Cabral: A Reassessment", *Journal of Modern African Studies,* vol. 19, no. 1, pp. 31–56

Chabal, Patrick. (1981) "National Liberation in Portuguese Guinea, 1956–1974" *African Affairs* vol. 80, pp. 75–99

Chabal, Patrick. (1983) "*Cabral: Revolutionary Leadership and People's War*", Cambridge University Press, Cambridge

Chabal, Patrick (1983) "Party, State and Socialism in Guinea-Bissau" *Canadian Journal of African Studies,* vol. 17, no. 2, pp. 189–210

Chabal, Patrick (2003) "*Cabral: Revolutionary Leadership and People's War",* Africa World Press, Trenton

Chailand, Gerard (April 1967) "Les maquis de Guinée Portugaise", *Les Temps Modernes,* 22, 251, p. 1868-1884

Chailand, Gerard (1969) "*Armed Struggle in Africa with the Guerilla's in Portuguese Guinea",* Monthly Review Press, New York

Chaliand, Gérard (8 Feb. 1973) "The PAIGC without Cabral: An Assessment. An Interview with Gérard Chaliand", *Ufahamu,* vol. 3, no. 3, pp. 87-95

Chaliand, Gerard (1973) "The Legacy of Amilcar Cabral", *Ramparts,* vol. 11, no. 1, p. 17–20

Chaliand, Gérard, and Vale, Michel (1977) "Amilcar Cabral", *International Journal of Politics,* pp. 3-17

Chilcote, Ronald H. (1967) "Nationalist Documents on Portuguese Guine and Cape Verde Islands and Mocambique", *African Studies Bulletin* , vol. 10, no. 1, pp. 22-42

Chilcote, Ronald H. (1968) "The Political Thought of Amilcar Cabral", *Journal of Modern African Studies,* vol. 6, no. 3, p. 373–388

Chilcote, Ronald H. (1972) "*Emerging Nationalism in Portuguese Africa: Documents",* Hoover Institution Press, Stanford

Chilcote, Ronald H. (1974) "Amilcar Cabral: A Bibliography of His Life and Thought, 1925–1973", *Africana Library Journal,* vol. 5, no. 4, pp. 289–307

Chilcote, Ronald H. (1977) "Guinea-Bissau's Struggle: Past and Present", *Africa Today*, vol. 24, no. 1

Chilcote, Ronald H. (1984) "The Theory and Practice of Amilcar Cabral: Revolutionary Implications for the Third World", *Latin American Perspectives,* vol. 11, no. 2, pp. 3–14

Chilcote, Ronald H. (1991) "*Amilcar Cabral's Revolutionary Theory and Parctice: A Critical Guide*", Lynne Reinner Publishers, Boulder

Clapham, C. (19 August 1983) "Africa's Philosopher King", *The Times Higher Education Supplement,* p. 12

Cohen, Sylvester (1998) "Amilcar Cabral: An Extraction from the Literature", *Monthly Review*, vol. 50, no. 7, pp. 39-47

Comitini, Carlos (1980) "*Amilcar Cabral: The Weapon of Theory",* CODECRI, Rio de Janeiro

Cortesão, Luiza (2011) "Paulo Freire and Amilcar Cabral: Convergences", *Journal for Critical Education Policy Studies,* vol. 9, no. 2, pp. 260-267

Crimi, B. (18 Novembre 1972) "Amilcar Cabral Prêt Pour l'Independence", *Jeune Afrique*, no. 619, p. 12-16.

Cruse, Harold (1975) "The Amilcar Cabral politico-cultural model", *Black World,* vol. 24, pp. 20-27

Dhada, Mustafah (July 1998) "The Liberation War in Guinea-Bissau Reconsidered", *The Journal of Military History*, vol. 62, no. 3, pp. 571-593

Dhada, Mustafah (1993) "*Warriors at Work: How Guinea was Really Set Free*", University Press of Colorado, Niwot, CO

Dadoo, Yusuf (1973) "Amilcar Cabral: Outstanding Leader of Africa's Liberation Movements", *African Communist,* no. 53, pp. 38–43

Davidson, Basil (Sept.-Oct. 1968) "The Revolt of Portuguese Guinea," *Tricontinental,* no. 8, pp. 89-91

Davidson, Basil (1969) "*The Liberation of Guine: Aspects of an African revolution*" Penguin, Baltimore

Davidson, Basil (Fall 1974) "Guinea-Bissau and the Cape Verde Islands: the Transition from War to Independence," *Africa Today,* vol. 21, no. 4

Davidson, Basil (1974) "*Growing from Grass Roots: the State of Guinea-Bissau*", Committee for Freedom in Mozambique, Angola and Guinea

Davidson, Basil (1981). *No Fist Is Big Enough to Hide the Sky: The Liberation of Guinea and Cape Verde: Aspects of an African Revolution,* Zed, London

Davidson, Basil (1984) "On Revolutionary Nationalism: The Legacy of Cabral" *Latin American Perspectives,* vol. 11, no. 2, pp. 15–42

Diop, Thierno (2001) "L'antidogmatisme d'Amilcar Cabral", *Bulletin de L'IFAN Ch. A. Diop,* tome 51, série B, n°. 1-2, pp. 221-236

Eckels, Jon (Jan-Feb 1976) "Amilcar Cabral: for the People. The Black Scholar , vol. 7, no. 5, *Black Popular Culture,* p. 42

Ferreira, Eduardo, and Cabral, Amilcar (1973) "Theory of Revolution and Background to his Assassination", *Ufahamu,* vol. 3, no. 3, pp. 49-68.

First, R. (1972) "Special Report: Portugal's African Wars", *Africa,* vol. 6, pp. 47-51

Fobanjong, John (2006) "Articulating Cabral's Regionalist and Pan-Africanist Visions", *African Identities, vol.* 4, no. 1, pp. 113-125

Fobanjong, John, and Ranuga, Thomas (Eds.) (2006) "*The Life, Thought and Legacy of Cape Verde's Freedom Fighter Amilcar Cabral (1924-1973): Essays on His Liberation Philosophy*", Mellen Press, Lewiston, NY

Gacha, M. (July 1976) "Eveil de la conscience nationaliste et stratégie révolutionnaire chez Amilcar Cabral", *Le Mois en Afrique*, no. 127, pp. 69-84

Galli, Rosemary E. (1986) "Amilcar Cabral and Rural Transformation in Guinea-Bissau", *Rural Africana, no.* 25, p. 26

Goldfield, Steve (1973) "Amilcar Cabral and the Liberation Struggle in Portuguese Guinea" *Socialist Revolution,* no. 13/14, pp. 127–30

Gomes, Crispina (2006) "The Women of Guinea-Bissau and Cape Verde in the Struggle for National Independence" In Fobanjong, John and Ranuga, Thomas (Eds.), *The Life, Thought and Legacy of Cape Verde's Freedom Fighter Amilcar Cabral (1924–1973): Essays on His Liber- ation Philosophy,* Mellen Press, Lewiston, NY, pp. 69-78

Henriksen, T.H. (1978) "People's Wars in Angola, Mozambique and Guinea-Bissau", *Journal of Modern African Studies*, vol. 14, no. 3, pp. 377-399

Houser, George and Henderson, Lawrence W. (Winter 1973) "In Memory of Amilcar Cabral: Two Statements", *Africa Today*, vol. 20, no. 1, pp. 3-6

Hubbard, Maryinez L. (1976) "Culture and History in a Revolutionary Context: Approaches to Amilcar Cabral", *Ufahamu,* vol. 3, no. 3, pp. 69-86

Hunt, Geoffrey (1978) "Two African Aesthetics: Wole Soyinka vs. Amilcar Cabral", *Marxism and African Literature,* pp. 64-93.

Idahosa, Pablo Luke (2002) "Going to the People: Amilcar Cabral's Materialist Theory and Practice of Culture and Ethnicity", *Lusotopie,* pp. 29-58

Ignatiev, Oleg Konstantinovich (1975) "Amilcar Cabral, *Filho de Africa: Narração Biográfica",* Prelo, Lisbon

Ignatiev, Oleg Konstantinovich (1975) "*Amilkar Kabral: Syn Afriki",* Izdvo Polit Litry, Moskva

Ignatiev, Oleg Konstantinovich (1975) "*Três Tiros da PIDE Quem, Porquê a Como Mataram Amilcar Cabral?*" Prelo, Lisbon

Ignatiev, Oleg Konstantinovich (1990) "*Amilcar Cabral",* Edicoes da Agencia de Imprensa Novosti, Muscova

Ishemo, Shubi (1993) "Amilcar Cabral's Thought & Practice: Some Lessons for the 1990s" *Review of African Political Economy,* no. 58, pp. 71-78

Ishemo, Shubi L. (March 2004) "Culture & Historical Knowledge in Africa: A Cabralian Approach", *Review of African Political Economy,* vol. 31, no. 99, pp. 65-82

Jinadu, Liasu Adele (1973) "*The Political Ideas of Frantz Fanon: An Essay in Interpretation and Criticism*" Ph.D. dissertation, University of Minnesota

Jinadu, Liasu Adele (1978) "Some African Theorists of Culture and Modernization: Fanon, Cabral and Some Others", *African Studies Review,* vol. 21, no. 1, pp. 121–138

Jinadu, Liasu Adele (1986) "*Fanon: In Search of the African Revolution*", KPI/Routledge and Kegan Paul, London

Kariamu Welsh-Asante (Dec. 1990) "Philosophy and Dance in Africa: the Views of Cabral and Fanon", *Journal of Black Studies,* vol. 21, no. 2, pp. 224-232

Keese, Alexander (2007) "The Role of Cape Verdeans in War Mobilization and War Prevention in Portugal's African Empire, 1955-1965", *The International Journal of African Historical Studies,* vol. 40, no. 3, pp. 497-511

Loomba, Ania (1998), "*Colonialism/Postcolonialism*", Routledge, New York

Loomba, Ania (Eds.) (2005) "*Postcolonial Studies and Beyond*", Duke University Press, Durham

Lopes, Carlos (1987) "*Guinea-Bissua: From Liberation Struggle to Independent Statehood*", Westview, Boulder, CO

Lopes, Carlos (2006) "Amilcar Cabral: a Contemporary Inspiration" *African identities, vol.* 4, no. 1, pp.1-5.

Lopes, Carlos (2006) "Amilcar Cabral's Legacy in View of the Challenges of Contemporary Ethics", *African Identities,* vol. 4, no. 1, pp. 127-140
Lopes, Carlos (2010) "*Africa's Contemporary Challenges: The Legacy of Amilcar Cabral*" Routledge, London

Luke, Timothy W. (1982) "Cabral's Marxism: An African Strategy for Socialist Development", *Studies in Comparative Communism,* vol. 14, no 4, pp. 307-330.

Luz, Amaro Alexandre da (January 20,1978) "Commemoration of the Fifth Anniversary of the Assassination of Amilcar Cabral" (Africa-Wide Information. Web. 20 Feb. 2013)

Lyon, Judson M. (1980) "Marxism and ethno nationalism in Guinea Bissau, 1956–76", *Ethnic and Racial Studies, vol.* 3, no. 2, pp. 156-168

Magubane, Bernard (Fall 1983) "Toward a Sociology of National Liberation from Colonialism: Cabral's Legacy", *Contemporary Marxism,* no. 7, pp. 5-27

Marcum, John A. (1973) "Guinea Bissau: Amilcar Cabral, the Meaning of an Assassination", *Africa Report,* vol. 18, pp. 21-23.

McCollester, Charles (March 1973) "The African Revolution: Theory and Practice", *Monthly Review*, vol. 24, no. 10, pp. 10-21

McCollester, Charles (March 1973) "The Political Thought of Amilcar Cabral", *Monthly Review* pp. 10-21

McCullock, Jock (1981) "Amilcar Cabral: A Theory of Imperialism", *Journal of Modern African Studies*, vol. 19, n° 3, pp. 503-511

McCulloch, Jock. (1983). "*Black Soul, White Artifact: Fanon's Clinical Psychology and Social Theory*", Cambridge University Press, Cambridge

McCulloch, Jock (1983) "*In the Twilight of Revolution: The Political Theory of Amilcar Cabral*", Routledge and Kegan Paul, London and Boston
Meintel, Deirdre (1994) "*Race, Culture, and Portuguese Colonialism in Cabo Verde",* Syracuse University Press, Syracuse, NY

Mendy, Peter Karibe (2006) "Amilcar Cabral and the Liberation of Guinea-Bissau: Context, Challenges and Lessons for Effective African Leadership", *African Identities,* vol. 4, no. 1, pp. 7-21

Moniz, Lino Vaz (2004) «Amilcar Cabral e Paulo Freire na era da Tecnologia Digital, «*BSB: UnB*

Morgado, Michael S. (1974) "Amilcar Cabral's Theory of Cultural Revolution", *Black Images, vol.* 3, no. 2, pp. 3-16

Moser, Gerald M. (1978) "The Poet Amilcar Cabral", *Research in African Literatures, vol.* 9, no. 2, pp. 176-197.

Mukandabantu, Angel Mwenda (1983) "The Political Thought of Amilcar Cabral: A Review Article", *Review of African Political Economy*, pp. 207-213.

Mwenda, Angel Alfred (1985) "*Amilcar Cabral and the theory of the revolutionary African petit-bourgeoisie*", Diss. University of Leeds

Nikanorov, Anatolii Vladimirovich (1973) "*Amilcar Cabral*", Novosti Press, Moscow

Nyang, Sulayman Sheih (1976) "The Political Thought of Amilcar Cabral, a Synthesis" *Odu: A Journal of West African Studies*, no. 13, pp. 3-20

Nzongola-Ntalaja. "Amilcar Cabral and the Theory of the National Liberation Struggle", *Latin American Perspectives* (1984): 43-54.

O'Ballance, Edgar (1973) "Amilcar Cabral: Life and Death of an African Guerrilla", *Army Quarterly & Defence Journal*, vol. 103, no. 4, pp. 442-451

O'Brien, J. O. (Summer 1977) "Tribe, Class and Nation: Revolution and the Weapon of Theory in Guinea-Bissau", *Race and Class*, vol. 19, no. 1, pp. 1-18

Oramas Oliva, Oscar (2003)»*Amilcar Cabral Un précurseur de l'indépendance africaine*», Indigo Cote Femmes, Paris, 199

Osorio, Owaldo (1980) "Amilcal Cabral: A Emergência de Poesia e o Decurso da Evolução Poética", In *Emergencia Da Poesia Da Em Amilcar Cabral: 30 Poemas*", Colecção Dragoeiro, Praia

PAIGC (1974) "*Guinea-Bissau: Toward Final Victory! Selected Speeches and Documents from PAIGC (Partido Africano da Independencia da Guiné e Cabo Verde*", LSM Press, Canada

"Peace Profile: Amilcar Cabral" (2003) *Peace Review : A Journal of Social Justice,* vol.15, Issue 2, pp. 233-240

Pélissier, R. (19-24 février 1973) "Guinée-Bissau: la Mort d'Amilcar Cabral," *Mois en Afrique*, no. 86, pp. 20-24

Perkins, Eugene (1976) "Literature of Combat: Poetry of Afrikan Liberation Movements", *Journal of Black Studies,* pp. 225-240

Peterson, Charles F. (2007) "*Du Bois, Fanon, Cabral: The Margins of Elite Anti-Colonial Leadership*", Lexington Books, Lanham

Pinto, Cruz, (1972) "Guinea-Bissau's Liberation Struggle against Portuguese Colonialism" *Freedom ways*, vol. 3, no. 12, pp. 189-195

Powell, M. (1993) "A Tribute To Amilcar Cabral, 12 September 1924 - 20 January 1973" *Review of African Political Economy,* no. 58, pp. 61-63

Press, Karen (1990) "The Role of Culture in the Revolutionary Process & the Struggle for National Liberation : Leon Trotsky, Mao Tse-Tung, Amilcar Cabral", *Spark 2,* pp. 5-9

Rabaka, Reiland (2009) "*Africana Critical Theory: Reconstructing the Black Radical Tradition, from W.E.B. Du Bois and C.L.R. James to Frantz Fanon and Amilcar Cabral*", Rowman & Littlefield Publishers, Lanham, MD

Rahmato, Dessalegn (1982) "*Cabral and the Problem of the African Revolution*", University Press, Addis Ababa

Riviere, C. (1977) "*Guinea, the Mobilization of a People*", Cornell University Press, London

Robinson, Cedric J. (May-June 1981): "Amilcar Cabral and the Dialectic of Portuguese Colonialism", *Radical America,* pp. 39-57

Rodney, Walter (December 18, 1963) "The Role of the Historian in the Developing West Indies" *The Social Scientist,* pp.13–14, 16

Rodney, Walter (1965) "Portuguese Attempts at Monopoly on the Upper Guinea Coast", *Journal of African History,* vol. 6, no. 3, pp. 307–322

Rodney, Walter (1966) "A History of the Upper Guinea Coast, 1545–1800", Ph.D. Dissertation, University of London

Rodney, Walter (1967) "*West Africa and the Atlantic Slave-Trade*", East African Publishing House, Nairobi

Rudebeck, Lars (1974) "*Guinea-Bissau: A Study of Political Mobilization*", Scandinavian Institute of African Studies, Uppsala

Rudebeck, Lars (1993) "Reading Cabral in 1993", *Review of African Political Economy,* vol. 20, no. 58, pp. 63-70.

Rudebeck, Lars (2006) "Reading Cabral on democracy" *African identities,* vol. 4, no. 1, pp. 89-98

Sarrazin, Chantal and Gjerstad, Ole (1978), "*Sowing the First Harvest: National Reconstruction in Guinea-Bissau*", LSM

Segal, Aaron (1973) "Amilcar Cabral: In Memoriam", *Third World,* vol. 2, no. 4, pp. 7–8

Segal, Aaron (2003) "The African Anti-Colonial Struggle: An Effort at Reclaiming History", *Philosophia Africana,*vol. 6, no. 1, pp. 47–58

Segal, Aaron (2006) "Amilcar Cabral and the Practice of Theory", In Fobanjong, John and Ranuga, Thomas (Eds.), *The Life, Thought and Legacy of Cape Verde's Freedom Fighter Amilcar Cabral (1924–1973: Essays on His Liberation Philosophy,* Mellen Press, Lewiston, NY, pp. 17–38)

Segal, Aaron (2007) "*Contested Memory: The Icon of the Occidental Tradition*", Africa World Press, Trenton

Sigrist, Christian (2010) "Amilcar Cabral" *Das Argument,* vol. 52, no. 4, pp. 223-235

Taiwo, Olufemi (1999) "Cabral", In Arrington, Robert L. (Ed.), *A Companion to the Philosophers,* Blackwell, Malden, pp. 5-12

Ulyanovsky, Rostislav (1984) "Scientific Socialism and Amilcar Cabral", *The African Communist*, n° 99

Urdang, Stephenie (1979) "*Fighting Two Colonialisms: Women in Guinea-Bissau*", Monthly Review, New York

Vambe, Maurice Taonezvi, and Zegeye, Abebe (2006) "Amilcar Cabral and the Fortunes of African Literature", *African Identities* , vol. 4, no. 1, pp. 23-44

Vambe, Maurice Taonezvi, and Zegeye, Abebe (2008) "Amilcar Cabral: National Liberation as the Basis for Africa's Renaissances", *Rethinking Marxism*, vol. 20, no. 2, pp. 188-200

Wallerstein, I. (July 1971) "The Lessons of the PAIGC," *Africa Today*, vol. 18, no. 3, pp. 62-68

Wick, Alexis (2006) "Manifestations of Nationhood in the Writings of Amilcar Cabral", *African identities,* vol. 4, no. 1, pp. 45-70.

Zartman, I.W. (Feb. 1964) "Africa's Quiet War: Portuguese Guinea" *Africa Report*, pp. 8-12

Zartman, I.W. (Nov. 1967) "Guinea: The Quiet War Goes On" *Africa Report,* pp. 67-72

Made in the USA
San Bernardino, CA
21 April 2014